Bosworth

By Chris Skidmore

Edward VI
Death and the Virgin
Bosworth

Bosworth

THE BIRTH OF THE TUDORS

Chris Skidmore

PHOENIX

A PHOENIX PAPERBACK

First published in Great Britain in 2013
by Weidenfeld & Nicolson
This edition published in 2014
by Phoenix,
an imprint of Orion Books Ltd,
Orion House, 5 Upper St Martin's Lane,
London WC2H 9EA

An Hachette UK company

1 3 5 7 9 10 8 6 4 2

ISBN 978-0-7538-2894-6

Typeset by Input Data Services Ltd, Bridgwater, Somerset

Printed and bound by CPI Group (UK) Ltd,
Croydon, CRO 4YY

The Orion Publishing Group's policy is to use papers that
are natural, renewable and recyclable products and made
from wood grown in sustainable forests. The logging and
manufacturing processes are expected to conform to the
environmental regulations of the country of origin.

www.orionbooks.co.uk

In memory of Lesley Boatwright

CONTENTS

PART FOUR: AFTERMATH

ILLUSTRATIONS AND MAPS

Louis XI, 1470 *(André Held/AKG Images)*

Charles VIII, 1485 *(AKG Images)*

Anne de Beaujeu, from the right wing of the Bourbon Altarpiece, Moulins Cathedral *(Giraudon/Bridgeman)*

Château de Suscinio, Sarzeau, France *(hemis.fr/Getty Images)*

Château de Largoët, Elven, France *(hemis.fr/Getty Images)*

Drawing of the tomb of John de Vere, 13th Earl of Oxford *(British Library)*

Stained-glass window depicting Reginald Bray *(Geoffrey Wheeler)*

Brass rubbing of Christopher Urswick *(Geoffrey Wheeler)*

SECTION TWO

Mill Bay, Pembrokeshire *(Author photo)*

Tomb of Rhys ap Thomas, St Peter's Church, Carmarthen *(Geoffrey Wheeler)*

Merevale Church, Warwickshire *(Author photo)*

Engraving of the Welsh Gate, Shrewsbury, by Hugh Owen *(Geoffrey Wheeler)*

The Blue Boar Inn, Leicester *(Geoffrey Wheeler)*

Brass rubbing of Sir Gervase Clifton *(Geoffrey Wheeler)*

Brass rubbing of Roger Wake *(Geoffrey Wheeler)*

Tomb of Simon Digby in Coleshill Church, Warwickshire *(Geoffrey Wheeler)*

Tomb of Sir John Cheyney in Salisbury Cathedral *(Geoffrey Wheeler)*

The fields where Richard III's last stand might have taken place *(Author photo)*

Battle of Bosworth, sixteenth-century relief *(Stowe School/SHPT)*

The view of the battlefield at Bosworth from the top of St Margaret's Church, Stoke Golding *(Author photo)*

Gold signet ring showing Richard III's insignia *(Geoffrey Wheeler)*

Cannon balls discovered at the battlefield site *(Bosworth Battlefield Heritage Centre)*

The Bosworth Crucifix *(Society of Antiquaries)*

Silver gilt boar badge discovered at the battlefield site *(Bosworth Battlefield Heritage Centre)*

Broken sword handle *(Bosworth Battlefield Heritage Centre)*

The Annunciation, from Richard III's book of hours, Ms 474 ff14v-15 *(Lambeth Palace Library/Bridgeman)*

Lead badge representing the Yorkist sun *(Bosworth Battlefield Heritage Centre)*

Gold badge of an eagle with a snake *(Bosworth Battlefield Heritage Centre)*

The gravesite of Richard III in Leicester City Council Social Services car park *(University of Leicester)*

The bones of Richard III *(University of Leicester)*

Richard III's skull *(University of Leicester)*

St James' Church, Dadlington *(Author photo)*

Henry VII, terracotta bust by Pietro Torrigiano, c. 1509–11 *(Victoria & Albert Museum, London/Bridgeman)*

MAPS

APPENDIX

ENGLAND, FRANCE AND BRITTANY DURING THE
WARS OF THE ROSES

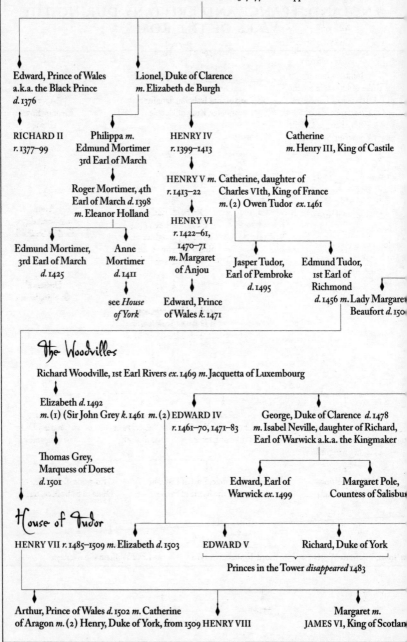

EDWARD III *r.* 1327–77 *m.* Philippa of Hainault

Edward, Prince of Wales
a.k.a. the Black Prince
d. 1376

Lionel, Duke of Clarence
m. Elizabeth de Burgh

RICHARD II
r. 1377–99

Philippa *m.*
Edmund Mortimer
3rd Earl of March

HENRY IV
r. 1399–1413

Catherine
m. Henry III, King of Castile

Roger Mortimer, 4th
Earl of March *d.* 1398
m. Eleanor Holland

HENRY V *m.* Catherine, daughter of
r. 1413–22   Charles VIth, King of France
m. (2) Owen Tudor *ex.* 1461

HENRY VI
r. 1422–61,
1470–71

Edmund Mortimer,
3rd Earl of March
d. 1425

Anne
Mortimer
d. 1411

see *House
of York*

m. Margaret
of Anjou

Jasper Tudor,
Earl of Pembroke
d. 1495

Edmund Tudor,
1st Earl of
Richmond
d. 1456 *m.* Lady Margaret
Beaufort *d.* 150

Edward, Prince
of Wales *k.* 1471

The Woodvilles

Richard Woodville, 1st Earl Rivers *ex.* 1469 *m.* Jacquetta of Luxembourg

Elizabeth *d.* 1492
m. (1) (Sir John Grey *k.* 1461 *m.* (2) EDWARD IV
r. 1461–70, 1471–83

George, Duke of Clarence *d.* 1478
m. Isabel Neville, daughter of Richard,
Earl of Warwick a.k.a. the Kingmaker

Thomas Grey,
Marquess of Dorset
d. 1501

Edward, Earl of
Warwick *ex.* 1499

Margaret Pole,
Countess of Salisbu

House of Tudor

HENRY VII *r.* 1485–1509 *m.* Elizabeth *d.* 1503

EDWARD V

Richard, Duke of York

Princes in the Tower *disappeared* 1483

Arthur, Prince of Wales *d.* 1502 *m.* Catherine
of Aragon *m.* (2) Henry, Duke of York, from 1509 HENRY VIII

Margaret *m.*
JAMES VI, King of Scotlan

Houses of Lancaster and York and the House of Tudor

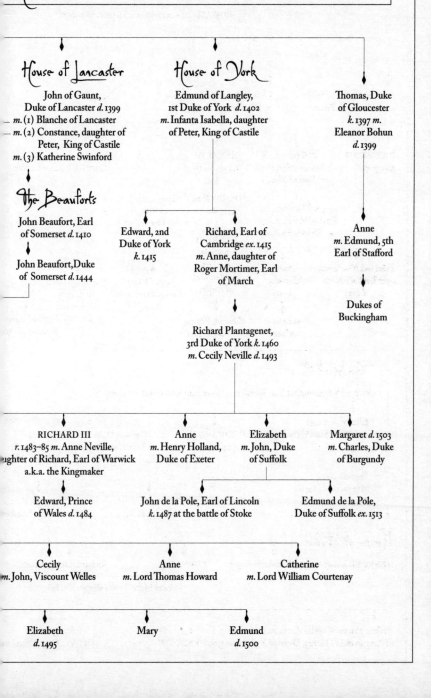

House of Lancaster

John of Gaunt,
Duke of Lancaster *d.* 1399
m. (1) Blanche of Lancaster
m. (2) Constance, daughter of
Peter, King of Castile
m. (3) Katherine Swinford

The Beauforts

John Beaufort, Earl
of Somerset *d.* 1410

John Beaufort, Duke
of Somerset *d.* 1444

House of York

Edmund of Langley,
1st Duke of York *d.* 1402
m. Infanta Isabella, daughter
of Peter, King of Castile

Edward, 2nd
Duke of York
k. 1415

Richard, Earl of
Cambridge *ex.* 1415
m. Anne, daughter of
Roger Mortimer, Earl
of March

Richard Plantagenet,
3rd Duke of York *k.* 1460
m. Cecily Neville *d.* 1493

Thomas, Duke
of Gloucester
k. 1397 *m.*
Eleanor Bohun
d. 1399

Anne
m. Edmund, 5th
Earl of Stafford

Dukes of
Buckingham

RICHARD III
r. 1483–85 *m.* Anne Neville,
daughter of Richard, Earl of Warwick
a.k.a. the Kingmaker

Anne
m. Henry Holland,
Duke of Exeter

Elizabeth
m. John, Duke
of Suffolk

Margaret *d.* 1503
m. Charles, Duke
of Burgundy

Edward, Prince
of Wales *d.* 1484

John de la Pole, Earl of Lincoln
k. 1487 at the battle of Stoke

Edmund de la Pole,
Duke of Suffolk *ex.* 1513

Cecily
m. John, Viscount Welles

Anne
m. Lord Thomas Howard

Catherine
m. Lord William Courtenay

Elizabeth
d. 1495

Mary

Edmund
d. 1500

INTRODUCTION

'The history of a battle is not unlike the history of a ball. Some individuals may recollect all the little events of which the great result is
the battle won or lost, but no individual can recollect the order in
which, or the exact moment at which, they occurred, which makes
all the difference as to their value or importance.'

The Duke of Wellington, 8 August 1815

The date 1485 is seared into our national memory. Learnt by every school
pupil, there is good reason to consider it one of the key events in British history. The battle of Bosworth, where the twenty-eight-year-old
Henry Tudor defeated Richard III, was the moment when the Tudor
dynasty was born.

Yet for all its fame as one of the most significant battles in British
history, Bosworth remains tantalisingly elusive to the historian. Compared to other battles that took place during the civil wars of the
fifteenth century, contemporary accounts of the battle are relatively
sparse. This book attempts to take a fresh look at the battle, drawing
together the widest possible range of sources, as well as investigating
unpublished manuscripts which shed new light on the period. This has
meant returning to the original documents, including the handwritten
manuscript of Polydore Vergil's *Anglia Historia*, one of the principal
sources for the battle now remaining in the Vatican Library in Rome,
in order to thread together as accurately as possible what might have
occurred during the morning of 22 August 1485.

Shakespeare's depiction of Richard III crying out on the battlefield,
offering to surrender his kingdom for a horse, has long been exposed
as the stuff of legend. What is often less clear is that Bosworth was
won not merely by the actions of Henry or Richard on the battlefield,
but through the actions, or inaction, of others present on that fateful
day. I have sought to understand these individuals' separate motiva-
tions, what drove each man to take up arms against his king, in order to

comprehend why Henry Tudor, against all the odds, was able to defeat Richard's army, a force twice the size of his meagre band of exiles, French mercenaries and Welshmen. In the centuries since Henry was crowned on the battlefield we have accepted a version of history which, from the moment that Richard's body lay still warm in the Leicestershire mud, was written exclusively by the winning side. Bosworth quickly became the providential story of good versus evil, of the innocent Henry, a David-like figure facing down the monstrous goliath of the tyrant Richard III. The truth, as this book attempts to reveal, was far more complex.

Yet rather than focus exclusively upon the movements of the battle itself, which, as Wellington wisely noted, can rarely be recalled with definitive certainty, *Bosworth* is intended to be more than just a detailed account of the battle alone. It charts the rise of the Tudors, at times an improbable saga of how Henry Tudor came to be crowned King of England. In doing so the book reveals a narrative of triumph against adversity, itself a gripping tale of how one man survived persecution and endured exile to seize the throne. Henry's journey to Bosworth is one of extraordinary perseverance; driven to flee to Brittany aged only fourteen, he spent his formative years as a prisoner, locked away in distant castles. It was a life filled with uncertainty and danger. On several occasions, Henry was forced suddenly to escape from one country to another, a fugitive whose claim to the throne would have seemed at best laughable.

The rise to power of the Tudors, a humble Welsh gentry family, in the space of just fifty years, was nothing less than remarkable. From Owen Tudor, a servant at the royal court who wooed the widowed Catherine of Valois, Henry V's queen, to the plight of their children, Edmund and Jasper Tudor, who rose through the ranks at court to join the most important noblemen of the realm, the Tudor story is one of romance and hardship. It is also one set against a backdrop of a bloody and brutal age, in which the politics of the fifteenth century gave way to civil strife, with the feuding houses of Lancaster and York descending into war. It was a time when men found themselves forced to make a choice between rival camps, when the wrong choice could lead to ruin or death. The Tudors were no exception. Henry Tudor's mother, the wily Margaret Beaufort, found herself on either side of the dynastic divide, before seizing her moment to help place her own son on the throne. From the instability caused by the vacuum of power left by Henry VI, through the battles of the 1460s and 1470s, Henry Tudor's survival lay not only in his mother's hands, but those of his dedicated uncle Jasper, who, almost like a surrogate father, ensured the boy's survival and masterminded his eventual triumph. With the ascendancy of Richard III, Henry found his own claim to the throne bolstered by hundreds of exiles from the English court; upon landing in Wales, he was joined on his march through the country by other leading figures such as Rhys ap Thomas. *Bosworth* charts their stories too, along with the many other actors on the stage who came together to forge the Tudor dynasty.

It is important to remember that Bosworth was not simply a culmination of Henry Tudor's victorious campaign, but is also the ending to the tale of how Richard III lost a kingdom. Henry's success owed everything to the tragic fate of the last Plantagenet king, whose rule seemed doomed from the moment he decided to seize the throne from his young nephew Edward V, right down to the dying moments of the battle, when Richard found himself deserted by his supporters and the king chose to throw caution to the wind and launch himself upon this young upstart pretender to his throne.

Since I began researching the book, for a battle fought more than half a millennium ago, events have moved fast. In 2010 news broke that the battle site had been 'rediscovered' two miles down the road from where it had been mistakenly believed to have been fought. More importantly, new finds relating to the battle, including more than thirty cannon balls, the largest collection of shot ever discovered from a medieval conflict in Europe, had been unearthed in the fields around the new site of the battle. Among the most treasured finds was a boar badge – as the emblem of Richard III, a clear sign of his army's presence in the location. It renewed a sense of determination in my own mind that the story of the battle was only just beginning to unfold. During the course of my research, which has taken me across the archives in Vannes, Nantes and Paris, returning to the remote castles where Henry Tudor was imprisoned during his youth, such as the Tour d'Elven, still hidden away in deep forest miles from habitation, I have sought to recreate as best as possible Henry's own experiences. By making use of the surviving French material detailing Henry's exile, down to the black fur gown he was given, I have tried to bring Henry to life, while recognising his utter dependence on his foreign hosts. Charting Henry's remarkable march through Wales in August 1485, one of the few successful foreign invasions of Britain, I attempted to recreate the journey myself, admittedly with the aid of my car, starting at the terrifyingly sheer cliffs of the Pembrokeshire coastline in sleeting rain, and ending up at the battle re-enactments of the Bosworth Battlefield Centre. My research even took me to the top of St Margaret's Church in Stoke Golding, clinging to a thirty-foot wooden ladder inside its tower as I peered out from the same spot where onlookers had watched the battle unfold over 500 years before.

Then in autumn 2012, as I had just finished the first draft of the book, a team of archaeologists from Leicester University made an announcement that hit the global headlines: beneath a council car park in Leicester, they had discovered the bones of a man believed to be Richard III. I rushed up to Leicester as soon as I heard the news, finding myself standing in a long queue that wrapped around the block, as I patiently waited my turn to enter the car park. At the front of the line, marshals wearing luminous jackets ushered the next group in, and they hurried forward as if desperate to get to the front of a rock concert. There was no music to be heard, yet the excitement among the chattering crowd felt as if the assembled throng were awaiting the arrival of a celebrity. Several months passed as tests were performed on the remains, until on 4 February 2013, just as this book was being sent to the printers, the announcement was made that the bones were indeed Richard's. A Postscript to the main text reveals the full extent of this discovery, and its implications for our understanding of Richard's final moments. It is perhaps just the latest twist in this compelling tale, rich with drama right to the end, as England's last Plantagenet king fought to his final breath, becoming the last monarch to die on a battlefield. There may be more still to discover, but for now, I hope that this book will help us understand not only one of our most important battles, but an event that opened one of the most dramatic chapters in British history, the reign of the Tudor dynasty.

A NOTE ON MONEY AND DATES

English monetary values are recorded as being in pounds (*l*) shillings (*s*) and pence (*d*), with twenty shillings in the pound and twelve pence in the shilling. The mark was a unit of account, with one mark being worth thirteen shillings and four pence, therefore 2/3rds of a pound. There are many pitfalls to estimating the value of currency across the centuries, however a useful guide is the National Archives' Currency Converter (see http://www.nationalarchives.gov.uk/currency) that suggests one pound in 1480 would have been worth an equivalent of £504.59 at 2005 prices, with one shilling worth an equivalent of £25.23 and one penny equalling £2.10. The standard unit of French money was the *livre tournois*, divided into twenty *sols* (later *sous*), which was worth twelve *dernier*. One *ecu* was worth the equivalent of six *livres tournois*. The value of the *livre tournois* to the pound fluctuated, however it is estimated that there were ten *livres tournois* in the pound, with one shilling being worth two *livres tournois*.

Dates are given according to contemporary sources that followed the Julian calendar in use at the time. With the adoption of the Gregorian Calendar in 1752, account should be taken of the fact that these dates do not match with the exact dates of our current calendar. The difference between the two calendars in the fifteenth century is nine days, so the Battle of Bosworth, while fought on 22 August in 1485, would have actually been 31 August in our contemporary calendar.

PROLOGUE

·—◆—·

7 August 1485

As the sun lowered beneath the horizon across the Milford estuary, a flotilla of thirty ships drifted across the mouth of the Haven, their sails billowed by a soft southern breeze. It had been a week since the fleet had sailed from the shelter of the Seine at Honfleur, but the ships had made fast progress in the balmy August weather. Onboard, sharpening their battle axes, knives and swords, over 3,000 men waited. They included a rabble of 2,000 Breton and French soldiers, many only recently released from prison, 'the worst sort', 'raised out of the refuse of the people', 1,000 Scottish troops and 400 Englishmen whose last sight of their country had been two years previously, when they had fled in fear of their lives.

The ships entered the entrance of the estuary where looking leftwards, the dark red sandstone cliffs, several hundred feet in height and impossible to scale, gave way to a small cove, hidden from sight from the cliffs above. High tide had passed an hour previously, allowing the ships to creep silently to the edge of the narrow shoreline for the troops to disembark. At first the Frenchmen seemed reluctant to move, fearful of what might be waiting on shore. Yet there seemed to be little sign of armed resistance, no troops shadowing the cliffs or boats patrolling the haven, in spite of reports that the previous year a company of men had been stationed there, ready to sound the alarm in case of invasion.

Their arrival had stirred no one. The nearest town of Dale was a mile and a half away, yet the bay was secluded from the sight of its castle by a large promontory. Only a watermill on the edge of the shore, fed by a stream running off the headland and into the bay, gave any sign of habitation. Soon the waters had clouded with sand as the men began to

I

heave cannon, guns and ordnance from the boats, leading horses from the ships and onto land.

From one of the boats stepped a twenty-eight-year-old man. Pale and slender, above average height with shoulder-length brown hair, he had a long face with a red wart just above his chin. Yet his most noticeable feature to those who had met him was his small blue eyes, 'cold and sober', which gave out the impression of energy and liveliness whenever he spoke. Stepping out of his boat, the man took a few steps forward on land he had last set foot upon fourteen years before. Kneeling down in the sand, he took his finger and drew a sign of the cross, which he then kissed. Then, holding up his hands to the skies 'meekly and devoutly' he uttered the words, 'Judica me deus et discerne causam meam'. It was the first line from the forty-third psalm: 'Judge and revenge my cause O Lord', which the soldiers now began to sing. As the words of the psalm echoed around Mill Bay in the darkening evening, one line in particular must have stood out above all others: 'O deliver me from the deceitful and unjust man.' The march across Wales to win a kingdom had only just begun. For Henry Tudor, his arrival to claim the crown of England was the end of a journey that had lasted his whole life. The moment of reckoning had arrived. All he could hope for was that God, at least, would take his side.

PART ONE:
BEGINNINGS

1

FORTUNE'S WHEEL

'But Fortune with her smiling countenance strange
Of all our purpose may make sudden change.'

John Paston III, The Paston Letters

No one knew when or how their relationship had begun. Or at least they chose not to know. She had been unable 'to curb fully her carnal passions', one contemporary wrote. Others would later excuse her behaviour, stating that she was 'but young in years, and thereby of less discretion to judge what was decent for her estate'. Everyone agreed, however, that Queen Catherine of Valois' latest relationship with her servant Owen Tudor was a highly unsuitable union.

Some said he was the bastard son of an alehouse keeper, others that his father had been a murderer on the run. In reality, Owen ap Maredudd ap Tudur was descended from the thirteenth-century Welsh prince Ednyfed Fychan. His ancestors had settled at Penmynydd in Anglesey, where his grandfather Tudur ap Goronwy had married Margaret, daughter of Thomas ap Llywelyn ab Owain of Cardiganshire, the last male of the princely house of Deheubarth. Tudur's marriage brought with it new powerful connections: Margaret's elder sister had married Gruffudd Fychan of Glyndyfrdwy, whose son was the Welsh prince Owain Glyn Dŵr. Tudur and Margaret had five sons, who as retainers of Richard II held important royal offices in North Wales, and whose wealth and influence were admired by poets of the day. Yet when their cousin Owain decided to raise a rebellion against 'the usurper' Henry IV in 1400, the brothers were forced to take sides between king and kin. Choosing the latter, they sealed their fates and the disgrace of the house of Tudur when the rebellion collapsed. The youngest of the five sons, Maredudd ap Tudur, fled into exile to continue the rebel campaign, and was still at large in 1405 when he was outlawed by the king

5

and his estates were confiscated. It is unlikely that his son Owen, born around 1400, ever had the chance to know his fugitive father.

How Owen ap Maredudd ap Tudur managed to enter into service in the English royal household is unknown. He may have done so through his service to Sir Walter Hungerford, whose retinue one 'Owen Meridith' had joined by 1420 and travelled with to France in 1421. The same year Henry V had married Catherine of Valois.

Catherine was the daughter of Charles VI of France, who in spite of his insanity, had managed to have twelve children with his notoriously promiscuous wife, Isabelle of Bavaria. Born in 1401, the youngest child of the royal couple, Catherine's destiny seems to have been fixed at an early age. As early as 1413, it was already being suggested that England and France might forge a closer union if she were to marry the son of the English king Henry IV, Prince Henry. His succession to the throne as Henry V, combined with his determination that his claim to the French throne be formally recognised, culminating in the English victory at Agincourt, delayed but did not end speculation that such a marriage could unite the two kingdoms. Catherine's beauty, captured in portraits sent to Henry, impressed the king enough to meet her in person in 1419. Entirely captivated, he kissed her hand, making her blush. In May 1420 the Treaty of Troyes was sealed, acknowledging Henry's claim to be heir to Charles VI at the same time as formalising a marriage between the French princess and the English king.

Catherine was eighteen at the time of her marriage. By twenty-one she was a widow and the mother of a nine-month-old boy, the new king Henry VI. The shattering news of her husband's death in August 1422 was followed two months later by the news that her father Charles had followed him to the grave. In name her son was now king of both England and France: in reality, power was placed in the hands of a minority council, led by Henry V's younger brothers, the Dukes of Gloucester and Bedford. Catherine remained at the royal court, occupied with the task of bringing up her young son, sitting beside him and holding his hand when he was required to make ceremonial appearances in public and in Parliament. In her letters at the time, she addressed herself as 'Catherine, Queen of England, daughter of King Charles of France, mother of the King of England, and lady of Ireland', yet all power had been stripped away: with no separate household of her own, she was dependent on the royal household for her upkeep which was strictly controlled by the minority council. Soon that was not all they wished to control.

Catherine's young age presented a problem to the king's Protector, Humphrey, Duke of Gloucester. While she continued to live in England with her young son, she might wish to marry again, perhaps to a subject, an idea as unthinkable as it would be a disgrace to the honour of the crown itself. Catherine's situation was almost unique: no queen who had outlived their royal husband had married again since the twelfth century, and even then they had taken the wise decision to leave England. There was the obvious fear that any husband of the mother of the king, regardless of his status, might try and involve himself in English politics, thereby threatening the position of the king's uncles in power. That fear became a terrifyingly real prospect for Gloucester when, in 1425, rumours began to circulate that Catherine had begun a relationship with Edmund Beaufort, the nineteen-year-old nephew of the chancellor and Bishop of Winchester, Henry Beaufort. Beaufort and Gloucester had fallen out on several occasions regarding the government of the realm; Gloucester was hardly going to allow Beaufort to gain any further influence over Catherine and the infant king.

When a petition by the commons appeared in the Leicester Parliament of 1426, requesting that Chancellor Beaufort should allow 'widows of the king' to marry as they wished upon payment of an appropriate fine, Gloucester's suspicions were confirmed. He would need to act to prevent Catherine's marriage becoming an issue that had the potential to undermine his own authority. That meant blocking Catherine from ever marrying for the foreseeable future. The following year, in the Parliament of October 1427 to March 1428, while Beaufort was conveniently out of the country campaigning in France, a statute was passed which forbade marriage to a queen without the king's permission on pain of forfeiture of lands and other possessions for life. Since the king remained a minor and would clearly be unable to grant any permission, it was ordained that permission to marry the queen could only be granted by the king when he reached an age of 'discretion'. Since Henry was only six years old, Catherine faced the prospect of being unable to marry for perhaps a decade, by which time she would be approaching thirty-seven. There was little Catherine could do. She could hardly protest without giving her intentions away; trapped by her own position as dowager queen and now the force of the law, she chose an altogether more extraordinary course of action.

Sir Walter Hungerford had been appointed steward of the royal household in April 1424. It was through his master's appointment that Owen Tudor became a servant in the royal household, in which Catherine remained until 1430. There is no evidence that he was keeper of Catherine's household or her wardrobe, as has been suggested. The sixteenth-century Welsh chronicler Elis Gruffudd noted that he was her 'sewer and servant'. Whatever his role at court, Owen Tudor was certainly in no position to begin a relationship with the widow of Henry V and the mother of the King of England.

Tradition has it that Owen Tudor and Catherine first caught each other's eye at a ball at court, when Owen drunkenly stumbled into Catherine's lap. Another tale, told in the mid-sixteenth century by a Welsh chronicler, related how it was Catherine who had first spotted the royal servant on a summer's day when he was swimming with friends in a river near the court. The Queen was instantly taken by the Welshman's handsome looks. She decided to play a game. Disguising herself as her chambermaid, she arranged to meet Owen in secret. The young man, unaware of the girl's true identity, attempted to force himself upon her, and in the struggle to free herself Catherine received a cut to her cheek. It was only when Owen came to serve the queen at dinner that he realised her true identity from the wound he had inflicted upon her, and ashamed of what he had done begged Catherine's forgiveness. The couple fell in love and soon were married.

One chronicler believed that Catherine's choice of husband was deliberate. In choosing a commoner, she hoped that the king's Council 'might not reasonably take vengeance on his life'. Others suggested later that she had married Owen since unlike her true love, Edmund Beaufort, Owen had no possessions to lose under the statute of 1428. According to a later source, as a Frenchwoman Catherine seems not to have understood the difference between the English and Welsh, and was intrigued that, when news of their marriage became known, Owen's 'kindred and country were objected . . . as most vile and barbarous'. Wishing to meet her husband's relatives, Owen sent for his cousins John ap Maredudd and Hywel ap Llywelyn ap Hywel, men who despite being of 'goodly stature and personage' were 'wholly destitute of bringing up and nurture'. When introduced to the queen, she spoke to them in several languages, but as Welsh speakers, they understood nothing and were 'not able to answer her', to which Catherine replied that 'they were the goodliest dumb creatures that she ever saw'.

If Catherine was indifferent to her new husband's humble origins, Owen remained conscious of the low status that being a Welshman at court brought. In 1432 he petitioned Parliament to be granted an exemption from the traditional restrictions placed upon Welshmen that treated him effectively as a second-class citizen. According to the grant he was from then on to be regarded 'as if he were a true English subject', although he was still unable to hold any royal office in any city, borough or market town.

This was of little consequence to Owen. He had secured his naturalisation and recognition as an English citizen less for himself than for his heirs. It must have been around this period that Catherine gave birth in secret to their first child, Edmund, followed soon afterwards by another son, Jasper. Henry VI now had two half-brothers who, although there was little chance that they could be considered members of the royal family and thereby eligible to be in line to the throne, would come to play an indelible part in English politics.

By 1436 Catherine was dying. She had been ill for some time, with, as she stated in her will, a 'grievous malady, in the which I have been long, and yet am, troubled and vexed'. She retired to Bermondsey Abbey where she died on 3 January 1437. She was buried in Westminster Abbey, where her wooden funeral effigy can still be viewed.

Without the protection of his royal wife, Owen knew his future was at risk, not least from Humphrey, Duke of Gloucester. Gloucester had been furious that Catherine had flouted his statute against her marriage, and that Owen 'had been so presumptuous . . . to intermix his blood with the noble race of kings'. Owen was also nervous what Henry VI's reaction might be to the news that had been kept from him until now: that his mother had taken another husband, and that by the time of her death Catherine had given birth to four more children – three sons, Edmund, Jasper and Owen and a daughter, Margaret, who died in infancy. Catherine had taken deliberate care when pregnant to seclude herself away from the court in London, giving birth in manor houses in the Hertfordshire countryside: Edmund had been born at Much Hadham, belonging to the Bishop of London, Jasper at Hatfield. Certainly when news of Owen and Catherine's marriage and their children was revealed, it came as a surprise to many, 'unwitting the common people till that she were dead and buried' as one chronicler observed.

It must have come as a considerable shock to Henry, who had visited Catherine at Bermondsey where he had given her a jewelled golden crucifix as a New Year's gift, to be told not only of his mother's death, but also that he had a stepfather and three half-brothers. Yet the king seems to have taken the news well; intrigued by his new family, he requested that Owen pay attendance to him at court.

Owen remained concerned as to the possible consequences of such a visit. He refused to come to court unless he received a promise from the king that he would be able to 'freely come and freely go'. Henry agreed, and instructed that Gloucester should inform the Welshman of his promise. Owen was at Daventry when he was told of the king's pledge by one of Gloucester's servants. Still he refused to come, stating that since there was no promise in writing, he could not be certain of the king's true intention. Nevertheless, Owen travelled to London where he sought sanctuary at Westminster, remaining there for 'many days'. Certain people who professed 'friendship and fellowship' eventually encouraged him to take up lodgings at a tavern at Westminster Gate. Soon after, he met the king. He told Henry that he believed he had been the victim of false allegations that he had offended the king, and that Henry himself had been 'heavily informed' against him. Owen declared that he was innocent, submitted himself to the king and offered to answer any accusation directly.

Owen returned to Wales, but at some point afterwards he was arrested, according to the council document that discussed his imprisonment, 'at the suit of the party', and placed in Newgate gaol. Had the king's word been broken? It was to be the subject of a meeting of the council in July 1437, which ruled that Owen had been granted safe conduct only once, and having 'freely come and freely gone', he could not assume the privilege of safe conduct twice. His arrest had been entirely within the law.

Who exactly was 'the party' that had issued a suit against him? The minutes of the council meeting to discuss Owen's fate point to the reason for his arrest, noting pointedly that he had 'dwelt' with the queen. Equally revealing are Gloucester's actions at the meeting, demanding personally a declaration of the council's ruling confirming the verdict under the Great Seal. It was probably through Gloucester's influence that the council also stated its belief that Owen held some 'malicious purpose or imagination' and that he should remain 'in ward'. To release him, they argued, would risk 'any rebellion, murmur or inconvenience'. Owen was to remain imprisoned until further notice. Gloucester had finally obtained his revenge.

Owen's imprisonment was to be a brief one. Sometime in late 1437 or early 1438, he had managed to escape from Newgate gaol during the night 'at searching time' with the help of his priest. The escape was a violent one, with Owen 'hurting foul' his keeper in the attempt. The attempt proved ultimately futile. Both Owen and his priest had been recaptured by March 1438, handed over to the sheriffs of London who were later pardoned for having 'allowed' Owen's escape in the first place, and returned to Newgate. By July, Owen was transferred to the more comfortable surroundings of Windsor Castle, where he remained incarcerated 'for particular causes' for a year, until he was granted an order from the king to move freely, dependent upon a substantial bail of £2,000 and 'his good behaviour towards the king and his people', though Owen was forbidden from entering Wales or the Marches. On 10 November 1439 a general pardon was finally granted for all offences he had committed, with the bail being cancelled on New Year's Day 1440, allowing Owen the chance to live free from recrimination within the king's household.

In the aftermath of their mother's death, Edmund and Jasper Tudor fared much better than their father. By July 1437 they had been placed in the care of Katherine de la Pole, the sister of the Earl of Suffolk and the abbess of Barking. They remained under her supervision at Barking until March 1442, when Henry VI began to take a personal interest in their upbringing and ordered his half-brothers to appear at court. Henry's chaplain John Blacman later wrote how the king, 'before he was married, being as a youth a pupil of chastity . . . would keep careful watch through hidden windows of his chamber, lest any foolish impertinence of women coming into the house should grow to a head, and cause the fall of any of his household. And like pains did he apply in the case of his two half-brothers, the Lords Jasper and Edmund, in their boyhood and youth; providing for them the most strict and safe guardianship, putting them under the care of virtuous and worthy priests, both for teaching and for right living and conversation, lest the untamed practices of youth should grow rank if they lacked any to prune them.' The third son, Owen, seems to have chosen a monastic life rather than enter the court. As Edmund and Jasper approached adulthood, however, the king's interest and enthusiasm for the welfare of his half-brothers was soon to change their lives dramatically.

While Edmund and Jasper Tudor spent their childhood in the secluded environs of Barking abbey, outside the political world at court, after nearly two decades of stable government led by the minority council, events were about to take a turn for the worse.

In 1437, the year of his mother's death, Henry VI brought his minority to an end. He had recently turned sixteen, and was keen to remove himself from the shackles of his minority council: three years earlier, aged thirteen, he had to be reminded that he was not yet old enough to take decisions. The king had been a precocious learner, whose tutor had noted how he had 'grown in years, in stature of his person, and also in conceit and knowledge of his royal estate, the which cause him to grudge with chastising'. Now Henry was determined to rule as a fully adult monarch, with all the personal duties and responsibilities that medieval kingship brought.

Yet something was not quite right. Even Henry's chaplain, John Blacman, whose hagiographical biography of the king helped raise Henry to saint-like proportions, and should therefore be treated with caution, admitted that the king was 'a simple man, without any crook of craft'. An exceptionally pious young man, his chastity seemed to go against the grain of what might have been expected from the traditional debauchery at court. As one nobleman was to discover to his cost when, organising a show of young women 'with bared bosoms' in order to entice the king, Henry, covering his eyes, fled in anger shouting, 'Fy, fy, for shame, forsothe ye be to blame'.

More worryingly, Henry spurned the tedious tasks of administration, preferring to be left in his study, absorbed in reading religious works. To fill his place, Henry allowed himself to be led by his advisers, in particular his chief minister, William de la Pole, the Earl of Suffolk, whom one chronicler described as England's 'second king'. Was Henry simply too young to properly lead the country? Or was there another reason why the king was unable to fulfil his duties effectively? Rather than deal with the important issues of the day, such as the control of English territories in France, Henry seemed more interested in establishing centres of learning such as Eton College and King's College, Cambridge.

In council Henry appeared simple-minded, often agreeing to the last piece of advice offered to him, only to change his mind just as suddenly as a decision had been taken. Easily swayed and lavish with his patronage, he allowed Suffolk to place his allies in key positions at court, the running costs of which were becoming ruinously expensive. Outside the king's household, rumours began to spread. A yeoman from Kent was reported in 1442 to have said that Henry was a lunatic like his grandfather, the French king Charles VI, who, believing he was made of glass, refused anyone to come near him fearing he would shatter into pieces. 'The king was a natural fool,' a Sussex man declared publicly in 1450, 'and would ofttimes hold a staff in his hands with a bird on the end, playing therewith as a fool.' 'Another king must be ordained to rule the land,' he presaged, stating that 'the king was no person able to rule'.

If Henry was mentally unstable, it is likely that he suffered from some form of hereditary schizophrenia, though perhaps in his younger years the disease had not fully manifested itself as it would do so with disastrous consequences later in Henry's life. His condition did not prevent him from marrying the fifteen-year-old Margaret of Anjou in March 1445; the queen arrived a month later and was crowned in Westminster in May. Margaret's influence as a teenager must have been limited, but there was no doubt that her arrival changed the political dynamics at court. Henry had been keen to bring peace to England and France; now Margaret, along with Suffolk, would push for a solution, opening negotiations that sought a peace treaty. In 1445 England seemed to hold the advantage: occupying Gascony, Anjou, Maine and Normandy in addition to territory around Calais. All this Henry was prepared to throw to the wind in order to obtain his cherished peace.

In December 1445 Henry wrote secretly to Charles VII promising to surrender Maine and Anjou.

No one was more aghast at Henry's manoeuvres for a French peace than the king's uncle, Gloucester. As Henry V's sole surviving brother, he saw himself very much as the guardian of English ambitions of conquest in France. Since Henry had no heir, Gloucester remained heir presumptive: the influence of the 'Good Duke' remained an uncomfortable presence for those who argued for the war to end. In 1442 an attempt had been made to discredit Gloucester when his wife Eleanor was accused of plotting the king's death through sorcery. In February 1447 Gloucester was arrested. Five days later the duke was dead, probably from a stroke brought on by the stress of his incarceration; but despite his body being exposed to public view, rumours began to spread that he had been deliberately put to death. As one chronicler wrote, 'some said he died of sorrow; some that he was murdered between two feather beds; and others said that a hot spit was put in his fundament. And so how he died God only knows.'

Gloucester's death opened up the way for peace negotiations with France to be concluded, implementing the secret agreement to cede Anjou and Maine to the French king Charles VII. The fortress town of Le Mans was surrendered in 1448 in return for agreement that a truce between the two countries be extended for a further two years. Behind the dealings, as ever, was Queen Margaret who wrote to Charles, her uncle by marriage, telling him 'in this matter we will do your pleasure as much as lies in our power, as we have always done already'.

Gloucester had not been the only nobleman concerned about the direction Henry and his advisers, the Earl of Suffolk and Margaret of Anjou among them, were leading the country. In the autumn of 1445 Henry had recalled his cousin Richard, Duke of York as commander in chief. York was furious, especially since he had not been paid his expenses or salary for several years, amounting to the enormous sum of £38,666. The duke was posted to Ireland as the King's Lieutenant there, no doubt to remove him from the scene: as one chronicler wrote, 'envy reared its head among the princes and barons of England, and was directed at the duke, who was gaining in honour and prosperity'. Out of sight, York smouldered, watching and waiting as the English kingdom in France that he, along with his ancestors, had fought for, fell apart.

For those who warned that the French truce was a prelude for Charles VII's ambitions to reconquer France, time would soon prove them correct. In July 1449 Charles VII tore up the terms of the truce and declared war, launching a full scale invasion of Normandy. The English were taken by surprise, and by October 1449 with their defences in disrepair, Rouen had fallen. It was to be the first of a series of castles, strongholds and towns that would fall without resistance. By August 1450 the English had been driven out of Normandy. It was a political disaster: 'We have not now a foot of land in Normandy', one observer wrote, almost in a state of shock.

The consequences of military failure reverberated across the realm as popular discontent broke out into open rebellion. The blame for English losses in France was placed squarely on Henry's small clique of advisers, most notably a gang of three who were identified as being responsible for the king's most disastrous decisions: Suffolk, the king's confessor William Ayscough, Bishop of Salisbury and Adam Moleyns, Bishop of Chichester. Within six months they were all dead: executed not through judicial trial, but killed at the hands of furious lynch mobs. In January 1450 Moleyns had been set upon by a mob of soldiers and seamen at Portsmouth; his death sparked further risings in Kent and London, alarming the king enough to issue orders that every member of the royal household was to be supplied with a bow and sheaf of arrows, 'for the safety of our person'. To calm public resentment, a scapegoat was required: Suffolk, having first been placed in the Tower, was banished from the kingdom for five years. Not even this punishment could save him: as he set sail in early May, his ship was intercepted off the coast of Dover by a small fleet lying in wait for him. He was dragged aboard a ship, the *Nicholas of the Tower*, where with a rusty sword, his head was cut off 'with half a dozen strokes' and his corpse dumped upon the sands at Dover.

The government blamed the lawlessness of the Kentish men for Suffolk's murder, and threatened reprisals: the sheriff of Kent even threatened to turn the entire county into a deer forest. The threats were ill-judged. A large uprising, led by a shadowy figure named Jack Cade, stirred by the penniless soldiers returning home from France, descended upon London in June 1450, with a large rebel army gathering at Black-heath. The royal army was caught in an ambush and defeated; as Henry VI fled northwards, it seemed as if all order had broken down. On 29 June the rebels burst into the chancel of a Wiltshire church where William Ayscough was saying Mass, dragging him up a nearby hill where he was put to death. Five days later, Cade's army entered London, capturing two noblemen who were summarily tried and executed. Matters were getting out of hand as the rebels rampaged through the streets in an orgy of violence, theft and mob rule; Londoners turned against them, forcing Cade upon promise of a pardon to disband his army, which quickly dispersed and fled. Of course the pardon meant nothing: Henry was determined to get retribution, and within ten days Cade had been hunted down and killed, his dead body beheaded and quartered, with his head placed on a spike above London Bridge. In marked contrast to his peaceful nature, the king ordered a 'harvest of heads', making sure that he personally attended each execution. It was a futile policy of extreme violence that merely alienated those protes-tors who had believed that Henry, if only removed from the grip of his advisers, would have taken their side. The rebellion had achieved nothing. None of the rebels' demands was met, nor were their petitions heard. Instead it had exposed the reality that Henry's kingship was a sham; it was not merely his advisers who were to blame, but Henry's own weakness and his incapacity to govern that lay at the heart of the collapse in order.

As men pondered the consequences of what had taken place that summer, in early September a ship docked at Beaumaris Harbour in Anglesey. From the boat, Richard, Duke of York stepped out onto the sands of the beach. His arrival would shortly transform the monarchy for ever.

York's arrival at Anglesey posed more questions than it offered answers. Why had he abandoned his office, and why had he done so unan-nounced? What had he hoped to achieve by returning home? Did he intend to take advantage of the government's current weakness? What was certain was that from the moment he stepped ashore, York would become a dynamic force in English politics for the next decade.

The timing of his arrival, coming so soon after the defeat of Cade's rebellion, seemed too much of a coincidence. Some had suspected the duke's involvement in Suffolk's death; his wealth and contacts certainly could have provided for the fleet of ships that had apprehended Suffolk and inflicted his grisly death. The demands set down by Cade's rebels had also included the request that Henry should appoint to his council 'men of his true blood', naming 'the high and mighty prince, the Duke of York' as a particular example, complaining that he had been 'exiled from our sovereign lord's person by the suggestions of those false traitors the Duke of Suffolk and his affinity'.

Upon landing, York's claim that he was 'not against the king and desired nothing but the good of England' appeared to be a convenient fiction, especially given his proximity in blood to the crown. Arguably, since the deaths of the Dukes of Gloucester and Bedford, York had a strong claim to be the heir apparent as closest in line to the throne. Born in 1411, York's father was Richard, Earl of Cambridge. Cambridge was the son of Edmund Langley, Duke of York, the fourth son of Edward III. His mother was Anne Mortimer, a descendant of Lionel, Duke of Clarence, Edward III's second son. This gave York two separate claims to royal descent, though admittedly one was through his mother that had passed through the female line, weakening its veracity. Nevertheless York's ancestry provided a compelling case that he should be considered Henry's heir, particularly since the childless Richard II had considered the Mortimers his natural heirs. It was surely for this reason that Jack Cade had titled himself 'John Mortimer' in his official petition – the choice of surname had been deliberate, since Cade had wanted to remind people of the Mortimer claim to the throne held by York.

There was another rival claim to the throne to possibly match York's, depending on whether one considered bastards to be acceptable heirs. Edmund Beaufort, Duke of Somerset, was the fourth son of John Beaufort, the eldest of the illegitimate children of John of Gaunt, the Duke of Lancaster. Gaunt himself was the third son of Edward III, whose legitimate marriage to his first wife Blanche bore him the future king Henry IV. Unfortunately for the Beauforts, the stigma of being born out of wedlock, the result of an adulterous affair, meant that no such claim to the throne could exist, despite Gaunt's later marriage to his mistress Katherine Swynford. In spite of his bastardy, John Beaufort had been declared legitimate by Parliament in 1397, an act which was confirmed by John of Gaunt's eldest legitimate son, Henry IV, in 1407. Henry had added the important proviso that the Beaufort line should never succeed to the English throne, yet it remained unclear whether royal declarations could alter the fact that the Beauforts were sprung from an illegitimate union. It did not prevent the family from becoming one of the most powerful families in the country, being granted the earldom of Dorset and later the dukedom of Somerset, though their income remained largely derived from the crown. Since Edmund's older brothers Henry and John were both dead by 1444, he became the head of the family and the upholder of the Beaufort claim.

Discussions over who might succeed the king were bound to surface. Each of Henry's uncles had died without leaving an heir: the king had become the only surviving legitimate male member of the house of Lancaster. After six years of marriage, Margaret of Anjou had been unable to conceive a son and heir, and it seemed as if her marriage to Henry would prove barren, a point that was not lost upon the mobs during the summer of 1450: one reason given for William Ayscough's summary execution was the belief that he had urged Henry to pursue a life of celibacy. Were Henry to die, the choice would have to be between the competing claims of York and Somerset's Beaufort inheritance. It was a choice that would one day resurface.

Somerset was a controversial figure. In his early life his rumoured affair with Catherine of Valois caused political scandal; he had proved a successful military leader during the siege of Harfleur in 1439, but his conduct in the French wars came under persistent attack with allegations that he had been more interested in safeguarding his own position than securing national victory, hoarding weapons in his own castle.

York despised Somerset, whom he considered a coward. Not only had Somerset taken the duke's place as Lieutenant of France, he had presided over the loss of Normandy, surrendering the town of Rouen to Charles VII in person. Unlike York, who paid heavily for the military expenses he incurred in office, having lent the crown £26,000, Somerset was reimbursed for his costs while York remained unpaid. After his failure in France, it seemed that Somerset was now on the point of seizing the rewards of power in England: having been created a duke to match York's status in 1448, Somerset returned from France in August

1450 to be appointed to the prestigious office of Constable of England, something which York must have baulked at.

Somerset's return must have been the trigger for York's appearance on the shores of Anglesey; indeed, before leaving Ireland, York had written open letters to the king defending his conduct, promising that he meant Henry no harm, but instead he called for the removal of those 'traitors' who were working against the king's best interest. Of these, York singled out Somerset for 'encompassing the destruction of his two kingdoms' since he had 'been responsible for the shameful loss of all Normandy'.

York first travelled to Ludlow Castle where, having raised a force of around 4,000 men in the Welsh Marches, he began his march to London. Henry issued an order for the duke and his men to be intercepted and arrested, but York managed to give them the slip, and arriving in Westminster on 29 September, sought out Henry, who had taken refuge in his apartments. Forcing his way inside the king's privy chamber, York swore his loyalty to the king, but insisted that his advisers must go. Henry was in no position to refuse to bargain, yet as a compromise he agreed that a new council would be formed, with York at its helm, with a new Parliament being summoned to pass legislation to address the national debt (which stood at £372,000 in 1449) and remove the king's councillors who were considered to have lined their own pockets. For the public, York was a figure of fresh hope. The duke had great expectations to live up to, but he knew that he could do nothing without the king's support. Yet Henry refused to remove Somerset from his position. Exasperated, the duke overplayed his hand when he allowed one of his supporters to present a bill calling for York to be recognised as the king's heir. Outrage ensued, and Parliament was promptly dissolved.

York's journey had ended in failure. Somerset remained in the ascendant, having by now amassed crown pensions and offices worth £3,000 a year. In 1451 he was further appointed captain of Calais, placing at his disposal the country's largest military base. Yet military failure in France continued. As the French began to march on Calais, York held Somerset personally responsible. He began to plan a coup to replace him, writing to several towns in early 1452 seeking their support for his enterprise against 'the envy, malice and untruth of the said Duke of

Somerset . . . who works continually for my undoing'. Few stirred, yet York marched his troops to the outskirts of the capital, where negotiations began in earnest to prevent armed conflict breaking out. Henry apparently agreed that Somerset should be put on trial for his conduct during the French wars in return for York pledging his loyalty to the crown; believing the king, York rode to meet with Henry at Blackheath. When the duke entered the king's tent, he found Somerset standing at Henry's side. It was a trap: accompanied by only forty of his men, York was forced into submission, riding back to London alongside the king as though he were his prisoner. Despite having committed treason, the duke was fortunate; it was decided not to put York on trial, probably for fear that the occasion might easily become a trial of Somerset's conduct in the wars. Instead, before being released in March 1452, York was made to swear an oath of loyalty before a great assembly of nobles in St Paul's, declaring that any future misconduct would be declared treason. Humiliated and completely defeated, York withdrew from the court to spend the next eighteen months in self-imposed exile.

Emboldened by his victory, Henry looked to strengthen his position even further, promoting key allies such as the Earl of Worcester to Treasurer, and the Earl of Wiltshire to Lieutenant of Ireland, where he replaced York. The king even decided that he would renew the war against France, taking an army across the Channel to defeat Charles VII's forces. Surprisingly, the tide seemed to turn for the English under the ferocious and skilled military leader, John Talbot, Earl of Shrewsbury.

It was against this backdrop of recovery and success that Henry decided to make one of his boldest political gestures: on 23 November 1452, he raised his half-brothers Edmund and Jasper Tudor to the rank of earls. Henry had already recognised both brothers as his kinsmen by providing for their education and upbringing; now he was prepared to go further, recognising their importance as members of the house of Lancaster. Henry's intentions can be guessed at from the choice of titles he was to bestow upon Edmund and Jasper. Edmund was to become the Earl of Richmond, Jasper the Earl of Pembroke. Both titles retained especial significance to the king: the earldoms of Richmond and Pembroke had previously been held by Henry's uncles, John, Duke of Bedford and Humphrey, Duke of Gloucester. Since the two Tudor brothers, despite having French royal blood in their veins, had no claim to the English throne, raising them to the higher ranks of the nobility could hardly endanger Henry's own standing. Their formal recognition as the king's half-brothers would help Henry to reinforce his own family interest, creating new standard bearers for the Lancastrian dynasty. It also helped to remove both men from any focus of political discontent, binding them close to the king to whom they owed so much.

The official investiture took place after the Christmas holidays, when on Friday 5 January 1453, the two brothers, having been provided with a new wardrobe of velvet clothing, furs and cloth of gold, appeared in front of the king attired in their ermine robes to be formally created earls. Two weeks later, they were summoned to Parliament. When Parliament opened in March, the House of Commons presented a petition to the king requesting that Jasper and Edmund be recognised formally as his legitimate brothers, born of the same mother as 'uterine' brothers. They also requested that Henry release both brothers from any legal penalties arising from their father's Welsh origins. The very fact that the request was made is remarkable in itself: Edmund and Jasper were the first Welshmen to enter the ranks of the English peerage.

As earls, both Jasper and Edmund would need a substantial income to sustain their positions at court. Between November 1452 and July 1453, both brothers were given substantial grants of landed estates that gave them each an annual income of £925. Edmund's lands were concentrated in the honour of Richmond, containing the fertile and prosperous lands on the eastern side of the country, between Norfolk and Yorkshire. Jasper received the honour of Pembroke, based around Pembroke itself, together with the lordships of Cilgerran and Llanstephan in south-west Wales; many of his estates were grouped around the great estuary of Milford Haven. Since their political activities were largely to be focused at court, both brothers would also need a townhouse or 'inn' within the capital. Edmund was granted Baynard's Castle, a large fortified house on the banks of the Thames, while Jasper was given a house in Brook Street, Stepney.

Titles and lands were not the only prizes that Henry had decided to bestow upon his half-brothers. On 24 March 1453, Edmund and Jasper were given joint custody, the 'wardship', of the nine-year-old Margaret

Beaufort, the daughter of the late John Beaufort, the elder brother of Henry's despised adviser Edmund Beaufort. Henry's expectation was not merely that the brothers would look after the girl. With the rights of wardship came the right to marry her. It was time, Henry believed, that one of the Tudor brothers at least should take a bride.

In particular, in granting Margaret Beaufort's wardship to the Tudors, Henry had Edmund Tudor's marriage in mind. As one writer later recorded, he intended to 'make means for Edmund his brother'. Margaret was not only one of England's richest heiresses in the 1450s: she was descended from the royal blood of Edward III, albeit through the illegitimate line borne from the relationship between Edward's son, John of Gaunt and his mistress Katherine Swynford, who had given birth to Margaret's grandfather, John Beaufort. In many ways, the Beauforts held a similar position to that of the Tudors. Both families were descended from royal blood, though both were tainted by accusations of illegitimacy. It was made clear that neither family, despite their nearness of blood, would ever be considered legitimate heirs to the throne.

Since John of Gaunt and Katherine Swynford later married, their son John was declared legitimate by both the parliaments of Richard II and Henry IV, though any claim to the throne that his heirs might have was specifically ruled out. Beaufort had been created the Earl of Somerset and Marquis of Dorset by Richard II in 1397, with his lands granted to him around the West Country, focused on his residence at Corfe Castle on the Dorset coast. The story of the family then turned to tragedy. Margaret's father John had succeeded to the earldom in 1418, yet his life had been wasted as a prisoner of war, having been captured at the battle of Bauge in 1421. Imprisoned in France for seventeen years, he was unable to marry until 1442, aged thirty-eight. His release had cost him £24,000, half the value of his inheritance, leaving him 'impoverished' and bitter at the hand life had dealt him. Desperate to win back his ransom, Beaufort persuaded the king to allow him to lead a major expedition through France. Elevated to the rank of Duke of Somerset for the campaign, Beaufort's expedition was a disaster, achieving no military success and leaving the crown with a bill of over £26,000. The fiasco caused Beaufort to be banished from court; retiring to the

West Country in disgrace, he died shortly afterwards, possibly taking his own life.

Aged just forty, John Beaufort left behind a pregnant wife and his sole surviving heir, his daughter Margaret, a few days short of her first birthday. The duchess of Somerset's second child did not survive, leaving her daughter as sole heiress. Margaret's wardship was a valuable commodity, one which Henry VI decided to grant to the Earl of Suffolk, in reward for his 'notable services' rendered to the country. Six years later, shortly before his exile and death off the coast of Dover, Suffolk decided that his only son, the seven-year-old John de la Pole, should marry Margaret, then aged six. He had originally intended that John should marry Anne Beauchamp, the daughter and sole heir of the Earl of Warwick, but she had died at the age of five in 1449. The hasty decision was taken between 28 January and 7 February 1450, while Suffolk remained in the Tower. It was obvious Suffolk considered it an urgent necessity to provide for his son's future, though the decision sparked further suspicion that he was attempting to control the succession to the crown, using his son's marriage to Margaret to obtain a claim to the throne. Suffolk's death brought an end to the prospect of Margaret and John de la Pole remaining in permanent union. Their betrothal was easily enough annulled: despite the fact that a papal dispensation had been sought and a marriage contract agreed, since Margaret had entered into her marriage contract with Suffolk before she was twelve, under canon law she was not bound to fulfil it. This allowed Henry the freedom to once again grant Margaret's marriage, this time to Edmund Tudor.

At so young an age, it is unlikely that Margaret would have known much about her marriage to John de la Pole. But three years later, making her first visit to court in February 1453 accompanied by her mother, the experience would leave a lasting impression upon her. She was treated with kindness by the king, who provided 'his right dear and wellbeloved cousin Margaret' with new clothes worth 100 marks. But it would have been the display of ceremony and the lavish clothing such as the blood-red dresses worn by Margaret of Anjou and her ladies in waiting at the St George's Day celebrations that April that gave the young Margaret her first introduction to the dramatic reality of power and its political stage.

Many years later, her memory faded and her childhood recollections hazy, Margaret told her chaplain John Fisher how she believed in her own mind she had faced a choice between John de la Pole and Edmund Tudor. Unable to decide, she was urged to pray to St Nicholas, 'the patron and helper of all true maidens, and to beseech him to put in her mind what she were best to do'. She had been given the night to decide and 'the morrow after make answer of her mind determinately'. In her dream, she remembered how a man dressed in white had visited her, 'arrayed like a bishop', who told her to choose Edmund Tudor as her husband.

Margaret's marriage to John de la Pole was annulled the same month she arrived at court, with her wardship formally being granted to the Tudor brothers on 24 March 1453. Her marriage to Edmund seems to have taken place formally in 1455, when they travelled to Lamphey in Pembrokeshire. Edmund and Margaret's marriage had taken place during a period of relative good news for the Lancastrian dynasty, for in March 1453 it was announced that Queen Margaret was pregnant. Within months, however, the country would once again be thrown into turmoil.

No one could be sure what exactly had caused Henry VI to collapse at his hunting lodge at Clarendon near Salisbury one day in August 1453. Unable to move or speak, he was 'so lacking in understanding and memory and so incapable that he was neither able to walk upon his feet nor to lift up his head, nor well to move himself from the place where he was seated'. It was believed that the king had suffered 'disease and disorder of such a sort'. No one understood then the medical realities of psychiatric illness, perhaps a form of hereditary schizophrenia inherited from his Valois ancestors. What everyone did know was that the king's mental collapse was very serious indeed, threatening the very foundation of the Lancastrian dynasty.

One possibility is that the queen's pregnancy may have placed strain upon a man uncomfortable with physical intimacy. More likely to have damaged Henry's mental state had been the events of the previous few weeks, when on 17 July the Earl of Shrewsbury's army in France had been overwhelmed at Castillon, and the earl himself killed in the cannon fire. Defeat at Castillon in effect brought with it the end of the Hundred Years War.

For two months news of Henry's collapse was kept secret in the hope that the king might recover. Yet not even the joyous news of the birth of his son and heir, Prince Edward, on 13 October 1453 could wake Henry from his catatonic state. When Queen Margaret presented their son to the king, he reacted 'without any answer or countenance, saving only that he looked on the Prince and cast his eyes down again without any more'. It was a situation which everyone realised could not continue.

For Richard, Duke of York, it was a second chance: as the most senior nobleman in the realm, while the king remained incapacitated, he had a strong claim to be recognised as Protector. Recognising the threat to his own position at court, Somerset was understandably reluctant to include York in any council negotiations about what should be done, though this did not prevent York from returning to London by November 1453, accompanied by a large retinue of armed men. The stage was set for an inevitable confrontation.

Throughout the winter, both factions sought to fill the vacuum of power. Margaret of Anjou demanded that she be declared regent of England and have 'the whole rule of this land'. It was to prove a step too far. Many noblemen who previously had refused to take York's side, Jasper and Edmund Tudor among them, understood the idea of a French Queen, the niece of their French enemy Charles VII, would be politically impossible. By January 1454 the Tudor brothers had formed an alliance with York, it being reported that 'the Earls of Warwick, Richmond and Pembroke come with the Duke of York, as it is said, each of them with a goodly fellowship'. Margaret's intervention ensured that the council's sympathies shifted towards York, agreeing to nominate him as the King's Lieutenant in February 1454. As armed retinues of various noblemen swarmed through London, tensions began to mount.

Matters came to a head when the appointment of a new chancellor became a political necessity following the death of the previous holder of the office Cardinal Kemp in March 1454. A crisis of authority opened up since only the king could signal who should take his place. The council rode to Windsor to discuss the matter with Henry. In vain, they tried three times to speak with the king, 'to the which matters they could get no answer nor sign, not for any prayer or desire, lamentable cheer or exhortation, nor for anything that any of them could do or say, to their great sorrow and discomfort'. Recognising that Henry would be incapable of taking any decision, it was decided that York should be appointed Protector, the chief councillor with responsibility for the defence of the realm.

York's success lay not merely in Henry's incapacity; the duke had managed to win more noblemen to his cause as a series of local conflicts between magnates had broken out, contesting lordships that had been parcelled out unwisely and often to separate parties by the crown. National politics and local authority had become polarised, as members of the gentry and minor nobility sought protection from great lords such as York. The most significant feud was the longstanding rivalry between the Nevilles and the Percys in Yorkshire, which had degenerated into an armed brawl between both sides in August 1453. When the king did nothing to prevent the violent behaviour of the Percys, who held the royal office of the Warden of the East March, against the Nevilles, it was clear that the Nevilles would have to look elsewhere for help. York was closely associated with the Nevilles, having married the youngest daughter of Ralph Neville, the Earl of Westmorland. Matters were made worse for the family in June 1453 when Somerset was granted estates in Glamorgan, previously held by the twenty-five-year-old Richard Neville, Earl of Warwick. It was to prove the final straw for the earl, who now sided with York in order to oust Somerset.

As Protector, York moved quickly to establish his position. Somerset had been sent to the Tower in November 1453, shortly after York's arrival in the city, having had charges of misconduct in France once again brought against him. York had every intention of keeping him there. In the meantime, York replaced key positions in the council with his allies: his brother-in-law, the Earl of Salisbury, was made Chancellor, Thomas Bourgchier was made Archbishop of Canterbury while York himself took over the captaincy of Calais. Margaret of Anjou was ordered to be removed to Windsor, where she was effectively placed under house arrest.

Then on Christmas Day 1454, Henry suddenly recovered from his illness, waking as if from a coma, not knowing 'where he had been whilst he hath been sick till now'. Henry's recovery of his faculties turned a tragedy into a national disaster. York was dismissed as Protector; in his place returned Henry's old friends and former advisers, including Somerset, who was released from prison in February 1455. York and his associates left London in disgust, without taking formal leave from the king. Somerset now began to plot their destruction, summoning Parliament to meet in May 1455 'to provide for the king's safety'. It was soon clear that York was to be placed on trial. The duke knew that if he were to fight for his survival he would have to act first. Military force seemed to be his only option.

On 1 May 1455 Henry departed London, riding with a large company of noblemen, including Jasper Tudor, intending to journey to Leicester. Spending the first night at Watford, they continued on to St Albans. There York was waiting with an armed force. Negotiations began in earnest, as heralds passed messages from one camp to another. York's demands, however, were uncompromising: Somerset was to be handed over, to be imprisoned. This Henry refused. As the talks continued, York's patience was wearing thin. After the herald had returned from his third mission, the duke had waited long enough. 'Now,' he is said to have replied, 'we must do what we can.' The Rubicon had just been crossed.

Street fighting broke out between the king's men and York's. It was soon clear that York was winning the 'battle'; many of Henry's household, who had been set upon even before they had the chance to arm themselves, fled into the surrounding countryside. Some raced for the abbey doors, in the hope of finding sanctuary. Others simply had to make do with the nearest building for shelter as the Yorkist troops streamed through lanes and back gardens into the town. The king sought shelter in a tanner's cottage as his standard was abandoned in the street, but not before he had been injured, wounded in the neck. When York discovered what had happened to the king, he ordered that he be removed to the abbey for his safety. His real target, Somerset, had barricaded himself into a local inn. There was to be no escape. As York's men surrounded the building and broke down the doors, Somerset resolved to die fighting and was said to have killed four men by his own hand in his final charge before he was hit first by an axe then set upon and hacked to death.

What part Jasper Tudor played in the fighting must have been limited. He had little military training or experience to take an active role in the fighting. The scenes of death, of the hail of arrows that had descended upon them, leaving many of Henry's household with face, neck and arm wounds, would have left a lasting impression upon him. The abbot of St Albans recalled the horrific scenes of violence that Jasper must also have witnessed: 'here you saw a man with his brains dashed out, here one with a broken arm, another with his throat cut, a fourth with a pierced chest'. It also left Jasper with a resolve that there might still be another solution to violence. With Somerset dead, perhaps reconciliation might be possible. Jasper would now play a critical role in attempting to bridge the two factions together.

Henry was taken back to London, riding alongside York. He had become effectively a prisoner of the Yorkists, even if they still claimed that they were the loyal servants of the king. When Parliament was summoned several weeks later in May, both Tudor brothers were ordered to attend. One of the most pressing issues was to stabilise the nation's finances, which had been placed under severe strain by the king's lavish grants of land and office. Now, in a grand Act of Resumption, all grants which Henry had made since the beginning of his reign were cancelled. There were however to be a small number of exemptions: as members of the royal family, Edmund and Jasper were to keep all their estates and offices. York could hardly have been pleased, but he recognised that he needed to build a broad coalition of support, and that the Tudor brothers had the potential to be his allies.

Shortly after the battle, Henry suffered a second breakdown. Both brothers knew that Henry's government could not continue in its present form with the king at the helm. In November 1454 they had both attended a council meeting which drew up ordinances to reform and, more importantly, reduce the size of the king's burgeoning household which was costing £24,000 a year to run despite its income being only £5,000. They sympathised with York's demands that more economical government was needed. Yet it was becoming increasingly difficult to retain a foothold in both camps. While their loyalty to their half-brother the king was beyond question, Edmund and Jasper were not convinced that Margaret of Anjou should lead the Lancastrian party. As the rift between York and Henry's court grew deeper, the more difficult it would become for the Tudor brothers to balance their loyalties to both the king and the security of the realm.

*

When Parliament reassembled in November 1455, York was reappointed as the king's Protector. Neither Edmund nor Jasper Tudor were present for the opening ceremony. Instead Edmund had been sent to Wales as the king's official representative, tasked with upholding royal authority there. It was a formidable challenge. Parts of the country had remained a lawless land ever since the end of Owen Glyndwr's rebellion forty years previously, with local rivalries between landowners often breaking out into violent quarrels, exacerbated by the fact that most offices were held by absentee noblemen who handed power and authority to their agents to act as deputies on their behalf. Exploiting their position for their own financial and political gain, effective government in many regions of south and east Wales had broken down. York himself had placed William Herbert of Raglan to deputise for him in his lordship of Usk, while the Duke of Buckingham had handed control of his lordship in Brecon to the Vaughans of Tretower. Both families, the Herberts and the Vaughans, now wielded significant authority on behalf of their masters.

The most influential force in the region, however, was Gruffydd ap Nicholas, whose unchallenged power in south-west Wales Edmund was now expected to curb. York was concerned about Gruffydd ap Nicholas's control, especially since the duke had recently replaced Somerset as constable of Carmarthen and Aberystwyth castles. Having moved to Lamphey in Pembrokeshire by September 1455, two miles east of his brother's castle at Pembroke, Edmund embarked on restoring royal authority to the region.

Gruffyd ap Nicholas resented the arrival of the young and inexperienced Edmund who himself had no lands in Wales. By June 1456 the two were 'at war greatly', with Gruffyd having occupied castles at Aberystwyth, Carmarthen and the fortresses of Carreg Cennen and Kidwelly on the Carmarthenshire coastline. Edmund fought hard to win back lost territory, with some limited success, managing to retake Carmarthen Castle. Yet as he continued to pursue his royal duties in the king's name, the political tide had begun to turn. Edmund soon found that he was facing the very same man who had sent him to Wales in the first place.

The Duke of York's second protectorship had lasted until February

1456, when Henry once again recovered and dismissed him, though being 'in charity with all the world' had decided to keep York as 'his chief and principal councillor'. It was not Henry whom York had to fear: Queen Margaret, now a prominent figure in her late twenties, determined to protect her son's royal inheritance, was described as 'a great and intensely active woman, for she spares no pains to pursue her business towards an end and conclusion favourable to her power'. Margaret was desperate to rid her husband and his household from York's influence: she had twice witnessed the duke seize power, and with it the expenditure of her royal household and its available patronage significantly reduced. She was determined to avoid York gaining the upper hand once more. Touring the country looking for support, Margaret sought out allies, strengthening her party against the duke. With neither side prepared to show their hand, the atmosphere was one of mutual suspicion: 'My lord York . . . watches the queen and she watches him,' wrote one London correspondent. Slowly, England was drifting towards civil war.

In seeking to defend the king's royal authority, Edmund Tudor was now inadvertently drawn into conflict with York himself. Edmund's recapturing of Carmarthen Castle from Gruffyd ap Nicholas, though a task he had been commanded to achieve, was now taken as an act of hostility against York, who held the constableship of the castle. Having been stripped once again of his authority at court, York sought to re-establish his power in Wales, sending his retainers to take control of Carmarthen from Edmund. On 10 August 2,000 men from Herefordshire led by York's agents Sir William Herbert, Sir Walter Devereux, Herbert's brother-in-law, and the Vaughan family crossed the border into West Wales, seizing Carmarthen Castle and imprisoning Edmund Tudor. It was the first time that the Tudors had faced the personal consequences of having been caught in the crossfire of the civil troubles brewing between the Yorkist party and the court party of the king and the Lancastrian dynasty, with which they were now inextricably linked through both blood and title. Edmund was released from captivity shortly afterwards, but the conditions of his imprisonment may have hastened his contracting of some kind of epidemic disease, probably the plague. He never left the castle, and on 1 November 1456 finally succumbed to his illness. He was buried nearby at Greyfriars

Church, though his tomb, finished with a brass image of the earl, was later transferred to St David's Cathedral during the Dissolution of the Monasteries.

Edmund's death was mourned by Welsh poets, who described him as 'brother of King Henry, nephew of the Dauphin and son of Owen', comparing Wales without Edmund to a land without a ruler, a church without a priest, a beach without water. What the poet failed to mention was that Edmund was about to bequeath what was to become his greatest legacy; for in death he had left his young wife Margaret seven months pregnant with his child.

At twenty-six, Edmund Tudor was over twice his wife's age, who at twelve was two years younger than the accepted age of fourteen at which a marriage could be consummated. To attempt to conceive a child any earlier brought with it significant risk to both mother and child. But Edmund had ulterior motives for making Margaret pregnant at such a young age. With a landed inheritance that included estates in the south-west and the Midlands, together with other properties in Yorkshire and in Wales, Margaret's landed value was worth over £800 a year. Edmund knew that in law, if a living child were born to the couple, no matter how long it lived, as father he would become the official tenant of Margaret's lands, able to legally receive the income from her estates. It was a ruthless strategy, and given Margaret's small physical size – as her chaplain John Fisher admitted later, she was 'not a woman of great stature . . . she was so much smaller at that stage' – a significant gamble to take. But Edmund seemed to care little for his wife's physical welfare. His overriding concern lay more in the material welfare of his landed estates and wealth. The irony of Edmund's sudden death was that it would be Margaret, inheriting portions of Edmund's estate, who benefited most from the marriage agreement.

A difficult pregnancy was made worse by fears that the plague which had killed Edmund might have spread across the region. John Fisher recalled the danger surrounding Henry's birth, coming so soon after his father's death: 'while your mother carried you in the womb', he later told Henry in an oration, 'you narrowly avoided the plague of which your illustrious father died, which could so easily have killed an unborn child'. Behind the towering thirteenth-century walls of Pembroke Castle, Margaret took to her bed in a small room on the first floor of the great gatehouse to prepare for childbirth, a terrified thirteen-year-old uncertain not only whether she would survive the birth, but also what her future as a widow with a baby might be.

On St Anne's Day, 28 January 1457, Henry Tudor was born at Pembroke Castle. It was not an easy birth. For a time it seemed that in labour both Margaret and Henry were at risk of losing their lives, and the trauma of the birth left Margaret so physically damaged, if not mentally scarred, that she would never have children again. Henry would be her only child, strengthening what was to become a remarkable bond between mother and son. Years later, Margaret remembered in a letter how 'this day of Saint Annes, that I did bring into this world my good and gracious Prince . . . and only beloved son'. Even as she recovered from childbirth, Margaret swiftly took control of her son's destiny. One tradition recorded by the sixteenth-century Welsh chronicler Elis Gruffyd, related to him by some old men alive at the time, was that the baby had been baptised Ywain, Welsh for Owen, but upon hearing this, Margaret had insisted that the child's name be changed to Henry, perhaps to reflect the importance of his English identity over his Welsh origins and closeness to the Lancastrian dynasty. If true, it was one of the wisest decisions Margaret Beaufort was ever to make.

2

TO CONQUER OR DIE

••

I n March 1457, two months after giving birth, Margaret Beaufort departed from Pembroke Castle, travelling across harsh wintry tracks as she journeyed a hundred miles eastwards. She was accompanied by Jasper Tudor, who had returned to Wales upon news of his brother's death to ensure the safety of his sister-in-law and his newborn nephew Henry. It would mark the beginning of a lifelong bond between Henry Tudor and Jasper, who became over time a kind of surrogate father. Jasper himself was unmarried and without an heir; he knew that it would be on Henry's shoulders that the fortunes of his family would rest. As one Welsh poet wrote in an elegy composed shortly after Edmund's death, Jasper would do everything to protect his brother's baby son, whom the poet compared to a young deer who would one day grow into a proud stag.

For the moment, Jasper decided that Margaret must take a new husband as soon as she possibly could. The young girl had only been widowed for five months, and was still recovering from giving birth, but they both understood that given the political turmoil, it would be better for Margaret to choose a husband now rather than later have another forced upon her by the king, or whoever controlled him. For this purpose the destination of their journey was Greenfield, near Newport, the Duke of Buckingham's residence. Buckingham was one of the wealthiest peers of the realm, and the only English nobleman whose power might match the Duke of York. The duke was keen to marry his second son, Henry Stafford, to Margaret, mindful of her substantial landed estates which would enrich the family greatly. Since Henry Stafford and Margaret were second cousins, the couple needed a dispensation to marry. This was granted by the Bishop of Coventry and Lichfield on 6 April, with the official ceremony being celebrated the following January.

Jasper Tudor now turned to the task of finishing his brother's mission to bring peace and stability to South Wales. Sir William Herbert had remained at liberty, free to continue his lawless campaigns that included mustering armed men in Abergavenny, Usk and Glamorgan. At the end of March 1457, charges were brought against Herbert, Sir Walter Devereux and the Vaughan family. Henry, Margaret of Anjou, together with the Duke of Buckingham and Jasper Tudor arrived at Hereford to oversee their trial. It was difficult not to suspect foul play, though at the trial, no blame was laid upon Herbert, Devereux or the Vaughans, who merely claimed that they had acted with parliamentary authority. At the same time, the court party realised that simple vengeance for Edmund's death would prove counter-productive, with the potential for heavy sentences to be seen as an attack on York. Instead, Herbert was to be pardoned along with the Vaughans, though Devereux was gaoled until February 1458.

Whatever retribution Jasper had hoped to achieve for his brother's death, Herbert's release and amnesty must have been galling. He knew that Edmund's death, whether from the plague or violence, had been hastened by his arrest by the Duke of York's men. It was to mark a watershed moment for Jasper, who now broke off contact with York. His earlier dalliance with compromise and moderation had ended, as Jasper placed himself firmly in the king's camp, committed to the Lancastrian cause. He spent time at court in personal attendance upon Henry at Sheen, with 'no more Lords', though he preferred to leave the capital whenever possible, hiding himself from the realities of impending conflict by returning to his Welsh estates. Yet further rewards drew Jasper ever closer to the court party: following the death of the king of Aragon, Jasper was elected to take his place as a knight of the garter. He was even granted his own tower near to Queen Margaret's accommodation in the palace of Westminster where he could hold council meetings and keep his papers.

It was in Wales where Jasper, as Earl of Pembroke, was given greatest influence. In order to shore up the Lancastrian position in West Wales, in April 1457 Jasper was granted the constableships of Aberystwyth, Carmarthen and Carreg Cennen castles. Jasper himself began a programme of strengthening key towns and castles in south

Wales, including Tenby, whose walls were thickened to six feet at every point, while the town moat was widened to thirty feet. Jasper was also given a more prominent role in enforcing law and order in the region: in March 1459, together with his father Owen Tudor, he was given a commission to arrest several Welshmen. It seems that unlike Edmund, Jasper was successful in reconciling Gruffyd ap Nicholas and his sons with the Lancastrian cause, their previous hostilities put aside as both factions united to prevent further interference from York's men in Welsh affairs.

Margaret of Anjou continued to strengthen her position at court. She ruled as a monarch in almost name, with the king's letters being signed by her personally, expressing 'our great marvel and displeasure' if her commands were not followed. 'Almost all the affairs of the realm were conducted according to the Queen's will,' one chronicler wrote, adding tersely, 'by fair means or foul.' Yet Margaret needed the military strengths of York and the Earl of Warwick to prevent attempted invasions from the Scots in the north and, more worryingly, the French upon Calais. Reconciliation was attempted by both sides, when on 25 March 1458 the rival parties took part in a 'Love-day', marching arm in arm to a service at St Paul's Cathedral. What the country needed was not love-days, but an energetic and strong monarch who would be able to provide effective leadership. Everyone knew Henry VI was utterly incapable of this. Each party understood that the tensions were too great not to spill over into further civil war. 'I dread fearfully,' one observer wrote, that 'more mischief [shall] arise, and from the sores unhealed a scab will form, so large that nothing may restrain its growth.'

The festering tensions beneath the surface finally spilled over at Blore Heath, near Market Drayton in Staffordshire, when on 23 September 1459 the queen's forces clashed with a small force led by the Earl of Salisbury. The queen's side were driven away, and Lord Audley, the chamberlain of South Wales, was killed. Salisbury moved swiftly south, where he met York, the Earl of Warwick and other Yorkist noblemen at Ludlow. Their forces were far smaller than the king's army that was moving towards them. York and his allies issued a manifesto professing their loyalty; in response, Henry issued a pardon to all who would join his standard within six days. It was an effective tactic, for when on

12 October the two sides found themselves facing each other at Ludlow Bridge, despite York's forces being carefully entrenched, his troops melted away, refusing to fight against their anointed king, preferring pardon to death in battle. York, together with his son Edmund, was forced to flee into Wales.

York had been crushed and humiliated. Margaret was now determined to complete the victory. Parliament was summoned to meet at Coventry on 20 November. Vengeance was to be its sole aim: nicknamed the 'Parliament of Devils', the main bill of the session was a wide-ranging act of attainder that was to strip York, his sons the Earls of March and Rutland together with the Earls of Salisbury and Warwick – in total twenty-seven members of the nobility – of their titles and lands. Their estates were to be portioned out among Henry's loyal supporters. Once more the Tudors were to become the beneficiaries of others' misfortune. Owen Tudor was granted an annuity of £100 from manors forfeited by John, Lord Clinton, while in addition to being granted the rents from York's forfeited lordship of Newbury for seven years, Jasper was appointed as life constable, steward and master forester to York's lordship of Denbigh in North Wales. For Jasper, whose income had risen to £1,500 a year following Edmund's death and his inheriting of a number of properties jointly owned, the additional offices merely confirmed his status as the country's premier nobleman, especially since the disgrace of York, Warwick and Salisbury. With each grant, however, came resentment and increasing unpopularity from York's own men, who refused to give up their positions without a fight. Jasper was forced to lay siege to Denbigh Castle for several months, at a cost of £650. In order to defeat Yorkist resistance, Jasper was granted remarkable powers by the king to judge and execute rebels at his discretion, confiscating their goods and weapons, in addition to raising a force against any of York's men. It was testament to the strategic importance of Denbigh, which had been York's main channel of communication between Ireland and England. In granting his half-brother almost vice-regal powers, the king intended that Jasper would be entrusted with making Wales impregnable from further Yorkist invasion.

The Yorkist cause had been scattered – York had eventually found sanctuary in Ireland with his son Edmund, while his eldest son Edward of March had ridden south through the night, sailing with the earls of Warwick and Salisbury to Calais. Everything seemed to be in ruins, their followers captured or killed, their wealth and inheritance destroyed. But York refused to give in. He established himself as ruler of Ireland, claiming to be the King's Lieutenant. The duke recognised that in spite of his defeat, disillusion still prevailed in England. Nothing had changed since 1450; the king, incapable of rule, remained in the grip of a clique of advisers. The Parliament had moreover terrified the property-owning classes since, with its unprecedented attainders, stripping some of the greatest landowners of their property, it threatened to undermine the sanctity of inheritance. These fears the Yorkists were able to harness in streams of letters and broadsheets sent from Calais, denouncing the king's evil and grasping councillors, 'our mortal and extreme enemies' who had, they claimed, planned the attainders for their own enrichment. Where would their greed end? Presenting themselves as champions of good government, the Yorkists began to build up support for their cause in south-east England, where memories of the Lancastrian reprisals in the aftermath of Cade's rebellion remained fresh in the mind. Londoners had also become disenchanted with the Lancastrian regime, which seemed to have deserted the capital altogether for the Midlands, and whose commercial policies were badly affecting trade. By the summer of 1460, having made sufficient military preparations and reinforced by the Calais garrison, they were ready to descend upon England.

On 26 June 1460 the Earl of Warwick, together with York's eldest son, Edward, Earl of March and Richard Neville, Earl of Salisbury, landed at Sandwich in Kent with a force of 2,000 men, joining Salisbury's brother, William Neville, Lord Fauconberg, who had led an advance raiding party to defeat an attempt by the king's party to muster troops, 'like bees to the hive'. They were warmly welcomed, and their army swelled along the road from the coast to Canterbury as large numbers of Kentishmen rushed to join their standard. Before nightfall they had arrived at Canterbury, where the town threw open its gates. That evening the Yorkists knelt in prayer at Thomas Becket's tomb, before heading towards the capital. After the city authorities decided to admit them, the earls entered London in triumph on

2 July where they were welcomed by the mayor and the archbishop of Canterbury.

The Yorkists had no intention of remaining in London. Their aim was to confront the king, whose forces were gathering near Northampton. The Yorkist invasion had thrown the Lancastrian party into confusion; if an invasion were to have taken place, they had expected it would have come from Ireland, through Wales. Thrown into panic, Henry had refused to take refuge but instead, leaving his wife and son at Coventry, made his way slowly towards London. As news reached his troops that the Yorkists were advancing out of the capital, the king established his camp outside Northampton.

The Yorkist army arrived at Northampton on the evening of 9 July. Compared to Ludlow, when only six peers were prepared to lend their support, now seventeen members of the nobility joined their cause, bringing with them a superior force of arms and men. The Lancastrians were outnumbered, but their commander, the Duke of Buckingham, was steadfast in his refusal to negotiate. Battle was inevitable. The Yorkists drew their forces into three divisions, with orders to spare the king and the commons, but to slay any lords and knights. As the weather worsened and a heavy downpour began, the battle was decided after half an hour. Buckingham himself was killed defending the royal tent. He had resolved that he would always fight to the death; before the battle began, he had made his final will and testament. Included in its provision was 400 marks' worth of land for his son Henry Stafford and Margaret Beaufort. The king was discovered in his tent, and must have found it confusing that, after Warwick and March had declared their unreserved loyalty to him, he was to be led back to London a prisoner.

News of the king's capture left Margaret of Anjou still residing at Coventry with little option but to flee, seeking Jasper Tudor's protection at Harlech Castle. Jasper's influence in Wales could hardly be tolerated by the Yorkists: on 9 August 1460 Jasper was ordered to hand over Denbigh Castle. Jasper refused to obey 'royal' orders that he knew came not from his king. Instead, he would do everything in his power to frustrate and undermine his Yorkist enemies. Jasper Tudor's defiance was not the only problem that the new Yorkist regime faced. Margaret of Anjou had decided to flee to Scotland, where she enlisted the support of the Scottish King James III. In London, Warwick moved quickly to establish York's supporters in key positions of power while Parliament was summoned to meet in October, its principal aim to cancel the Acts of Attainder that had been passed in the previous year.

But still the Yorkist figurehead, the Duke of York himself, was absent, having remained in Ireland throughout the invasion. Now with the king finally within his control and the queen forced into exile, York planned his return, this time not as Protector but as a potential king.

York landed at Chester on 9 September. Making slow progress south, it was obvious that the duke's intentions had changed dramatically. His banners were emblazoned with the royal arms, trumpeters announced his arrival at each town along the route, his drawn sword was carried upright before him, a privilege granted only to kings. When he arrived at the capital three days after Parliament had assembled, the fanfare that greeted him was reserved for a monarch, as York made his way to Westminster. In a scene nothing short of remarkable, he entered the palace through the king's traditional entrance and approached the empty throne. In front of the assembled lords, he held out his hand, 'in this very act like a man about to take possession of his right'. There his hand hovered, in silence. York turned round, looking 'eagerly' for applause from the nobility nearby. But none came. In the awkwardness of the moment, 'at length' York withdrew his hand, once again turning to those standing 'quietly' around the royal canopy.

The embarrassing silence was broken by the Archbishop of Canterbury who suggested that the duke should speak first with the king. York retorted angrily: 'I do not recall that I know anyone within the kingdom whom it would not befit to come sooner to me and see me rather than I should go and visit him.'

York had badly miscalculated the support he would receive for his claim to the throne. He had defied Henry on five separate occasions over the past decade; it was clear that the nobility remained deeply distrustful of the man whose ambitions had destabilised a kingdom, throwing it into turmoil. But York was relentless. A week later, he formally submitted his claim, based upon his superior descent from Lionel of Clarence through his Mortimer relatives.

The judges were not prepared to pass a verdict, which they claimed was 'above the law and past their learning'. With stalemate likely to ensue, the Lords decided upon what they considered the best compromise, passing an act on 24 October formally recognising York as Henry's heir.

If the nobility believed their compromise would placate the kingdom, they underestimated the resolve and determination of Margaret of Anjou to protect her son's rights of inheritance. As soon as the news reached her of the plans to disinherit Prince Edward, she began planning for invasion, able to count upon her loyal Lancastrian supporters including Jasper Tudor and Somerset, together with the Earls of Northumberland, Wiltshire and Devon who one chronicler estimated would be able to raise a force of 15,000 men. The impending threat could hardly be ignored, and on 9 December a Yorkist force some 6,000 strong commanded by York himself left London, reaching Sandal Castle near Wakefield on 21 December where they spent Christmas. Any festivities were cancelled when it became clear that within the castle there was a severe lack of provisions to feed York's army. Dependent upon foraging missions into the surrounding hostile countryside, York realised that he could not hold out for long within the confines of the castle's walls.

On 30 December a force led by Somerset appeared outside Sandal. On the freezing cold day, as the winter afternoon began to darken, York took the decision to lead his men outside of the security of the castle, the duke himself charging down the hill at his opposing forces, where outnumbered and outflanked, he found himself 'environed on every side, like a fish in a net, or a deer in a buckstall'. York was dragged from his horse and killed, while his son, Edmund, Earl of Rutland was killed by Lord Clifford as he attempted to escape. The battlefield lay thick with the bodies of York's men; many others who were wounded died later in the bitter cold. The Earl of Salisbury was taken prisoner, and despite his attempts to bribe his gaolers, according to one chronicler, 'the common people of the country, which loved him not, took him out of the castle by violence and smote off his head'.

York's decision to leave Sandal Castle is shrouded in mystery. Later chronicles suggested that the duke had been the victim of treachery, deceived by the 'false colour' of his own side. Whatever the exact reason, the retribution and vengeance inflicted upon the dead bodies of the fallen was unprecedented. John Whethamstede, the abbot of St Albans, wrote how York's corpse was propped up on 'a little anthill' and a crown, 'a vile garland made of reeds', was placed on his head. Somerset and his men then approached the dead man, and bending their knees, mockingly cried, 'Hail King, without rule. Hail King, without ancestry. Hail leader and prince, with almost no subjects or possessions.' York's body was then decapitated, and his head was taken together with those of the Earls of Rutland and Salisbury to York, where they were placed upon spikes above Micklegate Bar. To add further insult, a paper crown was placed upon the duke's head, a reminder to all those who passed beneath the stone gate how fortune's wheel had turned so fast for the man who would be king.

The battle of Wakefield, as it became known, was an unmitigated disaster for the Yorkists. Not only had they lost their leader, but the road to London was now left open for Margaret and the Lancastrian army, which now swelled to 20,000 men as it made its way towards the capital, sparking a sense of general panic throughout the realm as men feared vengeance from this 'whirlwind of the north' which one abbot described as 'a plague of locusts covering the whole surface of the earth'.

When Edward, Earl of March, discovered the news of the death of both his father and his brother, he had been preparing his forces at Ludlow. His immediate instinct was to march towards London, intent on avenging York's death, yet his journey was curtailed with news that the Earl of Wiltshire had landed in south-west Wales with a force of French, Breton and Irish mercenaries. Wiltshire had joined forces with Jasper Tudor, bringing with him a large number of Welsh troops, as well as his own father, Owen Tudor. Together they had begun to march upon Hereford. The news caused Edward to change his mind and turn north. He succeeded in intercepting this new Lancastrian threat not far from his castle at Wigmore, on the rising ground near the river Lugg, known as Mortimer's Cross, between Ludlow and Leominster. With his father's cruel death and the humiliating treatment of his corpse still fresh in his mind, as well as the execution of his brother, Edmund, Earl of Rutland, Edward was determined to wreak vengeance upon the Lancastrian army.

It was Candlemas Day, 2 February 1461, when the two armies met in the freezing cold at Mortimer's Cross. Just before the battle, Edward looked up at the sky, where to his amazement, in the east not one, but three suns appeared, 'in the firmament shining clear'. This strange phenomenon was most likely caused by the optical illusion known as a perihelion, which appears in winter skies when light is refracted through ice crystals in the atmosphere, causing the apparition of multiple suns to form in the frosted air. Not knowing what was happening, the Yorkist troops were terrified at what they considered an ominous portent, until Edward himself knelt down on his knees and thanked God, taking the spectacle as a sign of divine favour, claiming that the three suns 'betoken the Father, the Son and the Holy Ghost'. From that moment, Edward took the sign of 'the sun in splendour' as one of the images for his badges, the golden sun of York.

Edward took to the field, where his Lancastrian opponents, caught out unprotected by a storm of arrows unleashed upon them as they advanced across the frozen ground, found their line beginning to collapse and within half an hour were soon routed, fleeing for their lives. Some 4,000 Lancastrians were killed, most of them Welshmen in Jasper Tudor's service. More soldiers were killed at Mortimer's Cross than the three previous battles combined. It was a sign of the unrestrained bloodshed that was about to be unleashed upon England.

Jasper Tudor and the Earl of Wiltshire had managed to successfully flee the battlefield. Others were not so fortunate. Owen Tudor, now a man in his fifties, was taken prisoner and removed to Hereford. Along with several other Lancastrian lords he was sentenced to die, yet it seems that Tudor still believed that as the king's stepfather, he would receive a pardon at the final moment. But the moment never came. It was not until Owen was led out to the block in the marketplace at Hereford and caught sight of his executioner wielding an axe, that he realised his fate. As the collar of his red velvet doublet was ripped off to expose his neck, in a mixture of defiance and amazement, he told the crowds, 'That head shall lie on the stock that was wont to lie on Queen Catherine's lap'. According to one chronicler, he then 'put his heart and mind wholly unto God, and full meekly took his death'. His head was set upon the highest part of the market cross, where a 'mad woman' took it upon herself to comb his hair and wash away the blood from his face, setting around his decapitated head more than a hundred burning candles.

Father for father, brother for brother; the pattern of the civil war was becoming gruesomely familiar, as each family sought to avenge the deaths of their own. For Edward, Owen's execution was some comfort for his father's own brutal end. As the wars drew on and families were torn apart fighting, fathers and sons hacked down on the field of battle, soon many more would be drawn into the blood feud of revenge and reprisal. As Jasper Tudor fled towards the sanctuary of Pembroke Castle a defeated man, he reflected on how both his brother Edmund and his father Owen had died at the hands of his Yorkist enemies. Only he remained to defend not only the Lancastrian cause, but his own house of Tudor, its hopes embodied in the small four-year-old child, his nephew Henry, whom he returned to at Pembroke. Jasper resolved that revenge would be his. In a remarkable letter that survives, written by the earl to his kinsman Roger Puleston three weeks after the battle, he fumed of 'the great dishonour and rebuke that we and you now late have by traitors March, Herbert . . . with their affinities . . . in putting my father your kinsman to the death, and their traitorously demeaning'. He now intended 'with the might of our Lord, and assistance of you and other our kinsmen and friends' to avenge his father's execution 'within short time'. There Jasper ended his brief letter to Puleston, 'trusting verily that you will be well willed and put to your hands unto the same, and of your disposition with your good advice there in we pray you to ascertain us in all haste possible, as our especial trust is in you'.

Little did Jasper Tudor realise then, that vengeance would take nearly quarter of a century.

Edward was still basking in his victory at Ludlow when news reached him that Margaret of Anjou and the Lancastrian forces had inflicted a massive defeat upon the Yorkist force led by the Earl of Warwick at St Albans on 17 February. In the confusion of the battle, it is difficult to comprehend why Warwick should have been defeated so comprehensively. The fact that not a single Yorkist lord was killed during the fighting suggests that Warwick's army never really engaged with their enemy. To make matters worse, the earl had failed to keep possession of his most valuable asset – the person of the king himself. Henry VI was discovered by Margaret's troops, sitting under an oak tree where he had watched the battle, laughing and singing.

With her husband back in her possession, all that was needed to complete Margaret's triumphant victory was to march into London to take charge of the country. But she did not. Instead she turned back, ordering her army to travel to Dunstable. Margaret's decision not to enter the capital was to prove disastrous. As soon as Edward had heard the news of what had happened at St Albans, he had immediately marched eastwards with his troops, where on 22 February he met with the humbled Earl of Warwick in the Cotswolds. Together they rode to London where, four days later they entered the capital where they were 'joyously received' as grateful Londoners threw open the gates.

Edward's entrance into London created fresh dynastic problems for the Yorkists. They held the capital, and with it the financial power and departments of state to control the country. Yet without possession of the king, they could no longer claim to act, as they previously had done, on the authority of Henry VI. Their solution would mark a complete break in the accepted order, ushering in a new phase to the civil wars. The Yorkists would create their own king; on 4 March, the eighteen-year-old Edward, Earl of March was proclaimed Edward IV in Westminster Hall, wearing a purple robe and holding St Edward the Confessor's sceptre in his hand. A formal coronation, however, would have to wait: Edward was determined that he must first defeat Henry in battle, the only true sign of divine favour for his new kingship.

As soon as he had entered the capital, Edward was already preparing for one final military confrontation, and 'acting faithfully in the Lord, girded himself with the sword of battle'. There was no small number of people willing to fight for their new king; an Italian visitor to London wrote how there was 'a great multitude who say they want to be with him to conquer or die'. The chance for God's judgement upon Edward's kingship came three weeks later when, on Palm Sunday, 29 March 1461, the Battle of Towton was fought in a bitter snowstorm.

Margaret of Anjou and her Lancastrian force had retreated towards York, where they had begun to regroup, sending for reinforcements from Wales and Scotland. Soon a titanic force estimated at 30,000 soldiers had gravitated to her standard. The Lancastrians also retained the support of the majority of the nobility, having the backing of nineteen peers compared to Edward's eight. Sensing the danger and eager to seal complete victory, Edward and his forces had arrived in Pontefract by 27 March, ready for a final showdown. Between them, the two armies numbered over 50,000 men, the largest show of force ever witnessed in England. When battle came, it was the weather which was to be a decisive factor in the Yorkist victory as the Lancastrians found the wind against them, and consequently found themselves trapped, blinded by the driving snow as arrows hailed down upon them.

Towton would earn its name as the bloodiest battle in English history. Twenty-eight thousand soldiers were killed during the ten hours of fighting, many drowning in the nearby river as they fled the battle. 'So many dead bodies were seen,' Warwick's brother George Neville wrote, 'as to cover an area six miles long by three broad.' Equally devastating for the Lancastrians were the six members of the nobility and forty-two knights who were either killed or captured and later executed. Towton was a complete and utter victory for the Yorkists. As Henry VI, Margaret of Anjou, their son Prince Edward and the remaining Lancastrian forces fled northwards across the border into Scotland, it is hard to contemplate a more crushing defeat. For Edward, it was a true vindication of not only his cause, but a sign of God's undeniable favour and support for his kingship.

Edward entered York in triumph on Easter Monday, where he was met by cheering crowds. One of his first actions was to order the removal of his father and brother's rotting heads from spikes on Micklegate Bar. In their place were skewered the heads of his defeated enemies who had been executed in the aftermath of the battle, including the Earl of Wiltshire and the Earl of Devon. As Edward and his army basked in victory, some could not help thinking that he had been denied what would have been the greatest prize of all – possession of the deposed Henry VI, Queen Margaret and their son Prince Edward. The failure to capture them would prove an expensive mistake. Having arrived in Edinburgh, they were now sheltered at the Scottish court. Edward demanded that the royal couple be returned 'without delay', yet he knew his orders had little chance of being obeyed. Instead, Margaret was free to continue to plot to regain her position, leaving the political situation far from certain. 'If the King and Queen of England with the other fugitives . . . are not taken', an Italian visitor wrote, 'it seems certain that in time fresh disturbances will arise'.

The presence of a rival king north of the border was not the only problem Edward had to face. Support for the Lancastrians in the country at large remained strong, especially in many parts of the north and west, including Wales and the Marches where Jasper Tudor and other Lancastrians remained in control of the key fortresses at Pembroke, Harlech, Carreg Cennen and Denbigh. In order to address the lack of authority that he possessed in Wales, on 8 May 1461 Edward appointed his loyal supporter Sir William Herbert as life chamberlain of South Wales and steward of Carmarthenshire and Cardiganshire. The appointment signalled Edward's intention that Herbert was to replace Jasper Tudor as the premier nobleman in Wales, a fact confirmed by Herbert's advancement to the peerage, being created Lord Herbert on 26 July.

Herbert was ordered to seize the county and lordship of Pembroke from Jasper. By the end of August, Herbert was back in Wales, ready 'to cleanse the country'. In the end there was little opposition, and the expedition proved more of a triumphal progress, with the well-fortified and provisioned Pembroke Castle capitulating on 30 September. Herbert secured not only the castle, but in doing so captured its most important inmate, the five-year-old Earl of Richmond, Henry Tudor.

Jasper seems to have been absent during Pembroke's capitulation. He may have believed that this great castle, in the heart of his own estates, would be able to withstand attack, or at least put up resistance in the form of a siege. Instead, he shifted his focus of opposition to North Wales where, assisted by the Duke of Exeter, on 16 October just outside Caernarfon they 'reared war'. It was a desperate effort, destined not to succeed. Jasper soon fled, probably to Scotland.

When Parliament met on 4 November, its immediate priority was the attainder and forfeiture of the estates of Henry VI's supporters. Jasper was near the top of the list. According to the Act of Attainder, they had 'divers times since the fourth day of March last past, stirred, laboured and provoked the enemies of our said Sovereign Lord King Edward the fourth, of outward lands, to enter into his said realm with great battle, to rear war against his estate within the said Realm'. Jasper was stripped of his lands and title as Earl of Pembroke. Not that this mattered to Jasper, who, believing that Edward was a usurper at the head of an illegal government whose decisions were not binding, continued to use the title, just as he continued to believe that Henry VI was the only true King of England. In exile, Jasper aimed for nothing less than the restoration of the Lancastrian monarchy.

Other Lancastrians demonstrated less commitment to their cause, and after the devastating losses at Towton, many came to terms with the new regime. Margaret Beaufort's husband Sir Henry Stafford had fought on the Lancastrian side at Towton, but upon Edward's victory he submitted himself to the Yorkist regime, obtaining a pardon for himself and Margaret. Margaret's estates were protected from confiscation, but she was to pay perhaps a heavier price: her separation from her young son Henry, who was placed in the custody of William, Lord Herbert.

Herbert was an intensely ambitious man. Victories against the Lancastrians in Wales had left him with a reputation as being, in the words of one Welsh poet, Edward's 'master-lock'. Determined to enhance his own power and arrange prestigious marriages for his daughters, in March 1462 he paid £1,000 for Henry Tudor's wardship. Herbert knew that Henry was a valuable commodity: unlike his uncle Jasper, the young boy had not lost his title in the recent attainders, remaining the Earl of Richmond. Realising Henry's future potential, especially if the king were to restore the earl to his estates, Herbert planned to marry him to his eldest daughter Maud. Henry's wardship was not the only one Herbert sought: the young Henry Percy, having recently inherited the title of Earl of Northumberland after his father's death in battle at Towton, joined Henry at Herbert's semi-regal court at Raglan Castle, where Herbert had begun an extensive rebuilding programme. It was there that Henry was to spend his childhood, remaining under the supervision of Herbert's wife Anne Devereux. At Raglan, perhaps realising that the young boy might one day marry her daughter, Anne ensured that Henry was well cared for. Even though, as the Tudor court historian Polydore Vergil admitted, Henry was 'kept as prisoner', he had been 'honourably brought up'. Henry's nurse was the wife of

Philip ap Howel of Carmarthen, who may have taught him to speak and understand Welsh. When one Welsh poet raised his concerns that Henry might be brought up an Englishman, not understanding the Welsh language, he wrote expressing his concerns that 'if he is a Sais' (an English-speaker) 'there is great malice'. In response another bard responded, reassuring him: 'you need not worry that he will become a Sais'.

Little is known about Henry's early childhood. His earliest biographer Bernard André wrote that Henry 'often suffered from ailments in his childhood'; as a result 'he was given a gentle rearing by his guardians'. He was educated by 'excellent and very upright tutors' and had been 'endowed with such keenness of wit, lively intellect, and capacity to learn'. André recorded how as a 'little boy he learned everything pertaining to divine worship quickly, and beyond the expectation of them all'. According to André, Henry showed a keen interest in listening and reading 'divine offices', while once he had been introduced to literature, 'surpassed all his contemporaries in the quickness of his understanding, no less than he had in learning his alphabet'. Henry's tutors included Edward Haseley, later Dean of Warwick, whom a grateful Henry later granted an annuity of £10 for services during his 'tender age', while he may have been given military training by Sir Hugh Johns, a local landowner and one of Herbert's men in Gower, who was also rewarded by Henry for services to him during his childhood. Another tutor was Andrew Scot, with whom Bernard André had managed to speak personally. Scot, by then a professor of Theology at Oxford, told him that he 'had never heard of a boy of that age so marked by quickness and capacity to learn'.

The special treatment offered Henry was entirely understandable. Already the boy's importance for the future of Wales was recognised by Welsh poets, who urged Herbert to take special protection to guard the five-year-old boy. 'Keep in your court,' one pleaded with Herbert, 'the young swallow, a man from Gwynedd. Your daughter wedded to him, give him sustenance and gold. Let no one exchange the man, let no one else have your fledgling.'

Having fled to join Margaret and Henry in exile at the Scottish court, Jasper Tudor had much to reflect upon. He had lost both his brother and father to the Yorkists; now he had to confront the painful news that his young nephew Henry had fallen into the hands of his enemy William Herbert. Despite what seemed a hopeless situation, Jasper was undeterred. He had already begun to plan how to win back the kingdom for the Lancastrians. The capture of a Lancastrian spy exposed a possible plot of international and implausible proportions to overthrow the new regime. Jasper Tudor and Exeter were to land at Beaumaris in Anglesey, while the Duke of Somerset, Lord Hungerford and the Duke of Calabria, Margaret of Anjou's brother, would land in Norfolk and Suffolk with an army of 60,000 Spaniards, with a third army of Frenchmen descending upon Kent. The initial invasion would supposedly be followed by another of nearly a quarter of a million men, commanded by the kings of Aragon, Portugal, France and Demark, as well as Margaret's father, René of Anjou. The mastermind behind the campaign was apparently John de Vere, the Earl of Oxford. Fantastical as the plans seem, there must have been a grain of truth behind them, for in February 1462 Oxford, together with his eldest son Aubrey, were arrested, tried and executed for high treason.

The failure of the coup left Margaret with little choice but to seek the aid of Louis XI of France, who had inherited the throne following the sudden death of Charles VII. Edward IV had hoped that Louis would be prepared to show him greater favour than his father, yet the new king, who was to become one of the most skilled and cunning statesmen of the time, recognised the diplomatic advantages that were to be won, and was more than prepared to countenance giving shelter to his cousin Margaret, at least for as long as it suited his purpose.

Having left her husband behind in Scotland, in April 1462 Margaret arrived in France, finally meeting with Louis XI on 5 June, where at the French king's magnificent chateau at Chinon in Touraine, secret negotiations began aimed at securing French support for the Lancastrian cause and a new invasion of England. By the time Jasper Tudor arrived at Chinon, the talks had been concluded and agreement reached, resulting in the Treaty of Tours being signed on 28 June, with Jasper Tudor's signature among those on the document. Its terms seemed generous: a hundred-year truce was agreed between Louis XI and Henry VI, with both sides pledging not to aid each other's enemies. Much to Edward's chagrin, the Lancastrians appeared to have pulled off the remarkable feat of achieving the full diplomatic support and financial backing of England's most powerful neighbour and adversary, paving the way for a fresh attempt to overthrow the isolated Yorkist regime.

Remarkable it was, but what Edward could not know was that the Treaty of Tours was only half the story. Four days before the treaty had been signed, Margaret and Louis XI had also come to a secret agreement in which Louis had agreed to lend Margaret 20,000 livre tournois, with a further promise of 40,000 crowns. This came at a heavy price: the loan was granted only on the condition that were Henry VI to be restored to the throne, then either Jasper or another Lancastrian supporter was to be made captain of the military base at Calais. The new captain would then have to swear an oath to hand over Calais to the French within one year, or otherwise repay the loan immediately. If Calais were handed over, then the 40,000 crowns would be further granted. It was an audacious bid from Louis, who can scarcely have expected that any English negotiator would have accepted his suggestion that Calais, England's last foothold on the French mainland that had been won by Edward III in 1347, might be sacrificed. The fact that the Lancastrians were prepared to countenance such a universally unpopular decision reveals just how desperate they were to secure both diplomatic and military support against the Yorkists. It is little wonder that they wanted to keep this hidden agreement as secret as possible.

Louis soon discovered a snag in his otherwise faultless scheme. In order to reach Calais, Louis's troops would need to cross Burgundian territory, something which Duke Philip of Burgundy refused outright. Having been denied access to Calais, Louis realised that the treaty was almost meaningless, and in the face of diplomatic pressure and threats from Edward IV, lost interest in equipping Margaret's expedition.

When Margaret set sail in October, she was accompanied by only 800 men. The voyage took her first to Scotland, where Henry VI boarded the fleet, which then sailed down to Bamburgh Castle, a fortress that had been left in the hands of Sir William Tunstall, a brother of one of Henry's chamberlains, who was prepared to surrender the castle to the Lancastrians. Jasper had sailed separately from France in time to take charge of the fortress, together with the Duke of Somerset. Meanwhile Margaret continued to Alnwick, successfully laying siege to the castle.

However, the threat of a large Yorkist force travelling northwards led by the Earl of Warwick broke her troops' resolve, and the decision was taken to turn back to Scotland. As they sailed away in flight, their fleet was struck by a storm, with four ships wrecked on the coastline by fierce winter winds. Margaret somehow managed to reach Scotland in a rowing boat, yet many soldiers and sailors were left to fend for themselves, stranded on Holy Island.

Deserted by their king and queen, Jasper Tudor and Somerset were left isolated and exposed at Bamburgh, and with supplies fast running out, their men had been reduced to eating their own horses. Their only vain hope lay in reinforcements being sent from Scotland. This did not materialise, and on Christmas Eve they were forced to surrender. Somerset accepted a pardon and swore loyalty to Edward IV, enticed by the reinstatement of all his lands and titles. This Jasper refused to countenance; instead he managed to negotiate a safe conduct to Scotland. Alnwick fell to Warwick's siege in early January. Only Harlech Castle, in the north-western tip of Wales, held out for the Lancastrians.

Margaret's mission had ended in failure, yet she remained convinced that the success of her cause lay in persuading Louis XI to grant further assistance, or at least in preventing the French king coming to terms with the Yorkist regime. For this reason, between mid-April and early May 1463, Jasper Tudor, together with the Duke of Exeter and other Lancastrian leaders, made another voyage from Scotland to Sluys in Flanders, where they journeyed to France to seek an audience with Louis. Margaret followed with her son Prince Edward in July, hoping that her heir's presence would convince the French king that hope remained in the Lancastrian cause. These hopes were dashed in October when Louis XI signed a joint truce with Edward IV and the Dukes of Brittany and Burgundy: each side promised to cease all hostilities for one year, and at the same time pledged not to assist each other's enemies. Edward had succeeded in neutralising the Lancastrians' greatest asset; disconsolate and frustrated, Margaret decided to travel to the sanctuary of her father, René of Anjou's residence, where she remained for the next seven years. Jasper remained in France until December, when he was granted 500 livre tournois to return to Scotland, the only source of refuge now open to the Lancastrian dissidents.

The Scottish government recognised that the Lancastrians were being frozen out diplomatically; they were unwilling to be left isolated alongside them. With Louis XI indicating as part of the new treaty with England that he was ready to abandon traditional French protection for Scotland, its government felt it had little choice but to open negotiations with England. On 9 December 1463 a truce was agreed with Edward at York, to last until the following October while discussions continued for a more permanent treaty. With the truce, Edward had obtained the crucial promise that he must have longed for: that the Scots would no longer aid the Lancastrians. Henry VI was asked to leave the country, departing St Andrews for Bamburgh. With nowhere else to turn and separated from his wife and son, it seemed as if his chances of being restored to the throne were all but over.

Edward could have been forgiven for thinking that he was now master of his own destiny. Through a combination of effective diplomacy and military strategy, he had driven the remaining Lancastrian resistance from almost every corner of the realm.

The pinnacle of this success had been the defection of one of the Lancastrians' most powerful supporters, Henry Beaufort, the Duke of Somerset. In light of the enmity that existed between Edward's father, the Duke of York, and Henry Beaufort's father, Edmund Beaufort, the first Duke of Somerset, the fact that reconciliation was possible must have seemed remarkable to many. Yet Edward had genuinely believed Somerset, or at least had wanted to believe him, so much so that, according to one chronicler, 'he lodged with the king in his own bed many nights, and sometimes rode a-hunting behind the king, when the king had no more than six men in his party, of whom three were the Duke of Somerset's men'.

For Edward's supporters, the king's willingness to pursue a policy of reconciliation seemed naive at best, with frustrating consequences: already the decision to place Sir Ralph Percy, who had defected alongside Somerset, in charge of Bamburgh had backfired when he handed the castle back to the Lancastrians in March 1463, once again giving them a vital foothold. The king's judgement was once again called into question when at Christmas 1463, without obtaining the king's leave, Somerset fled northwards to rejoin the side of his old master, Henry

VI. It was a bitter blow and unforgivable in Edward's eyes, and he soon launched a fresh campaign to crush the Lancastrians in the north.

Even though a fresh alliance with France was now out of the question, Jasper Tudor had refused to give up the fight. Now, heartened by Somerset's re-defection to the Lancastrians, he began to look for new opportunities to pursue, and new foreign powers to support the cause. This came in the form of Duke Francis II of Brittany. Francis sent an envoy to meet Henry and Somerset, who assured him there was still considerable support across the country for the deposed king, and the restoration of his kingship would still be possible, if only he might be supplied with food, materials and men. Having spent Christmas at the exiled Lancastrian court, the envoy returned at the end of February 1464, with letters from Henry to his wife Margaret, her parents and the Duke of Brittany. Jasper travelled to France soon afterwards, arriving in Brittany in March. He carried with him letters from Louis XI, who did not believe that his truce with Edward prevented him from requesting that Brittany should give aid to Jasper in order to assist his return to Wales. Francis obliged, and on 26 March ordered that Jasper should be provided with the protection of a fleet led by the vice-admiral of Brittany, Alain de la Motte. However, in June, in a characteristically sudden change of mind, Louis XI wrote to the duke criticising him for the support he had given to Jasper, prompting a confused Francis to reply that he thought he had only been carrying out the French king's wishes.

Meanwhile, in retaliation for Somerset's double-dealing, Edward announced his intention to lead a force against the Lancastrians in the summer. Since Somerset's defection, their cause had rallied and having gone on the offensive, several vital outposts had been captured which allowed them to control most of the countryside south of the border, and were threatening the Yorkist stronghold at Newcastle. Edward understood the urgency of the situation, and began to muster a massive royal army. A battle involving 5,000 Lancastrian troops took place at Hedgeley Moor on 25 April, resulting in a Yorkist victory, yet it was victory at the battle of Hexham on 15 May that ensured the virtual extinction of the Lancastrian cause. This time Edward would show no mercy. After the battle, over thirty Lancastrians were dragged out of their hiding places, rounded up and summarily executed, including

Somerset who had been captured in pursuit. Bombarded by the king's 'great guns' that caused its walls to crumble into the sea, Bamburgh soon capitulated. Henry VI was forced to flee into hiding, wandering the countryside until he was eventually captured in July 1465 and taken to the Tower.

It seemed that after nearly five years, Edward IV had finally succeeded in pacifying his kingdom, having weeded out the last remnants of Lancastrian opposition. While Margaret of Anjou remained exiled in 'great poverty' at her father's residence in France, only Harlech Castle, described by one contemporary as 'so strong' that 'it was impossible unto any man to get it', remained in Lancastrian possession.

Jasper Tudor also remained at large, though his exact whereabouts during these dark years are unknown. Surviving hand to mouth, he embarked on raids across North Wales, where his fame in frustrating the Yorkist regime was admired by Welsh poets, who wrote of his ability to command raiding parties from the Dyfi estuary. One ally upon whom Jasper relied for support was Gruffydd Fychan of Corsygedol, whose residence at Barmouth, the fifteenth-century stone house, Ty Gwyn, was celebrated in verse as being the location which Jasper used as his headquarters, planning his next moves. Ultimately, however, Jasper's fortunes as a renegade and a rebel without much of a cause would change little without the backing of a significant foreign power to provide the money and men necessary to embark upon a major invasion and pose a serious threat to Edward IV.

The tide of diplomacy had been in Edward's favour ever since his agreement with Louis XI. Yet this was soon to change when, against the best advice of his most powerful supporters, the Earl of Warwick included, Edward set his heart on concluding new alliances with the Dukes of Burgundy and Brittany in the spring of 1468. In doing so, he alienated Louis XI who, diplomatically isolated himself by the move, looked to seek revenge by once again taking up his cousin Jasper's cause. On 1 June 1468, having been courted by Jasper and Margaret of Anjou in turn, he agreed to provide Jasper with three ships and £293 5s 5d to allow the earl to travel to Wales. In reality it was a paltry investment, with no chance of making much impact, yet Louis was not interested in backing a full-scale invasion of England. He merely sought to embarrass Edward for the affront of spurning his diplomatic advances; making his next move across the board, Jasper Tudor was the nearest convenient chess piece.

A convenient pawn he may have been, but Jasper was determined to make the most of his opportunity. Landing in the Dyfi estuary near Harlech on 24 June 1468, he set out across North Wales, marching towards Denbigh, where in the process his forces swelled to 2,000 men. At the same time, Jasper decided to hold assizes and formal court sessions 'in King Harry's name', a gesture clearly designed to show that he considered Henry VI the rightful King of England. Jasper managed to capture Denbigh without difficulty, and in an act of open defiance burned down the new part of the town, leaving it 'clear defaced with fire', while Flintshire was so ravaged that it would struggle to pay taxes five years later. So impressive was the force and impact of Jasper's lightning raid, that news spread across the courts of Europe, with the Milanese ambassador in Paris reporting that in response Margaret of Anjou was also journeying to visit Louis, in an attempt to solicit further assistance.

Evidently rattled by the progress Jasper was making through Wales, Edward IV ordered William, Lord Herbert and his brother-in-law Walter, Lord Ferrers to raise a large army from across Gloucestershire, Herefordshire and the Welsh Marches to crush the insurrection. A force of some 7,000 men was split in two: one wing moved across the North Wales coast and into the Conway valley, where it was 'wasted with fire and sword', the other moved north from Pembroke; both were to converge upon Harlech Castle from the east and the south. Hopelessly outnumbered, the fortress surrendered with only slight resistance on 14 August. Jasper managed to escape his enemies and, according to the Welsh chronicler Elis Gruffyd, gave them the slip, managing to commandeer a boat from a gentleman 'living at Mostyn . . . at a place called Picton pool'. Mention of Mostyn suggests that the Tudors may have been helped by the Conway family; John Conway was the lessee of the township of Mostyn lordship, though help may have also been given by one of Jasper's kinsmen, Hywel ab Ieuan Fychan of Pengwern and Mostyn. In order to disguise himself, Jasper had to carry a 'bundle of pease pods' on his back, 'for fear that someone should spot him – for there were plenty to spy on him in those parts'. Boarding the boat, he managed to sail to Brittany 'more through the craft of the earl than the craft of the boatmen of Picton'.

In spite of the early success of his invasion, Jasper had suffered a devastating setback. The once impregnable fortress at Harlech had fallen, and with it was removed from Lancastrian possession their only toehold left in the kingdom. His humiliation was complete when in September 1468 Edward, delighted with the outcome, rewarded Herbert for his crushing of the rebellion and capture of Harlech with Jasper's own Earldom of Pembroke. Jasper was not the only person dismayed by Edward's decision to raise Herbert to the earldom, a sign of his rising favour and influence at court. Silently fuming, the Earl of Warwick watched as he saw a man he considered an upstart from relative obscurity take his place alongside him as an earl, his equal. For too long, Warwick believed, he had suffered in silence; action would need to be taken, and he, the kingmaker, would be the one to act.

'Now take heed,' wrote one contemporary observer, 'what love may do.' It was a lesson that Edward IV learnt to his peril. An attractive and energetic young man standing six foot three inches tall, with 'a goodly personage and very princely to behold', Edward IV had an eye for the ladies, particularly those at court, and he 'pursued with no discrimination the married and unmarried, the noble and lowly', casting off his conquests to other courtiers 'as soon as he had satisfied his lust . . . much against their will'. Nevertheless, for the security of the Yorkist dynasty, it was vital that the king should marry. The Earl of Warwick, believing that Edward owed him his kingdom, and that in turn all matters of English policy should come under his influence, had taken a strong interest in arranging a French marriage for Edward, and had entered into negotiations with Louis XI for the hand of the French king's sister-in-law, Bona of Savoy. The match would have secured a lasting peace between England and France, something which Warwick considered particularly vital given Louis's previous support for his Lancastrian cousins.

Edward refused to listen to the earl's reasoning. Early in the morning on 1 May 1464, Edward departed the court in secret. Why he did so, no one would find out until four months later, but the consequences of his actions that May morning would be politically explosive. Edward had married Elizabeth Woodville, the widow of Sir John Grey, who had died fighting for the Lancastrians at St Albans in 1459. Her mother was Jacquetta of Luxembourg, the aristocratic princess who had been married to the Duke of Bedford; Jacquetta had then gone on to marry Elizabeth's father, Richard Woodville, a humble member of the gentry. For a king to marry a commoner was unthinkable, let alone a woman who was four years older than him with two children from her previous marriage; when the king publicly announced that he was already married in September, the council was astounded, protesting that 'she was not his match, that however good and fair she might be, she was not a wife for so high a prince as he'. Edward would hear none of it. Clearly infatuated with his new bride, chroniclers wrote in amazement how they spent 'three or four hours' in bed, with some even claiming that Elizabeth had used witchcraft or sorcery to place a spell upon him. Still, for the old nobility like Warwick, accustomed to the order of rank and dignity, matters were about to get much worse.

The arrival of Elizabeth Woodville at court could scarcely have been greeted with greater controversy. Ambitious and determined to obtain advancement for her family, the new queen set about providing for her twelve brothers and sisters. Within a month of the royal marriage, her sister Margaret had been betrothed to the Earl of Arundel's heir; this followed with successive marriages for her sisters to the Duke of Buckingham and the heirs to the Duke of Exeter and the Earl of Kent. When her twenty-year-old brother John married the Duchess of Norfolk, in her sixties and on her fourth marriage, the court recoiled at the sheer indignity of the grasping family, prepared to make such 'diabolical' unions, all it seemed, for the sake of greed. It did not help matters that the duchess was in fact Warwick's aunt, but it was the planned marriage of Thomas Grey, Elizabeth Woodville's son from her first marriage, to Lady Anne Holland, the heiress to the Duke of Exeter, that caused Warwick's 'great and secret displeasure' since Lady Anne had previously been betrothed to the son of Warwick's brother, Lord Montagu. For the earl, a pattern was beginning to emerge: his family's influence was beginning to be slowly eroded by the upstart Woodvilles, as Warwick's uncle Lord Mountjoy was replaced as treasurer by Elizabeth's father, the newly created Earl Rivers. Warwick's position as premier nobleman and power-broker was under threat from a group of parvenus.

It was not merely his status at court that concerned Warwick; the earl had earned a significant reputation at the courts of Europe as the most powerful man in England, to whom Edward IV owed his throne: as one foreign chronicler remarked, Warwick 'might also be called the King's father as a result of the services and education he had given him'. Louis XI was intrigued by Warwick, and in an attempt to ingratiate himself with the earl, during the course of several embassies during the 1460s, had won him over to the idea of an Anglo-French treaty. When instead Edward, influenced by Earl Rivers, began to favour a treaty with Burgundy, England's largest trading partners, it was a public humiliation for Warwick, whose influence and control of the king had been exposed as a sham.

Relations between Edward and Warwick worsened when it was suggested as part of an agreement that Edward's sister Margaret of York should marry Charles, Count of Charolais, the eldest son of Duke Philip of Burgundy, while Edward's brother the Duke of Clarence should marry Philip's daughter Mary. Warwick was aghast. He had hoped that, without a male heir, and with the Woodville clan claiming most available aristocratic marriages for their own (indeed every English earl who had an available heir to marry had chosen for them a Woodville wife), he would be able to marry his two daughters to Edward's younger brothers, George, Duke of Clarence, and Richard, Duke of Gloucester.

Warwick had done much to flatter the two young men. Like Warwick, both brothers had been 'sorely displeased' at their brother's marriage, and had to witness the unedifying spectacle of their mother Cecily having to kneel in homage before the new queen at court. Warwick had taken Richard into his household as one of his 'henchmen' in 1465, where he was trained in the arts of war at Warwick's castle at Middleham in north Yorkshire. Yet Richard was still a boy, too young to have much influence at court; to begin with, Warwick's target was Clarence, the heir presumptive to the throne, in whom the earl would seek to fulfil his ambitions.

One chronicler wrote a circumstantial account of how in the autumn of 1464, shortly after Edward's announcement of his marriage, Warwick invited George, then aged fifteen, and Richard, aged twelve, to Cambridge where he suggested that Clarence should marry his eldest daughter Isabel, and Richard his younger daughter Anne. When

Edward discovered what had happened he summoned both boys to his presence, where they were ferociously reprimanded. For Edward, a marriage between Warwick's daughter and Clarence was out of the question. Clarence was heir presumptive; Edward and the Woodvilles would hardly allow Warwick's influence to extend to becoming yet another kingmaker.

For Clarence, the king's refusal to allow his marriage was an uncomfortable bridle. He had no other reason to be dissatisfied with his own position, having been appointed as the King's Lieutenant in Ireland in 1462, while in 1464 he had been endowed with the lands of the Earldom of Chester, traditionally reserved for the Prince of Wales, enriching his wealth to around £3,666 13s 4d a year. But it seems that, encouraged by Warwick, ambition had got the better of him.

By 1467 Warwick was once again pursuing the duke, complaining to him how Rivers and the Woodvilles controlled the court; offering to make Clarence King of England or governor of the realm, he told the duke that the entire country would support him. It was clear that some agreement had been reached when, as Jasper Tudor planned his attempted invasion in Wales, rumours circulated that a plot was planned at court. A shoemaker named Cornelius, under torture in the Tower confessed that several Lancastrian sympathisers had been conspiring with Margaret of Anjou, including Lord Wenlock, a close friend of Warwick's, and John de Vere, the thirteenth Earl of Oxford, Warwick's brother-in-law. Confessing his innocence, Oxford, whose own father had been executed as a traitor six years previously, was lucky to escape with his life. Others were not so fortunate. Several were charged in May 1468 for having plotted, with Margaret of Anjou, the 'final death and final destruction' of Edward IV and, found guilty, executed.

Further insult was heaped upon Warwick when his brother George Neville, the chancellor and Archbishop of York, who had been working hard to gain a papal dispensation for Clarence and Isabel's marriage, was sacked from his position as chancellor after he refused to meet representatives from Burgundy. Edward was determined to press ahead with his sister's marriage to Charles, and despite the dowry costing a ruinous 200,000 gold crowns (£41,666 13s 4d), the marriage took place in Flanders in July 1468, 'much against' Warwick's wishes, who now developed a 'deadly hatred' of Charles. Warwick understood that the marriage and alliance, which had brought England into partnership with Brittany and Burgundy, were part of a prelude to war against France. Two months before, the king had announced to Parliament that, with the new alliance with Burgundy, he intended to wage war on 'his old and ancient adversary', for which he obtained a substantial grant in taxation. In August Edward agreed to send 7,000 archers to assist the Duke of Brittany against France, and during the autumn months a fleet was actively being prepared at Portsmouth, ready to sail as part of a planned invasion of France to take place the following year.

In fact, in a calculated gamble, Louis had himself made peace with Brittany and Burgundy in October 1468, making any invasion practically impossible. For fear of humiliation, Edward hid the truth, claiming that Margaret of Anjou was preparing to invade England from Harfleur; he spent £18,000 on ordering the fleet to patrol the Channel instead. It was this kind of waste that confirmed contemporary writers' opinions that taxpayer's money was being frittered away, that law and order were breaking down with 'great riots and oppressions done to our subjects', with the king's councillors, especially the Woodvilles, enriching themselves at the expense of the common people. It was in this explosive atmosphere that rebellion broke out in the north in the spring of 1469, led by one 'Robin of Redesdale'. Robin's real identity may have been Sir William Conyers, the brother of Sir John Conyers, the constable of Warwick's castle at Middleham. In a familiar echo of the revolts of the 1450s, manifestos were circulated calling for the deposition of the king's evil advisers, in particular the Woodville clan. Worryingly, another rumour began to circulate that Edward himself was a bastard and that Clarence should be the rightful King of England.

In spite of initial attempts to crush the rebellion, the 'mighty insurrection' began to move south, numbering an estimated 20,000 men. When news of the rising unrest reached Edward, he decided to move north, waiting at Fotheringay Castle for reinforcements to arrive. These were slow in assembling, and when it became clear that none would be ready in time, Edward withdrew to Nottingham Castle to wait for Welsh troops that had been promised by William Herbert, the Earl of Pembroke. With the situation deteriorating daily, on 9 July, Edward wrote to Warwick and Clarence, both of whom had suspiciously not yet offered any military support, demanding that they show their loyalty. He received no response.

Five days earlier, Warwick, together with his daughter Isabel, Clarence and his brother-in-law the Earl of Oxford, had crossed the seas to Calais, where on 11 July, Warwick's daughter Isabel was married to Clarence in a hastily conducted ceremony. Warwick was now prepared to finally reveal his hand: issuing a declaration remarkably similar to the rebels' own, he stated his intention to save Edward from 'the deceiving covetous rule and guiding of certain seditious persons', named as Rivers, the Earls of Pembroke and Devon, who had caused the 'great poverty' of the realm, 'only intending to their own promotion and enriching'. Warwick landed at Canterbury on 16 July, receiving an enthusiastic welcome as he continued his march to London. Edward remained at Nottingham, still in the hope that Pembroke's army would reach him in time. Meanwhile, Robin of Redesdale's army continued to march southwards, intending to join with Warwick who had entered the capital.

William Herbert had departed from Wales with a large number of cavalry and infantry drawn from his Welsh estates, assuming that the Earl of Devon would later join him with a force of archers. Devon never arrived. The separation of the two forces was to prove fatal at Edgecote field near Banbury, when confronted by the lethal combination of Robin of Redesdale's rabble of an army and a reinforcement provided by Warwick's troops and Herbert's Welsh men-at-arms, both outnumbered and with no archers to protect them, were hacked down and overrun, suffering heavy casualties. Herbert and his brother were captured and taken to Northampton where they were beheaded the following day on Warwick's orders, without any legal justification.

Herbert had marched out of Raglan Castle with a formidable army of Welshmen. Joining him had been the twelve-year-old Henry Tudor, who would have witnessed the devastating outcome of the battle at Edgecote at first hand. In the panic of defeat, he was taken from the battlefield by Sir Richard Corbet, a gentleman who was married to a niece of Herbert's wife Anne Devereux, the Countess of Pembroke. In a later petition written by Corbet to Henry, Corbet declared that he had first served him 'after the death of the Lord Herbert after the field', when he had been one of the men who had 'brought your grace out of the danger of your enemies'.

When news of the battle reached Margaret Beaufort, then residing at her husband Henry Stafford's residence at Woking, in her anxiety she sent out messages to discover what had happened to her son. Although she had been separated from Henry since the fall of Pembroke Castle in 1461, Margaret had been allowed to remain in contact with her son, corresponding with him and visiting him on occasions, for instance in September 1467, when together with her husband she visited Henry, having paid ten shillings at Bristol to be taken across the Severn by boat to Chepstow where she travelled on to Raglan to be entertained for a week as Herbert's guests.

Hearing the news of the devastation of Herbert's forces at Edgecote, Margaret assumed that Henry must still be at Raglan. She sent her servant William Aykerig to ride immediately to Worcester, passing on a message for John Bray to ride to Raglan 'to my lord of Richmond'. Bray then travelled with his page from Worcester to Raglan, only to find he was not there.

Henry had in fact been led from the battlefield to the home of Herbert's brother-in-law Lord Ferrers, at Weobley in Herefordshire, where Bray arrived six days after beginning his panicked journey. There he found Herbert's widow Anne Devereux sheltering under her brother Ferrers' protection, where she had continued her duty of looking after her dead husband's ward.

Margaret's immediate concern was for the welfare of her son. Her household books record how twenty shillings was 'given in reward to Davy that waiteth upon my lord Richmond by my lady commandment at Weobley' with a further 6s 8d 'in reward to master Starky and to Richard Eton for my lord of Richmond'. If Henry was shaken from his experience, he recovered quickly enough to return to his archery practice, and was provided with twenty shillings by his mother 'for his disports to buy him bow and shafts'.

Warwick was not content with just William Herbert's destruction. In the aftermath of his triumph, Earl Rivers and his son Sir John Woodville, the husband of the elderly Duchess of Norfolk, were executed without trial, while other Woodville supporters, rounded up in hiding, soon met their deaths. It was a pyrrhic act of revenge. Unless Warwick, who claimed to be acting in the king's best interests, was prepared to depose Edward, replacing him with either Clarence or Henry VI, the earl could achieve little else. He had achieved his ambition of bringing the Woodvilles to heel, but what next? Without the support of the nobility, who had observed the summer's events with horror, Warwick could do nothing. He was caught in a trap of his own making.

Knowing that Warwick was powerless to act without deposing him, Edward remained calm. He had left Nottingham to travel south on 29 July, unaware of what had taken place at Edgecote. When news of the outcome of the battle reached him, he had been deserted by his forces and taken into custody by Warwick's brother, Archbishop George Neville at Olnet in Buckinghamshire. Placed in confinement at Warwick Castle before being moved to Middleham then Pontefract, he showed grace and affability, agreeing to every demand placed in front of him, biding his time. His captors could do nothing when, after sending out messages to his supporters to come to him, Edward declared that he wished to journey to London. He made a ceremonial return to the capital, where he was received with enthusiastic acclaim.

At first Edward behaved as if nothing had happened. 'The king himself', wrote one observer, 'hath good language of the lords of Clarence, of Warwick . . . saying they be his best friends'. Yet everyone, including Warwick and Clarence, knew that no matter how calm the king remained, the queen was unlikely to forgive the merciless execution of her father and brother.

On his return, Edward was welcomed with open arms. Warwick's uprising had left the country in a state of uproar, as an absence of authority allowed local feuds to erupt, with gentry families hoping to make the maximum political capital out of the uncertainty. For Margaret Beaufort, William Herbert's death had thrown Henry Tudor's future wide open. Having held Henry's wardship since 1461, the earl's death gave her the opportunity to provide a new settlement for her son. Just as she had acted quickly to secure her marriage after the death of Edmund Tudor, Margaret understood that she needed to move fast to ensure that Henry's own wardship was resolved. On 24 August 1469, while Edward IV remained a prisoner at Pontefract, Margaret rode with her husband Stafford to Clarence's residence in London, where she might best communicate with the duke who was currently based in Middleham. Clarence continued to hold her son's lands in the honour of Richmond; now Margaret hoped that an agreement might be reached whereby her son's lands would be eventually restored to him. It was a dangerous and risky strategy, especially given the current uncertainties; her husband Stafford was keen to appease Edward on his return to the capital, purchasing a new hat and spurs as he rode to meet the king on his arrival in London, but Margaret was determined to do best for her son, taking advantage of the situation to achieve the best possible bargain.

On 21 October at the Bell Inn in Fleet Street, Margaret Beaufort and Stafford, along with their 'learned counsel', dined with Lord Ferrers and the Countess of Pembroke's counsel to discuss Henry Tudor's wardship, consuming a meal of bread, pears, apples and mutton washed down with ale and wine at a cost of 5s 7d. The meeting seems to have been a success as, three days later, Margaret paid 4s 4d for letters patent to be written 'for my Lord of Richmond matter of the king's grant', while Sir Davy Thomas was paid 40s to ride to South Wales to find a copy of any previous documentation concerning Henry's 'reckoning'. When this proved inconclusive, Thomas Rogers was paid 2s 4d 'for the search in the chancellery' for 'the copy of my lord Pembroke patent for the ward and marriage of my lord Richmond'. A further 6s 10d was paid for 'searches in the Exchequer with Thomas Bayan clerk of the parliament and the writing of 2 copies of a act and a provision for my lord of Richmond matter'.

If Margaret had intended for a swift resolution to her son's position, her rashness had been a mistake. Edward's return to the capital was followed by the reward of his most loyal followers, including Stafford's younger brother John, who was created Earl of Wiltshire. Henry Stafford remained a mere knight; his wife's dealings with Clarence, of which Edward had grown suspicious, had possibly cost him a peerage. Even if she had wanted to, Margaret was unable to escape her own Lancastrian heritage. When Sir Robert Welles, the son of Margaret's stepfather Lord Welles, launched a rebellion in Lincolnshire, Edward crushed it with such force that the confrontation was over in minutes, earning the 'battle' its nickname of Losecoat Field, named after the haste at which the rebels had cast off their clothing and fled. When it was proved that the rebellion, which had called for every man to rally in the name of Clarence and Warwick, had been stoked by the two men, Edward condemned them both as 'rebels and traitors'. Warwick had anticipated that the fragile peace since their insurrection could not last for long; in encouraging rebellion, he had decided to make the first move. Now there was no other option but to flee the kingdom.

Meanwhile, Jasper Tudor had remained in exile in France. The records reveal that from October 1469 until September 1470 he had entered the service of Louis XI at the royal court, with the French king granting him a pension of 100 livre tournois a month. It was here that in May 1470 he welcomed some unexpected visitors that were set to transform both his and the Lancastrian fortunes.

Never before had England witnessed 'so many goodly men, and so well arrayed', wrote one observer, as Edward rode with his forces in hot pursuit of Warwick and Clarence. Having reached Manchester before the northern rising had been repressed, they turned and fled for Devon; Edward followed, determined to confront or capture these 'great rebels', covering a distance of 290 miles in eighteen days. When he arrived at Exeter, however, Edward discovered that he was already too late: his enemies had fled.

They had boarded a ship at Dartmouth, destined for Calais, currently held by Warwick's supporter, Lord Wenlock. They had managed to assemble their families to depart with them, including Clarence's nine-month pregnant wife Isabel. Arriving at Calais they found the garrison's guns turned against them, forcing the small fleet to hover a distance out at sea. The sound of the pounding guns prompted Isabel to go into labour, a desperate situation that endangered the lives of both mother and child, Clarence's heir, but still Wenlock refused to admit Warwick's ships, claiming that to do so would leave his friend in a 'mousetrap'. With nowhere else to sail, tossed in the storms of the Channel, Isabel miscarried, and her stillborn baby, a son, was buried at sea.

When the Duke of Burgundy refused Warwick permission to land at any port in Flanders, there was no other choice but to sail for France, where the party landed at Honfleur in the first week of May, exhausted and starving after nearly three weeks at sea. Hearing news of Warwick and Clarence's arrival, Louis XI realised that his opportunity had come. In return for his military support, the restoration of Henry VI to the English throne might fulfil his dream of establishing an Anglo-French military alliance against his rival Burgundy. That would mean a radical departure from the previous loyalties of English politics, necessitating an alliance between Warwick and the Lancastrians. Warwick could hardly be pleased with the thought of returning the Lancastrians to the throne, but he had come to realise Clarence's limitations and was desperate to cling to a scheme which might preserve his grip upon power. The greatest hurdle to Louis's plan would come in winning over a more than hostile Margaret of Anjou, who could hardly be expected to trust a man who had devoted a decade to destroying her husband and family. Yet, as Louis stressed, this was her last, and possibly only, chance. For a month, even Louis's mastery of the arts of diplomacy were tested to the limit as he negotiated with both parties for agreement. But, slowly, ambition proved too much a healer as both Margaret and Warwick were drawn into the French king's web.

At Angers on 22 July, Warwick knelt in front of Margaret of Anjou, begging her forgiveness. It was over a quarter of an hour before she would let him rise, so bitter was the queen for the wrongs the earl had done to her family. Three days later, her son Prince Edward was betrothed to Warwick's daughter Anne Neville in Angers cathedral. Plans were now drawn up for an invasion of England, with the aim of deposing Edward IV and placing Henry VI back on the throne. But Margaret, her distrust of Warwick so ingrained, refused to cross the Channel or allow her sixteen-year-old son to accompany him. Instead they would return to England only when the earl had successfully completed his mission and destroyed the man he had worked tirelessly to create as king. Warwick would leave his daughter Anne in France, almost as a hostage to bind the earl's loyalty. Instead Jasper Tudor would join the earl, along with the Earl of Oxford, who had made his own way to the French court.

For his part, Louis had agreed to provide the expedition with money, ships and men. Sixty French ships departed from La Hogue in Normandy on 9 September; four days later, after a calm journey unbroken by storm, the fleet reached Dartmouth and Plymouth, where the Lancastrian army disembarked after nightfall. Jasper set off for

Wales, while Warwick turned eastwards, towards London.

Edward had known for months that Warwick had entered into an agreement with Margaret to re-establish Henry VI on the throne, and that he planned to invade the kingdom. So why, when the moment came, was Edward ultimately caught unaware and unprepared? He had spent the winter strengthening naval defences on the south coast, arming a fleet and in signalling his determination to defeat the earl, had gone to the extremes of ordering the execution of twenty of Warwick's men at Southampton, having their bodies then cut into pieces and impaled on wooden spikes facing the sea so that they might be seen by passing ships. Confident that he had done enough to secure the south, Edward turned his attention northwards, where a spate of rebellions had broken out. Aware of the potential dangers of ignoring such risings, Edward swiftly moved to crush the opposition. It was to prove a costly miscalculation.

Edward was at York when he was informed on the eve of 13 September that Warwick, together with Clarence, the Earls of Oxford and Shrewsbury had landed in Devon and were advancing to London, their forces gathering such support as they went that their numbers had reached 30,000 men. Edward realised that he had misjudged the situation; stranded in the north, he now immediately began to march south, where he had badly overestimated the strength of his natural support base. He had only reached Doncaster, however, when, in the middle of the night, his minstrels burst into his bedchamber to inform him that Marquess Montagu, Warwick's brother whom Edward had stripped of the Earldom of Northumberland, was only a mile away and advancing in haste towards them with an armed force of 6,000 men to capture him.

Edward took the only decision open to him: together with his brother Richard, Duke of Gloucester, Lord Hastings, and his brother-in-law Anthony, the new Earl Rivers, alongside a few hundred household men, he galloped through the night to King's Lynn in Norfolk. Seizing two flat-bottomed boats from some Dutch merchants, he gave the ship's master the only payment he could find, 'a robe lined with fine marten's fur, promising to reward him better in the future'. Still wearing his armour, he set sail for the Low Countries. 'They did not have a penny between them and scarcely knew where they were going', wrote the Burgundian chronicler Commynes.

Edward's flight left Warwick to enter London unopposed, where he swiftly arranged for Henry VI to be led from his confinement in the Tower, 'not so cleanly kept as should seem such a prince', and moved to the adjoining palace where the earl knelt in front of him, professing his loyalty. Henry appeared 'amazed' as the man who had unmade him, made him king once more. Henry was swiftly paraded through the streets to St Paul's, where Warwick carried his train. As the crown was placed on his head, could Henry have understood what had happened, or what was happening to him? Five years of captivity had taken its toll on Henry's fragile mental state; described by one chronicler as 'a shadow on a wall', he was certainly not a full participant in the events which were now centring upon him as he sat in the coronation chair, 'submissive and mute, like a crowned calf'. Everyone knew it was Warwick who held the reins, as the earl issued a proclamation that, with Edward deposed, Henry had been restored as king, or as the document officially put it, had achieved 'his readeption to royal power'.

Warwick's invasion had been achieved with remarkable ease, but this could not mask the immediate problems facing the new regime. Law and order was breaking down as local feuds and rivalries across the country took advantage of the prevailing uncertainties to turn to open disputes and violence. The new government, hamstrung by its inability to reward its supporters, was therefore unable to confiscate or revoke any lands and offices for fear of triggering further unrest. Jasper Tudor might have hoped that, after the sacrifices his family had made, the years of exile and forfeiture of his lands, he would be rewarded for his pains. Instead he found that only his Earldom of Pembroke was returned to him. Even then he discovered that this could not be granted in its entirety; since William Herbert had been also been given the same title in September 1468, his son William had inherited the title. Technically two Earls of Pembroke now existed.

Jasper decided to turn his attention to ensuring that at least his young nephew Henry was well provided by the new regime. During the negotiations over his wardship during the previous year, Henry Tudor had remained at Weobley with the Countess of Pembroke. Immediately after Henry VI had been restored to the throne on 7 October, Jasper

Tudor travelled to Hereford where Sir Richard Corbet handed over the thirteen-year-old boy to his uncle. Jasper now rode with Henry to London, ready for the opening session of Parliament which had been summoned for 26 November. Henry was reunited with his mother Margaret, who was equally determined that, with the Lancastrians finally in the ascendancy, her son would be restored to his rightful inheritance of the honour of Richmond. To achieve this, nothing less than the king's own authority would be needed. It was decided that the young boy should meet with Henry, in the hope of impressing upon the king the need to restore his young nephew to his entitled lands. On 27 October, on a barge for which Reginald Bray paid 3d, Henry was rowed from London to Westminster for an audience with Henry VI. After the meeting, Henry, his mother Margaret, Stafford and Jasper dined with the royal chamberlain Sir Richard Tunstall.

We do not know what conversation took place between the thirteen-year-old Henry Tudor, growing in confidence and approaching his majority, and the child-like Henry VI, almost fifty, who, as one chronicler reported, had been 'bandied about as in a game of blind man's bluff', but it seems unlikely that the latter understood much of the circumstance or even the identity of the adolescent boy presented before him. Later, the meeting would be vested with almost supernatural significance, as the Tudors sought legitimacy through their connection with a Lancastrian past. Every straw, no matter how thin, needed to be grasped at. Henry Tudor's earliest biographer Bernard André wrote how, when Henry VI was enjoying a 'lavish banquet', while washing his hands he summoned Henry Tudor, 'and forecast that someday he would assume the helm of state, and was destined to hold everything in his grasp'. The king also apparently warned Henry to flee the realm, 'to evade the cruel hands of his enemies'. Several years later, no doubt having been influenced by André's own account, the Tudor historian Polydore Vergil wrote in his *Anglia Historia* how Jasper 'took the boy Henry from the wife of the Lord Herbert and brought him with himself a little after when he came to London unto King Henry. When the king saw the child, beholding within himself without speech a pretty space the haughty disposition therefore, he is reported to have said to the noble men there present, "This truly, this is he unto whom we and our adversaries must yield and give over the dominion".'

Related by later writers, the story was simply too good not to be told. The truth, however, will remain forever hidden. What the records do reveal is that shortly after his audience with the king, Henry Tudor enjoyed what little time remained of his visit with Margaret Beaufort, bonding as mother and son. On 5 November, Margaret, Stafford and Henry visited Guildford, at a cost of 10s 11d, with Margaret riding three palfreys on the journey. Further visits were made to Maidenhead on 8 November, where they stayed the night, buying firewood 'for my lord Richmond's chamber' at a cost of 7d. It was in the town that on 9 November, a new 'horsecloth' made of 1½ yards of white cloth was acquired for Henry at a cost of 16d, while eight new horseshoes purchased at Windsor for 14d were required to finish the journey. Arriving at Henley on Thames on Saturday 10 November, more fuel was bought for Henry's chamber, and more horses needed including three palfreys for Henry and four for Margaret. The total cost of the journey was £5 8s 4d. At the end of the journey on 11 November, Henry bade farewell to his mother and was returned to Jasper's custody, with whom he was to return to South Wales by the end of the month.

After Henry's departure, Margaret remained in London, though her son's welfare continued to be the focus of her attentions. On 27 November a meeting was arranged with the Duke of Clarence at Baynard's Castle to discuss the future of lands belonging to the honour of Richmond that traditionally accompanied the Earldom of Richmond, but which had been granted to Clarence by Edward IV. If Margaret had hoped for the restoration of her son's inheritance, she was to be sorely disappointed. Clarence refused to give them up, but a compromise was agreed that Henry would succeed to them after Clarence's death.

For Clarence, Henry Tudor's arrival at court and audience with the king had seemed ominous, perhaps a sign of things to come. The duke had been appointed as Lieutenant of Ireland in reward for his support for Henry VI's restoration, but this was hardly what he had bargained for when he had given his initial support to overthrowing his elder brother. Now, faced with Margaret of Anjou's return from France with her son Prince Edward, who was officially married to Warwick's daughter Anne at Amboise on 13 December, Clarence had found his own claim to the throne pushed aside.

Warwick's discarding of Clarence's royal ambitions was not the only harsh reality that the proud duke had to face when he returned to court. According to one contemporary account, Clarence found himself 'held in great suspicion, despite, disdain, and hatred, with all the lords, noblemen, and other, that were adherents and full partakers' of the Lancastrian side; the duke could not but feel that they 'daily laboured' to undermine him, 'and more fervently intend, conspire, and procure the destruction of him and all his blood'. It seems that from his exile, Edward understood that securing his brother's support would be critical to any mission that he was planning to win back his crown. He had previously sent a lady on a secret mission to the duke to 'persuade him not to be the agent of the ruin of his family' and to 'ask him to consider very carefully what room there was for him now that Warwick had married his daughter to the Lancastrian Prince of Wales'. Once again he made contact with his brother, urging him to consider defecting to his side.

Edward IV faced a bleak future. Having landed on the coast of Holland, the men who witnessed them disembark considered that 'never was such a beggarly company'. Hearing of Edward's arrival, Duke Charles of Burgundy was less than pleased; refusing to admit him to his court, Charles ordered that no subjects should provide aid or assistance to Edward and his entourage, whom he considered as embarrassing refugees and 'would rather the King had been dead'. An exiled king was the last thing he needed in his attempts to win over English support, which he hoped would be achieved by winning over the Lancastrians, sending them repeated messages of friendship. Hoping to avoid conflict with England, in January 1471 Charles was visited by the Lancastrian Dukes of Somerset and Exeter who attempted to persuade the duke to support Henry VI. Frozen out from international diplomacy, Edward and his men were forced to settle in Bruges, where he found lodging with his friend and former Burgundian ambassador to England, Louis de Gruthuyse.

As days passed in nervous frustration, Edward waited, watching whether the consequences of Warwick's deal with Louis XI would indeed mean war with Burgundy, something which would surely push Duke Charles into his arms. Stunned by how fast he had been brought to heel by Warwick's return, in darker moments doubts in his mind were bound to surface. He had attained the crown mainly as a result of his perceived strength against the background of Henry VI's unsuitability and weakness as king. In contrast, Henry's son, Edward, Prince of Wales, now aged seventeen, showed none of his father's character traits: in 1467, the Milanese envoy described how Edward, then a precocious thirteen-year-old who had grown up knowing little else but violence, 'already talks of nothing but of cutting off heads or making war, as if he had everything in his hands or was the god of battle or the peaceful occupant of that throne'. Perhaps Henry VI might even be persuaded to step aside and offer the throne to his son: if this happened, it would be more than likely that the country, of whom reports suggested that 'the more part of the people' were 'full glad' for the Lancastrian restoration, would prefer to support the peaceful accession of the prince rather than suffer violent conflict. If Edward did not act swiftly, the return of Prince Edward could easily mean that his window of opportunity would be closed for good.

Fortunately for Edward, Margaret delayed her departure from France, spending Christmas and the first few weeks of 1471 waiting for Warwick to return to France to collect her son and his daughter. It was a nonsensical idea, one which Warwick attempted to reject claiming lack of funds. In the intervening months he strengthened his own position, appointing himself Great Chamberlain of England and captain of Calais, as well as the king's Protector, yet his power base rested only on a few noblemen including his brother Montagu, Clarence, the Earl of Oxford and Jasper Tudor; to leave the country might end in disaster.

Warwick's mind was also elsewhere, wondering how to solve the diplomatic nightmare he now faced. Louis now expected his favour to be returned, making clear that he required Warwick to prepare, and raise taxation for, a force to fight in France against the Burgundians. In order to put additional pressure on the earl, Louis declared war on Burgundy in December 1470. Warwick continued to procrastinate, promising 10,000 archers and ordering the Calais garrison to go on the offensive against Burgundy. But with Louis keeping hold of Prince Edward and his daughter Anne, the earl was forced to declare war on Duke Charles and Burgundy in February 1471, to the amazement of

London's merchants who understood the devastation this would inflict upon England's trade with the Low Countries.

The situation was now too serious for Burgundy not to act. Duke Charles was forced to retaliate and was drawn into lending his support to Edward, who was summoned to the Burgundian court and given £8,000 'to assist his return'. Thirty-six ships were also hired for the expedition, which eventually set sail from Flushing across the stormy North Sea on 11 March. Few believed Edward stood any chance of recovering the throne. 'It is a difficult matter to go out by the door and then to try and come in by the windows', the Milanese ambassador wrote. 'Men think he will leave his skin there.'

Edward landed in Norfolk the following morning, but after his scouting party had been attacked, set sail again to land at Ravenspur in Yorkshire, three days later. His army, numbering just 2,000 men in total, had been scattered by storms and struggled to regroup deep in hostile Lancastrian territory. Edward was undaunted; he remembered how, when Henry Bolingbroke, the future Henry IV, had landed at Ravenspur seventy years before to claim the throne from Richard II, he had announced that he had come not as pretender, but merely to recover his rightful Lancastrian inheritance. Now Edward chose to emulate him, proclaiming that he had landed only to reclaim his Dukedom of York. To win over the city of York, that nervously refused to admit him, he came wearing the ostrich plumes of the Lancastrian Prince of Wales and made his supporters wear Lancastrian badges as a sign of their loyalty to Henry VI. He then made his progress southwards, managing to avoid Warwick's forces in a series of brilliantly paced marches and counter-marches. The turning point came on 4 April when, having decided to desert Warwick, Clarence, accompanied by 4,000 troops, was reunited with his brothers at an emotional encounter at Banbury, with 'right kind and loving language betwixt them'. Growing stronger by the day as the surrounding countryside he marched through flocked to his standard, Edward entered London in triumph on Maundy Thursday, 11 April, aided in part, one chronicler noted, by 'ladies of quality, and rich citizens' wives with whom he had formerly intrigued' who now 'forced their husbands and relations to declare themselves on his side'.

As Henry VI was once again shut up in the Tower, Edward was reunited with his wife and to the king's delight, his newborn son and heir Edward, who had been born on 7 November, while Elizabeth had taken shelter in the sanctuary of Westminster abbey. Edward's tactic of luring Warwick from the capital had been a remarkable success: with Henry VI in his possession and the force of the Tower and its artillery at his disposal, Edward felt confident enough to leave the capital, intent upon crushing the earl in one final battle.

3

EXILE

•◆•

Two kings, two dynasties, yet the outcome was likely to be the same: the beaten path to victory would be bloody and wreak destruction. It is hardly surprising that many did their best to avoid conflict altogether; Henry Percy, the Earl of Northumberland, who had much to gain from Edward's success, had failed to rise in support as Edward marched southwards following his landing at Ravenspur. But he had also failed to rise against him, and his inaction was praised as doing the king 'a right good and notable service', preventing his tenants, many of whom were Lancastrians with strong memories of Towton, from rising against Edward's invasion. Warwick had charged noblemen 'to come forth on pain of death' to support his cause, but Thomas, Lord Stanley chose to ignore the earl's summons, preferring instead to continue waging his private feud with the Harrington family over the possession of Hornby Castle in Lancashire. Warwick had written to Henry Vernon of Derbyshire on 23 March summoning him to march to meet him at Coventry, adding a postscript written in his own hand, 'Henry, I pray you fail not now as ever I may do for you. R. Warwick'. Vernon refused to move, calculating that the most sensible course of action was to err on the side of caution and stay put.

Family loyalties and ties would be tested to the limit. No more was this apparent than in the Stafford household. After Towton, Henry Stafford had submitted himself to Edward IV, earning a pardon despite his previous Lancastrian sympathies. Stafford had joined with Edward in crushing the Lincolnshire rising in 1470, despite the fact that the rebels included his wife's stepfather's son. Edward's flight and Henry VI's restoration to the throne had caused Stafford to consider his position. His wife Margaret Beaufort's desire to ensure that her son Henry Tudor would accede to his inheritance of the honour of Richmond had drawn the couple close to Henry VI and his household during the king's restoration. Margaret felt that she was close enough to brokering a deal with the existing regime with whom her sympathies naturally lay. Her son's future, after all, depended upon it.

Under the security of the new regime, Margaret felt able to return to her Lancastrian roots. When Margaret's cousin, the exiled Edmund Beaufort, Duke of Somerset, returned to England from Burgundy in February, he met with Margaret, dining on a meal of fresh salmon, eel and tench. Somerset naturally assumed that Margaret would support the restored Lancastrian regime, yet Stafford remained uncertain which side to support. Events would leave him with little time to decide. Edward's sudden return placed Stafford in an impossible dilemma. Should he back the king to whom he had previously pledged loyalty, or fall in with his wife's family? With Edward's landing and march to Coventry, the Duke of Somerset, uncertain himself whether to remain in the capital or to march west in the hope of meeting Margaret of Anjou's forces upon arrival, once again visited the couple at Woking on 24 March, spending four days there with his retinue of forty men. He laid out his plans to head for Salisbury in order to recruit a larger army, but still Stafford refused to join the duke. The discussions continued after Somerset's departure, with Stafford sending some of his men to Newbury for further talks, yet Stafford himself rode to London on 2 April, perhaps hoping to avoid any impending conflict.

Edward's decision to leave Coventry and march into the capital, seizing Henry VI, would force Stafford's hand. He had no option but to support Edward's cause. Ten days later he joined the Yorkist army as it marched out of London towards Barnet where Warwick and his forces were approaching with speed. The pace of events had taken Stafford by surprise. Riding out of London, he was not even armed for battle; his servant had to follow later with gussets of mail that might hopefully protect his master in the impending conflict. As Stafford prepared for battle, he wrote a hastily drafted will, naming Margaret, 'my most entire beloved wife', as his executrix, and if he should fall in battle, asked for 'my body to be buried where it shall best please God that I die'.

Warwick knew that the ultimate test of battle had arrived: unless he could defeat Edward, his future within the Lancastrian dynasty would be over, regardless of whether Margaret of Anjou and Prince Edward arrived from France. He had waited too long in the Midlands, mistakenly believing that Clarence could be relied upon to provide vital support. Nevertheless, the earl still held the advantage in terms of the size of his army, supposedly numbering 30,000 to Edward's 10,000 men.

After some initial skirmishes involving the advance patrols of both sides, the armies drew up half a mile north of Barnet on the evening of Saturday, 13 April. As darkness set in, and as both armies manoeuvred into position, blinded by nightfall, Warwick ordered his guns to bombard Edward's camp. As the deafening sound of cannon fired across the skies, it was soon clear that Warwick had mistaken how close the Yorkist force was to his own side, with the guns overshooting their intended target, much to Edward's relief. Quickly realising that his opponent had no idea of his position, he ordered his men not to return fire, while the entire army was placed under strict orders to remain in silence. The constant bombardment through the night from Warwick's guns began to produce a large cloud of smoke that blended into the thickening mist, creating an impenetrable screen between both forces. Determined that the earl's superior firepower should play no part in the battle, Edward decided to strike first.

Between four and five o'clock in the morning, in the half-light of dawn, a blast of trumpets signalled Edward's advance into the mist. The two forces were so close that both sides fell almost immediately to 'hand strokes', even before the gunners and archers had time to fire their weapons. On Edward's left, it quickly became clear that his troops were outnumbered by the Lancastrian right flank, commanded by the Earl of Oxford. After 'sharp' fighting, the Yorkist flank broke, with many taking to flight as Oxford's forces pursued them, while other Lancastrians, 'weighing that all had been won', rode 'in all haste' to London to announce that Edward had 'lost the field'. They were wrong.

Edward, unaware in the blinding fog that one flank of his army had collapsed, had continued fighting regardless, pushing Warwick's other flank back, in what became a close-set slogging match between men-at-arms on foot, led by Edward's own physical prowess and fighting skill. 'With great violence', one chronicler recorded, 'he beat and bore down before him all that stood in his way, and turning first one way and then another he so beat and bore down that nothing might stand in the sight of him'. In the mist and confusion, in which men 'might not profitably judge one thing from another', the steel of their armour pressed so tightly that even movement became impossible, the battle became like a scrum, with each side locked against one another. Slowly, however, the alignment of both sides began to turn ninety degrees as the Yorkists gained the advantage.

Having scattered the Yorkist left flank, Oxford's men returned to the battlefield, possibly to search for spoils among the dead (one chronicle recalled that they 'returned and fell to rifeling'), only to discover that the battle had not ended. Oxford immediately regrouped his scattered force in the dense mist, unaware that the battle had swung round in a direction that would mean he would be charging into his own side. As the sound of Oxford's charge grew near, Warwick's men mistook Oxford's livery badges of a star with streams that the earl's men displayed on their coats for Edward's badge of the Yorkist sun in splendour. Believing that a separate charge had been organised by the Yorkists, Warwick's forces began to shoot and fight against Oxford's men, 'supposing they had been King Edward's'.

By the time Oxford realised what was happening, it was too late. His forces had already fled, crying 'Treason! Treason!' Left to fight the battle alone, in the panic that ensued, Warwick's troops were overwhelmed by the combined forces of Edward and his younger brother, Richard, Duke of Gloucester. Ignoring the earl's plea to withstand a final charge, the Lancastrian soldiers, believing there was treason in their ranks, fled the field en masse. Soon Warwick had joined them, attempting to make his way to a nearby wood where he had tethered his horse in case he needed to escape. The opportunity never came. Edward had given orders that the earl should be taken alive, but even the king's orders could not save him. Amid the carnage, Warwick was recognised by a group of Yorkist soldiers who, surrounding the earl, battered him to the ground and beat him to death.

The battle had lasted three hours. It was barely dawn, yet already a thousand Lancastrians had been killed, along with 500 Yorkists. The significance of the battle and its outcome could not have been greater;

the kingmaker was dead, with the rest of the Lancastrian noblemen put to flight, including the Earl of Oxford, who escaped northwards to Scotland.

For those remaining in the capital, waiting for the outcome of the battle, to discover whether their husbands or sons had survived or been killed, it was a nervous time. As soon as she discovered that Warwick and the Lancastrians had been defeated, on 17 April Margaret Beaufort made all possible speed from Woking to the capital. She did not know whether her husband was dead or alive; in her anxiety she sent a rider to the battlefield at Barnet to discover Stafford's fate. In fact Stafford had been wounded, severely enough that he would play no part in any further military activities during the year.

Several hours after the battle, the bodies lying strewn across the field were loaded onto carts and taken away, including the corpses of Warwick and his brother Montagu, who were stripped and taken back to the capital to St Paul's where they were placed on public display. But the war was not over yet. As the evening light of Easter Sunday grew dim, a fleet of ships drew anchor at Weymouth. Onto the shore stepped Margaret of Anjou and her son Prince Edward. 'The world, I assure you', Sir John Paston, who had fought on Oxford's side at Barnet, wrote home, 'is right queasy, as ye shall know within the month; the people here feareth it sore. God hath showed himself marvellously like him that made all, and can undo again when him list; and I can think that by all likelihood shall show himself as marvellous again, and that in short time.'

Hearing the news of Warwick's defeat, Margaret of Anjou was 'right heavy and sorry'. Yet she had every reason to remain optimistic; the Lancastrian cause was certainly not lost, and without Warwick, she would no longer be compromised by an agreement she had only entered into with hesitation. The Duke of Somerset, himself experienced in battle on the Continent having fought among Duke Charles of Burgundy's army, soon joined her, and was appointed commander of her forces, which in addition to an army provided by the Earl of Devon, began to grow rapidly as the Lancastrians began to march northwards across the West Country. Meanwhile, Jasper Tudor had travelled westwards to South Wales, where he had begun to recruit a large Welsh army. The intention would be to avoid battle until both armies were able to join up creating a formidable force.

As Margaret and Somerset made their way first to Exeter before heading northwards to Bristol and the Severn Valley, Edward prepared for a second round of battle, sending out orders to fifteen counties for soldiers. Marching from London, he celebrated St George's Day at Windsor Castle and began his march westwards, knowing that he had to intercept Margaret and Somerset's forces before they had the chance to join with Jasper Tudor's. That meant ensuring that the Lancastrians did not cross the river Severn. Edward first moved cautiously, in case Margaret decided to change course and head for London, but his march soon picked up pace and by 29 April he had reached Cirencester, less than a day's march from the Severn at Gloucester. The king could still not be sure, however, of the Lancastrians' exact intentions; one moment it seemed they were heading towards Bath, luring Edward towards Malmesbury and away from the passage across the Severn, when in fact they journeyed in haste to Bristol, where they were welcomed and bolstered with a supply of arms, money and men. Then it appeared the Lancastrians were preparing to wage battle near Chipping Sodbury, but when Edward arrived there was no sight of any opposing army. In fact, Margaret and Somerset, sending advance patrols there, had deliberately sought to confuse Edward into believing that their direction had changed. Instead, having given the Yorkists the slip, they had headed west towards Gloucester with all possible speed. The race for the Severn was now on.

Outmanoeuvred, Edward had no chance of reaching the Lancastrian forces before they reached Gloucester. Instead he sent messages to its governor, ordering him to hold the town at all costs. The plan worked. When Somerset and Margaret arrived at Gloucester at ten o'clock on Friday, 3 May, they discovered that the town's gates had been closed. Somerset threatened to storm its walls, but it was an idle threat. His troops had already marched thirty-six miles through the night, across 'foul country, all in lanes and strong ways betwixt woods without any good refreshing'; they were exhausted, but were ordered to push on another twenty-four miles to Tewkesbury.

By now, both sides were running low on rations, and with neither food nor drink available, soldiers were forced to refresh themselves from muddied puddles, churned up from the carts that passed through them, that one chronicler wrote were barely fit for horses to drink from. Edward shadowed the Lancastrian advance, marching across the high ground along the western edge of the Cotswolds, where there were better marching conditions than the woodlands of the Severn vale below. As the day passed with the dazzling hot sun beating down upon them, the Yorkists managed to make speed and by late afternoon, having covered over thirty miles in a single day, reached Cheltenham. There Edward discovered that the Lancastrians had advanced to Tewkesbury; after a brief rest to allow his troops to refresh themselves, his force continued their march into the night until they stopped to camp within three miles of the enemy, taking what little sleep they could among the preparations for the clash they would face the following morning. Edward knew that defeat was unthinkable if he wanted to prevent Margaret and Somerset crossing the Severn and joining forces with Jasper Tudor. Regardless of all his previous victories, this was the battle he had to win.

As dawn broke, it was clear that the Lancastrians had chosen a strong defensive position, encamped on high ground to the south of Tewkesbury; in front of them were 'foul lanes and deep dykes, and many hedges with hills and valleys', making it practically impossible for any attack upon them: it was 'as evil a place to approach as could possibly have been devised', one chronicler noted.

Edward was undeterred. On Saturday morning, 4 May, he drew up his forces in three divisions or 'battles'. He placed his brother Richard, Duke of Gloucester, in charge of the vanguard on his left side, and Lord Hastings on his right while he himself remained with the main battle in the centre. Observing from his vantage point that there was a large wood to the left of the Lancastrian position, fearing that there might be Lancastrians lying there in wait ready to ambush his forces, he ordered that a squadron of 200 men-at-arms, mounted with spears, be placed near the wood. On the Lancastrian side, Somerset had chosen to command the right flank, placing the elderly veteran Lord Wenlock (who had fought in the first battle at St Albans nearly twenty years before) in charge of the centre of the army.

Edward made the first move, ordering his trumpeters to sound the advance. A soon as his archers and gunners were in range they opened 'right-a-sharp' fire. The Lancastrians attempted to return fire, but the ferocity of the Yorkist arrows which rained down upon them, together with the confined space of their defensive position, soon meant that Somerset found himself outgunned. Realising that his defensive line was in danger of being broken, he ordered that his men should attack Edward's main battle, using the ditches, sunken lanes and wooded terrain skilfully to launch a downhill attack. Somerset, however, had underestimated the strength of the Yorkist vanguard, which having been freed from attacking the Lancastrian defences, returned to Edward's aid. Somerset now found himself being attacked from both sides by Edward's and Richard's forces in fierce hand-to-hand combat. Somerset would have expected that his own central battle, led by Lord Wenlock, should have moved forward and engaged in the fighting, but for some reason, possibly due to the difficulty of crossing the rough terrain, Wenlock's forces remained motionless on the 'marvellous strong ground'.

Outnumbered, Somerset's force was slowly being driven back up the slope. It was at this point that Edward performed a masterstroke, ordering his 200 men-at-arms waiting hidden in the woods to launch a surprise attack into the side of Somerset's beleaguered troops. The duke's men scattered, 'dismayed and abashed'; some fled along the lanes, some into the park and down to the meadow by the river running alongside the abbey, but most would suffer the same fate of being cut down and killed as they ran. Somerset, however, refused to give up, making his way back to the Lancastrian centre whose troops had stood motionless at Lord Wenlock's order. Riding up to the aged nobleman, Somerset was in no mood for excuses; according to a later account, in a fury, he raged at Wenlock, and before he had a chance to respond, Somerset seized his battle axe and beat his brains out, though a more contemporary chronicle suggests that this dramatic confrontation never took place, with Wenlock being captured and executed after the battle.

As the division between the Lancastrian leaders had become horrifically apparent, Edward took the opportunity to engage with the diminished Lancastrian defensive line, now under the command of Prince Edward. Hacking away with battle axes and stabbing with swords, the hand-to-hand conflict did not last long. Already demoralised by their initial defeat, the front of the Lancastrian line gave way, leading to a mass flight towards the river Avon and the sanctuary of the abbey. Edward gave his soldiers permission to pursue the chase with ruthlessness, ordering that they should be killed and despoiled. The most significant victim was the seventeen-year-old Edward, Prince of Wales, who, having been recognised by his surcoat emblazoned with the royal arms, was hacked to death. The son of Sir William Cary, who had been in the service of the prince 'at the field of Tewkesbury', remembered how Edward had been 'slain for his true faith and allegiance' by 'the servants of the said King Edward the iiiith'. By the time the fighting had ceased, the bodies of the Earl of Devon and Somerset's brother, John Beaufort, also were among those littering the battlefield.

Meanwhile, Somerset and other Lancastrian leaders and men had fled into Tewkesbury Abbey, confident that the holy rights of sanctuary would protect them while they remained inside the building. At first, in the elation of victory, Edward offered a pardon to everyone inside the church. He soon decided to change his mind. In spite of the abbot's protestations, Yorkist soldiers burst into the abbey brandishing weapons and dragged the fugitives out with such violence that enough blood was spilt on the stone floors that the abbey needed later to be reconsecrated. According to one chronicler, Edward himself was there, sword in hand, and had to be brought to his senses by a priest bearing the sacrament aloft.

In the aftermath of battle, vengeance would be swift. Under the direction of his brother Richard and the Duke of Norfolk, the trial of Somerset and around a dozen prominent Lancastrian knights was swiftly organised and with sentence summarily passed, they were sentenced to death. Dragged out into the town's marketplace, they were quickly beheaded, though they were spared the indignity of being drawn and quartered, and were given honourable burials.

Margaret of Anjou had watched the battle unfold powerless from the tower of Tewkesbury Abbey. Somehow, realising that defeat was inevitable, perhaps watching the flight of her forces towards the abbey, she fled to a religious house near Malvern, where she was arrested three days later and taken to London.

Edward's victory at Tewkesbury could have hardly been more comprehensive; after crushing a significant attack on London organised by 'the Bastard of Fauconberg', an illegitimate son of Warwick's uncle, he marched into London in triumph on 21 May, 'ordering his standards to be unfurled and borne before him'. That same night, Henry VI died in the Tower. The official account declared that the king had died of 'pure displeasure and melancholy' upon hearing of the fate of his cause. Few believed it. John Warkworth, in his chronicle written around 1480, wrote how Henry had been murdered 'between eleven and twelve of the clock, being then at the Tower the Duke of Gloucester and many others'. The following evening, Henry's body was taken to St Paul's Cathedral, where his body lay in an open coffin, 'that he might be known'. The next morning it was escorted up the river to Chertsey Abbey for burial. According to the Milanese ambassador, Edward had 'chosen to crush the seed' of the Lancastrian dynasty. With Henry and his heir both dead and buried, the king could not have contemplated a greater success.

That 'great and strong laboured woman', Margaret of Anjou, no longer a queen but a childless widow and broken woman, was taken to the Tower where she remained in custody for four years until she was ransomed to Louis XI and returned to France. There was little chance that she might become the focus for any disaffection; she lived out her final days first in a chateau near Angers then at Dampierre, near Samur, where she died on 25 August 1482.

The Lancastrian dynasty had effectively been erased from history. 'In every part of England,' one commentator wrote, 'it appeared to every man that the said party was extinct and repressed for ever, without any hope of again quickening.' With Warwick dead, Edward was the master of his own kingdom. For the first time his throne, together with the future of the house of York, looked secure. On 3 July Parliament assembled to swear its allegiance not only to their undisputed king, but also to his infant son Edward, Prince of Wales, as their successor. In the joy of victory and the celebration of success, it was perhaps easy to forget or even dismiss the fact that the Earl of Oxford had fled to Scotland, or that Jasper Tudor remained at large in Wales, in control of Pembroke Castle, and with him, his fourteen-year-old nephew Henry Tudor, whose claim to the throne, in the aftermath of the Lancastrian destruction, now seemed so remote as to be almost insignificant.

*

Jasper Tudor had only just departed from Chepstow when the devastating news arrived that Margaret and Somerset had been 'vanquished' at Tewkesbury. He had marched from South Wales, in the hope of crossing into England to provide the additional troops he had been sent to raise, but had been unable to reach Margaret and her forces in time to prevent defeat. Realising that the scale of the defeat was so great that 'matters were past all recovery', he returned to Chepstow Castle, to consider what, if at all, the next possible course of action might be. Reflecting upon the disaster, he could have been forgiven for wondering what might have been if only Somerset had delayed battle until he had the chance to join him. According to the Tudor historian Polydore Vergil, he lamented 'that headiness, which always is blind and improvident' that had resulted in Somerset's defeat.

Secluded behind the defensive walls at Chepstow, high upon the Welsh bank of the river Wye, Jasper continued to seek advice from his friends about his next move. Together with Warwick's death at Barnet, the outcome at Tewkesbury altered radically the position of his own family. Whether he knew yet of Henry VI's death in the Tower, the death of Prince Edward had effectively destroyed the Lancastrian inheritance to the throne. Aside from the Duke of Exeter, one of the closest claimants to its lineage seemed to be his nephew Henry Tudor, currently residing in Pembroke Castle. With his mother Margaret forced to submit herself to Edward IV and make peace with the Yorkist regime once more, Jasper understood that the welfare of the boy lay in his hands alone.

Events left Jasper with little choice but to act decisively. Edward had sent Roger Vaughan of Tretower, described as 'a very valiant man', to arrest Jasper by trickery or some other secret means. Ten years previously, it had been Vaughan who had ordered the execution of Jasper's father Owen Tudor, after the battle of Mortimer's Cross; when Jasper 'being advertised' that Vaughan was approaching Chepstow, he was determined to have his revenge. Arresting Vaughan in the town before he had the chance to plan Jasper's own capture, he swiftly had him beheaded. According to a later report, facing his death upon the block, Vaughan pleaded for Jasper's mercy, but was met with the reply from Jasper that 'he should have such Favour as he showed to Owen his Father'.

Jasper understood that to secure his nephew's safety he would have to leave Chepstow immediately and travel to Pembroke Castle. He arrived only just in time, for Edward, hearing news of Vaughan's death, was already in pursuit. The king now sent Morgan ap Thomas, the grandson of Gruffyd ap Nicholas, to besiege Jasper and his household at Pembroke. Thomas had been a strong friend of the earl's, following his family's traditional loyalties to the Lancastrians, but it is more than likely that his decision to turn against Jasper was a personal one: he was married to one of Sir Roger Vaughan's daughters, and it seems that family loyalties on this occasion superseded previous alliances, especially considering the cold-blooded treatment his father-in-law had received at Jasper's hands.

There was little chance that Thomas would gain access to the impregnable fortress; instead he decided to encircle the castle, digging trenches and ditches around it so that 'there was no possible means of escape'. With all communications, including supplies and rations, from outside now prevented, Thomas intended to starve Jasper and Henry out of hiding.

Relief only came eight days later in the form of Morgan ap Thomas's younger brother David, who arrived at Pembroke with a force of 2,000 men, described as a 'ragged regiment, with hooks, prongs and glaives, and other rustic weapons', and began to attack his brother's siege. He was soon able to free Jasper and Henry, conveying them to Tenby. Jasper knew that the heavily fortified harbour would be able to hold out from any siege: the earl had himself ordered its walls to be strengthened in 1457. Six feet thick, with a continuous platform running around the top, the moat was also widened to thirty feet. But with William Herbert, the other Earl of Pembroke, and Lord Ferrers having been dispatched to crush any resistance in Wales and moving closer towards the region, to hold out for too long would be hopeless. Jasper understood that his and his nephew's safety could only be secured in flight.

A 'barque' was hastily prepared, provided by the prominent merchant Thomas White, mayor of the town several times between 1457 and 1472 and who had worked with Jasper on the town's reconstruction, and his son John. On 2 June Jasper, together with Henry and 'certain other his friends and servants', set sail for France, presumably to seek refuge at the court of Louis XI. However, storms blew the ship off course, and after apparently landing briefly at Jersey, they landed at the small port of Le Conquet, on the westernmost point of the peninsula, in north-west Finistère near Brest. Instead of disembarking in France, as Jasper had hoped, they found themselves in the territory of the duchy of Brittany, ruled by Duke Francis II. Initially, Jasper must have cursed what had seemed an ill wind that had blown them away from their planned destination; later, it would prove a remarkable stroke of fortune.

Jasper had hoped to seek the protection of his cousin the French king Louis XI, who had previously sheltered the earl at his court and had awarded him a pension. Arriving in Brittany as he had done, this was now out of the question. Instead, he would need to seek asylum at the court of Duke Francis. As soon as they landed, news reached Francis of the Tudors' arrival. Sending a 'good and safe guard' to meet the new arrivals to his shore, Jasper and Henry were accompanied to the ducal palace, the Château de l'Hermine at the walled hilltop city of Vannes, where Duke Francis II was residing. There Jasper 'submitted himself and his nephew to his protection'. The duke knew that both would be valued pawns in any future diplomatic games between France and England; he received his new guests 'willingly, and with such honour, courtesy, and favour'. Treating them as if 'they had been his brothers', he pledged to Jasper that he would protect him and his nephew 'from injury, and pass as their pleasure to and fro without danger'. The chronicler Philippe de Commynes was present at the duke's court when Henry and Jasper arrived at Vannes. 'The duke,' he observed, 'treated them very gently as prisoners.'

By late September, news of Jasper and Henry's escape was common knowledge. Sir John Paston wrote to his brother that 'it is said that the Earl of Pembroke is taken on to Brittany; and men say that the King shall have delivery of him hastily, and some say that the King of France will see him safe, and shall set him at liberty again'. When Edward IV heard the news of Jasper and Henry's escape and safe landing in Brittany, discovering that they had been 'courteously received and entertained' by Francis, he was furious: 'which matter indeed he took very greviously, as though his mind gave him that some evil would come thereby'. He sent secret messengers to Francis, promising great reward if he would hand over the earls.

The tactic backfired: Francis had already been 'very merry' when he discovered news of Henry's arrival, knowing that 'by having him in his grasp he could always command King Edward' since if the French king had obtained possession of the boy, 'he would have easily crowned him King of England'. Edward's expressed interest in obtaining Henry and Jasper, seemingly at any cost, only increased the value of his captives; 'the earls were so rich a prey' he was determined not to release them, and instead kept them more closely guarded than before. He could not return them to England, he told Edward's messengers, 'by reason of his promise and fidelity'; instead he would 'for his cause keep them so sure as there should be no occasion for him to suspect that they should ever procure his harm in any manner'. When the ambassadors returned to the English court with Francis's message, Edward was determined to ensure the duke stuck to his word, writing further to Francis, calling on his 'honour, good fame, and constancy' to keep Jasper and Henry under arrest, promising at the same time money, aid and 'huge gifts' if he would do so. Understanding the advantage that possession of the Tudors had brought him, Francis knew that he would need to prevent their escape. He ordered that Jasper's personal servants be removed, and that his own men were placed around the two earls, 'to wait upon and guard them'.

For Margaret Beaufort, news that her son had arrived safely in Brittany must have come as a blessed relief from the concerns that encircled her. On 4 October 1471 her husband Henry Stafford died; he had suffered from bouts of illness, possibly resulting from the injuries he had received at Barnet. He certainly never recovered from the outcome of the battle. She began the required period of a year's mourning, but already she was contemplating her next marriage; in choosing Thomas, Lord Stanley as her third husband, she had decided to forgo her former Lancastrian loyalties to bind her fortunes closely to those now in the ascendant at court.

Thomas Stanley had become one of the wealthiest noblemen in the kingdom, with large estates stretching across Cheshire, Lancashire and North Wales. For Stanley, marriage to Margaret brought with it the prospect of further augmenting his lands, providing him with a life interest in her estates; in return Margaret would be granted an annual income from Stanley's own lands. For Margaret, Stanley's power lay not merely in his wealth; his connections at court as steward of the king's household would provide Margaret with the opportunity to be restored to Edward's favour. In particular, the Stanley family had strong links with the Woodvilles; Thomas Stanley's son and heir George had first married the queen's elder sister Jacquetta, and had later been married to Joan, the daughter of George, Lord Strange. It was these connections that allowed Margaret to establish a presence at court; whatever reservations she may have had about the upstart queen, she remained silent, ingratiating herself, even attending upon the queen and her daughters on the occasion of the reburial of her nemesis, Richard, Duke of York, at Fotheringhay, in 1476.

Still Margaret's true loyalty lay undoubtedly with her son's welfare. Throughout Edward's reign, she would continue to hope for her son's eventual return from exile and into the king's favour. It was almost as if Henry was at the heart of every decision she was to make. Ten days before her marriage, on 2 June 1472, Margaret placed her paternal estates in Devon and Somerset in trust, with the provisions that the trustees of her estate were to create a separate estate of lands for Henry Tudor's inheritance. Ten years later, after Margaret's mother the Duchess of Somerset had died, Margaret would make further provisions for Henry. In a document drawn up in Edward IV's own presence in June 1482, her husband Thomas, Lord Stanley promised that he would not interfere with Margaret's Beaufort estates, and that lands to the value of 600 marks a year would be granted to Henry, 'called Earl of Richmond', upon certain conditions. Henry was to return from exile, and 'to be in the grace and favour of the king's highness'. The document was sealed by the king himself. Stanley later recalled that it was during Edward's reign that Margaret and others had discussed the possibility of Henry even marrying Edward IV's daughter Elizabeth of York, relating how the discussion had included the bishops of Ely and Worcester and a Papal representative as well as the king. The clearest evidence that, at some stage, Edward himself intended Henry Tudor to be restored to favour can be found in Margaret's own archives where, on the back of a copy of a patent of creation of Edmund Tudor as Earl of Richmond, is written in a faint, almost illegible hand the draft text of a pardon for 'Henry Earl of Richmond alias lord Richmond alias the said Henry son and heir of the late Earl of Richmond to be the said Richmond or also by the name'.

The date of the pardon, surviving as only a draft, is unknown, but that it reflects not merely Margaret's hopes, but Edward's genuine desire for Henry Tudor to return to England should not be in doubt. Edward seems to have been determined to reconcile former supporters of Henry VI to his kingship. Between 1472 and 1475, thirty attainders were reversed, and former Lancastrians were offered positions under the new regime. It was clear to many that no hope remained for the Lancastrian cause; many understood that the most pragmatic course was to accept God's judgement in battle, that Edward IV was indeed their rightful king. John Morton, the son of a Dorset squire, who had risen through the Lancastrian ranks as a successful lawyer and had taken part in the Parliament of Devils, made his peace with the new regime and by 1472 had been made Master of the Rolls, personally enjoying Edward's 'secret trust and special favour'. Morton later admitted that 'if the world would have gone as I would have wished, King Henry's son had had the Crown and not King Edward'. Yet now things were different: 'after that God had ordered him to lose it, and King Edward to reign', Morton accepted, 'I was never so mad that I would with a dead man strive against the quick'.

For men like Morton, the Lancastrian dynasty was over: Henry VI was dead, his son killed on the battlefield at Tewkesbury. Even Margaret Beaufort recognised that her son Henry would be best placed to one day return to court, to ingratiate himself with the Yorkist dynasty through marriage, as she herself had done. Yet there remained a few 'so mad' that they would refuse to admit that their cause was finished.

John de Vere, the Earl of Oxford, had been determined to crush the Yorkist cause. His father and his eldest brother had been executed by the Yorkists; it is hardly surprising that he was described as 'being disposed in extreme malice against the king'. Henry VI's restoration to the throne, the achievement of which Oxford himself played no small part, had seen the earl return from penniless exile in France to becoming one of the most powerful noblemen at court, bearing the sword of state during the procession at St Paul's in October 1470 in which the

Lancastrian king was formally recrowned. Oxford's influence at court was such that he had 'the rule of them and theirs', one contemporary wrote. Six months later, upon Edward's return and as he drew up his soldiers in preparation for battle at Barnet, Oxford knew that the Lancastrians had the advantage, both in terms of the number of men and artillery ranged against the Yorkist pretender. The battle had started to plan, with Oxford's men defeating the Lancastrian wing; only returning to the battle in the thick blinding fog did Oxford find that Warwick's troops had set themselves upon him. He was not to know of their fatal mistake, confusing the badges of his men with their Yorkist opponents. Instead, the earl had fled the confusion of the battle with the sound of the cries of 'Treason!' ringing around him.

Several days later, Oxford wrote to his wife, 'in great heaviness at the making of this letter; but thanked be God, I am escaped myself, and suddenly departed from my men'. Being among 'strange people' he had no money to even pay his messenger. Asking for all 'the ready money you can make, and as many men as can come well horsed', he requested that his own horse be sent 'with my steel saddles' to be covered with leather. 'You shall be of good cheer, and take no thought,' he ended his letter, 'for I shall bring my purpose about now by the Grace of God, whom you have in keeping.' This cryptic letter was the last the countess would hear from her husband for some time. The outcome of Tewkesbury and Henry VI's death put paid to any hope that Oxford might bring his 'purpose' about; not knowing where her husband was, the countess decided that in spite of her husband's optimism, the best course of action was to flee to the sanctuary of St Martin's church in London. Several years later, one chronicler wrote, she was reduced to such poverty that she had nothing to live upon, 'but as the people of their charities would give to her, or what she might get with her needle or other such cunning as she exercised'.

Still Oxford was determined to fight on. Over the next few years he was sighted in Scotland, Dieppe, making attacks on Calais, determined to become a sore thorn in Edward's side. On 28 May 1473 he arrived on the shore at St Osyth's, Essex, not far from his own ancestral estates. Oxford's hope of raising a hundred gentlemen in Norfolk and Suffolk who had agreed to give their assistance was dashed by the Earl of Essex and Oxford 'tarried not long'; shortly afterwards he was apparently sighted on the Isle of Thanet, 'hovering, some say with great company, and some say with few'. Oxford had hoped for French support for his endeavours, but with no chance of ever establishing a rival to Edward IV, and with France and Burgundy having come to a peaceful alliance, already the Duke of Burgundy had warned the French king 'not to keep the Earl of Oxford in his kingdom any longer' as part of their continued truce. Initially supportive of Oxford's enterprises, Louis began to change his mind. 'He fears art and fraud in the earl', one ambassador reported.

After spending the summer at sea in piracy, capturing passing ships and obtaining 'great good and riches', on the last day of September 1473 Oxford took the remarkable decision to seize the small garrison at St Michael's Mount in Cornwall. He had fewer than eighty men with him, but the fortress and the position of St Michael's Mount made it next to impossible to attack. It seems that Oxford was further assisted by the support of the nearby Cornish gentry, including Henry Bodrugan who, despite being tasked by Edward with recovering the garrison, pocketed the money he had been given for the commission for himself, and despite occasional outbreaks of fighting, including one occasion when Oxford was shot and wounded 'in the very face' by an arrow, was mostly content to meet with the earl each day under truce, supplying him with enough victuals and supplies to last until the following summer. When Edward realised what was going on, he transferred control of the siege to Sir John Fortescue; in addition to stepping up the ferocity of the attack upon Oxford's stronghold, he supplied Fortescue with 300 men, cannon and artillery from the Tower and four ships from the royal fleet carrying over 600 men that were able to cut off any chance of escape by sea. The siege began in earnest in late December, but Oxford's resistance ensured that it was not for another month, when tempted by the promise of pardon for his life if not his goods, that Oxford finally surrendered on 15 February.

Oxford would spend the next nine years imprisoned in Hammes Castle in the Calais pale. His stay was a comfortable one: at first fifty marks was set aside for his 'costs and sustenation', later increased to fifty Flemish pounds. A year after his surrender, Oxford and his two brothers were attainted, with all their lands and goods being declared forfeit to the king. One chronicler lamented the earl's downfall, stating how 'all was done by their own folly'. As the years drew on, in isolation Oxford struggled to come to terms with his own ruin, seeing no chance of restoration to his title and lands. In 1478 he took the drastic step of attempting to end his own life: John Paston was repeating well-known gossip when he wrote that Oxford was rumoured to have 'leapt the walls and went to the dyke to the chin', adding, 'to what intent I cannot tell; some say, to steal away, and some think he would have drowned himself, and so it is deemed'.

Despite Duke Francis's assurances that both Jasper and Henry Tudor would be guarded so that they would be unable to challenge his crown, Edward continued to press for both men to be returned to England. He also sought to ingratiate himself with Francis, in the hope that his support for Brittany against France might sway the Duke into handing over both the Tudors. In April 1472 he had sent his brother-in-law Anthony Woodville, Earl Rivers, together with a troop of soldiers, to join the duke's service. Having assisted the duke in repelling a French invasion on 11 September, Rivers negotiated a treaty with Francis at Châteaugiron, signalling both sides' desire for a joint Anglo-Breton invasion of France. In November, Breton envoys led by Guillaume Guillemet arrived in England to negotiate for further military aid. It seemed as if an agreement might be reached that, in return for military assistance, the Tudors might be handed over to Edward, but still Francis insisted that in light of his earlier promise to protect Jasper and Henry, he could not break his word. Francis's resort to chivalric honour was nothing more than an excuse; he was hardly prepared to give up his greatest bargaining tools quite yet, at least until he had gained everything he could from Edward in return. He would, however, restrict Jasper and Henry's movements further, something which Edward welcomed, writing to the duke pledging more money and aid to Brittany.

As a consequence, around October 1472 both Jasper and Henry were taken to Suscinio, one of the duke's country residences close to Sarzeau on the gulf of Morbihan, near St Gildas abbey. Set in a vast hunting chase on the Rhys Peninsula, enclosing the Gulf of Morbihan in southern Brittany, the castle itself was built in the thirteenth century to be used by the Dukes of Brittany as their summer residence. With several large rounded towers formed around a courtyard, it was both secluded and 'well sumptuous'. The keeper of the chateau was Jean de Quelennec, the admiral of Brittany since 1432, who had earned a reputation as both 'wise and judicious', and who gave his full support to protecting the Tudors, especially after rumours began to circulate that English envoys had been ordered to kill Henry if they were unable to secure his extradition.

Only a mile away from the sea, positioned as it was on the flat sandy expanse of the peninsula, it was soon apparent that Suscinio would be too exposed in the face of any attack or attempt to seize Jasper and Henry by ships landing nearby. The decision was made to take them back to the ducal court. In late 1473 both were at Nantes; in the absence of any further information, it must be assumed that Jasper and Henry accompanied Duke Francis's court as it moved between the centres of Vannes, Nantes, Rennes and the nearby rural manor houses favoured by Francis, such as Plaisance, Bernon or Suscinio.

Francis's decision to keep both Tudors close to him during this time was also influenced by the fact that it was not merely Edward who wanted to get his hands upon Henry and Jasper. The pair had intended to travel to the court of French king Louis XI, who had previously been a source of refuge to Jasper, formerly in receipt of an annual pension from Louis worth £1,200. Now the French king, treating both men as if they were members of his own household, wanted them in his own possession, back where he considered they had intended to travel had their voyage not blown them off course and where he believed they rightfully belonged. In 1474 Louis decided to send a series of detailed instructions to Guillaume Compaing, the dean of the church of St Pierre en Pont in Orleans and the French envoy at Francis's Breton court. Compaing was ordered to seek a meeting with the duke, requesting that both Jasper and Henry be freed. First, Compaing should explain the background behind their arrival in Brittany, when their intended destination had all along been France: 'considering the divisions in England, the Count of Pembroke, to avoid numerous perils and dangers there and save his life, has for a long time wanted to see the King':

The King considering this and that the Count of Pembroke is his first cousin, received him with good intentions and therefore kept him in his household and in his service, and gave him a pension as he is used to do with his servants around him. For some time and until recently, the Count of Pembroke continuously stayed in the king's estates, and went from place to place with the King to serve him and accompany him as do the rest of the household, and had the accord of the King that from then on the Count of Richmond his nephew, would be there all the same for the safety of his person, and to keep him out of harm's way, being so young and the road so dangerous. While the Count of Pembroke was in his service and kept by the King's pension, shortly before the Queen of England and the Prince of Wales last went into the Kingdom of England, came some news to Pembroke, and he was informed that if he wanted to come back to Wales, where his land and estates are, he would find great favours and would recover his land, and many times he was pressed in that direction by the people from over there. Hearing this, Pembroke came to the King, and told him of this, and supplicated him to be given permission to go to Wales to recover the land, a request that was so just and so measured, that everyone thought that the King could not disallow it. Therefore, to the great pleasure of the King, Pembroke, always remaining his servant, made his way to Wales. The King gave him all the favours he could because of their close family ties and so that he could recover, keep and defend his estates and land . . . When the Count of Pembroke arrived in Wales, he found great favours there, and was decently received, and he recovered most of his lands. But as the adventures of war came, these people met their enemies in Wales, and not for the best. At this moment, many favours he sought to have in this country were found wanting, and he and his nephew Richmond were in great danger, and he was for this completely unprepared. For these reasons, Pembroke and Richmond were advised to go to the King as their lord and single refuge, and that it would be his pleasure to welcome them as humble servants. Following this advice, Richmond and Pembroke boarded a ship with the intention to come before the King for the reasons mentioned. And as God had wished, they had such great torments of seas and wind, that they were forced into landing on the coast of Brittany, and came under great danger to the haven of Conquet where they were made safe, as they would have been in Harfleur or any port of the King. However, as it has been told to the King, and he has been warned, that some officer or other subject of the Lord of Brittany have taken or arrested Pembroke and Richmond, and any of those in their company, and seized all of their effects.

Since, Louis warned, 'there is no war between the King [Louis] and the Lord of Brittany, and that no harm has been made by Pembroke and Richmond to the Lord of Brittany and his land, it is very strange to the King that the Lord of Brittany would have been advised to seize and arrest Pembroke and Richmond, even though some have advised him to'. There had been rumours at the French court, he stated, that Francis has already freed Jasper and Henry, but 'doubting this to be true', he wished Compaing to 'very fondly pray' that they be released immediately, 'and the King would find great pleasure in this and be indebted to him'.

Louis had considered carefully in advance every argument that the duke might employ to justify his keeping both men. In order to counter each one, in case of any doubt, the king had already written the response for Compaing. If Francis were to reply that Jasper and Henry had landed without any arranged safe passage, or that since 'they or their people waged war against the subjects of the Lord of Brittany and similarly against the people of King Edward who is his ally', Compaing was to respond that neither Jasper nor Henry had 'ever landed in Brittany for warfare, and therefore upon their landing in Brittany they owe to be as safe there as in Paris'. If Francis could give 'particular cases of Pembroke and Richmond's subjects waging war against him' then Louis would offer sufficient reparation, but 'on this occasion the two cannot be gaoled, nor reasonably taken, arrested, nor held back'. As for the fact that Jasper had fought against Edward IV, Francis's 'friend and ally', Louis responded that this was not a 'sufficient cause' for arresting Jasper and Henry, since the whole of France was an enemy of Edward and the English; 'if it was desired in Brittany to take and keep all the enemies of King Edward', the French king concluded sardonically, 'one should conclude that all the French that come to Brittany should be taken and kept, which would be a very strange thing to allow to stand on such little grounds'.

In addition, Compaing was to give the uncompromising reply that 'the King understands not that Pembroke and Richmond be in any way the enemies of the Lord of Brittany, for the King holds them in his esteem as the servants of his household. And that if his servants and the people of the King's household were to be taken, it would seem therefore that the Lord of Brittany would want to lead a war against him, which the King does not think is what the Lord of Brittany wants, neither does the King have any intention of waging war for his part.' The menacing tone of Louis's intentions could hardly have been spelt out any clearer.

Louis concluded by demanding that Pembroke and Richmond should be 'freed frankly and swiftly' and sent to the French court and the king's person, 'to whom this shall come at a great pleasure, and which he will be indebted to him for'. Nevertheless, for all his threats and demands, Louis was a realist; Francis was hardly likely to cave in to his wishes immediately, but that did not preclude achieving part of his intentions. For now, Louis was willing to compromise. 'If the Lord of Brittany refuses to free Pembroke and Richmond with their people and goods,' he ordered, 'it shall be asked of him that he should neither take nor move them from his hands', with Louis requesting that a written promise or certification be made 'so that good faith be on paper, and so that the King can think about what can be done'.

It was around this time that Francis decided to separate Henry and Jasper. Facing demands from both Edward IV and Louis XI to hand over both Tudors, in doing so the duke made it difficult for both to be captured, their separation ensuring that he would at least hold on to one of his valuable captives. At the same time, Jasper's separation from Henry came as a relief to Edward, who could be assured that if the earl escaped, he would be unable to take his nephew with him, taking up his cause as a challenger to the throne.

The decision came as a sudden surprise to Henry, who was understandably anxious to learn that he was to be removed from his uncle Jasper's company, the man who had acted as his guardian and protector for much of his childhood and adolescence. Henry was reassured by Quelennec, who had been appointed by the duke to inform the earl of the intended separation, who explained that it was being done in his own interest and with no risk to himself, promising that once Henry's fortunes had changed, he would be 'as free as he could be in any place in the world where he would choose to retire'.

Jasper was placed in the fortress of Josselin, twenty-five miles from Vannes. Facing the river Oust, the castle had been rebuilt in the 1370s, with a great keep and prison tower being constructed. It was in this tower that Jasper may have been placed, at least until 1475. Meanwhile Henry was sent to the chateau of Largoët, a 144-foot, seven-storey-high octagonal tower, known as the Tour d'Elven, that had been rebuilt in the 1460s and remained unfinished, hidden deep within a forest. In January 1475 financial accounts record Henry being named as a 'prisoner' at Largoët; it seems likely that he would have been placed in rooms either on the sixth or seventh floors of the tower, which had been designated as secure rooms. Nevertheless, Henry's stay in this secluded and secure location would hardly have been one of hardship and harsh conditions. Largoët was in the possession of Jean de Rieux, the marshal of Brittany, who having made the offer to Francis II to take the young earl, treated Henry with both honour and care. Rieux also had two young sons, around Henry's age, with whom he may have shared his upbringing. It was certainly at Largoët that Henry continued his studies, becoming fluent in both French and Latin, while acquiring a taste for French courtly works and poetry heavy with classical allusion and allegory.

Only fragments of information concerning Henry's exile during the 1470s remain. Nevertheless they provide fleeting insights into Henry's formative years, secluded as they are from view. Preserved in the surviving financial records of the wardrobe accounts of Duke Francis for instance, is the following entry for May or June 1472: 'To my lord of Richmond for a long robe by gift of my said lord [the duke], seven ells of fine black velour, costing 4 royals a ell: £35; for lining the upper arms, half a third of black, cost 23d. And for the lining, four ells of changeable taffeta at 2 royals an ell, costing £10; and the making of each, sum £45 13s. To him for a short robe, an ell and a half of black Damask at £4 an ell, and padding, 1 ecu, total £7 2s 10d.'

From the description, one can almost envisage the young Henry, wearing his robe of black damask, padded with taffeta. In the city library at Arras, there survives a series of drawings by Jacques le Boucq, Hainault Herald. Though drawn in the sixteenth century, some were based on earlier portraits, now no longer extant. One includes Henry as a young man, a robe draped over his shoulders, thickly crumpled around his arms and wrists as he holds what appears to be an apple in his right hand. A cap with a badge on its right side covers his head and hair, which falls on either side of his face at chin height. Yet it is Henry's eyes, large and weary with dark lines forming beneath them that stand out, just as they would later do so for those who met him. It is tempting to imagine the image as Henry while still in exile, his simple dress a far cry from the world of majesty at the royal court.

The other glimpse we have of the young Henry is from the chronicler Philippe de Commynes, who managed to speak with him at the Breton court. Appearing relaxed, Henry told Commynes that 'since the age of five he had been guarded like a fugitive or kept in prison'. It is perhaps this sense of weariness, of a young man who, despite being only in his teenage years, had spent his entire life on the run, in danger of his life, that Henry's tired and determined eyes reflected.

With his own kingdom finally pacified and with the exception of Jasper and Henry Tudor's exile in Brittany, the Lancastrian cause firmly crushed, Edward felt able to turn his attention to the traditional preoccupation of English kings: their natural enemy of France. In spite of the massive erosion of territory that the English had occupied since the halcyon days of the 1420s, Edward had continued to style himself King of France, quartering his arms with French lilies. He had his own personal reasons to reclaim glory there, since having been born in Rouen when it was still under English occupation, he may have felt that it was his duty to reclaim some of the lost territories in Aquitaine and Normandy that his father had achieved military glory fighting for. The French king Louis XI had also demonstrated his own hostility to Edward's kingship, giving succour to the Lancastrian regime, and until recently had managed to remain a persistent nuisance, giving aid to the Earl of Oxford's missions across the Channel and into East Anglia.

Edward would have also had in mind the unifying effect that war could have on the realm. The past sixteen years of civil war had witnessed the death, through execution or on the battlefield, of thirty-nine peers. Military glory in France would help to repair the damage of the previous decade; success would prove God's judgement that Edward was rightfully England's king. In 1472 Edward's spokesman in Parliament argued that war might even prevent civil discord for the future. But war was costly, and that meant persuading Parliament to grant the king the power to raise additional taxation; in November 1472 a tax of one-tenth of all income from land was eventually granted. But Edward was still left with a significant shortfall, which he was forced to make up through borrowing from wealthier subjects, though few felt able to refuse to lend to the king in spite of the cost: Margaret Paston lamented to her son John that 'the king goes so near us in this country, both to poor and rich, that I know not how we shall live if the world amend'.

Careful alliances with France's neighbours Brittany and Burgundy would also need to be sought. Brittany's support was secured through a combination of sending 2,000 archers in April 1472 to counter French attacks upon Duke Francis's realm, together with an embassy, led by Earl Rivers, that led to the signing of the Treaty of Chateaugiron in September, which allowed the English to use Brittany as a territorial base from which to launch an invasion of France. Burgundy proved a harder bargain, but Duke Charles the Bold finally agreed to support Edward's claim to the French throne if he might be rewarded with territory in the Somme region. Hesitations and further diplomatic complications, however, meant that neither agreement lasted long enough for Edward to prepare for war. It would be another two years before he felt secure enough to finally launch his long awaited invasion.

By December 1474 detailed preparations were being made to ship over 11,500 men, the largest single army assembled for a military campaign in France, together with thirteen large siege guns and over 700 stone cannonballs, though Commynes admitted that the 'men seemed very inexperienced and unused to active service'. Nevertheless Edward crossed the Channel with his aristocracy, hungry for military glory, fully committed to what the king termed his 'great enterprise', with five dukes, three earls and at least a dozen barons boarding the boats for France that sailed on 20 June 1475. Upon his arrival, Edward had hoped to count upon Burgundy's support, bringing with them a large army to bolster his own troops. When Duke Charles arrived with only a small personal retinue, Edward knew that he was left with a huge problem. Without full Burgundian support, he did not have a chance of defeating the might of France. Already he had gone too far to turn back without suffering a humiliating defeat; the excitement in the air was palpable, with his men eager to engage with their long-standing enemy. 'If the Frenchmen will do us the day,' Thomas Stonor wrote from Guines on 19 July, 'it shall not be long before we meet.' A solution was provided by the French king who, unwilling to wage a ruinously expensive war, offered to negotiate a peace at Picquigny, near Amiens. Both armies marched in full battle array to the town, where Louis put on lavish entertainments for the English soldiers, including an enormous amount of food and wine, 'of which there was great plenty, and of the richest that France could produce'. The English took advantage with 'very great satisfaction', Commynes adding that 'not a drop of water was drunk'. Another account suggests that women were made freely available, but that 'many a man was lost that fell to the lust of women' having been 'burnt' by them, a euphemistic term for venereal disease, so that 'their members rotted away and they died'. While the soldiers revelled in an abundance of wine and women, behind the scenes a deal was swiftly hammered out, Louis agreeing to pay Edward 75,000 French crowns together with an annual pension of 50,000 crowns. In return, several trade agreements were concluded, as well as a private understanding that the Dauphin would eventually be betrothed to Edward's daughter Elizabeth of York.

It seemed, the Crowland Chronicler believed, an 'honourable peace'. But for many members of the nobility, realising what had taken place, the treaty was anything but honourable. In agreeing to a peace with France, Edward had left his brother-in-law Charles the Bold to be hung out to dry. Gone was the promise of military glory and the spoils of victory, the booty and expensive ransoms of French prisoners that many would have hoped to have earned. A peace was not what they had crossed the Channel for; for some, Edward's volte-face was too much to bear. The young Henry, Duke of Buckingham, withdrew from the expedition entirely and left for England together with his retinue before the negotiations at Picquigny were concluded. Yet the dissatisfaction at the king's capitulation struck right at the heart of Edward's government. Commynes wrote that when it came to arranging a formal interview with the French king, 'the Duke of Gloucester, the King of England's brother and some other persons of quality, who were not pleased by this peace, were not present at this conference'. For the first time, the king's younger brother Richard, usually a loyal mainstay of his realm, had chosen to publicly show his dissatisfaction with his brother's decision, though Commynes admitted that Richard, accepting the fait accompli, 'reconciled' himself to the peace, and shortly afterwards visited Louis at Amiens, where he accepted 'some very fine presents, including plate and well-equipped horses'.

Edward returned home to face the criticism that he had failed to wage a successful war, that taxation had been misspent, and that the king himself had acted dishonourably in letting down Charles the Bold of Burgundy. Yet it had been Charles himself who, due to his military commitments in Lorraine, had failed to deliver upon his promise to Edward of providing a full Burgundian force to fight France. It was to prove a costly mistake; by the end of the year he had launched a war against the Swiss, a viciously fought conflict that ended in Charles's death at the battle of Nancy in January 1477. Five years later, after Mary of Burgundy died falling off her horse in 1482, the Treaty of Arras resulted in the Duchy of Burgundy being subsumed into France, while the ducal title descended to Mary's son Philip the Fair. If there was one winner from Picquigny, it was undoubtedly Louis XI; calculating that the costs of Edward's pension was a small price to pay for peace, he was later heard to boast that 'I have chased the English out of France more easily than my father did; for he had to drive them out with armies, while I have seen them off with venison and good French wine.'

Edward could at least take consolation that the peace brought to a conclusion the problem of Margaret of Anjou, who had been imprisoned in the Tower since 1471; handed over to Louis upon payment of a ransom and the condition that she renounce her claim to the English crown and her lands in England. She lived on for another six years, suffering the further humiliation forced upon her by Louis to give up all claims that she had inherited from her father, René of Anjou. Living out her days in poverty and as a shadow of her former self, this exiled queen remained the sole testament to the fading memory of Lancastrian rule.

*

The terms of the treaty of Picquigny had included a promise from Louis XI that he would refrain from invading Brittany, a promise for which Edward now hoped Duke Francis would thank him. With this expectation of gratitude in mind, Edward decided to return to the vexed issue of Henry Tudor's exile in Brittany. The sudden death of Henry Holland, Duke of Exeter, while he was returning with the king's army from France had once more narrowed the bloodline of possible Lancastrian claimants to the throne: Exeter had been the grandson of Henry IV's eldest sister, and on his return journey he had drowned at sea, leaving no heir.

While Henry Tudor remained in exile, Edward believed that the Yorkist dynasty could only be secure once he was captured. In spite of the birth of a second son, Richard, in August 1473, in addition to his heir, Edward, Prince of Wales, Edward could not forget that Henry was 'the only impe now left of King Henry the 6th's blood', whose survival left the king in 'perpetual fear' that his own dynasty might one day be challenged.

With the new treaty signed, Edward turned his mind to removing this one remaining thorn in his side. Once again the king sent ambassadors to Francis at Nantes, headed by the Chester herald Thomas Whiting, with a large sum of gold to ease the negotiations. Ordered to report that Edward wished to arrange a marriage for Henry with one of his 'affinity', by which means the prospect of civil war would finally draw to an end, they requested that Henry should travel back to England with them. Francis listened to the ambassadors courteously; after they had spoken, he repeated his well-worn arguments that, having sworn a promise to his captives, he 'might not lawfully' release Henry. The ambassadors persisted, pressing Francis with ever greater sums of money for his compliance. Eventually the duke, 'wearied with prayer and vanquished with price', agreed to hand over Henry, having been convinced that Edward intended to marry the earl to his eldest daughter Elizabeth of York.

Henry was taken from Largoët, where he travelled with the English ambassadors to St Malo, where a ship was waiting to embark on the journey to England. Henry's fate seemed to have been sealed. In the hands of Edward's ambassadors, his return to an uncertain fate in England seemed inevitable. Henry seems to have understood the consequences of his sudden uprooting: in his 'agony of mind' or perhaps in dissimulation, he 'fell by the way into a fever', delaying their departure.

It would prove a crucial delay. It seems that Francis's decision to allow Henry's return to England had been taken without consultation with members of his council: when the news reached the Breton court of the duke's capitulation, many were shocked, none more so than one of Francis's trusted councillors Jean du Quelennec, Vicomte du Fou and admiral of Brittany since 1432, 'a man of such reputation among the nobles of Brittany'. When Quelennec discovered what had occurred, he rushed to the court, where he presented himself to the duke, his appearance so grave and 'very sad and heavy without speaking' that Francis demanded to know what was wrong.

'Most noble duke,' Quelennec is supposed to have answered, 'this paleness of countenance is unto me a messenger of death.' Francis had forgotten the promise he had given, he argued, and instead delivered 'that most innocent imp, to be torn in pieces by bloody butchers, to be miserably tormented, and finally to be slain'. When Francis denied it, Quelennec pressed the duke: 'Believe me most noble duke, Henry is almost lost already, whom if you shall once permit to step one foot out of your jurisdiction, all the world shall not after that be able to save his life'.

At length Francis was persuaded by Quelennec to change his mind and reverse his decision. There was no time to lose: three days had already passed, with the ambassadors' departure, taking with them their precious cargo, imminent. Francis immediately sent his treasurer Pierre Landois to halt the ship setting sail. With 'great celerity' Landois arrived at St Malo where with 'long talk' and 'counterfeiting some business' managed to delay the ambassadors' departure. Discovering Henry 'almost dead', Landois arranged in secret for the earl to be conveyed to a secure sanctuary in one of the chapels within the town. When the English ambassadors discovered what had happened, they were furious; not least concerned for their own safety, 'thus spoiled both of money and merchandise . . . they should not return home altogether void'.

Desperate to prevent their catch from slipping out of their grasp, the ambassadors decided to lure Henry out of sanctuary. When they arrived at the chapel, however, they were met with a hostile reception from townsmen who had surrounded the chapel, determined that Henry's rights of sanctuary would be observed. In further negotiations, Landois claimed that it was through the ambassadors' own negligence that Henry had managed to enter sanctuary, yet gave a promise that the earl 'should either be kept in sanctuary . . . or else should be committed to ward again with the duke, so as there should be no cause to fear him'.

When the ambassadors returned bringing news of Henry's near capture, Edward was 'very sorry', though he was 'eased' by the promise that the earl would remain under ward. With the threat of his capture lifted, Henry's illness miraculously cleared and 'pretty well amended', the earl returned to the ducal court. Still, the threat of uncertainty remained; Henry remained too valuable a prize for other courts in Europe not to take an interest in seeking his possession. Louis XI continued to pressure Francis for both Tudor exiles to be released; when he discovered that Henry had narrowly escaped being handed over to Edward, the French king was disturbed enough to send a new mission led by the admiral of Guinne, Guillaume de Souplainville, to Nantes just before Christmas 1476, with de Souplainville being ordered to demand from Francis that Henry and Jasper be handed over to him. Met with a flat refusal, he returned to France empty-handed in early 1477. Faced with an increasingly hostile French king who, regardless of his promises given in treaties, seemed bent upon ending Brittany's independence, Francis understood that one day he would need to come to terms with Edward's demands and decide the fates of his Tudor captives.

The money Edward had acquired from his French pension, together with the commercial returns which ended a restriction in trading between English and French merchants, leading to an expansion in the cloth and wool markets, had left him 'an extremely wealthy prince'. The king was even able to live off his own revenues, which coming after years of Lancastrian profligacy, was a remarkable achievement; with his kingdom at peace and his rivals silenced, one chronicler considered the years of his reign after 1475 as ones of 'glory and tranquillity'.

The one exception to this newfound tranquillity was the king's brother George, Duke of Clarence. He had never recovered Edward's trust after his defection to the Lancastrians, but the king could not ignore the fact that his brother was of royal Yorkist blood, and as such he felt duty-bound to recognise the duke as the pre-eminent nobleman in his realm, allowing him to inherit his wife's vast Neville inheritance and forcing his younger brother Richard to surrender the office of Great Chamberlain to Clarence after the duke had complained to the king that it was more deserving of his status.

Edward's attempts at reconciliation with his brother had come in the face of Clarence's continued intractable nature. Throughout the 1470s, his loyalty remained suspect; there were rumours that he had stayed in contact with the Earl of Oxford, while behind the scenes he attacked the king's policies. Slowly, one chronicler observed, 'each began to look upon the other with no very fraternal eyes'. Clarence had also never come to terms with Edward's marriage to Elizabeth Woodville, making no secret of 'his bitter and public denunciation of Elizabeth's obscure family'; in doing so, he set himself aganist the queen who 'remembered the insults to her family and the calumnies with which she was reproached'. According to the Italian Dominic Mancini, 'she concluded that her offspring by the king would never come to the throne, unless the Duke of Clarence were removed; and of this she easily persuaded the king'. In the end, however, it proved that Clarence alone would become the author of his own destruction.

Clarence had accompanied Edward to France, but on his return his behaviour became erratic, especially after the death of his wife Isabel in childbirth in December 1476. 'It was noticed,' the Crowland Chronicler observed, 'that the duke was gradually withdrawing more and more from the king's presence, hardly uttering a word in council, not eating and drinking in the king's residence.' When in April 1477 he arranged for the abduction of a former servant in his household, convinced he had killed the duchess by giving her 'a venomous drink of ale mixed with poison', having him tried and summarily hanged at Warwick Castle, Edward realised that his brother had become dangerously unhinged. A month later, when an Oxford astrologer was arrested for attempting to use magic against the king, under torture he confessed that a member of Clarence's household, Thomas Burdett, had been involved in creating a horoscope that calculated the deaths of the king and the Prince of Wales. Both were tried and found guilty on 20 May and taken to Tyburn where they were hanged, drawn and quartered. Clarence's mistake was to question the decision not privately, but in public, insisting that the condemned men's declarations of innocence be read out to the council. Edward was furious, deciding his brother had tried his patience too far. Within a month, Clarence was arrested and placed in the Tower. When Parliament convened the following January, Edward had decided there would be no second chances for his wayward brother. The charges against Clarence were vague and unsubstantiated, but there would be no doubt that the king's will would prevail: the duke was convicted of treason. After the speaker of the House of Commons demanded an immediate execution, Clarence was dispatched on 18 February 1478, the method of his death remaining mysterious, with Dominic Mancini writing a few years later that 'the mode of execution preferred in this case was that he should die by being plunged into a jar of sweet wine'.

If Richard disagreed with Edward's treatment of his brother, which amounted to nothing less than judicial fratricide, he remained silent. He had stuck loyally to his brother throughout; in contrast to Clarence, his fidelity to the king never wavered, following Edward into exile in Flanders and returning with him in triumph, fighting in both battles of Barnet and Tewkesbury. Victory had brought Richard the spoils of war, namely the offices, estates and perhaps above all influence exerted by the Earl of Warwick in the north. Now, with Clarence's death, Richard would reap further reward, with his son Edward being created Earl of Salisbury, one of Clarence's titles, three days before the duke's murder; six days after, Richard was reappointed as Great Chamberlain and given a greater share of the late Earl of Warwick's inheritance that had previously been denied him. Richard and Clarence had argued bitterly over the inheritance, since both were married to Warwick's daughters who had claim to the lands, to the point that one foreign observer reported that Richard 'was constantly preparing for war with the Duke of Clarence'. But brotherly disagreements did not mean that Richard would willingly accept his brother's execution. According to Mancini, he was 'so overcome with grief' that he was 'overheard to say that he would one day avenge his brother's death'. He withdrew to his estates in the north and, according to the Italian observer Dominic Mancini, who had arrived in England in the early 1480s, was rarely seen at court; preferring instead to keep 'himself within his own lands'.

Meanwhile the king revelled in his newfound wealth, 'very often dressed in a variety of the costliest clothes very different in style' from what contemporaries had been used to, as the Crowland Chronicler described: 'the sleeves of the robes hung full in the fashion of the monastic frock and the insides were lined with such sumptuous fur that, when turned back over the shoulders, they displayed the prince (who always stood out because of his elegant figure) like a new and incomparable spectacle set before the onlookers'. Edward's expensive tastes in clothing were not the only excesses that the king had taken to indulging in. In addition to his constant womanising, that Thomas More later claimed was 'insatiable, and everywhere all over the realm intolerable', Edward, who had once displayed the slim physique of a warrior, had taken to eating too well. At Picquigny, Commynes had observed that Edward was 'a very good looking, tall prince' but that 'he was beginning to get fat and I had seen him on previous occasions looking more handsome'. In middle age, the king had begun to take his feasting to extremes. 'In food and drink he was most immoderate', Mancini observed, adding that 'it was his habit, so I have learned, to take an emetic for the delight of gorging his stomach once more'. As a result, the king's once 'fine stature' ('previously he had been not only tall but rather lean and very active') had 'grown fat in the loins'.

When Edward fell ill and his condition deteriorated suddenly, resulting in his death on 9 April 1483, aged just forty-two, the king's demise came as a surprise to many: he was 'neither worn out with old age nor yet seized with any known kind of malady', the Crowland Chronicler wrote. Mancini related the popular opinion that 'they say another reason for his death was, that he, being a tall man and very fat though not to the point of deformity, allowed the damp cold to strike his vitals, when one day he was taken in a small boat, with those whom he had bidden go fishing, and watched their sport too eagerly. He there contracted the illness from which he never recovered, though it did not long afflict him.' Possibly Edward died of a stroke, termed by Commynes as 'apoplexy', resulting from 'the limits of his excesses'; what matters is not exactly how the king died, but the very fact that he had died now, leaving his heir Edward, Prince of Wales to inherit his throne aged just twelve. A child king upon the throne was the last thing that

Edward would have wanted to leave behind; in 1377 and 1422 the realm had managed to establish a regency council to mask the inadequacies of minority rule, yet given the instability of the previous decades, and the novelty of the Yorkist monarchy, a new chapter of uncertainty was about to be opened.

PART TWO:

ASCENT

4

USURPATION

•—•

As Edward lay on his deathbed, he had managed to add 'several codicils' to his will. According to Dominic Mancini, he had directed that Richard should become sole protector of his young son Edward V. Richard himself had been in the north at York when he was taken by surprise by the suddenness of his brother's death. On hearing the news, he had summoned the northern members of the nobility to him to 'hold a solemn funeral ceremony' where they pledged their loyalty to 'the king's son; he himself swore first of all', while he sent 'most pleasant letters' to Queen Elizabeth consoling her and promising 'to come and offer submission, fealty and all that was due from him to his lord and king, Edward V'.

As the dead king's body lay in state at Westminster, a sense of unease over the future direction of the realm had already descended. John Gigur, the warden of Tattershall College in Lincolnshire, wrote to his patron, the Bishop of Winchester, on 19 April, beseeching him 'to remember in what jeopardy your College of Tattershall standeth in at this day; for now our Sovereign Lord the King is dead, we know not who shall be lord nor who shall have the rule about us'. As noblemen and prelates gathered in the capital for the king's elaborate funeral ceremony, behind the scenes a debate raged among royal councillors between two sides, that of the king's blood family, his mother Queen Elizabeth and her wider kin the Woodvilles, and noblemen at court who had resented their rapid rise to power and now feared the influence that they might hold over the young king.

Edward had been fully aware of the problems that his queen and her kin had created at court; the constant quarrels between the Woodvilles and other members of the nobility had annoyed him, 'yet in his good health he somewhat less regarded it, because he thought whatsoever business should fall between them, himself should always be able to rule both the parties'. Many at court continued to blame the queen for Clarence's death, while the Woodvilles had failed to shake off their reputation as parvenus; 'they were certainly detested by the nobles', Dominic Mancini wrote, 'because they, who were ignoble and newly made, were advanced beyond those who far excelled them in breeding and wisdom'.

To the evident discomfort of many, including Edward's close friend William, Lord Hastings, the steward of the household Thomas, Lord Stanley, and more traditional members of the aristocracy such as Henry Stafford, Duke of Buckingham, the Woodvilles had slowly been tightening their grip upon some of the key offices of state: by the beginning of 1483, the queen's brother, Anthony, Earl Rivers was the master of the Prince of Wales's household, his brother Sir Edward Woodville was shortly to take command of the navy while another brother Lionel was Bishop of Salisbury. The Marquess of Dorset was deputy-governor of the Tower of London.

The Woodvilles seemed to hold every card. The young king remained in the possession of Earl Rivers at Ludlow, while Dorset had seized all of the king's treasure and munitions in the Tower, which he was now guarding. At the first meeting of the council, they sought to press home their advantage. Their military strength was increased with the council's decision to give command to Sir Edward Woodville of 2,000 men at a cost of £3,670 to set sail with the royal fleet at the end of April, ostensibly to tackle ongoing piracy in the Channel. The date of the coronation was also hastily arranged; despite calls from some 'who said that everything ought not thus to be hurried through' and that the ceremony should wait for Richard's return from the north, the date was quickly fixed for 4 May. 'We are so important,' Thomas Grey, the Marquess of Dorset, is reported to have replied, 'that even without the king's uncle we can make and enforce these decisions.'

The Woodvilles made it clear that it would be unacceptable for Richard to become sole protector, fearing that if he did so, they 'would suffer death or at least be ejected from their high estate'. When it came to a vote, their superior numbers meant that instead, it was resolved that 'the government should be carried on by many persons among whom the duke . . . should be accounted the chief'. In a tense showdown, other members of the council were not going to allow the Woodvilles to get their own way entirely; 'the more foresighted members' argued that the family 'should be absolutely forbidden to have control' of the king until he reached his majority. An argument also broke out concerning the number of horsemen that should accompany the king into London, with Hastings protesting that he would rather flee to Calais, where he was captain of the garrison there, than await the king's arrival with a large army. Hastings' determination to limit the new king's retinue grew out of fear: 'He was afraid that if supreme power fell into the hands of the queen's relatives they would then sharply avenge the alleged injuries done by that lord. Much ill-will, indeed, had long existed between Lord Hastings and them.'

Eventually Queen Elizabeth, 'desirous of extinguishing every spark of murmuring and unrest', agreed to his demands, writing to her son's household in Ludlow that his numbers that accompanied him to the capital should be limited to 2,000 men. It was to prove a significant concession, the full consequences of which Elizabeth and the Wood-villes had underestimated. They had also underestimated Hastings, who had no intention of not allowing the dead king's wishes to be observed. Hastings was a devout Yorkist, whose father had been a retainer to Richard, Duke of York. Hastings' star rose with Edward's accession to the throne; he followed him into exile, and was rewarded for his loy-alty with the lieutenancy of Calais, replacing Rivers who had angered Edward by planning to go on crusade in Portugal. During the 1470s, as his wealth and influence increased, including his appointment as Lord Chamberlain, Hastings emerged as Edward's chief adviser and confidant. He intended to remain loyal to his former master's wishes to the last.

Hastings also understood that unless Richard was granted the pro-tectorship, his own future at court was under threat. Queen Elizabeth had never forgiven Hastings for being 'the accomplice and partner' of the king's 'privy pleasures', especially since he had quickly taken to living with the dead king's mistress Elizabeth Shore immediately after Edward's death. Hastings had apparently also continued to maintain 'a deadly feud' with the queen's son, Thomas, Marquess of Dorset, resulting from a quarrel over mistresses that they both 'attempted to entice from one another'; two days before his death, Edward had attempted to reconcile the two men, though 'latent jealousy' still remained.

For these reasons Hastings remained convinced that as the king's brother, Richard was the best person to act as the young king's guardian. The duke was also Hastings' 'long standing' friend 'in whom he had the greatest trust', from whom he probably hoped he might receive advancement if Richard was granted the protectorship. He now sought to do everything in his power to ensure that this happened.

After the council meeting had ended, Hastings sent messengers to Richard, informing him of the outcome of the council meeting and its decision to prevent Richard from taking up his position as Protector. He urged Richard to leave the north immediately and to 'hasten to the capital with a strong force'; at the moment he felt 'alone in the capital' and believed his life was 'not without great danger, for he could scarcely escape the snares of his enemies'.

Hastings was confident, however, that if Richard brought a 'strong force' with him, he would easily be able to match the two thousand troops that Rivers had been limited to bringing to London for the coronation. He also broached a more radical course of action, urging Richard to intercept Edward and his household before they had the chance to enter the capital. Richard would need to take the young king 'under his protection and authority' before he entered London, seizing his household men around him 'before they were alive to the danger'.

Receiving Hastings' message, Richard understood that he needed to act fast. He began to mobilise his forces to march south, but to avoid this being seen as an overtly hostile act, he sent letters to both Queen Elizabeth and the council seeking to reassure them of his loyalty to Edward V. In his second letter, however, Richard insisted that he was best placed to act as his nephew's protector. Making the contents of this letter public, it was reported that

he had been loyal to his brother Edward, at home and abroad, in peace and in war, and would be, if only permitted, equally loyal to his brother's son, and to all his brother's issue, if perchance, which God forbid, the youth should die. He would expose his life to every danger which the children might endure in their father's realm. He asked the councillors to take his deserts into consideration, when disposing of the government, to which he was titled by law, and his brother's ordinance. Further, he asked them to reach that decision which his services to his brother and to the State alike demanded: and he reminded them that nothing contrary to law and his brother's desire could be decreed without harm.

The letter apparently had 'a great effect' on the public, who 'now began to support him openly and aloud, so that it was commonly said by all that the duke deserved the government'. A popular general, whom Parliament had formally congratulated several months earlier for his victories over the Scots, Richard had seemingly won the people over to his side. Marching to London, he was determined to claim guardianship of his nephew and seize control of the office he believed was rightfully his own.

News of Edward IV's death had been slow to reach Ludlow, where the new king had been residing, devoting himself to riding, hunting and 'other youthful exercises', with a messenger only reaching the prince to inform him of his father's death and his accession five days later on 14 April.

As Prince of Wales, Edward had been guarded at Ludlow by his uncle Anthony Woodville, Earl Rivers. Rivers had been chosen as the Prince's mentor on account of his learned background; fluent in several languages, he was one of the most cultured figures at the Yorkist court. Rivers had also built up a reputation as an excellent jouster who had fought at Barnet and Tewkesbury. An influential patron of literature, he was considered 'a kind, serious and just man'.

As soon as Rivers received news that Edward had acceded as king, he prepared to depart from Ludlow for the capital 'with all convenient haste', yet a delay of almost ten days to collect an adequate number of forces meant that Richard was able to dictate proceedings. Sending letters to the young king and Rivers, enquiring 'on what day and by what route he intended to enter the capital', he asked if 'they could alter their course and join him, that in their company his entry to the city might be more magnificent'.

Rivers had little reason to decline Richard's request; he certainly had no reason to suspect the duke, whom only several weeks before he had accepted as an arbitrator in a dispute he was having with his Norfolk neighbours. On 24 April the young king and Rivers set off from Ludlow with no more than the 2,000 soldiers that the council had agreed should accompany him.

Richard had departed from York on 23 April with a retinue of 600 'gentlemen of the north'. Encouraged by Hastings' messages, the duke had left the north knowing that he was not alone in his determination to face down the Woodvilles. In the weeks since Edward's death, he had sought support from members of the nobility who might be considered hostile or threatened by their takeover. In doing so, the duke had 'allied himself' with Henry Stafford, the second Duke of Buckingham, 'uniting their resources'. Buckingham had never forgotten how he had been forced to marry one of the queen's sisters as an eleven-year-old boy; embittered that he had gained nothing from the marriage which he had 'scorned' on account of its 'humble origin', he hoped to take his own revenge on 'the queen's kin'.

By 29 April both Richard and Buckingham had reached Northampton, where they received news that Rivers and Prince Edward were fourteen miles away at Stony Stratford. On the evening of 29 April, leaving the new king and his household at Stony Stratford, it was arranged for Rivers and Sir Richard Grey to ride to Northampton, where they were greeted by Richard 'with a particularly cheerful and merry face, and sitting at the duke's table for dinner, they passed the whole time in very pleasant conversation'. After dinner, they were joined by the Duke of Buckingham, and they continued their conversation late into the night.

The following morning, they set out to rejoin the young king. Just outside the town, Richard and Buckingham struck. Rivers and Grey were arrested and sent under close guard ominously to Pontefract Castle, in the heart of Richard's northern estates. Both dukes now hurried to intercept the king, who had remained at Stony Stratford and was unaware of Rivers' arrest. When Richard arrived he ordered the arrest of his servants and his chamberlain, the aged Thomas Vaughan. Orders were sent out for the rest of the household to depart 'at once, and that they should not come near any places where the king might go, upon pain of death'.

Richard approached the young king with a 'mournful countenance', explaining to him why he had been forced to arrest Rivers and Grey and dismiss his household, claiming these 'puny men' had been responsible in part for his father's death, encouraging the debauchery that had ruined his health. Richard further claimed that he had discovered plans to ambush him on the road to the capital, and that it was 'common knowledge that they had attempted to deprive him of the office of regent conferred on him by his brother'. For the sake of the young king's security, Rivers and the entire household needed to be 'utterly removed' since they were prepared, Richard believed, to 'dare anything'.

Edward, who in spite of his young age was already displaying signs of 'talent and remarkable learning', was not convinced. Refusing to believe his uncle, he defended Rivers and his servants, telling Richard that they had been appointed by his father, 'and relying on his father's prudence, he believed that good and faithful ones had been given him'. He had seen 'nothing evil' in them himself, and wished to keep them. Edward's independence of mind must have been disturbing for Richard. It was clear that while the king might be too young to govern by himself, he was certainly no child, with the force of character to express his own opinions. Bishop John Russell believed that the king possessed a 'gentle wit and ripe understanding, far passing the nature of his youth'. To hear him defending his Woodville relations, Richard must have recognised that he could hardly rely upon the king's support; though his uncle, Richard must have been a remote and unknown figure to Edward, in contrast to his mother's family, with whom the king had grown up and whose influence was evidently already deep set. The king continued to argue with his uncle, declaring that he had 'complete confidence in the peers of the realm and the queen' to make arrangements for his minority, yet he eventually agreed to submit himself to his uncle's authority, realising that he was powerless to refuse Richard's demands.

When rumour of what had taken place at Stony Stratford reached London, Queen Elizabeth fled in the night with her children into sanctuary at Westminster. By the morning, confusion reigned as the capital began to take sides. 'You might have seen the partisans of one side and of the other, some sincerely, others dissimulating because of the confusing events, taking this side or that'. A rumour began to spread that Richard had brought his nephew 'not under his care, but into his power, so as to gain for himself the crown'.

In this atmosphere of fear and uncertainty, Richard knew that his entrance into the capital would need to be carefully stage-managed. To counter the rumours that he intended to claim the crown as his own, Richard made full use of letters, sent to the council and the city authorities, to repeat what he had told Edward, that 'he had rescued him and the realm from perdition, since the young man would have fallen into the hands of those who, since they had not spared either the honour or life of the father, could not be expected to have more regard for the youthfulness of the son'. In contrast, 'no one save only him had such solicitude for the welfare of King Edward and the preservation of the state'.

The self-appointed saviour of the nation, when Richard entered London with Edward on 4 May 'in regal style', with a force of 500 men, each solemnly dressed in black, he brought with him cartloads of weapons, stamped with the Woodville arms, that were supposedly to have been used in an armed takeover that the duke now claimed he had thwarted. Playing the role of the loyal uncle of the king, determined to do what was in his nephew's best interest, Richard ordered that every nobleman in the capital together with the mayor and aldermen of the city of London 'take the oath of fealty' to the king; it was taken that 'this promised best for future prosperity' and was 'performed with pride and joy by all'.

Richard's entrance into London had seen him effectively acclaimed as the king's official Protector. Richard himself was confident that he could act as the king's regent 'on account of his popularity', while it was reported that members of the nobility 'even said openly that it was more just and profitable that the youthful sovereign should be with his paternal uncle'.

At the next meeting of the council on 10 May, Richard was appointed Lord Protector, with the appointment scheduled to last until at least the king's coronation, which was now set for 22 June. Everyone 'now hoped for and awaited peace and prosperity in the kingdom'. Hastings, having himself helped to engineer the transfer of power, was 'bursting with joy over this new world', grateful that it had taken place 'without any killing and with only so much bloodshed in the affair as might have come from a cut finger'.

In spite of his new authority, 'commanding and forbidding in everything like another king', it soon became clear to Richard that power was not quite what it seemed. He would soon feel bridled by the council; as the Crowland Chronicler remarked, he might only govern 'with the consent and the good will of all the lords'. When Richard attempted to have Rivers and Grey condemned as guilty of treason for planning to ambush him and conspiring his death, he was blocked, with the council refusing to do so, casting doubt on the evidence that any ambushes had been planned and arguing that even if they had been planned, since Richard was not Protector then, no treason had been committed.

The decision must have prompted Richard to reassess the vulnerability of his own position. He had been granted the protectorship for a period of six weeks only, until the coronation, when the decision would be reviewed. By that time, the tables might have once again turned in favour of the Woodvilles. With Rivers and Grey now potentially soon to be freed, it would not be long before they would seek revenge for their treatment. He had wrested control of the king from the Woodvilles, preventing their immediate dominance in the vacuum of power following Edward IV's death, but they remained far from crushed, and their presence in London was acutely felt. Before fleeing into sanctuary, after hearing news of Richard's capture of the king, they had attempted to assemble an army; this had ultimately been in vain, since the noblemen they approached 'were not only irresolute, but altogether hostile to themselves', but the city remained divided along factional lines, with men loyal to the Woodville party flocking to the queen's side at Westminster. Queen Elizabeth's flight into sanctuary had taken the king's younger brother Richard, Duke of York, out of Richard's grasp, and left a potential alternative power base within the capital. 'A great cause of anxiety which was growing,' the Crowland Chronicler wrote, 'was the detention in prison of the king's relatives and servants and the fact that the Protector did not show sufficient consideration for the dignity and peace of mind of the queen.' Sir Edward Woodville also remained at large, having escaped from the capital the day before Richard's arrival, setting sail with the royal fleet.

Richard had immediately set about strengthening his own position and dismantling the Woodvilles', replacing Archbishop Rotherham, a friend of the queen's, with John Russell, Bishop of Lincoln, as chancellor. He also ordered the Woodville lands to be seized, even though there were no legal grounds for the forfeiture. It was the first sign that Richard was prepared to flout the law for his own advantage.

Learning that Sir Edward Woodville's fleet still lay at anchor in the Downs, Richard sent troops to defend Sandwich and Dover, as well as giving the vital control of the castles of Porchester in Hampshire and Carisbrooke on the Isle of Wight, previously held by the Woodvilles, to his own supporters. He offered a free pardon to all men that would desert the fleet, though Woodville had countered any prospect of desertions by placing armed guards on each ship. Two Genoese carracks were placed in a particularly awkward position; they had no intention of becoming involved in internecine civil war, but only to remain on good terms with whomever happened to be in power. Plying their guards with drink, having overcome them, they managed to escape, setting sail under a blast of trumpets for London. In the confusion, the rest of the fleet scattered. Still Woodville managed to escape with two ships; more significantly he had managed to take with him £10,250 in English gold coin that he had seized from a carrack docking in Southampton water, using his position as 'uncle unto our said sovereign lord and great captain of his navy' to persuade the unsuspecting ship owner to hand over the money on the condition that it had been forfeit to the crown with a promise that an equivalent value in English merchandise would be offered in compensation. Sailing across the Channel, Woodville's chosen destination was Brittany, where he not only intended to find solace at Duke Francis II's court; he hoped to form a remarkable reconciliation with Henry Tudor.

Sir Edward Woodville's escape was not the only problem Richard had to countenance; discovering 'from his spies' that Thomas, Marquess of Dorset had escaped from sanctuary at Westminster, believing that he was 'hiding in the adjacent neighbourhood' the duke ordered his men to hunt him out with dogs, searching the crop fields and woods around the capital, though despite this 'very close encirclement' Dorset was nowhere to be found.

Meanwhile Richard continued to shore up his own support by rewarding those who had colluded with him in seizing the protectorate. John, Lord Howard, for instance, was appointed chief steward of the Duchy of Lancaster south of the Trent; the day after, on 15 May, he presented Richard with a gold cup weighing 65 ounces. Many rewards went to men who had been loyal supporters of Edward IV himself, a recognition of Richard's desire to retain a continuity between his regime and the old, hoping that he might be able to keep a stable balance of power. Of seventy grants that he made in the following month, only five of the sixty-four recipients had any definite links with the duke himself before his protectorate; in contrast, fifteen grants went to men who had been in Edward IV's household, while many existing positions were probably retained by the former king's men.

Yet it proved impossible to recognise the vital support that Buckingham had given the duke, without granting him an extraordinary share of royal patronage. On 10 May, as a sign of Richard's dependence upon the duke, Buckingham was appointed chief justice of both North and South Wales, in addition to being made constable and steward of all fifty-three castles and lordships in Wales and the Marches and being given supervision of the king's subjects in Shropshire, Hereford, Dorset, Somerset and Wiltshire, with the power to raise both armies and revenue in these areas.

In contrast, Hastings' only reward came in the office of master of the Mint. Perhaps aggrieved by his paltry share of patronage, his 'extreme joy' at Richard's appointment as Protector had within 'a very few days' turned 'into sadness'. If Hastings' doubts about Richard's true intentions had begun to grow, he seems finally to have spoken out on 9 June, when the council met to discuss the details of the coronation. It seems that during the meeting Richard broached the issue of the king's younger brother, Richard, Duke of York, remaining in sanctuary at Westminster. As the date of the coronation neared, Richard argued that York should attend the ceremony as next in line to the throne. It would be 'improper' for the king's brother not to be there, but this would mean his removal from his mother Queen Elizabeth in sanctuary. Hastings seems to have offered resistance to either forcing the duke to be removed from Westminster, or breaking the rights of sanctuary; perhaps he felt by now that Richard's motives were highly suspect. Though the details of the council discussions remain obscure, they were evidently protracted, with the meeting lasting for four hours.

It seems that the council meeting was to prove the final straw for Richard. Not only did he feel his power was being been tempered, but it seemed that, with just two weeks before the coronation, there was a real chance that the Woodvilles might be able to re-establish their authority after his temporary protectorship had ended. It was hard to forget that, aged twelve, Edward was himself only three years away from attaining his majority; already he had shown his independence of mind, daring to disagree with Richard to his face. Once he had acceded to the throne, free to make his own decisions, would he forgive his uncle for arresting Rivers and his own household? If Richard were to secure his own future, he would need to act fast; it was obvious that as matters stood, that future would soon be in doubt.

He decided to strike first. The day after the council meeting, Richard wrote to the mayor and city of York, urging them to send as many men 'as ye can make defensibly arrayed' in order to

aid and assist us against the queen, her blood, adherents and affinity, which have intended and daily doth intend to murder and utterly destroy us and our cousin, the Duke of Buckingham, and the old royal blood of this realm, and as it is now openly known, by their subtle and damnable ways forecasted the same, and also the final destruction and disinheritance of you and all other the inheritors of prosperity and honour, as well of the north parts as other countries that belong to us.

Letters were also sent to the Earl of Northumberland, who began to raise men in the East Riding the day after the letter had reached York. For what purpose Richard intended this large army to march on London was yet to become apparent. Only the duke himself knew what his next moves were to be; within days, they would leave a kingdom stunned.

It was a sunny morning on 13 June when the council met at the Tower of London at nine o'clock. The day before, Richard had chosen to divide the council that morning, so that 'part met at Westminster, part in the

Tower of London where the king was'; later, his reasons for doing so would become brutally apparent. Arriving at the council chamber, the duke seemed in a good mood. He even asked John Morton, the Bishop of Ely, to fetch him a 'mess' of strawberries from the walled garden of the bishop's house across the city. Richard's purpose for getting Morton out of the way would soon become clear.

Once the meeting began, Richard excused himself and left the room. When he returned, his mood had changed. Appearing with 'a sour and angry countenance', he sat down at the council table. Suddenly he banged his fists on the table. Someone outside hearing the noise took it as a signal, and began to shout 'Treason!' Before the council members could understand what was happening, the room was filled with men 'in harness, as many as the chamber might hold'. Hastings, Thomas Rotherham, Archbishop of York, and Oliver King, the king's secretary, were seized in the struggle, which saw Thomas, Lord Stanley struck across the face.

Before anyone could challenge the duke or his armed men, Hastings was led out into the courtyard, where after 'scarce leisure' to make a confession, he was summarily executed, beheaded with a sword 'on the stock of a tree'. He had been killed, Mancini mused, 'not by those enemies he had always feared, but by a friend whom he had never doubted'. The Archbishop of York and the Bishop of Ely were spared execution 'out of respect for their order', but instead were led from the capital to be imprisoned in Wales.

As soon as Hasting's dead body was carted away to be buried, Richard explained to the council he had uncovered yet another conspiracy against him. Involving Queen Elizabeth, witchcraft and Edward's former mistress Elizabeth Shore, its highly improbable combination of authors meant that few believed it, with many suspecting that 'the plot had been feigned by the duke so as to escape the odium of such a crime'.

'All men generally lamented the death of that man', one observer reported; nevertheless, no one dared to speak out. 'All praised the Duke of Gloucester for his dutifulness towards his nephews and for his intention to punish their enemies. Some, however, who understood his ambition and deceit, always suspected whither his enterprises might lead'. Hasting's execution had cowed men into silence, 'expecting something similar' if they dared to demonstrate any resistance, so that Richard and Buckingham 'thereafter did whatever they wanted'.

The method of Richard's sudden attack on Hastings, followed by accusations of a conspiracy, was almost identical to his treatment of Rivers and Grey several weeks before. This time, however, Richard had learnt the lesson of dispatching his rival as soon as he could. Yet even if the implausible details of any conspiracy related by Richard can be discounted, it was clear that the duke himself sincerely believed that some kind of conflict would soon arise, compromising his ability to rule as Protector. The timing of Richard's decision to arrest and execute Hastings itself must be questioned: if the attack had been pre-planned, why did Richard not wait until his northern troops had arrived in the capital, leaving him in a much stronger position, or until he had the Duke of York in his possession? It seems that, far from being carefully orchestrated, Richard had been forced into acting before it was too late. Perhaps Hastings had discovered Richard's plans to assemble a force to march on London; or that at the lengthy council meeting on 9 June, he had expressed enough resistance to Richard's plans to have the Duke of York removed from sanctuary that Richard realised that Hastings' loyalties lay not with him but with the princes. Hastings had agreed to Richard's seizure of the protectorship since he considered it in their best interests to be brought up with their uncle instead of his enemies the Woodvilles; he did not, it seems, consider that interest went as far as to forcibly remove one of the children from the holy protections offered by sanctuary. For his resistance, Hastings had to go. 'And thus was this nobleman murdered,' the author of the Great Chronicle remarked, 'for his troth and fidelity which he bare his master', Edward V.

Hastings had been at the head of a court party that had defended the young king's interest above all other; he had been, Polydore Vergil remarked, the person in whom 'the nobles who favoured King Edward's children had reposed their whole hope and confidence'. Now, 'without justice or judgement, the three strongest supports of the new king were removed', the Crowland Chronicler observed. In destroying Hastings, Richard had evidently not acted alone, but in concert with several noblemen. Mancini relates that it was Buckingham who had alerted Richard to secret meetings between Hastings, Morton and Thomas Rotherham in each other's houses. The armed men who seized Hastings had been placed in charge of John, Lord Howard's son, Thomas Howard. With their continued support, Richard was now in complete control. There was to be no turning back.

With the king already in his possession in the Tower, two days later Richard now moved to seize his younger brother, Richard, Duke of York from sanctuary at Westminster. Already he had also sought to secure the possession of Clarence's young son, Edward, Earl of Warwick, fearing that 'this child, who was also of royal blood, would still embarrass him'.

On the morning of 16 June, the sanctuary was surrounded by troops, described as 'a great crowd, with swords and clubs'. As the head of a delegation to Queen Elizabeth, Richard sent the eighty-year-old Thomas Bourgchier, the Archbishop of Canterbury, accompanied 'with many others', who remonstrated with the queen to give up her younger son into his care, promising that York would be returned to her after the coronation. She had heard the arguments over and over for the past few weeks, but the elderly prelate's pleading, 'in order to prevent a violation of the sanctuary', suggested that she realised that if she did not give up her son voluntarily, he would be taken from her by force. In the end, seeing herself 'besieged' and the 'preparation for violence', she gave up her son.

With both the princes now in his hands, Richard did not hesitate to show his real intentions, 'not in private but openly'. Later the same day, Richard issued writs cancelling the Parliament that had been summoned for 25 June; quietly, as the day neared to the appointed coronation date, Richard postponed the coronation to 9 November, as business in the exchequer and the chancery effectively ceased. Simon Stallworth wrote to Sir William Stonor on 21 June, barely containing his nervousness at the situation, 'for with us is much trouble and every man doubts everyone else'. With a 'great plenty of harnessed men' surrounding Westminster Abbey, reports continued to spread that 20,000 armed men that had mustered at Pontefract on 18 June were now heading to the capital from the north, 'in frightening and unheard of numbers'. As the day neared to the originally appointed coronation date of 22 June, instead there was 'privy talking in London that the Lord Protector should be king'.

Two days before the original coronation date, orders were issued by the mayor that every man was to observe a night-time curfew, with a watch carefully appointed. When the date of the coronation arrived, the only spectacle was provided by Dr Ralph Shaa, who preached a sermon from St Paul's cross outside the cathedral, declaring Edward V and his brother illegitimate on the grounds that Edward IV had not been validly married to Elizabeth Woodville due to a pre-contract he had apparently previously entered into with a lady at court, Elizabeth Butler. Shaa even went so far as to cast doubt upon the former king's own legitimacy, suggesting that he had been born out of an affair, though this charge was swiftly dropped. The arguments themselves were irrelevant. The purpose of the sermon was to give backing to what had already been decided: that Richard should instead claim the throne as his own. When Buckingham repeated the same charges in an eloquent speech at the Guildhall on 25 June to the city authorities, for a 'good half hour', only a small number of men could bring themselves to cry out 'yea, yea' and even then they had done so 'more for fear than love'. But with armed men stationed outside the building, the Londoners felt that they had little choice but to support Richard's claim.

As Richard was being petitioned to take the throne, several hundred miles away at Pontefract Castle an altogether different spectacle was taking place. Acting as judge, the Earl of Northumberland presided over the trial of Earl Rivers, Thomas Grey and Thomas Vaughan, reaching a verdict that they were all guilty of treason. Rivers had suspected that his own end was near, and had made his will two days earlier. All three were executed the same day, their bodies thrown into a common grave.

On 26 June, together with the mayor, Buckingham led a delegation of noblemen and aldermen to Richard's mother's residence at Baynard's Castle where they requested that Richard accept the crown. After a symbolic hesitation, Richard agreed, and 'attended by well near all the lords spiritual and temporal of this realm' rode to Westminster Hall where, in a ceremony conspicuously modelled on his brother's accession back in 1461, he 'thrust himself into the marble chair' of the king's throne and was declared king. With his coronation fixed for 6 July, Richard wrote to the Calais garrison informing them of the decision, explaining simply that although Edward V had been recognised as the rightful heir, this had only taken place since men were 'then ignorant of the very sure and true title which our sovereign lord that now is, King Richard III, hath and had the same time to the crown of England'.

The change in Richard's appearance could hardly have been starker. Previously dressed for months in mourning black, he now clothed himself in the royal purple, riding through the capital surrounded by a thousand attendants. Richard III took instantly to the trappings of majesty, acting every part a king. When, six days before his planned coronation his 'northern men', numbering between five and six thousand men, had finally arrived in the capital, camping on Finsbury Fields, Richard 'himself went out to meet the soldiers before they entered the city; and, when they were drawn up in a circle on a very great field, he passed them with bared head around their ranks and thanked them'. Stationed at intervals on every street in London, they were to provide a menacing reminder of Richard's formidable strength and supreme authority.

The coronation on 6 July was no less an impressive occasion, with Richard dressed in a gold and blue doublet, covered by a purple gown trimmed with ermine. His new queen, Anne, was carried in a litter with five ladies in waiting. Buckingham's pre-eminence as kingmaker was underlined by his role as master of ceremonies at the coronation, having the 'chief rule and devising' of the ceremony, carrying the white wand of high steward. John, Lord Howard had stood at Richard's right hand when he had assumed the throne on 26 June. Two days later the price of his collusion was paid in the form of political reward when he was created Duke of Norfolk, together with his son who became Earl of Surrey, while William, Viscount Berkeley was raised to the Earldom of Nottingham.

The creations were the first in a series of appointments designed to bolster the new king's authority. No longer dependent upon the pretence of maintaining the status quo of his dead brother's household, Richard began to refashion the court and council to his own making. His close friend Francis, Viscount Lovell was appointed chief butler and Lord Chamberlain, William Catesby, who may have played a part in the downfall of his former master Hastings, became Chancellor of the Exchequer, while Sir Robert Brackenbury became Master of the King's Moneys and constable of the council. The council was packed with Richard's own supporters, including Lovell, Brackenbury, Lord

Scrope of Bolton, Sir Richard Ratcliffe, Scrope's brother-in-law, Sir James Tyrell and Sir Richard Fitzhugh.

Despite being 'wounded, seized and imprisoned' during Hastings' arrest, Thomas Stanley had managed to regain the king's favour, being appointed steward of the household, attending the coronation where his wife Margaret Beaufort bore the queen's train in the procession to Westminster Abbey. According to Polydore Vergil, Richard had decided it was best to come to terms with Stanley, fearing that his son George, Lord Strange 'soon should have stirred up the people to arms somewhere against him'. It seems that Richard was also intending to try and heal old wounds, or at least to neutralise the threat that he believed Henry Tudor, still in exile in Brittany, posed.

Evidence of this attempt at reconciliation came the day before the coronation, on 5 July, when Margaret and Stanley had been invited to court to an audience with Richard and his chief justice William Hussey at Westminster, where Richard gave his support to Margaret's claim to a ransom debt due to her that she was attempting to obtain from the Orleans family in the courts in Paris. Margaret had arrived at court with the intention of not merely resolving her financial affairs; according to the Tudor chronicler Edward Hall, she had taken the opportunity of approaching the Duke of Buckingham shortly after Richard's accession, asking him to intercede with Richard on her behalf for Henry's return to the English court. In order to aid the chances that the king might accept Henry's return and subordination to the Yorkist regime, she proposed that Henry might take one of the Woodville daughters in marriage, the arrangement of which she would leave to the king, 'without any thing to be taken or demanded for the same espousals but only the king's favour'. The prospect of Henry's marriage with Edward IV's daughter Elizabeth of York seems to have been keenly discussed as a means by which to bring the exiled Tudor home. Thomas Stanley himself later recalled how he had heard his wife and 'divers and other noble and illustrious persons' discussing a possible marriage for Henry Tudor with Elizabeth of York, while others remembered that it had been discussed by the Duchess of Buckingham, the Bishop of Worcester and the Bishop of Ely.

Since his narrow escape from capture seven years before, Henry had been taken by Duke Francis to the fortified walled town of Vannes, to be guarded near to his own ducal palace of the Château de l'Hermine in order to prevent his possible capture. By October 1476 Henry had been placed under the guard of Vincent de la Landelle. Landelle had been born into a small gentry family from the Oust valley forty kilometres east of Largoet; he had gone on to serve as a soldier in the duke's retinue since at least 1454, and was now in receipt of a pension from the duke of £60.

Henry's uncle Jasper had also been returned to Vannes, to be guarded by Bertrand du Parc. Du Parc had begun his career as a ducal lance in the early 1460s, even being sent in 1462 to carry money to Margaret of Anjou, then residing at Rouen. His efficiency ensured that he quickly rose up the ranks, being given charge of 100 lances in 1468 and being granted a series of important captaincies; later, in 1477, Bertrand received a series of commissions to inspect and repair various fortifications across Brittany, while in 1478, he was appointed captain of the frontier castle of Fougères, the most powerful and highly fortified military site in the region. Further promotion came when Bertrand became master of the duke's artillery in 1481, receiving a pension of £400 in addition to providing him with a company of 50 lances and 75 archers. It seems that throughout this time, Jasper Tudor remained with Bertrand, in his keeping between 1475 and 1483, with money still being allocated for the earl's upkeep in Bertrand's guard in 1483.

Meanwhile, separated from his uncle, Henry was placed in the custody of a series of guardians, minor Breton gentry whose conservative tastes and modest lifestyles perhaps had an impact on Henry's own formative mind. After departing from La Landelle's custody, by the early 1480s Henry had become attached to the household of Jean Guillemet, a member of the Guillemet family of La Lande-es-Glemet who had served with the marshal of Brittany since 1454, and was in receipt of an annual pension from Francis of £60. The family seem to have been both prosperous and well-connected at court, with Jean's brother Guillaume having been sent to England previously as an envoy to negotiate at Edward's court. In 1481 Henry was transferred to the custody of Louis de Kermene, a member of Francis's ducal ordonnance who had been in his service as a man-at-arms as early as 1474 and whose estates, like Guillemet, lay in the diocese of St Brieuc. Together with his son Giles, de Kermene was part of the ducal bodyguard, suggesting that the duke had taken the decision to keep the earl close to his own court. The following year, Henry was moved once again to the charge of Jean de Robichen, another member of the ducal ordonnance whose growing importance at court would see him being appointed as keeper of Nantes Castle by 1489.

At the time of Edward IV's death, Henry was probably living among the duke's personal bodyguard in Vannes, residing at the duke's residence of the Château de l'Hermine. It was at Vannes that on 2 February 1483, Henry can be found making an offering of £6 7s 1d at the holy day of the Purification of Our Lady at the cathedral in the town. By now, Francis was increasingly recognising Henry's value, with the budget for his upkeep being increased from £2,000 between 1481 and 1482 to £2,200 in 1483. In comparison, £607 10s was set aside for Jasper, including £40 for the earl's personal expenses.

Upon Edward's death, it seems that Francis no longer felt bound by his promise to the dead king to keep both earls under close guard, allowing both Henry and Jasper the freedom to travel across his dukedom. Two payments among the duke's accounts record that in the summer of 1483, Guillemin du Boys, described as an 'archer', was paid £37 'for a horse which we took from him and gave to the lord of Pembroke'. One Germain Gentilhomme was also paid £27 10s 'for buying two small horses as well as for conducting a stableboy and a palfreyman, sent by us, to serve the lords of Richmond and Pembroke'.

Richard was understandably concerned about this relaxation of these restraints upon a man who, no matter how distant in blood, might just be recognised as retaining a claim to the English crown. He was not going to allow Henry to become a magnet for political dissidents who might seek to flock to Tudor in the hope of dethroning his own fragile monarchy. Already Richard had witnessed Sir Edward Woodville's escape across the Channel with two ships from the royal fleet and an enormous sum of money; now he was determined that 'provision was made that the king's enemies, desirous to disturb all things, might not be able to call home again into England Henry Earl of Richmond'.

On 13 July 1483, eight days after his meeting with Margaret Beaufort and Thomas Stanley, Richard sent his confidential agent, the cleric Thomas Hutton, described as a man of 'pregnant wit', to Duke Francis's court, where he was ordered 'by all force of fair words and money' to secure guarantees from the duke that he would continue to 'detain the earl in perpetual prison at least'.

Richard's immediate priority was to ensure that Sir Edward Woodville would not be able to find shelter at the duke's court. In addition to attempting to resolve the issue of piracy between the two nations, Hutton was instructed to discover 'the mind and disposition of the duke against Sir Edward Woodville and his retinue, practising by all means to him possible to ensearch and know if there be any intended enterprise out of land upon any part of this realm'. Henry's name was not specifically mentioned, but Francis's response, which came around Hutton's return to England on 26 August, when the duke's own envoy was given his instructions for negotiation with Richard, made clear that Francis understood who exactly was Richard's intended target.

Francis knew that he had in his hands an important bargaining tool – he was not prepared to give him up easily. His demands to Richard were little short of blackmail. Despite protesting his friendship in the conventional manner, the duke declared that since Edward IV's death, the French king Louis XI 'has several times sent to the duke to pray and request him to deliver to him the lord of Richmond his cousin'. Adding that Louis had already made 'great offers', Francis assured Richard that he had 'given him no inducement, fearing that the said King Louis would thereby create annoyance and injury to some of the friends and well-willers of the duke. In consequence of which the said King Louis gives great menace to the duke of making war upon him, and the appearances are great'. This was to be a prologue to Francis's demands, and what specifically he wanted from Richard. The new king was about to be given an important lesson in the intransigence of diplomatic negotiations.

Given France's 'great power of men of war, artillery and finances', the duke argued, Brittany would be unable to hold out without England's support. The consequences of this, Francis suggested, would mean that he would be helpless but to give over Henry to the French king: 'Whereby of necessity the duke might be compelled to deliver to the said King Louis the said lord of Richmond, and to do other things which he would be very loath for the injury which he knows the said King Louis would or might inflict upon the king and kingdom of England'.

Of course, Francis indicated, there was an alternative course of action. If Richard was determined to avoid Henry Tudor being sent to France, the duke's loyalty to his new regime could be bought; but it would come at a significant price. Before his death, Edward IV had sent envoys to Brittany in early 1482, in a final attempt to try and win over possession of Henry; taking with them £3,000 in silver bullion, Edward also made the significant promise of sending 4,000 archers at a month's notice from Plymouth to serve in Brittany for three months at his own expense. The promise to send archers remained unfulfilled since Francis had chosen to delay requesting the force, but now the duke sought the same promise to be delivered by Richard, this time with even greater demands placed upon the English forces and the king's finances. 'In maintaining the amities and treaties heretofore made between the said late King Edward and the duke', Richard would need to 'succour the duke against the said King Louis if he commence war against the duke, and send him for part of his succours the number of 4,000 English archers, furnished with good captains and a good chief, and paid for six months at the expense of the said King of England'. This would need to be done within a month of any request being made, and if Francis needed extra support, another two or three thousand archers 'furnished with good captains' were to be sent the following month. 'And so doing the duke will await the fortune of war, such as it shall please God to send him, rather than deliver into the hand of the said King Louis the said lord of Richmond'.

Francis' demands were hopelessly unrealistic and out of any sensible proportion. Military aid to Brittany on this scale had been agreed before, in 1468, 1472 and 1475, yet only against the backdrop of a triple offensive between Brittany, Burgundy and England against France, with a commitment of a full English invasion of France. Six thousand archers alone would stand little chance of taking on the might of France. To Richard, it must have seemed little more than blackmail, yet at least Francis had shown himself ready to do business. To keep Henry Tudor where he wanted him would come at an enormous cost, but it was a cost worth considering. In the event, the death of Louis XI on 30 August, plunging France into its own internal troubles with the accession of the eight-year-old Charles VII, for the moment removed any threat of imminent war between France and Brittany. Henry, however, remained a free man. If Richard had hoped to secure his capture or close imprisonment, his failure to do so would prove a costly mistake.

5

REBELLION

•◆•

It was noted at Richard's coronation that neither the former king Edward nor his younger brother Richard had been present. Instead, both had remained imprisoned in the Tower. The Great Chronicle recorded how they had been spotted 'shooting and playing in the garden of the Tower by sundry times'. Mancini believed it was after Hastings' execution that the young king's attendants had been removed from him. Only his physician John Argentine was allowed to visit Edward, who apparently 'reported that the young king, like a victim prepared for the sacrifice, sought remission of his sins by daily confession and penance, because he believed that death was facing him'. Both Edward and his brother were then moved into the 'inner apartments' of the Tower where they 'began to be seen more rarely behind the bars and windows'. Soon they 'ceased to appear altogether'.

According to the Crowland Chronicler, the princes remained in the Tower 'with a specially appointed guard'. In the south and south-west, he recorded, people began 'to murmur greatly', planning how to 'release them from such captivity'. Secret assemblies were held, though others held conversations openly, 'especially those people who, because of fear, were scattered throughout franchises and sanctuaries'. No one seemed to know what fate had exactly befallen Edward and his brother, though some began to fear the worst. 'After his removal from men's sight', Mancini had seen 'many men burst forth into tears and lamentations' when Edward's name was mentioned; 'already there was a suspicion that he had been done away with'. 'Whether, however, he has been done away with, and by what manner of death, so far I have not at all discovered.'

Meanwhile, shortly after his coronation, Richard felt confident enough to leave the capital to make a progress outside of London, in an attempt not only to increase public recognition of his kingship, but his own popularity. Through each town he passed he made grants that were designed to please. Gloucester had its liberties confirmed with a new city charter, while at Tewkesbury, the scene of the bloody massacre at the monastery after the battle in 1471, Richard promised to repay a large debt owed by his dead brother Clarence. Dr Thomas Langton, Bishop of St David's, accompanied Richard, writing in a letter to the prior of Canterbury how the new king 'contents the people where he goes best that ever did Prince for many a poor man that hath suffered wrong many days have been relieved and helped by him and his commands now in his progress. And in many great cities and towns were great sums of money give to him, which all he hath refused. On my troth, I never liked the conditions of any Prince so well as his. God hath sent him to us for the weal of us all.' There then follows a faint Latin sentence, which reads: 'I do not take exception to the fact that his sensuality [*voluptas*] seems to be increasing.' Langton was later himself a recipient of Richard's continued generosity; several months later, at Canterbury, he was given a purse filled with £33 6s 8d in gold, six capons and a gold bead.

Still the rumours surrounding the princes' fate would not go away. The Great Chronicle reported that 'men feared not openly to say that they were rid out of this world'; nonetheless as to the manner of their deaths, there were 'many opinions, for some said they were murdered between ii feather beds, some said they were drowned in malmsey and some said that they were stykkid with a venomous poison, but how so ever they were put to death, certain it was that before that day they were departed from this world'. As men grew increasingly nervous that the two young children's safety was at risk, it seems that an attempt was made to free both the princes from their confinement in the Tower. Evidence for the episode itself is scant, but on 29 July Richard wrote a cryptic letter to his chancellor, declaring how 'certain persons of such as of late had taken upon them the fact of an enterprise, as we doubt not ye have heard'. What this 'enterprise' exactly involved is possibly related by the Elizabethan antiquary John Stow, who claimed to have read indictments that no longer survive, that 'there were taken for rebels against the king, Robert Russe sergeant of London, William Davy pardoner of Hounslow, John Smith groom of King Edward's stirrup, and Stephen Ireland, wardrobe of the Tower, with many others'. The accused were said to have planned 'to have set fire to divers parts of London, which fire whilst men had been staunching, they would have stolen out of the Tower the Prince Edward and his brother the Duke of York'. Having been tried at Westminster, the men involved were condemned to death, drawn behind horses to Tower Hill and beheaded, with their heads displayed upon spikes at London Bridge. Stow's account is further given credence by a contemporary French chronicler Basin who believed that in total fifty Londoners had been involved in the attempt and the group had hoped for more, though the city had failed to support the rising.

The fact that two royal servants, one based in the Tower, had taken part in the attempt is revealing, especially when John Smith, as groom of the stirrup, had been under the command of John Cheyney, the master of the king's horse, at least until Richard's accession. But the indictment made further revelations, 'that they should have sent writings into the parts of Brittany to the Earls of Richmond and of Pembroke and other lords'. With the failure of the attempt, or if in its process it was discovered that Edward and his brother were already dead, there would now be a new focus to the campaign of dissent.

As August passed, it was becoming clear that resistance to Richard's new regime was increasing. According to one London chronicler, 'many knights and gentlemen' intended 'to have subdued Richard' since it was rumoured 'he also put to death the two children of King Edward, for which cause he lost the hearts of the people. And thereupon many gentlemen intended his destruction.' On 13 August the land of John Welles, described as 'the king's rebel', was granted to John, Lord Scrope of Bolton. In an evident sign of his own nervousness at the growing unease, on 17 August Richard ordered 2,000 Welsh bills to be sent to him in 'all haste'. Eleven days later, a commission was appointed to investigate treasons and felonies committed in London and the Home Counties, to be led by the king's 'dearest kinsman', the Duke of Buckingham.

When it was reported that Elizabeth of York and her sisters, remaining in sanctuary with their mother, had been advised to flee overseas in disguise, 'so that if any human fate, inside the Tower, were to befall the male children, nevertheless through the saving of the persons of the daughters the kingdom might someday return to the rightful heirs', Richard was fast to act. Troops were commanded to surround the perimeter of the abbey, 'men of the greatest strictness' who gave the entire neighbourhood 'the appearance of a castle and a fortress'. John Nesfield was appointed captain, sending orders that all entrances and exits were to be closely guarded, 'so that no one inside could get out and no one from outside could get in'.

One woman considered it a challenge worth overcoming. Weeks before, Margaret Beaufort had sought the king's assistance in returning her son home from exile in Brittany, yet even then the possibility of Henry marrying one of the Woodville daughters was strong in her mind. With the result of these negotiations inconclusive, she now looked elsewhere to fulfil her ambitions. When it seemed that the princes would not be leaving the Tower, Margaret had begun 'to hope well of her son's fortune', especially if Henry might somehow be able to one day marry Elizabeth of York, thereby ensuring that 'the blood of King Henry the Sixth and of King Edward to be intermingled by affinity', and allowing Henry to launch a credible assault upon the throne. Determined not to let 'so great opportunity' pass, Margaret would first need to gain Queen Elizabeth's support for the match, contacting her in sanctuary without raising Richard's suspicions.

It seemed an impossible task, yet Margaret was confident that it could be done without the king suspecting a thing. Contact between the two women was to be established by means of a physician they shared, the Welshman Lewis Caerleon, 'a grave man and of no small experience' with whom Margaret was accustomed 'oftentimes to confer freely with all, and with him familiarly to lament her adversity'. Caerleon had been a leading intellectual at the Lancastrian court, who had offered a horoscope to Henry VI in 1441, and who had written extensively on astronomy and mathematics. By 1482 he had taken to practising medicine in London, where he continued to serve the queen from her sanctuary, a position which had enabled him to slip through the net of armed guards surrounding Westminster.

The Tudor historian Polydore Vergil is the only source for the episode; despite writing from the evident position of hindsight, and thereby able to mould his narrative of events into a seamless plan, Vergil's account, which should therefore be treated with caution, reveals the painstaking efforts that Margaret Beaufort took to foster and secure her son's claim to the throne. Margaret informed Lewis Caerleon of her plan to marry

Elizabeth to Henry, ensuring that Richard 'might easily be dejected'. Requesting that Lewis visit Queen Elizabeth in sanctuary and 'deal secretly with the queen of such affair', for several weeks, Lewis carried messages between Queen Elizabeth and Margaret Beaufort, who remained in London, residing at Thomas Stanley's house in the capital. Lewis erred initially on the side of caution, broaching with the queen the idea of Henry marrying her eldest daughter, as if it was 'devised of his own head'. Elizabeth, by now probably aware that her two sons were dead, agreed; being 'so well pleased' with the idea, she ordered Lewis to return to Margaret and 'promise in her name that she would do her endeavour to procure all her husband King Edward's friends to take part with Henry her son, so that he might be sworn to take in marriage Elizabeth her daughter'.

As soon as Margaret gained news that Elizabeth Woodville was supportive of the plan, she ordered Reginald Bray, her long-standing and trusted servant, whom she had known since he had managed the estates of her late husband Henry Stafford, and who would now become 'the chief dealer in this conspiracy' to 'draw into her party, as secretly as might be' those men who had been members of Edward IV's household, and were still considered loyal to the memories of the dead king and his children. Within a few days, Bray had contacted Sir Giles Daubeney, Richard Guildford and John Cheyney, securing their support through an oath 'of every man particularly'. At the same time, Queen Elizabeth had managed to make her own friends 'partakers of this devise and business' to prepare for rebellion 'with all speed convenient'.

Elizabeth Woodville had remained in contact with her son by her first marriage, Thomas, Marquess of Dorset, and her brother Lionel Woodville, the Bishop of Salisbury, both who had managed to escape into hiding. Both would now be critical to organising a network of plotters around Kent, Wiltshire and Berkshire, and Devonshire. Some of the gentlemen who joined their side had well-established connections with the Woodvilles, including Sir Richard Haute and John Guildford. But many were the former household men and servants of the dead king, likely contacted by Reginald Bray. They included Edward's brother-in-law Sir Thomas St Leger, the master of his horse Sir John Cheyney, the treasurer of his household Sir John Fogge and other chamber knights including George Brown, William Norris, William Stonor, William Berkeley, Giles Daubeney, and Edward's former secretary Peter Courtenay, currently the Bishop of Exeter. Many were able to draw their brothers and sons into the rebellion, including Courtenay's distant kinsman and head of the family Edward Courtenay, who may have hoped that in supporting a successful change in regime, he might be able to win back the confiscated family title of the Earldom of Devon. Courtenay's own participation in the rebellion points to a new dimension not only to the revolt, but to the entire dynamic of the political scene: a diehard Lancastrian, the very fact that Courtenay would decide to join forces with loyal household men of his own Yorkist nemesis is a remarkable indication of the determination and strength of feeling to unseat Richard from the throne.

While the strength of the proposed rebellion gathered, Margaret ordered a young priest, Christopher Urswick, who had entered her household on Caerleon's recommendation and whom she had granted the rectory of Puttenham the previous December, to prepare to travel to Brittany to inform her son Henry about what she had planned for him, 'to signify unto him all that was done with the Queen' and the prospect of his marriage to Elizabeth of York, and no doubt urging him to prepare to launch an invasion to return to England as soon as he possibly could. Before Urswick was able to depart, Margaret received remarkable news from Reginald Bray.

Bray had journeyed to visit John Morton, the Bishop of Ely, who had been placed under the Duke of Buckingham's custody at Brecon Castle following Richard's seizure of Hastings in the Tower. Born in 1420, Morton had impeccable Lancastrian credentials, having served Henry VI faithfully 'and nevertheless left it not nor forsook it in woe'. He had been taken prisoner at Towton, yet still refused to switch his allegiance. Instead he escaped from the Tower to face penniless exile abroad with Margaret of Anjou and her son. He accompanied her on the road to Tewkesbury, and only then, once her son had been killed and Henry discovered dead in the Tower, did he submit himself to the Yorkist cause. He had served Edward IV with similar loyalty, as he later admitted, 'so was I to King Edward faithful chaplain', adding, 'and glad would have been that his child had succeeded him'. Richard's usurpation of the throne had seen Morton's faithfulness to the Yorkist regime sorely tested; now he prepared to return to his Lancastian roots.

Bray brought news not merely of Morton's support for the rebellion, but of his captor's too. Hearing Bray relate what the bishop had told him, Margaret must have regarded the Duke of Buckingham's decision either with disbelief or suspicion, or both. The duke hardly had reason to be dissatisfied with his share of the rewards of power that Richard's usurpation had brought; the beneficiary of an enormous share of crown lands and castles in Wales, making him the effective viceroy of the country, he had been further rewarded on 13 July with lands from the Duchy of Lancaster worth £1,100. In spite of these staggering rewards, not to mention his renowned hostility towards the Woodvilles, Buckingham had chosen to turn against his master. Margaret must have asked herself why; indeed, to this day it is difficult to understand how the duke himself reached the decision he did.

Of course, being an ambitious man, Buckingham could have been considered to have a claim to the throne himself; as a great-grandson of Thomas of Woodstock, the youngest son of Edward III, the duke may have believed that he could take advantage of the rebellion to seize the crown himself. Polydore Vergil recorded that there was a rumour that Buckingham had deliberately persuaded Richard to usurp the throne 'by means of so many mischievous deeds' in order that, 'being hated both of God and man', the public reaction against Richard might allow the duke to sweep to power himself.

The duke's own reasoning was perhaps rather more prosaic. If Richard fell, Buckingham knew that he would fall with him; it would be impossible to countenance his survival in a new regime given the role he had played as Richard's right-hand man in the usurpation. It may have been that Buckingham, understanding the scale of the rebellion and the support it was gathering from both loyal Yorkists and Lancastrians such as Edward Courtenay, may have decided to throw his lot in with the rebels before it was too late. It was also apparent that Henry's claim to the throne was being widely spoken of; the Great Chronicle of London recorded how 'word sprang quickly of a Gentlemen being in the parts of Brittany named Henry and son unto the Earl of Richmond'. If Henry was already emerging as the strongest candidate to challenge Richard's crown, even if Buckingham considered his own claim to be stronger, it would be politic to hide his own private ambitions for now.

The influence of Morton upon Buckingham should also not be discounted. Sir Thomas More, who admired Morton as 'a man of great natural wit, very well learned and honourable in behaviour, lacking no wise ways to win favour', suggests that the bishop induced Buckingham to turn against the king, reminding him of his Lancastrian heritage and that the only way to bring an end to civil discord that had plagued the country for so long was for the strongest Lancastrian claimant, Henry Tudor, to seek the throne, finally placating the Yorkists by marrying Elizabeth of York.

Of course, there is no reason why Buckingham could not have reached a decision through a combination of his own instincts for self-preservation and Morton's entreaties. Either way, recognising the need to make a decision and perhaps giving himself the opportunity to later influence the Tudor claimant, Buckingham decided on Morton's advice to send a message to Henry, 'inviting him to hasten into the Kingdom of England as fast as he could reach the shore to take Elizabeth, the dead king's elder daughter, to wife and with her, at the same time, possession of the kingdom'. According to the attainder of the rebels passed in the Parliament of January 1484, Buckingham had 'on the 24th September by his several writings and messages by him sent, procured and moved Henry calling himself Earl of Richmond and Jasper late Earl of Pembroke being there in Brittany, great enemies of our sovereign lord, to make a great navy and bring with them an army from Brittany'.

As soon as Margaret heard news of Buckingham's defection she recalled Urswick; in his place she sent Hugh Conway, a former servant of Edward IV since 1465, who had married a younger sister of the Lancastrian Earl of Devon who had been executed in 1461. Conway also had an affinity with the Stanley family, coming from north-west Wales with his father taking one of the Stanley's relatives as his second wife; with connections to both Queen Elizabeth and Margaret, given his role at the Yorkist court together with his own family background steeped in Lancastrian heritage, he was perhaps the perfect agent to be sent to Henry to convince him of the prospect of a union between the two houses. Conway took with him 'a good great sum of money' raised by Margaret, and was ordered to urge Henry to make ready his return as soon as he possibly could, advising the earl 'to arrive in Wales, where he should find aid in readiness'. At the same time, to be sure that the message reached Henry, Richard Guildford and Thomas Rameney were also sent to Brittany, embarking from the Kentish coast. All three messengers, 'having speedy passage', arrived at the Breton court at the same time where they found Henry 'at his own liberty' at Francis's court.

As soon as he heard the news, Henry 'rejoicing wondrously' immediately gave thanks to God. He then approached Duke Francis, to whom he explained 'all things' with him, 'showing that he had conceived an assured hope of obtaining the realm of England, and prayed therefore that the same might be brought about both by his good help and assent'. In return, Henry promised, 'which when so ever ability should serve he would not fail to requite'.

In spite of the money that Thomas Hutton's mission had recently gifted him, together with Hutton's own pleadings that Henry should be placed 'again into ward', Francis agreed to aid Henry 'and willingly gave it'. With his neighbour France in a weakened state as a result of the minority of the new king, Charles VII, Francis felt confident enough to lend his support to Tudor's mission. He had also turned against Richard, who had so far refused to acknowledge his demands for 4,000 archers to be sent to his kingdom as a condition for peace; it is likely that Henry would have promised him this, and indeed anything else he demanded, in return for his support. Francis must have regarded any financial aid given now as an investment which, if Henry's invasion proved a success, would be returned in spades. There were perhaps more personal reasons touching Francis's own fragile dynasty within the duchy that had influenced his decision. In particular, he had been resentful of Richard's decision to depose Edward V, who since 1481 had been pledged to marry his daughter and heiress apparent Anne. The removal and disappearance of the young king had in consequence destroyed Francis's own careful plans for his dynasty.

While Henry began to prepare to launch a fleet across the Channel, Francis made a considerable financial commitment to the invasion, totalling some 13,000 crowns, in addition to providing a fleet of seven ships manned with around 515 men. His accounts reveal a detailed breakdown of the payments made to those who were to set sail with

Henry '*a devoir faire le passaige des sires de Richemont et de Penbroc en Englettere*'; he paid 513 livre tournois 6s 9d to Pierre Guillaume, 'master of a pinace of St Malo' weighing forty tons and with forty combatants, 'to make the passage of the Lords of Richmond and Pembroke to England' serving between 1 September to 30 November. Jean Le Barbu, master of the barque belonging to Alain de la Motte, sire de Fontaines and vice-admiral of Brittany, was paid 720 livre tournois for his vessel weighing 60 tons and with 60 combatants, serving from 1 September to 29 November. Derien le Du, captain of the ship *La Margarite* from Brest, weighing 160 tons and with 98 men on board was paid 1,227 livre tournois 12s, while Jean Pero, captain of the ship *La Michelle* from Auray, complete with 75 men and active from 13 September was paid 975 livre tournois. Another resident from Auray was Geoffrey Estrillart, the town's receiver since 1474, who had equipped his ship, the *Marie* of Auray weighing 90 tons with 69 combatants, and sailed from 14 September to 30 November, was paid 852 livre tournois 10s 9d. Louis Berthelot, the captain of the ship *La Tresoriere* from St Malo, sailing with 50 combatants, was also reimbursed for 200 livre tournois. Finally, while Henry was gathering his fleet together on 30 October at the fishing town of Paimpol, on the north coast of Brittany, Duke Francis's men arrived with a loan of 10,000 crowns.

It was a 'prosperous wind' that saw off the fifteen ships that accompanied Henry on his journey to England; mid-voyage, it had turned into a 'cruel gale' as a 'sudden tempest' scattered the fleet, each being separated 'from one way from another' so that some were blown back onto the Normandy coast, others into Brittany. Henry's own ship was 'tossed all the night long with the waves'. As dawn broke and the wind calmed, the chalk cliffs of the south coast and the haven of Poole harbour came into view. Shaken by the storms and their sleepless night, in the gloom of morning light the devastating impact of the storm was revealed: only Henry's and one other vessel had made it through the night. As the ships drew closer to the shore, there was even worse news. The shoreline was 'beset with soldiers' from Richard's army. Henry commanded that no man should land until the rest of the fleet had time to regroup. In the meantime, he sent across several men in a single skiff to the shore to find out the identity of the guards. Navigating the boat out to within hailing distance of the soldiers who, encouraging them to land, called out that they had been 'sent by the Duke of Buckingham to escort Henry to the camp, which he had nearby with his flourishing army, so that they could join forces and pursue the fleeing Richard'.

When the boat returned, passing on the message, Henry instantly suspected a trick. Despite waiting for the remainder of his fleet, after several hours it was clear that nothing was coming into view. Deciding to abandon the venture, the two ships hoisted sail on the back of a strong wind. It was only when, the following day, having been battered by storms that forced him to land, miles away from his intended destination, at St Vaast-la-Hougue on the Cotentin Peninsula in Normandy, that Henry learnt that the rebellion had been ruthlessly crushed and the Duke of Buckingham executed.

Richard had remained on his royal progress, passing through Pontefract and Gainsborough, reaching Lincoln on 11 October. It was here that he received the astounding news 'by means of spies' that not only was a chain of revolts about to break out across the country, but also that his most powerful nobleman the Duke of Buckingham was about to join the rebellion. Stunned by the revelation, Richard wrote to Chancellor Russell, calling for the immediate delivery of the Great Seal. Russell had been unwell, and had informed the king that due to 'such infirmities and diseases' he would be unable to travel on the progress himself. Yet Russell had retained the Great Seal, the official stamp of royal authority, in his possession. If Richard were to raise a large army of men, he would need to send out a summons whose validity could only be confirmed by the wax stamp of the Great Seal appended to any document. He needed the seal urgently. Writing to Russell, demanding that the stamp of the seal be sent to him as soon as possible, a postscript at the bottom of the letter, written in Richard's own hand, could barely disguise the king's disbelief and disgust at his former friend Buckingham's treason:

> We would most gladly ye came yourself if ye may, and if ye may not We pray you not to fail but to accomplish in all diligence our said commandment to send our seal incontinent upon the sight hereof . . . praying you to ascertain Us of your news. Here loved be God is all well and truly determined and for to resist the malice of him that

had best cause to be true, the Duke of Buckingham, the most untrue
creature living whom with God's grace we shall not be long till we
will be in that part and subdue his malice. We assure you there was
never false traitor better provided for . . .

Richard's determination to crush the rebellion was impressive. Even
the Crowland Chronicler admitted that 'he exerted himself in the promotion of all his views in no drowsy manner, but with the greatest
activity and vigilance'. An army was summoned to assemble at Leicester ten days later on 21 October; before it set out from the city, Richard
offered a pardon to all commoners and yeomen who laid down their
arms. For the ringleaders of the rebellion, there would be no such forgiveness. Denouncing them as 'traitors, adulterers and bawds', Richard
issued a remarkable proclamation in which he denounced Dorset as
having dishonoured 'sundry maids, widows and wives' while the rest
of the rebels were guilty of 'the damnable maintenance of vices and
sin as they had in times past, to the great displeasure of God and evil
example of all Christian people'. A price was put on their heads, dead
or alive: for the man who captured or killed Buckingham, he would be
awarded £1,000 or lands worth £100 a year; 1,000 marks or lands worth
100 marks a year was placed on the Marquess of Dorset's head and
the capture of the Bishops of Salisbury and Exeter; for other knights
associated with the rebellion, Richard would award 500 marks or lands
worth £40 a year. The king remained careful however to ensure that
men did not 'rob, spoil or hurt any of the tenants, officers or other persons belonging to the said Duke . . . so that they raise not nor made
commotions or assemblies'.

It seems that the rebellion had been co-ordinated to begin on 18
October, St Luke's Day. The plan was for the Kentishmen and men
from Surrey, Sussex and Essex to have launched an attack on the capital, thereby diverting Richard and his forces from the greater rebellion
that was planned for Wales and the West Country. In Kent, however,
revolts broke out early, so that on 10 October the Duke of Norfolk was
able to report to John Paston that 'the Kentishmen be up in the Weald
and say that they will come to rob the city'. If rebellion in Kent had
erupted prematurely, it would have led to the entire plan unravelling
before other areas where revolt was planned, in Wilshire, Devonshire

and Wales, were adequately prepared. Dispatching a force to Gravesend, Norfolk was able to prevent the Kentishmen from crossing the Thames to join with men from Essex. Meanwhile the rebels in Surrey were cowed into withdrawing to Guildford, where they hoped for the arrival of their main army from the west.

When 18 October arrived, just as planned, outbreaks spread across several key towns across the south. In the south-west, the Marquess of Dorset appeared from hiding to lead a rising in Exeter with Edward IV's brother-in-law Sir Thomas St Leger, Sir Robert Willoughby and the Courtenays; at Guildford, Edward IV's knights, Sir John Guildford and Sir George Browne and Edward Poynings rose up; other rebels met at Newbury, Berkshire, led by the queen's brother Sir Richard Woodville, and two knights from Edward's household, Sir William Noreys and Sir William Berkeley of Beverstone, and at Salisbury, including John Cheyney, Edward IV's Master of the Horse, and his esquire Sir Giles Daubeney. Others who joined the rebellion were former MPs, Justices of the Peace, respectable members of the gentry and stalwarts of their local communities. These were not desperate men, with little possessions and nothing to lose; they were the very bedrock of society whose decision to turn against the new king was a devastating blow to Richard's authority in the southern counties.

On the same day, Buckingham raised the standard of revolt at Brecon, yet already his efforts to raise rebellion were in trouble. It was soon apparent that the army that he had hoped would gather to his standard had failed to materialise, with only his closest household men, Morton and the academic Thomas Nandike, later described as a 'necromancer of Cambridge', providing his paltry army with any support. Even his own retainers that the duke had hoped would join him had, perhaps lured by the prospect of material reward, chosen to remain loyal to the king. The duke's retainer Thomas Vaughan, the son of the late Sir Roger Vaughan who had been executed by Jasper Tudor, probably had his own reasons for refusing to join a rebellion designed to aid the Tudor claimants to the throne. Instead he chose to turn against the duke, and keep a diligent watch over the surrounding countryside. Other tenants of the duke, who by all accounts was a 'sore and hard-dealing man' and far from popular, preferred to simply stay at home.

It is striking that, in the list of men attainted for their support of

Buckingham, not a single Welsh name is mentioned; in contrast, twenty-two gentlemen from South Wales were later to be rewarded with annuities. In a marked contrast with the risings in the south, not one of Edward IV's former household men in the region felt able to join forces with a man they considered had been complicit with Richard's usurpation and the disappearance of the princes; some may have even felt that the duke himself was to blame for their deaths. Others, like John Mortimer who had been forced to give up his constableship of Monmouth, were still dejected from having lost their own offices to Buckingham when the duke had been awarded his vast empire in Wales and the Marches.

But it was the absence of any recognisable noble support that dealt a death blow to Buckingham's chances of raising a successful rebellion. Despite being out of favour with Richard, Gilbert Talbot, the uncle of the young Earl of Shrewsbury who controlled his Shropshire estates during the earl's minority, refused to mobilise. Most notably, it was the failure of the Stanley family to support Buckingham that ended the duke's chances of success. Given Margaret Beaufort's key role in the uprising, the duke would have hoped to win support from her husband Thomas Stanley, his brother Sir William Stanley and Thomas Stanley's son by his first wife, George Lord Strange. Strange was in Lancashire in October 1483, perfectly placed to join the revolt. Buckingham clearly expected to win his support: as news of the rebellion gathered, Strange's secretary wrote how 'messengers cometh daily both from the king's grace and the duke into this country'. The conflicting pleas for support had thrown the surrounding countryside into confusion: 'people in this country be so troubled'. Even Strange's secretary did not know which side his master would choose. 'My Lord Strange goeth forth from Monday next [20 October] with 10,000 men' he wrote, adding 'whither we cannot say'. In the end, Strange chose to sit on his hands. Again, personal ambition dictated the choice of the family's inaction. Buckingham's new influence in Wales and the Marches had provided an unwelcome challenge to the Stanleys' own power base in North Wales and Cheshire; since Buckingham had been granted a remarkable extension of his power in the Welsh Marches, including the constableships of all the royal castles in Wales, his new authority had been resented by the Stanleys, whose followers were reluctant to co-operate with the duke and hand over possession of several castles. They were hardly likely to lend their support to a rebellion whose success would only likely lead to further enrichment of the duke's estates and influence in the region.

News of the premature uprising in Kent had allowed Richard to be forewarned of Buckingham's intended moves. Armed men were sent into Wales, encircling the duke, 'in readiness to pounce on all his domestic possessions as soon as the duke moved a foot away from his house'. Again, the encouragement of reward was dangled in front of the men, with Richard promising them 'the prospect of the duke's wealth for themselves'.

Humphrey Stafford was commanded to destroy the bridges and ferries that crossed into England. His efforts were aided by a deluge that lasted ten days, turning the river Severn and the Avon into raging torrents, sweeping away their banks and making both completely impassable. Unable to cross either river, Buckingham would be prevented from joining up with the rebels in the south. The duke had managed to make his way as far as the Forest of Dean when he realised that, cut off by the forces of nature, he was trapped. Returning to find that his castle at Brecon had been seized and plundered by Thomas Vaughan and his brothers, Buckingham fled to Weobley, leaving his young son and heir Edward with a nurse who dressed the young boy as a girl in order to escape capture by Richard's men. Arriving back at Weobley, where he was joined by John Morton, the duke took the only option that was open to him: changing his clothes, he disguised himself as a labourer and took refuge in a pauper's cottage near Wem in Shropshire. He was soon discovered, possibly through the treachery of his servant Humphrey Bannister, who betrayed the duke 'for fear or money', although the Crowland Chronicler relates how Buckingham's hiding place was given away by the fact that 'the supply of provisions taken there was more abundant than usual'.

Arrested and taken to Shrewsbury, on 31 October the duke was handed over to Sir James Tyrell and taken under armed guard to Salisbury, where Richard had journeyed with his army. The duke pleaded to be granted an audience with the king. This Richard refused; instead, he was executed in the market place in front of the king and his army on All Souls' Day, 2 November, the method of his execution by the axe being the one concession to the duke's royal ancestry. The following day, confident that the rebellion was all but over, Richard marched westwards, determined to crush the rising. News of Buckingham's execution had left the rebels 'so dismayed that they knew not which party to take'. A brave final stand was made at Bodmin on 3 November, when Peter Courtenay, Bishop of Exeter, and Edward Courtenay issued their own proclamation, declaring a call to arms to their 'other king' Henry VII. It was to be a hopeless last stand as the king's forces marched into Exeter, and a general sense of panic erupted. The Courtenays, together with Thomas, Marquess of Dorset and other members of the nobility and gentry who had conspired in the rebellion and 'as many of them as could find ships in readiness' took to the seas, bound for Brittany. John Cheyney and Giles Daubeney made their escape together with another rebel from Exeter, John Halwell, on a boat belonging to Stephen Calmady from Devon.

A ruthless search for those hiding in the shelter of friends or the protection of sanctuary ensued. Richard's own brother-in-law Thomas St Leger, the husband of his sister Anne, was unfortunate enough to be captured. In an attempt to save his life, 'innumerable sums' of money were offered, but Richard was in no mood to forgive such an act of betrayal from a member of his own family. St Leger was hung from the scaffold, drawn and quartered on 12 November.

Those more fortunate arrived across the Channel with tales of miraculous escape. The Cornish knight Sir Richard Edgecombe, who had previously sent money to Henry in exile, had been tracked down by Richard's men and chased through woods near his house at Cothele on the Tamar gorge. He was only saved through his own quick thinking when, with Richard's men closing in on him, 'fast at his heels' and his capture and likely death imminent, he found a large stone and placing his cap on top, rolled it into the water. Making a large splash, the rangers, 'looking down after the noise and seeing his cap swimming, thereon supposed that he had desperately drowned himself, gave over their further hunting'.

Those who joined Edgecombe in flight from Exeter included the Marquess of Dorset and his young son Thomas Grey, the Courtenays, Sir Robert Willoughby, Sir Thomas Arundell, the head of one of the most important families in Cornwall with strong Lancastrian sympathies, and whose sister was married to another fleeing rebel, Sir Giles Daubeney. Elsewhere, in spite of the failure of their risings and being in the less advantageous position of being distant from the coast, other leading rebels were able to slip the king's net, boarding boats destined for across the Channel. They included Bishop Lionel Woodville, Sir Edward Woodville, John Welles, Sir John Cheyney and his two brothers, together with Sir Giles Daubeney and Edmund Hampden who had taken part in the Salisbury rebellion; in Kent, the brothers Thomas and William Brandon, along with Richard Guildford and Edward Poynings had also managed to escape, as had the Newbury rebels Sir William Berkeley and John Harcourt. Bishop John Morton, faring better than the Duke of Buckingham, had fled Weobley into the marshy wastelands of the Fens in his diocese, before crossing unnoticed into Flanders where he was joined by Christopher Urswick. It proved to be nothing less than an exodus of some of the most influential members of court, and most valued members of the southern gentry.

In total, over 500 Englishmen had decided they had no other choice but to weigh anchor and set sail for an uncertain future with an equally unknown figure, whose remote claim to the throne remained their only hope. In desperation, each of their futures had become forged to a mysterious young Welshman whom most had never even met.

Richard returned to London triumphant, even though no battle had been fought. The cost of his expedition, however, had come 'at no less expense than if the armies had fought hand to hand'. Still, even the king understood that, with the successful flight of so many rebels across the sea, joining Henry's standard, his victory was a pyrrhic one. The rebellion had been defeated, yet its authors had lived to return to fight another day. As Richard pondered the consequences of the violence that had occurred that autumn, together with the fundamental breakdown in the natural order, he grew increasingly agitated, 'vexed, wrested and tormented in mind with fear almost perpetually of the earl Henry and his confederates return; wherefore he had a miserable life'. He was determined more than ever 'finally to pull up by the roots all matter of fear and tumult and other by guile or force to bring the same about'.

*

Exhausted from their journey and the battering that they had received as their ships were tossed around in the stormy seas of the Channel that had left them washed ashore miles from their intended destination in Brittany, Henry and his party spent three days on the coast refreshing themselves from the 'toil and travail'. Having sent his ships onward to Brittany, Henry was determined to return with part of his company on foot. In order to seek permission to pass through Normandy, he sent ambassadors to the new French king Charles VIII. A Breton chronicle written by Alain Bouchard suggests that when Charles VIII's guardian, the twenty-two-year-old Anne of Beaujeu discovered Henry had landed in France, she sent him to Charles VIII 'where he was welcomed with honours', and after remaining for a few days at the French court returned to Brittany where he was finally able to inform Francis II and his treasurer Pierre Landais 'of his misfortunes' and return to Vannes.

In fact, nothing could have been further from the truth. For the French government, plagued with its own internal problems since the death of Louis XI several months before, no effort was made to take advantage of Henry's desperate situation. The French regency government might have been expected to intercept him and take possession of a man whom Louis himself had sought to obtain for his own political purposes, but instead it chose only to take pity on the failed pretender, sending François, lord of Lau to meet him. Henry was given an escort by Henri Charbonnel to the monastery of Saint-Sauveur de Redon, at a cost of 1,051 livre tournois 12s 6d, where he was then freed to make his journey back to Francis II's court in Brittany. The decision of the French to let Henry slip through their hands might be seen as a missed opportunity, yet it also reveals how low Henry's stock had fallen on the international stage; after his ignominious return, with his fleet scattered and rebellion at home having been mercilessly crushed, Henry could be considered little more than an impoverished exile, whose defeat had called into question his usefulness as a diplomatic counter, let alone any chance of recovering the throne, his claim to which was at best remote. The dire reality of Henry's fortunes was summed up by the chronicler Commynes who, reflecting on what had taken place, noted that although 'God had suddenly raised up against King Richard an enemy', it was judged that

Henry 'had neither money nor rights to the crown of England'.

When he finally reached Brittany, Henry was informed that Buckingham was dead. Matters could hardly be worse, Henry must have considered, as he 'much lamented' the devastating news. But there was to be a glimmer of hope. For Henry had not arrived in Brittany alone. Henry was told how that, since the failure of the rebellion, those who had managed to flee England had sought protection in exile at Duke Francis's court. Most prominent among them was Queen Elizabeth's brother, Thomas, Marquess of Dorset, who had arrived together with a 'great number' of English gentlemen at Vannes shortly before. They now looked 'to seek' Henry and make contact with him.

Polydore Vergil records that Henry travelled to the ducal capital at Rennes, where he sent for Dorset and the other exiles who had arrived at Vannes. Uncertain whether Henry himself 'had fallen into the hands of King Richard', when Dorset and his followers learnt that Henry had arrived safe back in Brittany they 'rejoiced wondrously' and travelled quickly to Rennes, where after 'much mutual congratulation made' they spent several days in 'dealing in their cause'.

If the number of English exiles who sought out Henry were at first few, as men made their individual journeys towards Francis's court, the numbers soon swelled into a colony of several hundred. Their rebellion may have ended in failure, but the effect of that failure had been for each man in his desperation to throw in his lot with Henry Tudor. Many of course had been loyal to Henry's cause from the beginning, coming as they had from the households of his mother Margaret Beaufort and Thomas Stanley; Richard Pigot and John Browne had both been involved in the arrangements made by Margaret and Stanley for the inheritance of her estates in 1482; other exiles such as Sir John Risley, Seth Worsley and John Edward had strong connections with Thomas Stanley's own affinity.

For others, however, coming face to face with Henry, an unknown Welshman who many probably had never even heard of before Richard's usurpation, let alone ever considered a serious challenger to the throne, the experience of meeting the exiled Lancastrian must have been muted. For those once loyal Yorkists, men who had fought against Henry's own relatives in the civil wars, the very act of paying him homage must have seemed nothing less than bizarre. Edward IV's household men such

Henry Tudor holding the red rose of
the House of Lancaster, in a copy of
a lost portrait painted in around 1500.

chard Plantagenet, Duke of Gloucester
d later King Richard III.

After her husband Henry V's death, Katherine of Valois embarked on an affair with a servant at court, Owen Tudor.

Edmund Tudor (left) married Margaret Beaufort (right), who became pregnant with Henry at the age of twelve. Edmund did not live to witness the birth of his son, Henry Tudor; but Margaret would become his most devoted and loyal protector.

Henry VI, the last Lancastrian king. His mental frailties and weak kingship provoked the civil wars of the fifteenth century.

Margaret of Anjou, Henry VI's wife and fierce defender of the Lancastrian cause.

Pembroke Castle, where Henry Tudor was born in January 1457.

Edward IV (left), whose controversial choice of bride, Elizabeth Woodville (right), caused divisions among the York royal family.

Anthony Rivers presents a work of literature to Edward IV, whose eldest son Edward, the future Edward V, is at his side.

Elizabeth of York, Edward IV's eldest daughter and future wife of Henry Tudor. Their marriage would unite the houses of Lancaster and York.

Richard, Duke of Gloucester, his wife Anne Neville and their son Edward of Middleham, as depicted in the Rous Roll.

William Catesby, one of Richard's loyal dependants, whose support was crucial in Richard's seizure of the throne. He was also one of the few men on Richard's side at Bosworth to be executed after the battle.

John, Lord Howard, first Duke of Norfolk. Norfolk's support for Richard's usurpation was rewarded with a dukedom. He loyally served the king, and led the vanguard of Richard's forces into battle at Bosworth.

A French drawing of the young Henry Tudor.

The tomb of Duke Francis II of Brittany in Nantes Cathedral.

LOVYS XI
ROY DE FRANCE

CHARLES ·8·

uis XI (left), whose son Charles VIII (right) inherited the French throne aged thirteen. His
ency council, led by his sister Anne of Beaujeu (below), gave support to Henry Tudor after
flight to France.

chateau at Suscinio, in Morbihan,
ttany, where Henry and Jasper Tudor
e sent by Duke Francis in 1472.

The fortress of Largoët, situated near the
town of Elven north-east of Vannes. At
fifty-seven metres high its great keep, known
as the Tower of Elven, is the tallest in France.
Henry spent eighteen months imprisoned on
the sixth floor.

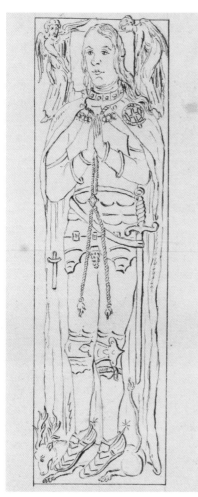

The former Lancastrian Reginald Bray, one of Margaret Beaufort's household servants, played a critical role in Buckingham's rebellion, recruiting supporters among the gentry.

The Lancastrian, John de Vere, Earl of Oxford, whose arrival at Henry Tudor's exiled court in 1484 proved a turning point for Henry. Oxford successfully led the vanguard at Bosworth, with Henry's forces reliant on his military expertise.

Christopher Urswick, Margaret Beaufort's confessor. His decisive action in travelling to Brittany in 1484 to warn Henry Tudor of the danger in remaining at Duke Francis' court prompted Henry's flight to France.

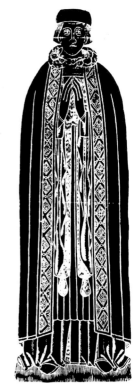

as Sir Giles Daubeney, or Edward's standard bearer John Cheyney, the Master of the King's Horse, must have reflected in a state of disbelief the course of events that had witnessed their lives transformed, to the extent that they now came to find solace in the company of a man their dead master had spent years in vain attempting to capture. Other men came to Henry with their own personal grievances still agonisingly fresh in their minds. John Harcourt had been a prominent member of William Lord Hastings' retinue before his master's execution. Then there was the Woodville affinity, represented by Sir Edward Woodville, Thomas, Marquess of Dorset and Lionel Woodville, Bishop of Salisbury, whose authority as the king's relatives had evaporated upon Richard's accession; still in mourning for the disappearance of Edward V and his brother and still uncertain as to the eventual fate of Queen Elizabeth and her daughters imprisoned in sanctuary at Westminster, a burning sense of revenge must have crowded out any reservation they might have of turning to their former Lancastrian foes for support.

It was a remarkable assortment of men from every variety of political background; only their hatred of Richard and their own pitiful sense of desperation united them. Yet in desperation, only desperate measures could suffice. At Bodmin, Henry had been proclaimed as 'the other king', though this claim had been made in haste, as the dying embers of revolt flickered away. Now those who sought Henry's side had little choice but to consider this unknown Welshman their candidate for the throne. It mattered little that Henry's claim to the throne may have been weak. If it was the only claim that they could cling on to in the hope of deposing Richard, it was claim enough. Yet Henry also recognised that if he were to hold his coalition of exiles together in support of his candidacy, he would need to go further.

In the previous months his mother Margaret had sought to raise the prospect of a marriage between Henry and Edward IV's eldest daughter Elizabeth of York, thereby cementing an unheard-of alliance between the houses of Lancaster and York, uniting the country around a joint claim to the throne held by Henry and Elizabeth together. Now Henry was willing to reassure his Yorkist converts that he would take the young princess as his bride. Moreover, he was determined to impress upon his Yorkist supporters that he would place past divisions behind him by creating a tangible and lasting union between the Lancastrian and Yorkist dynasties. Henry himself recognised that his claim to the throne would not stand scrutiny as merely a step-nephew to Henry VI; through marriage to Edward IV's daughter, however, the royal family that he hoped to create would have its bloodline from Edward III descended from several branches, strengthening its legitimacy and his right to rule as king. For the Woodvilles and those members of Edward IV's Yorkist household, Henry's pledge to marry Elizabeth of York gave them renewed hope that rather than merely campaigning for an unknown Lancastrian usurper, they would be restoring their own family name and fighting for the memory of their dead king, returning the legitimate ruling line of the house of York, in the person of Elizabeth of York, back to the throne.

Before the Woodvilles and the Yorkist exiles would commit their support to Henry's cause, they first demanded that Henry commit himself under oath to the marriage. This took place on Christmas Day, 1483. The Breton chronicle suggests that the alliance was sworn in the cathedral at Vannes, in the presence of the Duchess of Brittany, though Vergil places the ceremony at Rennes:

> The day of Christ's nativity was come upon, which, meeting all in the church, they ratified all other things by plighting of their troths and solemn covenants; and first of all earl Henry upon his oath promised, that so soon as he should be king he would marry Elizabeth, King Edward's daughter; then after they swore unto him homage as though he had already been created king, protesting that they would lose not only their lands and possessions, but their lives, before they would suffer, bear, or permit, that Richard should rule over them and theirs.

Henry had 'almost an assured opinion' that, despite the failure of his first invasion, his position was now strengthened. If any future invasion were to be a success, however, he would need to secure Duke Francis's backing, convincing him that his initial investment in the escapade in November had not been wasted. Henry returned to the duke, reporting what had occurred and at the same time urging him to provide more aid and money, 'that he might return forthwith into his country, much desiring his presence', promising that he would repay 'what so ever he should receive, and in time to come plentifully requite the duke's singular liberality with all endeavour, care and diligence'. What other promises Henry made have gone unrecorded, though an understanding must have been reached between the two men that if Henry were successful, as king he would commit to securing and preserving the fragile independence of Brittany against the might of France.

By this time Francis was an ill man, who seems to have suffered from bouts of mental fragility and seizures, leaving him unable to conduct affairs of state for months at a time. Consequently, most decisions of state were taken by the duke's influential treasurer Pierre Landais. Landais's decision was an easy one to make; for the moment, it seemed that Richard had left him with little choice but to support Tudor against the background of a fierce naval war that raged in the Channel between the two countries, as Richard was determined that Brittany would be made to pay the price for their support for Henry. As the situation deteriorated, on 15 December 1483 Francis had issued musters to resist any possible invasion by English forces. Richard continued to order that Breton ships in the Channel be plundered, while in early 1484 a commission was issued to the Yorkshireman Thomas Wentworth to captain a squadron of ships 'to resist the king's enemies of Brittany and France', with a separate commission being issued to John, Lord Scrope of Bolton in March 1484. The mayor and aldermen of London were ordered to sieze all Breton property and ships. Landois must have felt that he had little choice but to support any form of resistance to the English king, whose actions were strangling the country's trade and finances. Once again Francis promised Henry aid, allowing the earl to begin preparations for rigging another naval force, 'and made himself ready for the sea, that he should not be hindered from any attempt by latches of time'.

6

THE CAT, THE RAT
AND THE DOG

·•·

Christmas festivities at Richard's court were held with unrivalled splendour. Two hundred and seventy-five pounds of silver plate were purchased specially for £550, even though royal treasures including a gold-plated helmet that had belonged to Edward IV had to be pawned to pay for them. Robes for the king and queen were purchased at a cost of over £1,200 together with costly gems from a Genoese dealer. There had not been, Commynes wrote after hearing descriptions of Richard's magnificence, a king who reigned with greater splendour 'these last hundred years'.

It was a time to reflect upon the past and to consider the future. Richard's overarching desire was to now repair the damage that had been wrought by last autumn's rebellion, restoring the country to peace. In a proclamation issued in December 1483, he stated that 'His Grace is utterly determined that all his subjects shall live in rest and quiet, and peaceably enjoy their lands, livelihoods and goods, according to the laws of this land'.

Parliament had been summoned to meet on 6 November, but rebellion had caused it to be postponed until 23 January. It was obvious from the start that the assembly would be nothing more than a rubber stamp. The choice of Speaker, Richard's confidant and councillor William Catesby, who had never sat in Parliament before, typified the obedient nature of the institution. The Crowland Chronicler believed that 'such terror affected even the most stout-hearted men among them' that the commons would agree to the king's every wish.

Richard's first intention was to have his title as king formally ratified in statute; since it was Parliament that 'maketh before all things most faith and certainty', the king hoped that both houses would be able to legitimate his own claim to the throne, removing the 'divers doubts, questions and ambiguities' that had been 'moved and engendered in the minds of divers persons, as it is said'. Richard hoped that, with Parliament's official consent to his kingship, this would remove 'all occasion of all doubts and seditious language', 'quieting men's minds'. A statute, the 'Titulus Regius', was introduced into Parliament, underlining Richard's claim to the throne: the preamble to the statute stated how, due to the invalidity of Edward IV's marriage, his children were to be deemed illegitimate. Instead Richard was to be presented as the natural successor to the Yorkist crown, and the people's choice as king. To highlight the fact, a raft of legislation aimed at reforming the land tenure system and, in criminal justice, the right to bail were combined with a commitment on Richard's part to end the highly unpopular practice of royal benevolences. In doing so, even Polydore Vergil would pay Richard the backhanded compliment that 'he began to give the show and countenance of a good man, whereby he might be accounted more righteous, more mild, more better affected to the commonalty'.

The main purpose of Parliament's assembly, however, was to legalise a massive confiscation of the lands and offices of men who had taken part in Buckingham's rebellion. One hundred and four individual attainders were passed, including thirty-three from Wiltshire, twenty-eight from Kent and Surrey, eighteen from Exeter and fourteen from Berkshire. 'So many great lords, nobles, magnates and commoners, and even three bishops, were attainted', the Crowland Chronicler commented, 'that we nowhere read of the like even under the triumvirate of Octavian, Anthony and Lepidus. What great numbers of estates and inheritances were amassed in the king's treasury in consequence!'

The large number of attainders underlined how Buckingham's rebellion and the outbreaks of revolt across the south and southwest had created a vacuum of authority at a local level, as many of the key members of the gentry, crucial for establishing order, had either been executed or fled abroad to join Henry Tudor in Brittany. The attainder of so many men also left Richard with a dilemma of how exactly he should fill the gap left by the rebels. He was determined not to allow his authority to be questioned ever again. Southern counties such as Kent had an intractable history of disorder and lawlessness, stretching back to Jack Cade's rebellion in 1450 and the Peasants' Revolt of 1381.

The king's solution was to rely ever more on a close knit group of his loyal dependents to fill the gap, displaying the enormous degree of trust that Richard was prepared to place in a handful of his closest advisers. Over thirty grants were made, redistributing the lands of the attainted rebels into the hands of Richard's own household. Sir Richard Ratcliffe was granted lands in south-west England worth 1,000 marks a year, well in excess of what a lord might be expected to accumulate. His secretary John Kendall was bestowed lands and presents worth £450 a year; Robert Brackenbury £400 a year; Sir Thomas Montgomery, a member of Richard's council, £412 a year; Sir William Catesby £323 11s 8d a year. In total, Richard granted away over £12,000 in lands and annuities. His aim of securing support through financial reward had its precedence in the early years of Edward IV's reign, and in the reign of Henry IV, where £24,000 a year was spent on annuities alone, yet Richard's actions reveal the price that needed to be paid to buy support in order to shore up an insecure and unstable regime.

What this wholesale transfer of lands and offices could not buy was repaired relations with the rest of the country. In fact, it would ultimately breed further resentment at the confiscation of the rebels' property and offices, and the men who were chosen to replace them. In the absence of any appropriate men from the southern counties, Richard was forced to rely upon the network of northern gentry that he had cultivated during his years leading the campaigns against the Scots in addition to the gentry close to his northern estates. This resulted in a large number of northern men now being appointed to lands and offices hundreds of miles south from their homelands; for instance, Thomas Huddleston from Cumberland became sheriff of Gloucestershire, Edward Redmayne from Yorkshire became sheriff of Somerset and Dorset, Halnath Mauleverer, also from Yorkshire, was appointed sheriff of Devon. This left Richard wide open to the accusation that he was deliberately attempting to secure a widely feared 'invasion' of northerners into the south, hardly aiding the king's popularity. The Crowland Chronicler believed that Richard had 'planted' his northern followers, 'to the disgrace and loudly expressed sorrow of all the people in the south, who daily longed more and more for the hoped-for return of their ancient rulers rather than the present tyranny of these people'.

One of the 'northern' gentry who Richard had chosen to reward was Sir Marmaduke Constable. A member of one of the wealthiest northern knightly families from Flamborough in the East Riding of Yorkshire, Constable, like his father, was a retainer of the Earl of Northumberland. Yet Richard's coronation saw Constable naturally place his loyalty towards the crown. He had served under Edward IV during his expedition to France in 1475, and had also seen military service under Richard at the capture of Berwick in 1482.

In spite of his northern background, Richard decided that he needed experienced and trusted men such as Constable to restore order in the south. By December 1483 he had become a Knight of the Body, possibly even one of the king's councillors, and placed on the commission of the peace for Kent. For six months Constable was given several posts, including heading the investigation to value the estates of rebels within the county, as well as becoming steward of the manors of Tonbridge, Penshurst and Brastead, whose residents, possibly after displaying signs of resistance to Constable's command, were ordered by the king during a personal visit to Sandwich on 22 January 1484 not to 'take clothing or be retained by any man, person or persons whatsoever' but instead to attend upon Constable, whom Richard had 'deputed and ordained . . . to make his abode among you and to have the rule within our honour [of Tonbridge] and the lordships foresaid'. By April, the receiver of Tonbridge was also ordered to pay Constable £27 10s for his living expenses in the lordship.

No sooner had Constable submitted his first receipts than Richard decided that his services were required elsewhere, implanting him in the Midlands. It was an indication of how few reliable men Richard felt able to trust during his quest to restore order in his realm. This time Constable was granted a host of Duchy of Lancaster posts across Leicestershire, Derbyshire and Staffordshire, including steward of the honour of Tutbury, constable of Tutbury Castle and steward of the lordship of Newcastle-under-Lyme, steward and constable of the High Peak, steward of the lordship of Ashbourne, and steward and constable of Castle Donington. By May 1484 he had been appointed a commissioner of array for Derbyshire, and sheriff of Staffordshire in November. With office also came welcome material reward, with an annunity of £89 16s 8d from the honour of Tutbury, as well as the lordships and manors of Braunstone and Market Bosworth in Leicestershire. Constable's own kinsmen from the north were also rewarded, including Sir Gervase Clifton of Clifton in Nottinghamshire; a nephew of the Archbishop of York and an esquire to the body of Edward IV, Clifton was married to a relative of Constable's. He was granted extensive lands formerly belonging to the Duke of Buckingham in Derbyshire, Leicestershire and Huntingdon.

Men like Marmaduke Constable and Gervase Clifton owed their livelihoods to Richard, who could be confident of their loyalty; yet while Richard sought to refashion the gentry of the southern counties in his own image through his steadfast supporters, still the traditional power structures mattered, and could hardly be ignored. It was less easy to win the support of the nobility, none of whom owed anything to the king. Nevertheless, Richard was confident that, with enough royal patronage their support could be bought. The king was aided by the fact that the depletion of their ranks through the executions and deaths in battle during the civil wars meant that the size of the nobility had shrunk dramatically: twenty-six peers attended the Parliament in 1484, compared to fifty-one in Edward IV's first Parliament in 1461. With a reduced peerage, Richard was able to focus his attention of rewarding those whose support he was confident of securing.

Again the pattern of patronage was a familiar one, as Richard sought to bestow both office and annuities, essentially yearly salaries paid for by the crown, on the nobility he believed could be bought. John de la Pole, the Earl of Lincoln, the son of the Duke of Suffolk and Richard's sister, was granted lands worth £333 2s 5d in addition to receiving an annuity of £176 13s 4d. Lincoln was further rewarded with the office of King's Lieutenant in Ireland in October 1484 and made president of the newly established Council of the North. Other members of the nobility who were close supporters of Richard included Francis, Viscount Lovell, the chamberlain of the royal household, who was rewarded with the offices of chief butler and Constable of England, and given grants of lands from Buckingham's forfeited estates in Oxfordshire, Berkshire and the Thames Valley worth £400 a year, though it seems that Lovell, given his close proximity to the king, chose to spend most of his time at court. William Devereux, Lord Ferrers, was rewarded with an annuity and lands in Hertfordshire worth £146 a year. John, Lord Audley, was appointed a royal councillor with an annuity of £100, as was John, Lord Dudley, who was further rewarded with lands worth a similar amount for his services in putting down Buckingham's rebellion. Henry, Lord Grey of Codnor was granted lands in Norfolk, Suffolk and Rutland worth £266 13s 4d, while John, Lord Dinham, received lands worth £133 6s 8d for his loyalty during the rebellion. Richard did not worry about the mounting costs upon the crown's finances: most importantly, the king hoped he had purchased loyalty and devotion.

Still, it was the most important members of the nobility, the dukes and earls of his realm as well as super magnates such as Thomas, Lord Stanley who, in controlling vast geographic areas of the country within their lordships, mattered most. At his accession, Richard had managed to secure power with the support of the four most powerful members of the nobility: Buckingham, John, Duke of Norfolk, Henry Percy, Earl of Northumberland and Thomas, Lord Stanley. Now only three of these pillars upon which Richard's kingship rested remained. Despite Buckingham's rebellion, the revolt itself had failed with the assistance of the other three nobles in crushing the rising. Howard, who had been created a duke by Richard shortly after his coronation, had been instrumental in suppressing the Kentish rebellion, while Northumberland had been active in raising troops in the north for Richard during the rebellion. And it had been Stanley's inaction in Wales and their heartlands in Lancashire and Cheshire that, in spite of his wife's troublesome plotting on behalf of her son, had meant that Buckingham's attempt at raising rebellion there collapsed.

If Richard was to continue to effectively control the kingdom, all would need to be rewarded appropriately. Richard's accession had not merely seen John Howard be raised to the Dukedom of Norfolk and his appointment as Admiral of England; the king had sought to vastly increase his landed estates. On 25 July 1483, Howard had been granted forty-six manors in Berkshire, Wiltshire and Cornwall; upon Rivers's death, he had also been given the profits of twenty-five manors formerly belonging to the earl. When Katherine Neville, the dowager duchess of the Mowbray Duke of Norfolk, who had died back in 1432, finally died in September 1483, her estates were granted by Richard to be split between the heirs, Norfolk, and William Berkeley, Earl of Nottingham. In addition to this, Richard further granted a sizeable portion of lands in East Anglia formerly belonging to the Earl of Oxford to Norfolk, and as well as promoting Norfolk's son Thomas Howard to the Earldom of Surrey, awarded him the staggering annuity of £1,100.

Henry Percy, Earl of Northumberland was appointed steward and chamberlain of England, and after Buckingham's downfall was rewarded with the duke's lordship of Holderness in Yorkshire, worth over £1,000 a year. The earl was also granted possession of the lucrative Brian lands in the south-west, formerly held by the Duke of Clarence, although Northumberland also had a claim to the lands. In addition to being appointed captain of Berwick in May 1483, seemingly an uninspiring promotion until its salary of £438 a month, or £5,000 a year, is taken into account.

Thomas, Lord Stanley had been one of the first to benefit from the duke's fall, receiving his lordship of Kimbolton on the same day of Buckingham's execution. Further rewards followed, with Stanley being appointed to Buckingham's former office of Constable of England in December 1483, together with an annuity of £100. Stanley's loyalty was further rewarded with large grants of lands within the Welsh Marches and Cheshire, in addition to the lordship and castle of Thornbury in Gloucestershire, worth £687 a year. Richard also sought to further extend the Stanley family's influence in North Wales to replace the absence of leadership left by Buckingham's execution. Stanley's brother Sir William Stanley was appointed chief justice of North Wales on 12 November and later given the constableship of Caernarfon castle, while one of their kinsmen, William Griffith of Penryhn, was made chamberlain of North Wales. In spite of these grants, Richard was unwilling to grant the Stanleys the degree of influence that he had been prepared to give to Buckingham; instead, other key offices in North Wales went to his northern followers, possibly as a deliberate check to prevent the Stanleys' power from growing too strong.

Richard's hesitation in rewarding Thomas Stanley and his family with what they might have considered their due is perhaps understandable given Margaret Beaufort's own involvement in the conspiracy and rebellion during the previous autumn, which if anything was clearly apparent from the number of her kinsmen and servants who were listed among the rebels. According to Polydore Vergil, Margaret was 'commonly called the head of that conspiracy'.

Many had been surprised, angry even, that Stanley had not only escaped punishment but had received reward; 'it went very hard,' Vergil observed, 'that Thomas Stanley was not accounted among the number of the king's enemies, by reason of the practices of Margaret his wife'. Some even suspected that Stanley himself had been one of the instigators of the rebellion, and if Vergil is to be believed, Stanley was interviewed by the council where he 'proved himself guiltless of all offence'. It is hard to believe that Stanley would not have at least been aware of his wife's intrigues, or even considered the prospect of raising his stepson to the throne. According to a later ballad that recalled the time of the rebellion, Thomas Stanley sent one of his retainers, Humphrey Brereton of Malpas, Cheshire, to Henry. Brereton sailed in one of Stanley's ships from Liverpool, near to one of Stanley's residences, with a large sum of money which he took to Henry, finding him at the Cistercian abbey of Begard, near Paimpol on the north coast of Brittany. While the evidence contained in the ballad cannot be verified, it is striking that it records Henry's residence as being near Paimpol, exactly the same location where Duke Francis II handed over his loan of 10,000 crowns on 30 October before the earl departed on his ill-fated voyage to England.

Laying aside Thomas Stanley's own involvement, how to deal with Margaret Beaufort posed a potential problem for Richard. He needed to retain Stanley's support; adding his wife's name to the list of attainders would hardly achieve this. Even if Richard had wished to pass an attainder against Margaret, the fact that her marriage settlement with Stanley in 1472 guaranteed the earl a substantial income from her estates, as well as the cessation of Margaret's legal rights to property would have jeopardised Stanley's own interest in his wife's estates, potentially alienating Stanley's support. Instead, Richard chose to spare Margaret, 'remembering the good and faithful service that Thomas, Lord Stanley hath done . . . and for his sake'.

Nevertheless, for Margaret herself the commensurate punishment could be considered equally harsh. She was to forfeit her right to all titles and estates, with all her properties being regranted to her husband. The material change may have been small, but for Margaret the significance could hardly have been greater. For a woman who fiercely guarded her independence, not to mention the protection of her only son's rights and inheritance, she was being reduced to the status of a humble wife, dependent entirely upon her husband and his survival; the body of her estates, now granted to Stanley for life, would upon his death revert to the king. Her rights to her mother's Beaufort inheritance were also cancelled, while lands that Margaret might have hoped to be given to Henry were granted away to others.

This was not the only punishment that Margaret would have to endure. The king's council also decreed that Stanley was to 'remove from his wife all her servants, and to keep her so straight with himself that she should not be able from henceforth to send any messenger neither to her son, nor friends, nor practice any thing at all against the king'. Effectively forced to renounce her independence, it can only have been a humiliating experience for Margaret. Yet reflecting upon what had taken place over the past months, she would have been able to retain the satisfaction that her efforts had not been in vain. Her son Henry had not only been greatly strengthened with the arrival of several hundred exiles from the rebellion to his side; then Margaret herself had set in motion Henry's claim to the throne, while the ceremony at Vannes on Christmas Day had finally brought to fruition her long cherished ambition that Henry might one day marry Elizabeth of York. For thirty years, Margaret had weaved through the dangers at court, as she sought incessantly to protect her only son; now she had come close to securing an unofficial acknowledgement that, should Richard be swept aside, Henry might be crowned king. For all this, she must have considered, her own confinement within her household was a small price to pay. 'Albeit in King Richard's days she was oft in jeopardy of her life,' a later account recalled of Margaret's persistence, 'yet she bore patiently all trouble in such wise that it is wonder to think it.'

Richard's decision not to deliver a more severe punishment to Margaret Beaufort was a sign of the king's own willingness at reconciliation;

members of Margaret's household who had been explicitly involved in the rebellion, including Reginald Bray and Sir Richard Edgecombe, were granted a general pardon, despite the fact that by this time Edgecombe had already made his way to Brittany. Later in the spring, Richard would decide to pardon a third of those attainted, drawing up a list of men he hoped to rehabilitate, including rebels such as William Berkeley of Beverstone, Walter Hungerford and William Brandon – even Sir John Fogge, a former treasurer of the royal household and a kinsman of the Woodvilles who had been pardoned by Richard after his accession to the throne, having been brought out of sanctuary at Westminster where he shook the king's hand. Fogge had raised rebellion in Kent, yet Richard still thought fit to pardon him for a second time.

Margaret was not the only woman that Richard sought to appease. Since the flight of the exiles from Buckingham's rebellion to Henry Tudor in Brittany, the king had been determined to obtain intelligence as to what his rival was planning. 'He had provided himself with spies overseas,' the Crowland Chronicler observed, 'at whatever price he could get them, from whom he had learned almost all the movements of his enemies.' As soon as Richard had received news of Henry Tudor's promise to marry Elizabeth of York at Vannes, the king understood the urgent need to neutralise the threat that Queen Elizabeth and her daughters, remaining in sanctuary at Westminster, posed. If he could gain possession of Elizabeth of York and her younger sisters Cecily, Anne, Katherine and Brigitte then he would be able to arrange their marriages himself, choosing suitably loyal husbands for each of them, thereby frustrating Henry's ambitions. Despite the fact that Elizabeth Woodville had been at the very centre of the plot to overthrow him, Richard now sought to extend the branch of peace. Sending messengers to her urging her and her daughters to leave sanctuary, he promised that he would secure their welfare. Queen Elizabeth, whose grief over the disappearance of her sons 'seemed scarce able to be comforted', was understandably suspicious. She had heard the same promises before, when she gave up her youngest son Richard to Archbishop Bourgchier in preparation for his brother's coronation; that was the last time she had had sight of him. Resisting Richard's entreaties, it was only 'after much pleading, and also threats had been employed', with the queen being 'very strongly entreated', that she finally caved in to the king's demands.

Before she would allow her daughters to leave sanctuary, Elizabeth first insisted that she would only do so on condition that the king swear a solemn and lengthy oath in front of an assembly of the nobility and bishops, together with the mayor and aldermen of London. Addressing the gathering on 1 March, Richard, his hands placed upon a bible, declared that

I Richard by the grace of God, King of England and of France and Lord of Ireland in the presence of you my Lords spiritual and temporal, and you Mayor and Aldermen of my City of London, promise and swear . . . upon these holy evangelies of God by me personally touched that if the daughters of Dame Elizabeth Gray late calling herself Queen of England, that is to wit Elizabeth, Cecille, Anne, Kateryn and Brigitte will come unto me out of the Sanctuary of Westminster and be guided, ruled and demeaned after me, then I shall see that they shall be in surety of their lives and also not suffer any manner hurt by any manner person or persons to them or any of them in their bodies and persons to be done by way of ravishment or defouling contrary to their wills, nor them or any of them imprisoned within the Tower of London or other prison, but that I shall put them in honest places of good name and fame, and them honestly and courteously shall see to be found and entreated and to have all things requisite and necessary for their exhibition and findings as my kinswomen.

Richard further promised that he would ensure that each of the daughters would be married to 'gentlemen born' with a dowry of lands worth 200 marks a year provided for each of them. For the queen, he pledged that retiring to the country, she would receive 700 marks a year. Ominously, the king also stated that she would be personally attended by 'one of the esquires of my body', John Nesfield, the man who had been appointed to encircle the sanctuary at Westminster with an armed guard; however, Nesfield was soon to be ordered to command a naval fleet at sea, suggesting that his appointment was a nominal one, and that the queen would be allowed to retire from court in comfortable seclusion.

Becoming increasingly unsettled and nervous of Henry Tudor's growing strength across the seas in Brittany, Richard also believed it necessary for not only his own title, having been confirmed by Parliament, but the future security of his family dynasty to be given wider recognition. A month after Parliament had been dissolved, Richard would summon leading members of the London livery companies to Westminster to hear the 'king's title and right' announced to them, in which it was explained how Richard took his descent from Henry II. As soon as he had managed to gain possession of the Woodville daughters from sanctuary, Richard ordered his nobility and the court to attend a ceremony by which they swore their allegiance to his son Edward, Prince of Wales as the king's sole heir. The Crowland Chronicler recorded how

By special command of the king there were gathered together in a certain downstairs room near the corridor which leads to the queen's quarters, almost all the lords spiritual and temporal and the leading knights and gentlemen of the king's household, the chief amongst whom seemed to be John Howard, whom the king had recently created duke of Norfolk. Each person subscribed his name to a certain new oath, drawn up by persons unknown to me, undertaking to adhere to the king's only son, Edward, as their supreme lord, should anything happen to his father.

Few could have imagined that barely a month later, their oaths would prove unnecessary. Richard and Queen Anne were at Nottingham castle when on 9 April, it was broken to them that the king's only son and heir, Edward had died. The news came as a complete shock. Prince Edward himself had been at Middleham in Yorkshire, when he had suddenly been taken ill, dying after a 'short illness'. The Crowland Chronicler provides a pained eye-witness account of the king and queen's outpouring of unrestrained emotion: 'You might have seen the father and mother, after hearing the news at Nottingham where they were staying, almost out of their minds for a long time when faced with the sudden grief'.

Only glimpses of Edward's short life can be gleaned from the surviving accounts at Middleham for the previous year; he had made a journey to the abbeys of Jervaux, Coverham, Wensleydale, Fountains and Pontefract, where he had made offerings of 15 shillings, 20d, 2s 6d, and 4 shillings. Other purchases included a book of hours covered in black satin and a Psalter, a gown of grey cloth, 6s 8d to his servants 'for running on foot beside my lord prince' and 100s for the wages of Jane Colyns, who must have been one of the prince's maids. As the young prince reached his maturity, it was clear that Richard intended for his son to play a full role in regional affairs; Edward had already been granted possession and nominal control of Richard's northern estates, and had been crowned as Prince of Wales during an elaborate ceremony at York the previous August. Richard's personal interest in his son's upbringing is perhaps testified by a manuscript copy of the popular classical military treatise *De Re Militari*, by Flavius Renatus Vegetius, essentially a handbook on how to prepare for war and win battles, that was in the king's possession. Its frontispiece is illuminated with the English royal arms and a griffin, the insignia of the Earl of Salisbury, the title to which Edward acceded in 1478.

Richard had wept genuine tears for the death of his only legitimate son; his grief had been compounded by the fact that so soon after 'so many solemn oaths' had been sworn to Edward, in whom 'all hope of the royal succession rested', he had lost his sole heir to the throne. Since his Queen Anne was only twenty-six, Richard could certainly hope for more children; in the meantime, however, he would need to appoint an heir presumptive. Shortly after Edward IV's death, it had been reported that Edward, Earl of Warwick, the eldest son of the Duke of Clarence, was reportedly in the royal court proclaimed heir apparent to Richard's son, and in both ceremonies 'at table and chamber' he was to be served first after the king and queen. Since Clarence had been found guilty of treason in 1478, it would seem strange that his son would suddenly be rehabilitated, especially since the boy, as the son of Richard's elder brother, possessed a claim to the throne far stronger that the king's own. Possibly, realising the danger that the young Earl of Warwick threatened since the death of his son, Richard ordered that he be sent to his residence at Sheriff Hutton; John Rous wrote that 'later he was placed in custody and the Earl of Lincoln was preferred to him'. With Prince Edward's death, Lincoln would also be chosen to supersede his positions in the north, ruling on the king's behalf from Sandal Castle, which had been appointed the headquarters of the Council of the North.

Dealing with the royal succession was not the only issue confronting the grieving king. Rumours once again began to circulate that Henry and his exiles were planning an invasion, and 'would shortly land in England, together with their leader, the Earl of Richmond, to whom all the outcasts, in the hope that a marriage would be contracted with King Edward's daughter, had sworn fealty, as to their king'. Richard had resolved to be adequately prepared for any forthcoming military action: not only had he directed a royal fleet, commanded by John, Lord Audley, to patrol the Channel in order to intercept any invasion during the early months of 1484, but he had also set about strengthening his arsenal of artillery and munitions in the Tower in preparation for conflict.

The arsenal had for a long time been the pride and joy of English kings, with an Italian visitor to London in 1475 observing how the king inspected his artillery in the Tower each day. Even as early as 1396, there was an available stock of fifty guns in the Tower, together with 4,000 lbs of gunpowder and 600 lbs of saltpetre. Early in the fifteenth century the privy wardrobe's functions were succeeded by the newly established ordnance office, with a master of ordnance. Henry VI appointed a London merchant, John Judde, to the office, after Judde had first attracted the king's attention by promising to provide sixty serpentines (a type of cannon), and twenty tons of saltpetre and sulphur, which he would deliver 'under certain reasonable contitions'. Within a month, he had provided twenty-six serpentines to the king, and claimed also to have cast three 'great serpentines to subdue any castle or place that would rebel'. In June 1460, while conducting a new delivery to the king, Judde was ambushed at St Albans and killed, according to one commentator, in 'a wretched end, as the caitiff deserved'.

On his expedition to France, Edward IV's artillery train comprised at least thirteen pieces of heavy artillery, including a huge cannon known as a bombard (called 'bumbardelle'), five 'fowlers', a form of long-range field gun, a 'curtowe' (a short-range field gun) and three 'potguns' or mortars. These were intended for use both in the field as well as sieges. There was an evident pride in the artillery pieces – both the 'long fowler' and the 'bumbardelle' were named Edward. Richard, it seems, shared his brother's enthusiasm for the latest technology on the battlefield; when, in 1480, Louis XI had sent him a huge bombard capable of destroying even the thickest of castle walls, Richard wrote to the French king thanking him for 'the great bombard which you caused to be presented to me', acknowledging that 'for as I have always taken and still take great pleasure in artillery I assure you it will be a special treasure to me'. Richard's choice of St Barbara to be among the patrons of the college that he founded at Middleham is also interesting in this context: St Barbara, whose murderer was killed by lightning, was the patron saint of miners, gunmakers and gunners, all of whom invoked her name against sudden and unexpected death.

An idea of the arsenal's operation in the Tower can be gathered from the king's command in February 1484 for the constable of the Tower to deliver seven serpentines on carts, twenty-eight hackebushes 'with their frames', one barrel of torch powder, two barrels of 'serpentine powder' as well as 200 bows, 200 bills, 400 sheaves of arrows, and ten gross of bowstrings to be sent to Scotland. Several months later in June, another order came for the delivery of two serpentines, 'two guns to lie on walls', twelve hackebushes, ten steel crossbows, sixty longbows, one hundred sheaves of arrows and two barrels of gunpowder. In order to re-equip supplies, twenty new guns and two serpentines were purchased from merchants at Southampton for £24 in March 1484.

Possession of the latest weaponry was one thing, how to correctly use it was another. Given the fleeting nature of battle in the campaigns of the civil wars, sieges had been few, leaving the English development of weaponry far behind the Continent. Commynes noted in 1477 that 'because the English had not fought outside their kingdom for so long, they did not understand siege warfare very well'. To address this, men from the Continent with sufficient expertise were drafted into the Tower. William Clowte 'of Gelderland' was employed as a 'gunmaker' along with William Nele, who was granted an annuity of 6d a day. Another Dutchman, Patrick de la Motte, was appointed chief cannoner and master founder of the king's cannon, with two other men from abroad, Theobald Ferrount and Gland Pyroo, who were taken into the king's service as gunners. The king's official armourer was Vincent Tetulior, paid a salary of £20. He had ordered for the Tower to be restocked with harnesses, complete suits of plate armour, with 164 being purchased from Breton and Genoese merchants for five marks a harness, totalling £560. Plated suits of armour were also specially bought from Antwerp.

In the face of the prospect of an invasion by Henry Tudor at any time, Richard considered that the country should be placed on a constant state of readiness, with men prepared for war if and when it came. In particular, the Crowland Chronicler noted how the king introduced a method of communication last used by Edward IV 'at the time of the last war in Scotland' of allocating a mounted courier for every twenty miles, each able to ride with the 'utmost skill and not crossing their bounds'. The result was that messages could be passed 200 miles within two days 'without fail by letters passed from hand to hand'.

When rumours of a possible attack reached Richard, no doubt from his spies on the Continent, in the spring of 1484, immediate action was taken, with the king issuing Commissions of Array on 1 May, mustering men from across the country to be prepared to take up arms within twenty-four hours' notice. An indication of the urgency of the summons can be found in the lists of those appointed, for the name of the recently deceased Prince Edward had failed to be removed by the time they were issued. The names of the commissioners responsible for raising troops reveal the extent to which Richard had become dependent upon the small group of trusted men he himself had chosen to reward for their loyal service: the North was to be raised by Northumberland and Lincoln, Yorkshire by Sir Richard Ratcliffe, Sir Gervais Clifton and Lord Scrope of Bolton, the Midlands by Lord Lovell, William Catesby and Marmaduke Constable, East Anglia by Norfolk and his son Surrey, together with the warden of the Cinque Ports, the Earl of Arundel and Sir Robert Percy, the Comptroller of the royal household.

In spite of this, Richard could be confident that he would be ready to face down any invasion, as he had been when he had crushed Buckingham's rebellion the previous year. 'The king was better prepared to resist them in that year,' the Crowland Chronicler wrote, 'than he would have been ever at any time afterwards'. Yet the rumours of Henry Tudor's planned arrival were just that, rumours. There would be no invasion, not this year at least.

As worshippers arrived at the great door of St Paul's Cathedral on the morning of 18 July 1484, they were greeted by a sheet of parchment, pinned to the door and flapping in the wind. Scribbled on the parchment was a simple rhyming couplet:

The Cat, the Rat, and Lovel our dog,
Ruleth all England under a Hog.

Those crowding round curiously to read the words would have understood fully the cryptic verse. It was aimed as a barbed attack on Richard's closest councillors: the 'Cat' stood for Sir William Catesby, the 'Rat' for Sir Richard Ratcliffe, and Lovel 'our dog', Francis Viscount Lovell, the king's councillors and friends who had been richly rewarded by their king, 'the Hog', a clear allusion to Richard's own heraldic device of the Boar, and whose influence and power throughout the country had come to be bitterly resented.

Just as soon as the doggerel had been torn down, a search was ordered for the author of the seditious verse. Soon after, William Collingborne, a gentleman from Wiltshire, was arrested and charged with the offence. Collingborne had been been a former servant of Edward IV, who seems to have fallen out with the new regime shortly after Richard's accession, being removed from his position on the commission of the peace in Wiltshire. What was perhaps more worrying was that he had been a household officer to Richard's own mother, Cecilly Neville. Richard had written to her in June 1484, just a month before the offending verse had been pinned to the door of St Paul's, explaining how he had replaced Collingborne, requesting that she 'be good and gracious lady' to his chosen replacement who would be 'your officer in Wiltshire in such as Collingborne had'.

At Collingborne's trial several months later, the seriousness with which Richard regarded the crime was reflected in the panel of the jury which included two dukes, thirteen lords, the lord mayor of London and nine judges. As the trial progressed, it was clear that Collingborne's treachery went far beyond lampooning the king's councillors. Ten days before he had decided to nail the sheet to the door of St Paul's he had offered one Thomas Yate £8 to travel to Brittany to deliver a letter he had written to Henry Tudor and his exiles declaring that they should do very well to return into England with all such power as they might get before the feast of St Luke the Evangelist next ensuing . . . And that if the said Earl of Richmond with his part-takers, following the counsel of the said Collingborne, would arrive at the haven of Poole in Dorsetshire, he the said Collingborne and other his associates would cause the people to rise in arms and to levy war against King Richard, taking part with the said earl and his friends, so that all things should be at their commandments.

Yate was also commanded by Collingborne to encourage Henry to send Sir John Cheyney to the French king, 'to advertise him that his ambassadors sent into England should be dallied with' until winter had passed, so that at the beginning of the following summer, Richard would seek to make war with France, 'invading that realm with all puissance' and 'so by this means to persuade the French king to aid the Earl of Richmond and his partakers in their quarrel against King Richard'.

The jury's guilty verdict delivered, Collingborne was condemned to death. Unlike most of the rebels in Buckingham's rebellion, whose method of execution was to be the relatively painless death of swinging from the gallows, Collingborne's end was to be a gruesome one. His body was dragged behind a cart of horses through the filth of the capital's streets to Tower Hill, where he was first hanged from the gallows. Just as he was close to gasping his final breath, he was cut down, collapsing to the floor. Hauled to his feet, he was thrown onto a table where his body was 'straight cut down and ripped', with his genitals also being castrated. The 'torment', the Great Chronicle of London recorded, 'was so speedily done' that Collingborne was able to look down as his executioner thrust his hand into his chest and pulled out his heart, crying, 'Jesus, Jesus, Yet more trouble!'

Collingborne's seditious verse may be the only example that survives, yet it was certainly not an isolated case, as rumours and written propaganda against the king circulated in the capital and beyond, stoked no doubt by Henry's exiled community in Brittany.

Still unsettled by rumours that Henry was planning an invasion that summer, Richard was determined to crack down on any possible further treason before it escalated into revolt, punishing those who he discovered had been in contact with Henry Tudor. The cook William Finch later recalled that he had been in service with Robert Morton, the nephew of John Morton, Bishop of Ely and formerly clerk of the Rolls before he had been dismissed from his office the previous summer, when he had travelled with Morton to join Henry in Brittany. When Finch decided to return, Richard's men were waiting for him: not only was he 'beaten and maimed' by Richard's servants, 'as it appeareth as well on his hands as other parts of his body', 'but also all that he had was taken from him'. On 6 July John, Lord Scrope of Bolton was ordered to try James Newenham, who had been pardoned the previous year, yet had 'lately confessed great treasons'. The same month Scrope was further appointed to investigate the treasons of several Cornishmen who had planned to send £52 to Robert Willoughby and Peter Courtenay in exile in Brittany, with the indictment accusing the men of aiding the rebels 'to the destruction of the crown'. In September Richard ordered that several persons in the West Country be arrested for actions 'against their natural duty and liegeance'. And to prevent any ships departing the country for Brittany, in August Richard sent out orders that no one was to fit out a ship without first making a pledge and giving securities that the vessel would not be used against the king's subjects or friends.

Of all the allegations contained in Collingborne's indictment, most concerning for Richard must have been the accusation that he had urged Henry Tudor to make contact with France. Since the death of Louis XI on 30 August 1483, the political situation in France had remained highly unstable. Louis's heir, the new king Charles VIII, was just thirteen years of age. The queen mother, Charlotte of Savoy, had been removed from power altogether by the late king, and suffering poor health died a few months later in December 1483. In the absence of any recognisable authority, a struggle broke out between Charles's eldest sister Anne of Beaujeu and the next in line to the throne, the senior prince of the blood royal, Louis, Duke of Orleans, who was also the husband of Charles VIII's younger sister.

The political infighting in France had become entangled with the equally factious political rivalries taking place in Brittany at the same time. Duke Francis, his mind failing through age, was becoming increasingly frail, 'by reason of sore and daily sickness'. The Breton government was being effectively controlled by Francis's treasurer and chief minister Pierre Landais, 'a man both of sharp wit and great authority'. Landais's supremacy was resented by other members of the Breton nobility, dissatisfied with their treatment at the hands of a man they considered base-born. Events took a dramatic turn after the sudden death in prison of Landais's rival, the deposed chancellor Guillaume Chauvin on 5 April 1484. Exasperated at Landais's control of the duke and his court, two days later a group of dissident nobles led by the Prince of Orange and the Marshal de Rieux stormed the ducal palace at Nantes, attempting to seize the confused Francis and force him into arresting Landais. The uprising failed and the conspirators fled, seeking sanctuary at Anne of Beaujeu's court. Recognising that Duke Francis had no heir apart from his young daughter, Anne realised the potential for an alliance that might eventually secure the union of France and Brittany, marrying Charles VIII to Francis's daughter Anne. Eventually an agreement, the Treaty of Montargis, was signed between the Breton nobles and the Beaujeu government on 28 October 1484.

Facing this dangerous challenge to his authority, Landais chose to forge an alliance with the dissident French nobles, known as the Orleanists, led by the Count of Dunois, Orleans' cousin. On Easter Day, 18 April, Dunois and Orleans arrived in Nantes to give Landais their backing. In order to defeat his rival Anne of Beaujeu, Landais's support for his cause was only part of Orleans' grand plan. He was to cast his net for support far wider: in an attempt to create a coalition against the Beaujeu government, he had made contact with Maximilian of Austria, the ruler of the Netherlands, and Richard, hoping to combine the support of his French nobility, Brittany, Burgundy and England, which would ensure that a rebellion against Anne would prove insurmountable.

Maximilian himself had also been encouraging Richard to invade France. He had been humiliated by the treaty of Arras in 1482, which had cost him the loss of Burgundy, Artois and the towns of the Somme; he also wanted to ensure that his son Archduke Philip was less dependent upon the regency government of Charles VIII. He sent an embassy to England with instructions to explain to Richard how the king's own interests would be served by joining a united alliance against France, and that this would be best achieved by going to Brittany's aid. When Richard remained hesitant to involve himself in an alliance with Brittany due to the shelter that the Breton government was providing for Henry Tudor, Maximilian suggested that negotiations should be opened up to persuade Duke Francis to 'leave the party' of the earl, with Maximilian proposing that he would personally act as the duke's surety and pledge.

Richard's own diplomatic situation was looking increasingly bleak. His attempt to establish a puppet regime in Scotland under the Duke of Albany had failed with Albany's flight to England. Though the Scots signalled their intentions to negotiate a peace, at the same time they continued their attacks on the English garrison at Dunbar. By April 1484 they had reaffirmed their traditional alliance with France. Meanwhile French ships had turned their firepower on English fleets in the Channel, and it was widely expected in London that a French invasion would take place in the summer. The French had already denounced Richard's usurpation as 'orgies of crime' at a council at Tours in the spring of 1484, declaring that 'Edward IV's children were murdered with impunity, and the crown transferred to their assassin by the goodwill of the nation'. On 5 April 1484 a French delegation, led by three councillors of Charles VIII, had even arrived in Brittany promising support for a new English venture under Henry Tudor. The French government's motives were highly suspect: though they assured Francis that he had the survival of Brittany at heart, in reality Anne of Beaujeu hoped that another invasion by Henry would distract Richard's naval fleet from the damaging piracy that was affecting French ships, at the same time as potentially weakening any prospect of English support for Francis against a French invasion of the duchy. The offer was too generous for Francis not to suspect that the French had their own agenda; nevertheless, work began on preparing a small fleet for Henry, a flotilla of six ships from the ports of Morlaix, St Pol de Jean and Brest, carrying 890 men.

Meanwhile Landais wanted to commit to Orleans' cause against the French regency government, yet he too had his hesitations. He knew that without English military support it would be a risky strategy to involve Brittany in a French civil war, when the consequence of failure might be a French invasion of his own nation. Landais needed

Richard's own commitment to join in the attack. In return, he would use the one card that remained: handing over Henry Tudor. Already Richard had sent messengers to the duke, though finding Francis incapacitated, they dealt solely with Landais, promising him the yearly revenues of the confiscated lands belonging to Henry and his exiles if he agreed to place them in custody.

It was a tempting offer. Since arriving in Vannes after the failure of Buckingham's rebellion, the English exile community had been at liberty within the town, where the cathedral accounts offer glimpses of their activities there, recording their offering of 6 livre tournois 7s 1d during the celebrations of the feast of the Purification of the Blessed Virgin on 2 February. Yet the presence of over 400 exiles within the confines of the town's walls was becoming a burden on the townspeople; the city burgesses had donated 2,500 livre tournois to the impoverished exiles, while the canons of Vannes Cathedral had loaned the English 200 livre tournois, a sum they would later complain in 1498 had yet to be repaid. The chronicler Commynes also noted how the exiled community was becoming an equal financial burden upon Francis's finances: in June 1484 he gave 3,100 livre tournois to the Englishmen for their lodging; in addition, he paid a pension of £400 to the Marquess of Dorset and his men, £200 to John Halewell, £100 to Robert Willoughby and Sir Edward Woodville, in addition to a monthly sum of £100 'for his people' that totalled £900 for nine months. Tensions between the English exile community and native Vantois were also becoming apparent, with Duke Francis even obliged to grant compensation of 200 livre tournois to the widowed Georget le Cuff, whose husband was killed by one of the exiles.

On 8 June 1484 a truce between Brittany and England was finally agreed at Pontefract, to last until 24 April 1485. According to Landais, Richard sent his envoy 'le petit Salazar', a Spanish captain who had fought for Maximilian in the Netherlands up to 1483, to negotiate the terms of the truce, revealing the influence that Maximilian had behind the scenes. Central to the agreement was a promise by Richard to provide Brittany with a force of archers, yet rather than the 4,000 archers Francis had demanded the previous year, Richard would only agree to sending 1,000 archers. Jean Lesquelen had been sent to Richard to hold him to his promise that the men would be sent; Guillaume Guillemet was also sent with seven ships to ensure their safe arrival. Meanwhile Landais made plans for Henry Tudor's imminent arrest, preparing to sacrifice the young man he had sheltered for the past thirteen years for the sake of his own political advantage.

7

A CONFEDERACY OF REBELS

•◆•

H enry had remained at Vannes throughout August and into September, unaware of the diplomatic negotiations that were secretly conspiring against him. On 15 August and 8 September 1484 he is recorded in the cathedral accounts as having attended Mass there, making small offerings of alms. In the same accounts, several entries below, there appears an offering from '*le grand escuier d'Engleterre*' – most likely James Tyrrel, Richard's Master of the Horse. The net around Tudor was closing rapidly.

If Richard soon expected to have his enemy in his grasp, he could have hardly countenanced the turn of events that would leave his carefully laid plans in tatters. The king could have been forgiven for believing that John Morton, now living in exile in Flanders after his near escape from England the previous autumn, remained a relatively harmless threat to his regime. Yet Morton's intervention would now prove decisive. When the bishop was secretly informed of Landais's negotiations with Richard 'from his friends out of England', possibly from Margaret Beaufort or even Thomas Stanley, who would have been present during council negotiations over the truce with Brittany, Morton managed to get notice to Henry of the trap that was being laid around him. Sending his agent Christopher Urswick, one of Margaret Beaufort's chaplains who had travelled to Flanders to join Morton, to Henry at Vannes, Urswick impressed upon Henry the danger that he was in, urging the earl to 'get himself and the other noble men as soon as might be out of Brittany and into France'. Henry immediately sent Urswick on to the French court at Angers to request Charles VIII's permission for Henry to enter France.

Anne of Beaujeu could hardly believe her good fortune. With the mounting threat of Orleans' invasion backed by Burgundy, Brittany and

England, possession of Henry Tudor would be the perfect diplomatic counter to threaten Richard, possibly dissuading him from providing aid to Brittany. She immediately accepted Urswick's request.

Urswick returned to Henry, informing him of the news. He had already begun to plan his escape. Secrecy was vital. Only a few of his men were trusted with the plan, including his uncle Jasper, who was instructed to lead a delegation of only a handful of men who were told that they were to ride in convoy along well-known routes to visit Duke Francis, who at the time was staying near the French border while he recuperated from his illness. Jasper had been given the secret instructions that when he arrived at the French border, 'he should suddenly turn aside and make straight for France'. This they did 'without intermitting any one moment of time' and continued across into France, aiming for Anjou.

Two days later Henry himself left Vannes, accompanied by five servants, on pretence of visiting a friend who lived in the nearby countryside. His departure raised little suspicion, especially since there remained several hundred of his followers within the city walls. When he had travelled five miles outside of the city, he turned off the highway into a nearby forest, where having changed his clothes so as to appear dressed in 'a serving man's apparrel', 'and followed one of the servants who was acting as guide on this journey. He travelled with such speed, following no definite route, never stopping save to rest the horses until he had come into the territory of Anjou and rejoined his followers.'

Landais had been finalising plans to send a number of specially chosen men under 'trusty captains' to seize Henry, under the pretence that they were 'to accompany him on his return to his homeland', when he heard the first news of Henry's escape. Immediately he sent out men on horseback in pursuit, with orders that if they could overtake Henry they were to arrest him and return him to Brittany. It was to be in vain: arriving at the French border after a breakneck chase, they discovered that Henry had passed into France 'scarcely an hour' before.

When the 400 English exiles left behind at Vannes, having no knowledge of Henry's flight, discovered what had happened, 'they were overcome with such fear that now they despaired for their safety'. Fortunately it seems that when Duke Francis, recovering from his most recent episode of incapacity during which he had been 'ignorant of all the practice' of his treasurer, discovered what had taken place, he was furious with Landais, 'taking it in evil part' that Henry had been forced to flee. Whether through compassion or guilt, he was determined to make amends, sending for Edward Poynings and Sir Edward Wood-ville, where he announced that he would provide them with the necessary money 'to bear the charges of their journey' and commanded them to follow Henry to France. His accounts detail the costs of the duke's remarkable act of generosity: Sir Edward Woodville, Sir John Cheyney and Edward Poynings were rewarded with a gift of 100 livre tournois each, as well as 20s for each of the 408 exiles still stationed at Vannes, totalling 708 livre tournois.

When Henry was rejoined with his exiled companions, he was 'won-derous glad', sending back a message to the duke thanking him 'for the safety of himself and all his company', which he promised 'in time he would not fail to requite'. For those exiles Henry had left behind and who had been saved by the duke's intervention, the reunion came as a relief; still the fact that Henry had abandoned them to their fate must have been galling, perhaps raising questions in their own minds about the sheer ruthlessness of the young man who had been prepared to sacrifice their lives for his own.

Charles VIII and the royal court were at Montargis when he was informed on 11 October that Henry had arrived in his kingdom. The French royal council immediately issued an order for the governor of Limousin, Gilbert de Chabannes, Lord of Curton, to meet with Henry 'who has left Brittany in order to come over here, to entertain him, have him welcomed and housed in towns wherein he shall pass'. Through which towns Henry made his journey is not known, although the same day the French council issued a similar order to the bailiffs of Tou-raine to join with Chabannes and accompany him 'as long as the said Richmond be in Chartres, which is the place it was ordered he should be taken to'. Chartres was not the most direct route from Vannes to Montargis, but it may have been Henry's chosen place of rest after his flight across the border. A Monsieur de Sees and Guy de Laval were also sent to meet with Henry, along with a clerk carrying 2,000 francs, which were be distributed to Henry's men 'as he shall order'. By 4 November Henry had moved to Sens, sixty miles east of Montargis, and the French council further issued a commission for Monseigneur de La Heuze, 'to house Richmond's people in the town of Sens, up to the number of around 400, and have them given what utensils, supplies, as should be required, at a reasonable price'.

The previous day the French king had sent out a letter to towns across France describing how Henry and Jasper had come to him, 'accompanied by five or six hundred English, able to rally more as he should wish', intending to give their support 'and recover the Kingdom of England from the enemies of the French crown'. Acknowledging their service graciously, Charles had ordered for 'good and great provisions' to be made to them. When Henry finally arrived at Montargis, he was granted an audience with Charles VIII who 'promised him aid, and bade him to be of good cheer, for he would willingly show his goodwill'. According to the chronicler Jean Molinet, Henry was received at the French court with 'great joy'; 'he was very pleasant, an elegant character, and a fine ornament in the court of France, where he called himself King of England'. Henry was 'well loved and looked after' at the French court, Molinet remarked, though he added that Henry's welcome reception had been 'more so to irritate King Richard than by deference' to Henry himself.

When Richard discovered that Henry had fled to France, his first thought was to secure the English fortifications in the Calais pale, including the garrisons at Guisnes and Hammes Castle. For the past eleven years, Hammes had also acted as a prison for the Lancastrian magnate John de Vere, the Earl of Oxford, who finally had been arrested after his ill-fated attempt to seize St Michael's Mount in 1473. Despite the fact that the earl seems to have attempted suicide after Clarence's fall in 1478, jumping from the castle walls into the moat below, Richard knew that he could not risk the earl joining Henry Tudor now that Henry had managed to seek sanctuary in France. Throughout the 1460s, as a diehard Lancastrian, Oxford had fought to frustrate Edward IV's kingship. The earl's military reputation could hardly be in doubt; in spite of his defeat at Barnet, Oxford was one of the foremost soldiers of his generation, with the Crowland Chronicler referring to him as '*miles valentissimus*' or 'a most doughty knight'. Richard would have also understood the earl's personal animosity towards him; aside from his imprisonment, in December 1471, all of Oxford's lands had been granted to Richard. After Richard became king, he had granted Oxford's manors to his supporters, including twenty manors to the Duke of Norfolk. Richard had also forced his mother, the Countess of Oxford, to hand over her estates to him, reducing her to beggary and desperation, 'by heinous menace of loss of life and imprisonment'. If there was one man Richard would have hoped to keep under lock and key, it was Oxford.

On 28 October Richard sent a Calais guard, William Boulton, to transfer the earl back to England. By the time Boulton arrived at the garrison in Hammes, it was too late. Oxford had escaped; his 'escape' had involved taking with him both Sir James Blount, the captain of Hammes Castle who had been Oxford's guardian since 1476, and John Fortescue, 'the gentleman porter of Calais, suborned by the earl'.

The military implications of the defections could not have been more serious. Hammes was now held nominally in Henry's name by Blount's wife. Whereas Oxford's hatred of Richard's regime was understandable, much less comprehensible was the decision of Blount and Fortescue to defect to Tudor. It seems that James Blount's defection may have had its reasons in the current uncertainties of the times: Blount had been a servant of William, Lord Hastings, who had been captain of Calais from 1471 to his death in 1483. After his fall, Hastings had been replaced by Lord Dinham, while Hastings' brother Ralph was replaced by Blount's brother, John, Lord Mountjoy. However, Mountjoy fell seriously ill, and in March 1484 Ralph Hastings, returning to favour, was granted the reversion of Guisnes after Mountjoy's death. Perhaps Blount expected the office to be his: in any case, the fact that Richard was willing to overlook former Hastings men like Fortescue and Blount, suggested that as Richard's position grew stronger, they were both in danger of being replaced.

The Burgundian chronicler Jean Molinet alleged that another influence had been behind Sir James Blount's decision to free his captive and join Oxford in flight, with Thomas Stanley persuading Blount to release Oxford, sending messengers to the captain 'asking of him that he should free the Lord of Oxford with immediate effect, so that he could come to France' and join Henry.

Further bad news came closer to home when, on 2 November, it was reported that treasonous words had been spoken at Colchester by several gentlemen, including Sir John Risley, his servant William Coke, Sir William Brandon, the esquires William and Thomas Brandon, Sir William Stonor and a weaver, John Sterling, who were later all alleged to be conspiring with Henry Tudor and the Earl of Oxford. It was alleged that the conspirators had plotted the king's destruction, before taking a boat from Essex, making their way to Henry Tudor. Had they been in contact with the earl? Oxford certainly seems to have maintained contact with his friends in England. He later wrote of one such friend, William Page, that 'before the king's coming into this realm demeaned himself as well to his grace as unto his friends and was right loving to me and mine'. The links between the accused and Oxford were unmistakable: William Coke had been a servant of the earl's in 1471 and had even suffered in the service of his lord at the hands of one Gilbert Debenham. Sir John Risley had held office in Oxford's former lordship of Lavenham, while John Sterling was from Castle Hedingham, Oxford's ancestral home. Tellingly, Risley was a friend of John Fortescue, who joined Oxford in his flight from Hammes. The fact that the two men had now chosen to turn against Richard would have been a devastating blow for the king; Sir John Risley was a former esquire to the body of Edward IV, who had supported Richard in 1483. Equally, Fortescue's previous loyalty to the Yorkist regime had been impeccable; as sheriff of Devon and Cornwall, he had personally taken Oxford prisoner at St Michael's Mount.

When Henry discovered that Oxford had arrived at the French court, 'he was ravished with joy incredible'. Henry knew that he could trust Oxford 'more safely than in any other'. Previously, he had felt isolated among a growing community of Yorkists, whose dedication to his cause had stemmed from his opposition to Richard and 'by reason of the evil state of time', Henry had been their last hope. Oxford, by contrast, had always fought for the Lancastrian cause. Henry now had 'one of his own faction to whom he might safely commit all things'. There can be no doubt that Oxford's arrival marked a change in Henry's fortunes: for Vergil, it was a sign of 'God's assistance' and 'heavenly help'. For the first time, Henry could believe that his cause stood a chance, and he began 'to hope better of his affairs'. Nevertheless, Oxford's arrival would have surely proved difficult for some of Henry's new backers: Yorkists such as Thomas Grey, Marquess of Dorset, Sir

Edward Woodville and Giles Daubeney now had to come to terms with a man who had fought bitterly against the Yorkist regime and had steadfastly refused to accept Edward IV's kingship.

Henry had never met Oxford before, but he would have known that the earl brought not only military expertise. His previous stays in France in 1471 and 1473 would have left him acquainted with the French court. His diplomatic experience may have proved useful to Henry, especially in the regency administration of Charles VIII. Oxford's arrival with military reinforcements also proved to the French government that Henry was a credible candidate whom it would be worth supporting. Still an English invasion was expected to be imminent; backing for Henry Tudor might, they considered, help distract Richard from a campaign in France. Following Oxford's arrival and the defection of men from the Hammes garrison, on 17 November the French royal council authorised for 3,000 livre tournois to be granted to Henry 'to help him dress his people', adding cautiously, 'for this time only'. There was to be no repeat of the generous pensions offered by Duke Francis, as it would soon became clear to Henry that his presence at court was of entirely secondary concern to the Beaujeu government.

Oxford's first task was to return with some 'choice followers' to Hammes, which having been left in the command of Blount's wife had come under siege from the loyalist garrison of Calais headed by Lord Dinham, who spent £500 of his own money besieging its fortifications. On his arrival, Oxford pitched camp not far from the castle; after distracting Dinham's forces, Thomas Brandon and 'thirty stout men' managed to make their way into the castle through a secret passage which took them across a nearby marsh. Once inside the castle, renewing the fortifications and munitions, they 'pressed the enemy harder than usual from the walls, while Oxford attacked them no less vigorously from the rear'. Soon Dinham agreed to call a truce, allowing the entire garrison to depart with Oxford 'with all their goods'. After these gaining terms, Brandon and Oxford marched off with seventy-three men to rejoin Henry 'safe and sound'.

The Earl of Oxford's arrival at the French court not only transformed Henry's fortunes, encouraging the French government to place their support, however limited, in his cause, it was also to transform Henry's own ambitions. The earl quickly became one of Tudor's principal advisers, pressing his strong Lancastrian sympathies upon Henry to claim the crown as his right through his Lancastrian descent through his Beaufort inheritance. The Woodvilles and other Yorkist exiles, facing the prospect of a return to the old divisions and recriminations that a full Lancastrian revival might bring, must have looked on in horror.

The French government needed Henry to go further – in order to legitimise their own decision to grant their support, in their own eyes, Henry's claim had to be made far stronger. He would have to be considered the legitimate heir to the Lancastrian dynasty. Thrusting aside the realities of the complex web that was the English royal family tree, the French came up with their own solution. In his letter of 4 November setting out his reasons for giving Henry Tudor aid, Charles VIII simply declared that he did so for Henry was the '*fils de feu roy Henry d'Anglettere*': in other words, that he was the younger son of the dead Lancastrian king, Henry VI. The statement was as extraordinary as it was disingenuous. The French government clearly knew that Henry was nothing of the kind, understanding entirely the Tudors' origin; his uncle Jasper had been present at Louis XI's court between October 1469 and September 1470, while Louis himself had displayed a clear knowledge of both Henry and Jasper's trials in exile in his letter to Duke Francis II demanding their return. The French had previously recognised that Henry VI's only son was Prince Edward, who had stood as godfather to Charles VIII himself when he was younger at Amboise on 30 June 1470. A month later, France had agreed that in the event of the failure of Prince Edward to produce an heir, the English succession should fall on the Duke of Clarence and his heirs, with a treaty, the Act of Accord, signed in front of the entire French council.

Henry Tudor's limited claim to the throne was well understood by contemporaries on the Continent. As Commynes stated, 'Tudor was a member of the house of Lancaster, but he was not the closest claimant to the crown, whatever one may say about it, at least as far as I understand it'. Molinet remarked how Henry 'was quite far removed from the crown of England regarding his bloodline' yet he commented that 'however[,] he aspired to it very strongly later'. If Henry himself had doubts about the wisdom of claiming the throne both so directly and under false pretences, he remained silent: it was, he possibly considered, a price worth paying. Instead, buoyed on by Oxford and, according to Molinet, Thomas Stanley, who said that there were 'great and powerful lords, with others in great quality, allied together' who 'promised to make him the King of England would he go to Wales with an army', caught up in the enthusiasm of the moment, Henry seems to have been convinced by his inflated claim to the crown. The previous year, when he had embarked upon his first attempt at seizing the throne, there had been no mention of the royal title in Henry's correspondence, with the earl signing the receipt for his loan from Francis II as simply 'Henry de Richemont'. Now, sending out letters to England and Wales to those he hoped would support his cause, he inscribed them with the royal style 'H.R.' and sealed them with his own official signet. His readers could be under no doubt of Henry's royal pretensions:

> Right trusty, worshipful, and honourable good friends, and our allies, I greet you well. Being given to understand your good devoir and intent to advance me to the furtherance of my rightful claim due and lineal inheritance of the crown, and for the just depriving of that homicide and unnatural tyrant which now unjustly bears dominion over you, I give you to understand that no Christian heart can be more full of joy and gladness from the heart of me your poor exiled friend, who will, upon the instance of your sure advertise what powers ye will make ready and what captains and leaders you get to conduct, be prepared to pass over the sea with such forces as my friends are preparing for me. And if you have such good speed and success as I wish, according to your desire, I shall ever be most forward to remember and wholly to requite this your great and most loving kindness in my just quarrel.
>
> Given under our signet.
>
> H.R.

For someone seeking the crown, as Henry's letter patently made clear, Henry Tudor was prepared to make a radical break with tradition; neither Henry Bolingbroke in 1399 nor Edward IV in 1471 had declared their real intentions in advance of their landing, merely stating that they wished to be restored to their noble titles. Only Richard of York had been bold enough to assert his claim to the throne, a rash move that had backfired upon the duke. As his letter stated, Henry planned to invade England at some stage 'to the furtherance of my rightful claim due and lineal inheritance of the crown'; perhaps Henry had managed to agree a compromise with the Beaujeu regime, avoiding the ridiculous charade that he should be considered Henry VI's son, something which would have undoubtedly destroyed any shred of credibility in Henry's cause, but by claiming 'lineal inheritance' this would allow the French to continue their deception in their own minds. For Henry, and the audience who would have read the letter, it could only have meant his Beaufort descent through his mother, meaning a restoration of the Lancastrian dynasty. The wisdom of putting his claim into writing, at the same time as setting out the nature of that claim, would soon be questioned.

For Richard, whose nervousness about his rival's movements had increased since Henry's arrival in France, effectively placing him out of reach, discovering news of the letters provided the king with an opportunity to turn Henry's grandiose claims into his own propaganda attack. In August 1484 the king had hoped quite literally to bury the memory of the Lancastrian dynasty, ordering the body of Henry VI to be exhumed from Chertsey Abbey, where pilgrims had steadily flocked, convinced of the dead king's saintly powers, to be reburied at St George's chapel in Windsor. When it was disinterred, Henry's body apparently smelt 'very pleasantly scented'; it was 'certainly not from spices', one commentator observed, 'since he was buried by his enemies and butchers'. Leafing open the corpse's shroud, it was found to be 'for the most part' uncorrupted, 'the hair in place, and the face as it had been except it was a little sunken, with a more emaciated appearance than usual'.

Richard now hoped to bury Henry Tudor's chances of gaining support, exploit the uncertainties surrounding the Welshman's true intentions, that must have been circulating both at court and in the country at large: if Henry claimed rightful inheritance to the throne by his Lancastrian descent, would his succession mean that the clock would be turned back to 1471, or even earlier to 1460, annulling all royal grants of land and gifts of office that had taken place during the intervening years under the Yorkist dynasty? And what price would the French place upon their support of the young pretender? The last time France had sheltered the Lancastrians in exile, the cost had been the secret treaty of Chinon in 1462, in which the Lancastrians were willing to surrender Calais to the French in order to gain their support. Would Henry now do the same? No one could be sure exactly what shady deals might have been arranged in the anterooms of the French court.

On 7 December, Richard ordered his chancellor to prepare a proclamation against Henry Tudor. For the first time Richard was prepared to acknowledge the seriousness of the threat that his rival posed. Peter Courtenay, Bishop of Exeter, Thomas Grey, Marquess of Dorset, John, Earl of Oxford, Sir Edward Woodville and Jasper Tudor were all named as 'rebels and traitors disabled and attainted by authority of the high Court of parliament', adding for effect that 'many be known for open murderers, adulterers, and extortioners contrary to truth, honour and nature'. Having 'forsaken their natural Country', the proclamation continued, they had first sought protection from the Duke of Brittany, yet somewhat bizarrely, the proclamation declared they had promised the duke 'certain things which by him and his counsel were thought things too greatly unnatural and abominable for them to grant, observe, keep and perform. And therefore the same utterly refused.' In this rewriting of history, the rebels, 'seeing that the said duke and his counsel would not aid and succour them nor follow their ways', had chosen to depart in secret to France, where they had come 'under the obeisance of the king's ancient enemy Charles, calling himself King of France'. They now intended, Richard alleged,

to abuse and blind the commons of this said realm the said rebels and traitors have chosen to be their Captain one Henry late calling himself Earl of Richmond which of his ambitious and insatiable covetousness stirred and excited by the confederacy of the king's said rebels and traitors encroacheth upon him the name and title of the Royal estate of this Realm of England. Whereunto he hath no manner, interest, right or colour as every man well knoweth. And to the intent to achieve the same by the aid, support and assistance of the king's said ancient enemies and of this his Council of France to give up and release in perpetuity all the title and claim that kings of England have had and ought to have to the Crown and Realm of France.

According to the proclamation, Henry was prepared to give up all English claims to Normandy, Gascony, Calais, Guisnes and Hammes to France. If this was not enough, for good measure Richard was determined to play on the fear of the instability and terror that a forthcoming invasion might bring: 'the said Henry Earl of Richmond and all the others the king's rebels and traitors aforesaid have intended at their coming to do the most cruel murders, slaughters, robberies and disherisons that ever were seen in any Christian Realm'. If these 'inestimable dangers' were to be 'eschewed . . . to the intent that the king's said rebels and traitors may either be utterly put from their said malicious purposes or soon discomfited if they enforce to land', the king's subjects were 'like good and true English men to endeavour themselves at all their powers for the defence of themselves, their wives, children, goods and inheritances against the said malicious purposes and conspiracies which the ancient enemies of this land have made with the king's said rebels for the final destruction of the same land as is aforesaid'. Meanwhile, the proclamation ended on a note of reassurance, Richard as sovereign and 'a well willed, diligent and courageous prince . . . will put his most royal person to all labour and pain necessary in this behalf for the resistance and subduing of his said enemies, rebels and traitors to the most comfort, weal and surety of all and singular his true and faithful liegemen and subjects'.

The following day, despite the obvious difficulties that the wintry weather might bring to the proceedings, commissions of array were issued to most English counties, ordering that men be ready prepared upon half a day's notice in case a sudden alarm was raised of the rebels' invasion, with separate orders going out to the commissioners to perform a military census of the their local regions, with specific instructions set down from the king that 'they on the king's behalf thank the people for their true and loving dispositions shown to his highness in the last year for the surety and defence of his most royal person and of this his Realm against his rebels and traitors, exhorting them so to continue', before requiring that the commissioners should each 'diligently enquire' of every bailiff, constable and any other officer of towns or villages within their local area 'the number of persons sufficiently horsed, harnessed and arrayed as by every [one] of them severally were granted to do the king's grace service before the old commissioners whensoever his highness should command them'. Meanwhile coastal towns such as Harwich were placed on alert, with their defence being committed to Richard's loyal supporters.

For the moment, as musters began to be taken across the country, Richard was determined to enjoy the Christmas celebrations that year. As the twelve days of festivities passed, few failed to notice not only the luxury and the splendour of the celebrations, including the Crowland Chronicler, who observed that 'during this Christmas feast too much attention was paid to singing and dancing and to vain exchanges of clothing between Queen Anne and Lady Elizabeth'. For the Epiphany celebrations, Richard himself took a 'distinguished part' in the festivities, appearing wearing his crown in the great hall at Westminster, 'as though at his original coronation'.

The same day, as he returned to his chamber, Richard was informed by his 'naval spies' that 'in spite of his royal power and splendour, without any doubt, his enemies would invade the kingdom or make an attempt, as soon as the summer came'. Hearing the news, in a somewhat odd reaction, perhaps hiding his own anxieties, according to the Crowland Chronicler, Richard was apparently delighted, wanting 'nothing better than this' since he declared openly, victory 'would put an end to all his doubts and misfortunes'.

During the winter of 1484 and approaching 1485, Henry waited anxiously. Contrary to his initial hopes and warm words from Charles VIII, at the French court it was proving difficult to garner any kind of support that he might have previously hoped for. Having told his English supporters in exile that he intended to once more cross over the Channel as soon as he possibly could, further delay was scarcely an option. Polydore Vergil later related how, in order to reassure them, Henry 'was compelled to go and make earnest suit to every man particularly'. Yet Henry knew that while the French remained uncertain whether to support a fresh invasion, he would have little chance of success.

Charles VIII and his Beaujeu government had more pressing matters to deal with than preoccupy themselves with Henry's cause. Internal strife within France persisted as the tensions between Anne of Beaujeu and Louis of Orleans mounted. In early 1485 the Beaujeu government had been forced to leave Paris to establish their court at Montargis, leaving the capital in the hands of Louis of Orleans, who had begun to mount an increasingly hostile campaign against Anne of Beaujeu. In January Orleans announced his intention of 'liberating' Charles VIII from his sister Anne. French resources were also being drawn increasingly into Flanders, where since the death of Mary of Burgundy in 1482 the three Flemish towns of Ghent, Bruges and Ypres had gained physical control of the infant Archduke Philip, ruling the country in his name to the exclusion of Maximilian of Austria's claim to be regent of the region. Tensions remained high between both sides until war finally broke out in January 1485. A French army was sent into Flanders under Philippe de Crevecoeur, seigneur d'Esquerdes.

Desperate not to be left behind, Henry tagged along with the court and 'sought there to bring to pass his suit', requesting once again that Charles 'take him wholly to his tuition, so that if he and his confederates should be in safety they might all likewise also acknowledge the same received at his hand'. Henry's pleading worked: on 20 January Charles wrote from Montargis, stating that recently there 'came before us our very dear and well-beloved cousin Henry of Richmond, requiring help to recover the Kingdom of England which belongs to him, and considering the proximity of lineage between us, considering that it is the person in the world who has the most apparent right to the Kingdom of England, we will cater for him and his people for the time he spends here, and take the decision to help him in his business and deeds, which may amount to a large sum of money'.

Still, there was to be no guarantee of men, or money for that matter, without a royal decree and the permission of the Parlement in France. Henry's uncertainty would for the moment continue, as he agonised over his future direction; the chronicler Adrien de But caught the mood of speculation when, describing the mustering of an army under Esquerdes, he observed how some thought that it might be used for an attack on Calais, while others held that it was to assist Henry Tudor in his mission. In the end, it was sent to reinforce the Flemish towns against Maximilian.

Soon, contrary to the earlier reports that he had received, news reached Richard from his spies that Henry had been 'hindered amongst the French by reason of the time' and had grown 'weary with continual demand of aid, that he profited nothing, nor that anything went forward with him, but that all things which he diligently had devised fell out not well'. The king appeared with renewed confidence, 'as though he had vanquished the whole wars, and had been delivered from all fear', though, considering earlier reports that a landing would be planned for the summer, he remained convinced of the need to prepare for the defence of his kingdom.

First money would be needed. By late February Richard decided to finance the extra cost of military operations and defences by sending out urgent appeals for loans to his nobility and gentry. Royal commissioners were appointed and given a copy of a letter from the king, with which to approach potential lenders. 'Selected men were sent out . . . who extorted great sums of money from the coffers of persons of almost every rank in the kingdom, by prayers or threats, by fair means or foul'. The sums requested were as high as £200, though most were for £40, to be paid back at 'Martinmas next coming' (11 November). 'Assuring you that accomplishing this our instant desire and hearty prayer ye shall find us your good and gracious sovereign lord in any your reasonable desires hereafter'. With the prospect of Henry's invasion imminent, there must have been doubts that the king would honour his debts. The decision to raise a loan was bound to be unpopular – this Richard must have known, having abolished the practice of 'benevolences', so-called voluntary gifts to the king in the Parliament of 1484. That he still needed to do so suggests the king was in serious financial difficulties.

Royal servants were assigned counties and were issued with individual letters, containing the amount of money requested, but most were left with the names of the recipient blank, to be decided at their discretion. In Oxfordshire, Berkshire and Buckinghamshire, Richard Croft and Thomas Fowler were given thirteen blank letters and five addressed to specific gentry. They were also given a crib-sheet with formulae to persuade lenders to part with their money. The money was needed for the defence of the realm, something which 'every true Englishman' should agree. Commissioners were also advised to flatter their victims, approaching them with the weasel-like words that the king personally 'writeth to you before other, for the great love, confidence and substance that his grace hath and knoweth in you'. The first letters were sent out on 21 February, aiming to raise £9,000; in March letters to bishops and religious houses sought £4,390, further letters sent out represented a further £15,000. The response was disastrous. Some money drifted into the chamber – half of all loans that totalled £4,400 on the Easter receipt roll were likely from the commissioner's efforts – yet this represented but a fraction of what had been expected. Some men such as Roger Harecourt paid up, loaning 200 marks, though he had been asked for £200. The status of the commissioners chosen must have been partly to blame. Once again they were not local figures, and came from humble backgrounds, such as Walter Grant, a yeoman of the queen's chamber who was appointed a commissioner for Worcestershire, Warwickshire and Leicestershire.

Richard was also convinced that, since the debacle of Oxford's escape, urgent action would need to be taken to shore up his authority in the Calais garrisons. Sir James Blount's defection had called into question the suitability of Blount's elder brother Lord Mountjoy as Lieutenant of Guisnes; already seriously ill, on 22 January he was replaced by James Tyrell, a sign of the growing urgency with which Richard viewed the deteriorating situation. Tyrell had however been one of the king's main supporters in Wales, playing a leading role in the restoration of authority after Buckingham's fall. Now Tyrell was simply removed from his job there and ordered to reside in Guisnes. To compensate for his absence, Richard merely sent out orders to Welsh officials and gentry 'to accept' their absentee lord 'as their governor and leader as he hath been heretofore, notwithstanding that the king sendeth him to Guisnes'. Government was expected to continue by proxy.

Despite his efforts in besieging Guisnes, Lord Dinham was dismissed from his post as governor of Calais. On 11 March, in a sign of how few men the king could rely upon to defend the town, Richard appointed his illegitimate son John the captain of Calais and commander of its three fortresses; since John was under twenty-one, he was escorted there by Robert Brackenbury, with his authority ultimately wielded by a royal council.

If Richard was determined to prepare for every eventuality for the defence of his kingdom, he was equally convinced that he could erode Henry's morale and support base by winning back those disaffected Yorkists who had fled in exile after Buckingham's rebellion. Realising the potential backlash that Henry's ill-advised declaration of his Lancastrian claim might have upon those men who had previously fought against the Lancastrian regime and whose future welfare now seemed in doubt if Henry attempted to seize the throne, Richard believed that their reconciliation to his authority would be perfectly possible, especially since he had now managed to win over Elizabeth Woodville. Issuing promises of a pardon if they might return to the fold, his offer was met with considerable success; on 12 January Queen Elizabeth's brother Richard Woodville and John Fogge submitted themselves to the king, and were bound over for 1,000 marks to secure their pardons. Other former rebels soon followed, including Richard Haute, the Woodville kinsman Reginald Pympe, Roger Tocotes, Amyas Paulet and William Overdale. A general pardon was even offered to Elizabeth Blount and Thomas Brandon and thirty-seven men who had defected from the Hammes garrison. Robert Ratcliffe, who had sailed with Edward Woodville's fleet in 1483, was welcomed back to England and rewarded in April 1485 for 'good service to the king . . . in foreign parts'.

The greatest prize, however, came with the flight of Thomas Grey, the Marquess of Dorset from Henry's camp. Dorset had already received letters from his mother, pleading with him to return home. Now, faced with the prospect of his own authority over Henry being supplanted by the Lancastrian stalwart Oxford, Dorset had 'despaired of Henry's success' when according to Vergil he had 'been corrupted by Richard's promises'. In January 1485 Dorset sent his Portugese agent Roger Machado to Flanders, with instructions to meet the commander of the Flemish armies, Jacques de Savoie, who was battling against Maximilian's armies, possibly in the hope of securing a safe haven there. Suddenly, in the middle of the night, he fled the French court at Paris, aiming for Flanders. As soon as Henry discovered Dorset's escape, having most likely been informed by Machado, he was 'deeply disturbed'. Seeking Charles VIII's permission to have the marquess tracked down, every highway was immediately searched, until Humphrey Cheyney managed to hunt down Dorset in the town of Compiègne. Cheyney managed to 'persuade' the marquess to return to the French court, though it would be surprising if a threat of force had not been used. Dorset's attempted escape must have been a serious blow to Henry; for the moment, he must have been relieved that Dorset had failed in giving Richard the propaganda coup he had hoped for. More worrying, the marquess's escape had revealed the divisions in his own camp over which he was struggling to control and maintain discipline while the prospect of French support for an invasion remained a far-flung promise. Shaken by the entire episode and its potential consequences, Henry resolved that he could hardly trust Dorset again.

Confident of the appeal of his pardons, Richard even felt able to offer the same to John Morton, with the pardon granted under the Great Seal, a sign of the king's personal commitment to forgiveness. Richard had underestimated the bishop. Morton 'held him off by fair and wise excuses, till he had more experience of the sequel'. Meanwhile he made his way to Rome, where on 31 January his signature can be found in the register of the Santo Spirito fraternity. The purpose of Morton's visit seems likely to have been to seek a papal dispensation from Pope Innocent VIII for a marriage between Henry Tudor and Elizabeth of York, since both were descended from John of Gaunt. If Morton hoped that a marriage might still one day be possible, equally he had underestimated the king, for Richard was about to move to crush any chance of Henry Tudor marrying his intended bride.

THE SPIRAL OF DECLINE

•‑•‑

I t had been at the Christmas festivities at court when men began to
notice that something did not seem right. What caught the eye of
most spectators in particular had been 'the vain changes of dress, similar in colour and design, presented to Queen Anne and the Lady Elizabeth'. Since her release from sanctuary the previous March, Elizabeth
of York had spent her days at the king's court. Together with her sisters,
described by one chronicler as 'beauteous maidens', Elizabeth, on the
cusp of turning nineteen years old in February 1485, had grown into
a tall beauty with golden hair, the image of her mother. Her striking
presence was bound to have an effect, though the rumours that began
to circulate were unexpected nonetheless. According to the chronicler,
this 'caused the people to murmur and the noble and prelates greatly to
wonder thereat; while it was said by many that the king was bent, either
on the anticipated death of the queen taking place, or else, by means
of a divorce, for which he supposed he had quite sufficient grounds, on
contracting marriage with the said Elizabeth'.

Part of the rumour, it seemed, would soon be proved true: it was not
long after Christmas, the Crowland Chronicler recorded, that Queen
Anne 'fell extremely sick'. The queen grew increasingly frail, unable
to attend functions and ceremonies at court. The disease was possibly
tuberculosis, which would explain why Richard 'entirely shunned her
bed, declaring that it was by the advice of his physicians that he did
so'. While Anne lay sick in her bed, rumours of the queen's death had
begun to spread. According to Vergil, the queen had confronted Richard, blaming him for spreading them. The king's decision to 'forbare
to lie with her' and reports that he had begun 'to complain much unto
many noble men of his wife's unfruitfulness, for that she brought him
no children', fuelled the gossip that Richard wanted Anne dead. Yet

there seems no reason to doubt the king's genuine affection for 'his dearest consort' for whom, in the months of her disease, he made a grant of £300 to a university college which in the previous year he had decreed an annual Mass for their 'happy state'. As the agony of the queen's disease increased, Richard threw himself into the distraction of hawking, ordering commissions to be sent out on 8 and 11 March to search for falcons and other birds to be purchased 'at price reasonable in any place within this realm' as 'thought convenient for the king's disports', as well as sending five men abroad for the same purpose.

Just after nine o'clock on Wednesday 16 March, in the south-eastern sky the morning light began to darken as the sun began to disappear behind the curved shadow of the moon's disc, until its light had almost completely extinguished. For almost five minutes, darkness descended upon the world. An eclipse was considered an omen of the worst kind. Later that day the funereal toll of the great bell at Westminster began to resound, announcing the death of Queen Anne.

Anne was buried 'with no less honours than befitted the interment of a queen'. Just as soon as her embalmed body was lowered into the ground, fresh rumours began to circulate that Richard hoped to marry again – this time to Elizabeth of York. Richard was forced to deny in public 'in a loud and distinct voice' that 'such a thing had never once entered his mind', with the king convening a meeting of the mayor and citizens of London on 30 March at the priory of St John in Clerkenwell to denounce the accusations. The Crowland Chronicler believed the opposite to be the case, revealing that the king's own councillors 'very well knew to the contrary'. In particular, Sir Richard Ratcliffe and William Catesby, men 'to whose opinions the king hardly ever dared to offer any opposition', had warned Richard directly 'to his face' that if he did not repudiate the rumours that he might attempt to marry his niece in front of the mayor and commons of London, the consequences would be serve. The 'opposition would not be offered to him by merely the warnings of the voice,' they warned. 'For all the people of the north, in whom he placed the greatest reliance, would rise in rebellion against him, and impute to him the death of the queen, the daughter and one of the heirs of the Earl of Warwick, through whom he had first gained his present high position; in order that he might, to the extreme abhorrence of the Almighty, gratify an incestuous passion for his said niece'.

Twelve Doctors of Divinity were summoned to assert that no dispensation would ever be granted by the pope for such a marriage, 'in the ease of such a degree of consanguinity'. According to the chronicler, there were other reasons for Richard's advisers to fears such a marriage: if Elizabeth ever became queen, 'it might at some time be in her power to avenge upon them the death of her uncle, Earl Anthony, and her brother Richard, they having been the king's especial advisers in those matters'.

The king's denial did not prevent rumours from spreading across the country. These were clearly troubling to Richard, who was determined that they should be prevented from spreading beyond the capital. On 19 April a letter from the king, signed by him two weeks earlier, was read out at the Guildhall in York:

> Trusty and wellbeloved, we greet you well. And where it is so that divers seditious and evil disposed persons both in our city of London and elsewhere within this our realm, enforce themselves daily to sow seed of noise and slander against our person and against many of the lords and estates of our land to abuse the multitude of our subjects and avert their minds from us if they could by any means attain to that their mischievous intent and purpose; some by setting up of bills, some by messages, and sending forth of false and abominable language and lies, some by bold and presumptuous open speech and communication one with another, where through the innocent people which would live in rest and peace and truly under our obeisance, as they ought to do, [have] been greatly abused and oft times put in danger of their lives, lands and goods as often as they follow the steps and devises of the said seditious and mischievous persons to our great heaviness and pity; for remedy whereof and to the intent the truth openly declared should repress all such false and contrived inventions, we now of late called before us the mayor and aldermen of our city of London together with the most sad and discreet persons of the same city in great number, being present many of the lords spiritual and temporal of our land, and the substance of all our household, to whom we largely showed our true intent and mind in all such things . . . where we also at the same time gave straightly in charge as well to the said mayor as to all other our officers, servants

and faithful subjects wheresoever they be, that from henceforth as
often as they find any person speaking of us or any other lord or
estate of this our land otherwise than is according to honour, truth
and the peace and restfulness of this our realm, or telling of tales
and tidings whereby the people might be stirred to commotions and
unlawful assemblies, or any strife and debate arise between lord and
lord or us and any of the lords and estates of this our land, they take
and arrest the same persons . . . the furnisher, author and maker
of the said seditious speech and language be taken and punished
according to his deserts, and that whosoever first find any seditious
bill set up in any place he take it down and without reading or showing the same to any other person bring it forthwith unto us or some
of the lords or other of our council . . .

It seems highly implausible that Richard would have wished to
marry his own niece, whom he himself had declared illegitimate eighteen months before. But the king was planning to marry again, as soon
as he possibly could. He was also planning for Elizabeth of York's marriage. Already he had arranged for her sister Cecily to be married to
Sir Ralph Scrope, a younger brother of Thomas, Baron Scrope who
was nevertheless looked down upon as ' a man less than her in rank'; he
now began to negotiate a marriage for Elizabeth with the cousin of the
Portugese king, John II, Manuel Duke of Beja who would later become
King Manuel I. Less than a week after his wife's death on 22 March
Richard sent Sir Edward Brampton, a converted Portugese Jew, to the
Portugese court to offer the king's hand in marriage to King John's
elder sister, the Infanta Joana. In arranging this double marriage, Richard was conscious that he might be able to destroy Henry Tudor's claim
to be the sole descendent to the Lancastrian dynasty, since the living
descendents of Henry IV's sister Philippa, who had married John I of
Portugal, were to be found in the Portugese royal family. The Portugese
Council of State clearly understood the king's reasons for the marriage,
stating that the union between Richard and the infanta would unite
'as one the party of Lancaster, and York – which are the two parties of
that kingdom out of which the divisions and evils over the successions
are born'. By marrying off Elizabeth of York at the same time as marrying the Lancastrian heiress Joana 'straight away', Richard knew that

he was in reach of defeating the challenge that Henry Tudor posed; as the Crowland Chronicler observed, 'it appeared that in no other way could his kingly power be established, or the hopes of his rival be put an end to'.

Polydore Vergil reported in the manuscript of his history that Henry was at Rouen while a fleet was still being equipped at Harfleur when the rumour reached him that Richard was planning to marry Elizabeth of York. Henry was 'suddenly seized by anxiety'; unable to decide what to do, being 'in two minds', he spoke of his fears only to the Earl of Oxford. Confiding in the Earl of his 'great quandary', Henry understood that if Richard did marry Elizabeth, his plans for a union between the houses of Lancaster and York would be thrown into jeopardy. Henry also believed that he would be unable to marry any of her younger sisters 'for reasons of prestige'; if he did not, however, he would face the prospect that 'all Edward's friends would abandon him'. It was clear that Henry, approaching his one Lancastrian confidant in secrecy, felt constrained by his Yorkist supporters, whose agenda for supporting the earl was to restore one of Edward IV's children to the throne, rather than lend their wholehearted support to himself alone. Already the Marquess of Dorset's attempted defection had shaken Henry's faith in his Woodville supporters; he recognised that if Richard managed to marry Elizabeth of York, the king's reconciliation with the Woodvilles would be complete, leaving him without any hope of claiming the throne without their support.

Oxford, perhaps with an eye for obtaining an entirely Lancastrian succession, agreed that the price of abandoning a Woodville marriage would likely result in further defections. After a protracted discussion, both agreed that 'another marriage affinity should be sought as a way of acquiring prestige'. Their chosen candidate was Katherine Herbert, a sister of William Herbert, the Earl of Huntingdon, both of whom Henry had known growing up in Herbert's father's household at Raglan in the early 1460s. According to Vergil's manuscript history, in a sentence the Italian thought later wise to delete, Henry knew Katherine 'well and loved'. William Herbert himself had been married to a Woodville, which may have also influenced Henry's thinking if he hoped to retain any of his Yorkist exiles. Whether Henry would succeed in gaining Herbert's support seems doubtful. On Richard's accession, William Herbert had been a staunch supporter of Richard during Buckingham's rebellion. He was rewarded for his loyalty with his appointment as justiciar of South Wales and steward of the Duchy of Lancaster lands there, in addition to being appointed chamberlain of the Prince of Wales. Herbert's elevation to royal favour was confirmed with his betrothal to Richard's illegitimate daughter Katherine, that brought with it a landed endowment worth around £1,000 a year.

Despite the earl's newfound favour, the Herbert family must have been aggrieved that their previous authority in Wales, when the first Earl of Pembroke had been regarded as Edward IV's 'master lock', had not been restored under Richard. During the later years of Edward's reign, the family became involved in violent clashes with the Vaughan family, and the second earl had been forced to surrender his earldom with its accompanying Welsh lands, receiving instead the title of Earl of Huntingdon, with a smaller landed endowment in Somerset and Dorset. If William Herbert had hoped to restore to his family their coveted Earldom of Pembroke, Richard's new grants of land were instead located in the south-west, confirming Edward IV's decision to move the family influence outside of Wales. Perhaps Henry believed that with the Earldom of Pembroke also nominally held by his uncle Jasper, he might be able to buy their support by offering to restore the family to the title.

Since his days at Raglan, Henry understood the network of alliances that the Herberts surrounded themselves with. The family were linked through marriage to Henry Percy, Earl of Northumberland, a nobleman of a similar age to Henry Tudor; he had grown up with Northumberland as childhood friends when they had both been wards at Raglan castle. Later Northumberland had married one of Katherine's sisters, Maud Herbert, in 1472. Henry hoped that through the prospect of a Herbert marriage and his former youthful friendship, Northumberland might come to his aid.

It seems surprising that Henry would have considered Northumberland a candidate for supporting his cause, especially since the earl had been instrumental in placing Richard upon the throne, colluding in Rivers's execution. For his pains, Northumberland had been rewarded handsomely: appointed to the royal office of great chamberlain, he had also been rewarded with the cherished de Brian inheritance, which included lands in Devon, Dorset, Gloucester, Kent, Somerset, Suffolk and Surrey. In his homeland of the north, he was granted vast influence of power as the king's representative as warden-general of the Marches, the office of captain of the Berwick garrison worth a staggering £5,000 a year in salary, as well as being granted the lordship of Holderness, confiscated from the Duke of Buckingham, which was worth over £1,000 a year.

Yet the grants of office, wealth and land could not hide the fact that the earl felt his traditional Percy authority in the north constantly undermined by the king. Whatever Richard might have promised him, Northumberland had known for a long time that his influence in the north would always be curtailed by a king whose own northern interests threatened to undermine his ability to raise an affinity and attract men to his side. After the fall of the Earl of Warwick, Richard had been granted a large share of the Neville patrimony around which he quickly sought to construct his own powerbase. He soon fell into conflict with local noblemen such as Northumberland, who felt that Richard was drawing his own men away from him, with retainers who had previously pledged their loyalty to the earl taking offices and fees from Richard instead. This conflict of loyalties eventually had to be resolved by Edward IV, who summoned both men to his council at Nottingham in 1474, to hammer out an agreement between the two men. As a result, Northumberland had promised to be Richard's 'faithful servant' and to do him service 'at all times lawful and convenient', while Richard pledged in turn to be the earl's 'good and faithful lord at all times, and to sustain him in his right afore all other persons'. He would 'not ask, challenge, nor claim any office or offices or fee that the said earl hath of the king's grant, or of any other person or persons . . . nor interrupt the said earl nor any of his servants in executing or doing of any of the said office or offices by him or any of his servants in time to come'. Richard was not to accept or retain any servant that had previously been 'retained of fee, clothing or promise' by the earl. Nevertheless, the agreement could only have been viewed by Northumberland as nothing other than a compromise by the Yorkist brothers, whose regime threatened to freeze out his influence in the north.

Northumberland had been wrestling with these tensions when in exile Henry had attempted to contact the earl. According to Vergil's manuscript, Henry sent Christopher Urswick to discuss a possible alliance with Northumberland 'as quickly as possible'. When Urswick arrived in the north, however, he could find 'nobody to whom he dare pass on the commission to the earl' and was forced to return to Paris 'without accomplishing anything'. Later, when he came to write up his printed work, Vergil glossed over the fact that there seems to have been no appetite for the match or for Northumberland's support, claiming instead that 'the roads were so blocked that not one of them could get through to him'. Nevertheless it is possible that Henry had not given up on his belief that his old friend might eventually provide support to his cause.

Still the slow drip of defections to his camp gave Henry some hope. During the spring, he was joined at the French court by 'very many Englishmen, who either did flock continually out of England', including William Berkeley of Beverstone, who had already been pardoned once by Richard in March 1484 after his uncle and his brother-in-law had provided 1,000 marks in the promise of his good behaviour; they lost their money. Other converts to his cause included those Englishmen 'studious of learning' in the French city, studying at the university there. Among them was Richard Fox, described by Vergil as 'a man distinguished for both his good moral qualities and his good brain'. Henry was soon impressed by 'outstanding loyalty'; coming to quickly trust the young man, he took Fox into his service, making him 'a sharer of his plans and kept him always in his secrets', including his plans for 'the other marriage tie'.

As Richard struggled to contain the damaging rumours surrounding the queen's death and the accusations that he had hoped to marry his own niece, his authority seemed to be ebbing away. With no other men than his northern supporters to turn to, he was becoming a victim of his own decision to focus too much power in too few hands. It seemed as if the king's men, alien to the southern heartlands they had been rewarded with, were regarded, and often acted, as invading foreigners. An enquiry in the New Forest would later find that 500 deer had been killed in Richard's reign by 'the northern men'. Soon, as resistance to their enforced rule increased, some had begun to take the law unto their own hands, with Sir Ralph Ashton's sons being forced to seize land in

Kent. Ashton himself, a Lancashire man, had acquired a reputation for brutality that had earned him the nickname of the 'Black Knight' not only on account of his black armour, but for his ruthless punishments meted out after Buckingham's rebellion, when Richard had given him the power to try treason cases 'without formalities or appeal'. Tradition records that he sentenced his victims to being rolled downhill in barrels filled with spikes. Yet he remained an indispensable upholder of Richard's kingship: on 29 April 1485 Ashton was appointed a vice-constable to proceed against and try crimes of *lèse-majesté* 'summarily and plainly without noise and show of judgement on simple fault'. As instances of rebellion began to increase, Richard was determined to make an example of those who crossed his authority. This time there were to be no further pardons. Sir Roger Clifford, captured near Southampton, was tried and condemned to death at Westminster, to be executed on Tower Hill. Passing the sanctuary of St Martin's le Grand on his journey to meet his death, he nearly succeeded in escaping when his confessor and crowds nearby almost dragged him to safety, but the king's officers shouted for help; brought under restraint he was taken to the block. To those watching, it merely confirmed the growing suspicions that Richard was a tyrant, leading a merciless regime.

These demonstrations of power proved in vain, as even Richard's own household had begun to make their own individual decisions to leave the king's side. John Mortimer, an esquire of the king's body seems to have defected to Henry around February 1485; Peter Curteys, the Keeper of the Wardrobe, who had furnished Richard for his coronation procession, fled into sanctuary at Westminster in May.

Rumours now 'grew daily' that Henry and his followers were 'making haste and speeding up the plans for their invasion of England'. Welsh bards wrote poems, celebrating Henry Tudor's hoped-for return. According to the poet Robin Dhu, 'This is the time for our deliverance, the time for our little bull to venture forth . . . There is a longing for Harry, there is hope for our nation.' Another poet, Gruffydd ap Dafydd Fychan, looked forward to 'the youth from Britanny' defeating 'the Saxons'. Others believed that the Thames would run red with Saxon blood, a gruesome image taken from Merlin's prophecy in Geoffrey of Monmouth's *Historia Regum Britanniae*.

Richard ordered further preparations for the urgent defence of his kingdom, stockpiling weapons. On 15 March 1485 the constable of the Tower, Sir Robert Brackenbury, was paid £215 7s 5d for money owed to him for performing his duties, including 'the provision and reparation of our ordnances and artilleries' there. Fifty bows, a hundred sheaves of arrows, a barrel of gunpowder, fifty armed spears and three carts of ordnance were ordered from the Tower on 29 March for the defence of Harwich. On 12 May a warrant was sent to Calais, requesting two barrels of gunpowder, three hundredweight of lead and two serpentines.

Yet Richard remained uncertain if an invasion would take place, and where exactly Henry planned to land. His spies were unable to provide 'any certain information'. Richard's spies were at least correct that events were moving fast at the French court. While the court was at Evereux, news reached Charles VIII that the Duke of Orleans' rebellion had collapsed. Both Orleans and his ally Dunois had been raising troops in the Duchy of Alençon, but the decision was taken to disband any force gathered. On 23 March reconciliation took place between the Beaujeu government and Orleans. Almost overnight, France's preoccupations shifted from their own internal problems to the threat of a hostile invasion from the alliance between Brittany, Richard and Maximilian. Finally, France was ready to embrace Henry Tudor's cause for the sake of distracting England from attempting any hostile actions against them.

Still the French continued their charade that their pretender had a direct right to the English crown. When the court returned to Rouen, Charles VIII ordered that Henry should be treated as a prince of the blood in all public ceremonies. In the surviving accounts of Charles VIII's official entry into the city on 14 April, there is clear evidence of Henry's royal pretensions as dictated by the French king: Henry was described in the record as 'The Count of Richemont, they say the King of England'.

The royal ceremonies performed at the French court must have had a profound effect upon Henry, who observed as he rode into Rouen several pageants that had been deliberately organised on the roadside. Each had been crafted to express the hope and expectation that the young king Charles VIII brought to the realm, above all stressing his divine rights and authority as king to rule. One featured the anointing of Solomon, the king being played by a 'handsome and fair-haired boy representing our sovereign', who was wearing an azure robe decorated with sparkling fleurs-de-lis. Further along, another pageant again featured a young boy, this time appearing dressed as Constantine, both before and after his conversion to Christianity, with the transformation being represented by an official crowning, with his fleur-de-lis surcoat being changed for the dress of a crusader. For the first time, he experienced at first hand the hypnotic aura of the majesty and royal authority to which he himself aspired.

As preparations began to equip a fleet intended for his invasion at Harfleur in the mouth of the Seine, Henry was treated as if he were a king in exile. Two weeks later, when Henry attended the cathedral at Rouen on 28 April, walking beside members of the French royal family, he was styled 'princeps Anglie', though the clearest indication of Henry's new-found authority as a prince of royal blood came in the official order of the procession marking the feast of the Ascension on 12 May, where Henry, again being given the rank of 'princeps Anglie', walked behind the three French princes of the blood, the Dukes of Orleans, Bourbon and Lorraine.

The week before, Charles VIII had called upon the French equivalent of Parliament, the Estates, for further financial assistance for Henry Tudor's projected invasion. Since the previous meeting of the Estates, Charles stated, there had 'come to us our dear and beloved cousin the Count of Richmond, requiring help to recover the Kingdom of England which belongs to him, and whom in consideration of the close lineage we have in common, also considering that he is of all the people in the world the one with the most apparent claim to the throne of England, we have funded his and his people's stay for as long as he should remain here, do favour him in his deeds and businesses: that funding to our cousin and his people will reach great sums of money'. Still, with France remaining committed to supporting the Flemish towns against the might of Archduke Maximilian's onslaught, money remained tight. Yet within weeks the French army sent to Flanders found itself on the back foot; in June Maximilian had taken Bruges, with Ghent falling in July. It would be this collapse of French ambitions in Flanders, combined with the threat of an invasion by the English, that saw Charles VIII issuing orders on 25 June to mobilise forces against a possible

Anglo-Breton attack and finally pushed the French government into giving their unequivocal support to Henry Tudor.

During the spring of 1485, either out of respect or in mourning for the late queen, Richard chose to remain a recluse, hiding away at his court and shunning official ceremonies such as the annual Garter feast at St George's chapel on 23 April, preferring instead to send Lord Maltravers in his place. On 12 May, on the feast of the Ascension, Richard silently departed the capital for Windsor, before making his way to Kenilworth Castle in Warwickshire. On the evening of Wednesday 2 June, on the eve of the feast day of Corpus Christi, Richard chose to make a personal excursion, riding out together with his entourage to Coventry, where he had chosen to watch the Corpus Christi celebrations in the city.

The previous year Richard had attended the Corpus Christi celebrations at York. He must have mused upon what a difference a year had made. Then his wife and queen had been by his side. Now he was alone. Watching the celebrations, he would have seen the host being carried in its monstrance through Coventry's streets, followed by burning torches and incense, the ringing of the sanctus bell, and the priest walking beneath a canopy of rich cloth, robed in a cope, his arms and shoulders veiled. Pausing at certain 'stations' along the route, so that the bearers of the host could rest, dramatic interludes were performed; Coventry would later become celebrated for its own pageants, comprising at least ten plays, including the Shearmen and Tailors' pageant, and a nativity play that included a portrayal of the Massacre of the Innocents. Watching these, perhaps the king mused on the irony of the fates of his own 'innocents', the sons of Edward IV, about whose mysterious disappearance Richard remained tight-lipped, refusing to acknowledge their fates.

Richard had returned to Kenilworth by Monday 6 June, but three days later he had decided to ride northwards to his castle at Nottingham. The formidable fortress, built on an impregnable natural sandstone outcrop riddled with secret tunnels, dominated its surroundings with a view that stretched across to the distant horizon. It was a favourite residence of the Yorkists: between 1476 and 1480 Edward had spent over £3,000 on the castle, improving its living quarters with a new tower. In 1474 Richard Patyn had been commissioned to arrange the carriage of artillery to the castle, for which he was paid 4d a day for its custody. Richard had made alterations to the great tower, adding a timber loft with bow windows to make it, in the Tudor antiquary John Leland's words, 'the most beautiful part and gallant building for lodging'. Richard had last been here the previous summer, with his wife, when they had received news of his son's death. Tradition records that Richard referred to the castle as his 'castle of care', perhaps in reference to the solace he found there recovering from the traumatic news of the death of his heir. Now he returned to prepare for war.

Rumours had been 'increasing daily that those who were in arms against the king were hastening to make a descent upon England'. Yet despite the best efforts of his network of spies on the Continent, Richard still did not know at which port Henry might attempt to land. Prophesies and rumours suggested that Henry would land at 'Milford', but since Richard could not be certain whether this meant in Wales or at the port on the south coast, Lord Lovell was sent to Southampton to refit the royal fleet 'with all possible speed' and keep a 'strict watch upon all the harbours in those parts . . . if the enemy should attempt to effect a landing there, he might unite all the forces in the neighbourhood, and not lose the opportunity of attacking them'. Richard's decision to withdraw to Nottingham, into the centre of his kingdom, must be seen in the context of the prevailing uncertainty of where Henry's invasion might materialise. Like a spider in the middle of its web, Richard intended to be ready to subsume his rival, no matter in which corner of the realm he might attack.

Though Henry's invasion plan remained far from certain, Richard was taking no chances. The entire country would need to be placed on a war footing. It was at Nottingham Castle that on 21 June Richard signed a warrant for a second proclamation against Henry, to be issued two days later. The text remained mostly unchanged from the proclamation he had issued in late 1484, with the exception that Thomas, Marquess of Dorset's name had been removed, a clear sign that Richard remained committed to reconciliation with the Woodvilles. Still present were the charges that Henry was receiving French backing, and intended in return to give up the English claims to the French kingdom, but instead of briefly mentioning Henry as he had previously done as being 'late Earl of Richmond', Richard launched a full attack on his rival's parentage and legitimacy, claiming he was a man sprung from an illegitimate bed:

Henry Tydder, son of Edmund Tydder, son of Owen Tydder, which of his ambitiousness and insatiable covetousness encroacheth and usurped upon him the name and title of royal estate of this Realm of England, where unto he hath no maner interest, right, title, or colour, as every man well knoweth; for he is descended of bastard blood both of father side and of mother side, for the said Owen the grandfather was bastard born, and his mother was daughter unto John, Duke of Somerset, son unto John, Earl of Somerset, son unto Dame Kateryn Swynford, and of her in double avourty [adultery] gotten, whereby it evidently appeareth that no title can nor may be in him, which fully intendeth to enter this Realm, purposing a conquest. And if he should achieve his false intent and purpose, every man his life, livelihood, and goods should be in his hands, liberty and disposition, whereby should ensue the disinheriting and destruction of all the noble and worshipful blood of this Realm forever, and to the resistance and withstanding whereof every true and natural Englishman born must lay to his hands for his own surety and weal.

The theme of destruction also took on a greater sense of urgency than before, with Richard intent to emphasise that no one would escape the retribution that would take place if Henry's invasion were successful. No man, he claimed, would be spared:

And in more prove and showing of his said purpose of conquest, the said Henry Tidder hath given as well to divers of the said King's enemies as to his said rebels and traitors, archbishoprics, bishoprics, and other dignities spiritual, and also the duchies, earldoms, baronies, and other possessions and inheritances of knights, squires, and gentlemen, and other the King's true subjects within the Realm, and intendeth also to change and subvert the laws of the same, and to enduce and establish new laws and ordinances amongst the King's said subjects. And over this, and beside the alienations of all the premises into the possession of the King's said ancient enemies to the greatest aneantisement [reducing to nothing], shame, and rebuke that ever might fall to this said land, the said Henry Tydder and others, the King's rebels and traitors aforesaid, have extended [intended] at their coming if they may be of power, to do the most cruel murders, slaughters, and robberies, and disherisons that ever were seen in any Christian realm.

For the which, and other inestimable dangers to be eschewed, and to the intent that the King's said rebels, traitors, and enemies may be utterly put from their said malicious and false purpose and soon discomforted, if they enforce to land, the King our sovereign Lord willeth, chargeth, and commandeth all and everyche of the natural and true subjects of this his Realm to call the premises to their minds, and like good and true Englishmen to endeavour themselves with all their powers for the defence of them, their wives, children, and goods, and heriditaments against the said malicious purposes and conspiracies which the said ancient enemies have made with the King's said rebels and traitors for the final destruction of this land as is aforesaid. And our said sovereign Lord, as a well willed, diligent, and courageous Prince, will put his most royal person to all labour and pain necessary in this behalf for the resistance and subduing of his said enemies, rebels and traitors to the most comfort, weal, and surety of all his true and faithful liegemen and subjects.

Richard ended the proclamation by commanding that 'all his said subjects to be ready in their most defensible array to do his Highness' service of war, when there be open proclamation, or otherwise shall be commanded so to do, for the resistance of the King's said rebels, traitors and enemies'. That came the following day, 22 June, when Richard took the decision to reissue the Commissions of Array that he had sent out the previous December. This time, however, a sense of urgency ran through his letter to the commissioners sent out from his castle at Nottingham. 'Forasmuch as certain information is made unto us,' he wrote to the commissioners, 'that our Rebels and traitors associated with our ancient enemies of France and other strangers intend hastily to invade this our Realm purposing the destruction of us, the subversion of this our Realm and disinheriting of all our true subjects.' They were to muster their soldiers 'in all haste possible' after receiving the letter, 'according to our instructions which we send unto you at this time with these our letters. And that this be done with all diligence':

First. Forasmuch as the King's good grace understandeth by the report of his Commissioners and other the faithful dispositions and readiness that his subjects be of, to do him service and pleasure to the uttermost of their powers for the resisting of his rebels, traitors and enemies. The King's highness therefore will that his said Commissioners shall give on his behalf especial thankings unto his said subjects, exhorting them so to continue.

Item, that the said Commissioners in all haste possible review the soldiers late mustered before them by force of the King's commission to them late directed, and see that they be able persons, well horsed and harnessed to do the King service of war. And if they be not to put other able men into their places and that the money granted and gathered for the waging of them in towns, townships, villages or hundreds be ready in the hands of the constables, bailiffs or other sufficient persons to be delivered for the cause aforesaid when the case shall require.

Item, that the said Commissioners on the King's behalf give straightly in commandment to all knights, squires and gentlemen to prepare and ready themselves in their proper persons to do the King service upon an hour warning when they shall be commanded by proclamation or otherwise. And that they fail not so to do upon the peril of lessening of their lives, lands and goods. And that they be attending and awaiting upon such Captain or Captains as the King's good grace shall appoint to have the rule and leading of them and upon others.

Item, that the Commissioners make proclamation that all men be ready to do the King service within an hour warning whensoever they be commanded by proclamation or otherwise.

Item, to show to all lords, noblemen, Captains and others that the King's noble pleasure and commandment is that they truly and honourably – all manner [of] quarrels, grudges, rancours and unkindness laid apart – attend to execute the King's commandment, and every one of them to be loving and assisting the other in the King's quarrel and cause, showing them plainly that whosoever attempt the contrary, the King's grace will so punish him that all other shall take example by him.

The same day, a further letter was sent from Richard to every sheriff, ordering that upon receiving their instructions from the commissioners of array, they were to remain within their shire town or at least ensure that their deputy was present, 'where ye or he shall be surely found for the performing and fulfilling of such things as on our behalf as by our said Commissioners ye shall be commanded to do. Not failing hereof in any ways, as ye will answer unto us at your uttermost peril.' Only one text of an individual 'commission' survives, which Richard had sent to the county of Gloucester in 1484, though the instructions must have been the same for each county and would have likely remained unchanged when reissued:

For the safety and defence of our kingdom of England against the malice of rebels and our foreign enemies who intend to attack various parts of our said kingdom near the coast, we have appointed you jointly and separately to array and inspect all and singular men-at-arms and all other defensible men, both light horsemen and archers, dwelling within the said county, and when they have been arrayed and inspected in such array, to cause them to be set and put in thousands, hundreds and scores or otherwise as may be convenient and necessary, and lead them or cause them to be led to our presence with all possible speed to attack and expel the aforesaid rebels and enemies from time to time as the need arises from imminent peril. Also to hold and superintend diligently the muster or review of the same men-at-arms, light horsemen and archers from time to time as need shall arise. And we enjoin and command you and each one of you as strictly as we may that on the sight of these presents you will at once cause to be armed and arrayed and to come before you all and singular the defensible and able-bodied men of the said county and array and arm them according to their grades and ranks and when they have been thus arrayed and armed, to keep them in such array.

Commissions of array were the principal means by which kings were able to recruit forces for the defence of the realm. They had their origin in the obligations owed by men both living in shires and boroughs to give armed support to the king, dating back to Anglo-Saxon times. The arrangement was formalised during the thirteenth century, when the Statute of Winchester in 1285 set down the types of arms that men who owned goods or chattels of differing values were required to own in readiness in case they were called for service. The Statute described how:

Each man between the ages of fifteen and sixty shall be assessed and sworn to arms on a scale according to the value of his lands or chattels. Those who have lands to the value of £15, or chattels to the value of 40 marks, shall provide themselves with a hauberk, a cap of iron, a sword, a dagger, and a horse; those with lands to the value of £10, or chattels to the value of 20 marks, a hauberk of mail, cap, sword and dagger; land to the value of £5, a parpoint [padded doublet], cap of iron, sword, bow, arrows, and a dagger. Anyone whose lands are of less value than £2 shall be sworn to provide gisarmes [long-handled weapons with a curved blade and spike], daggers, and other cheap weapons; and similarly those with chattels of less value than 20 marks shall be sworn to provide swords, daggers, and other cheap weapons. Anyone else who can afford them shall keep bows and arrows, if resident outside a forest, and bows and bolts if resident within one.

Once all able-bodied men had assembled, grouped under their shires or boroughs, they were first sworn to allegiance. Leading members of the gentry, preferably knights with military experience, were appointed to raise individual companies for each shire, and to ensure that recruits were properly equipped, clothed, mounted and received pay. In 1327, in the face of rising costs as a result of increasingly sophisticated armour, a statute clarified that levies would only be expected to meet the costs of their arms as set down by the Winchester statute, while in 1343 it was agreed that men could be exempted from service if they paid a fine. In 1402 these statutes were once again confirmed, making clear that individuals would not have to meet their own costs and would receive wages for their service.

Once commissions had been sent out, all sheriffs, mayors, bailiffs, constables and officers were expected to assist the commissioners with their recruitment, issuing proclamations that every man between fifteen and sixty was 'to be ready in their said harness'. Constables of hundreds searched for all inhabitants 'of ability and harnessed to serve' in order to draw up a muster roll – a list of names and what weapons each man was able to bring with them.

Few of these documents have survived; however, a muster roll held at Bridport in Dorset in September 1457 reveals that 180 men with 'harness' presented themselves for inspection before the town's two bailiffs and constables. Around a hundred presented themselves with some form of arms; two-thirds of those had just a bow and sheaf of arrows, while seventy possessed further armour or weapons, including poleaxes, glaives, spears, axes, custills (two-edged daggers), bills, staves, a hanger (a short sword) and a gun. Some had incomplete pieces of armour that included harbergeons (jackets of mail or scale armour), pairs or gauntlets and brigandines (metal plate armour on material), leg harnesses and a kettle hat. Only ten owned the complete equipment expected for a man-at-arms: a sallet, a jack, sword, buckler and dagger, while another twelve lacked a buckler and dagger. One man was exceptionally equipped with two sallets, two jacks, three bows with sheaves, two poleaxes, two glaives and two daggers, but those whom the bailiffs considered of sufficient wealth to provide for additional equipment or arms (more shields, bucklers and sallets were required, while some men were required to double the number of arrows carried) were ordered to produce new equipment within two weeks, under pain of fine.

The Bridport muster roll indicates that the weapon of choice for most men was the bow and arrow. Another list of eighty men, complied for Sir William Stonor by constables of Ewelme in Oxfordshire, noted the preferred weapon of choice for their men, drawing up lists of archers, sometimes noted as 'good' archers, or whether they fought with a bill or staff (and whether they were 'able' at using it or not). Precise information was therefore available not only regarding the quality of weaponry that an area might present, but the quality of men that were to use it. The dependence on archery is understandable. As Sir John Fortescue argued in *The Governance of England*, completed in the 1470s, the might of England 'standith most upon archers, which be no rich men'. 'In my opinion archers are the most necessary thing in the world for an army', wrote Commynes, 'though they should be counted in thousands, for in small numbers they are almost useless'. The archer's rate of fire, which could reach ten or twelve arrows a minute compared to a crossbowman's two, led to the saying 'thicker than arrows in an English battle'. At archery, the English remained internationally renowned. They were 'the world's best', according to Commynes, while the Italian cleric Dominic Mancini, visiting England in 1482–3, was genuinely impressed by the sight of English archers mustered by Richard. 'Their bows and arrows are thicker and longer than those used by other nations just as their arms are stronger than other peoples', for they seem to have hands and arms of iron', he wrote. 'As a result their bows have as long a range as our crossbows. Almost every man has a helmet and each carries an iron shield and a sword which is as long as our sword, but heavy and thick as well.'

In announcing an immediate commission of array and muster of men throughout the kingdom, Richard was relying upon a centuries-old mechanism by which a king might prepare his kingdom for war. Throughout the civil wars, commissions of array had been used by both sides as a means of raising an army at short notice; frequently, men would be 'well and defensibly arrayed', to be prepared for service upon an hour's warning. It was all very well in theory, but how effective could the arrays be? In reality, arrays often suffered from being perilously slow: in 1469 Edward IV had to cancel a campaign against northern rebels, 'finding that the common people came to him more slowly than he had anticipated'. Then there was the problem that communities were only prepared, or could only afford, to pay for soldiers' wages for a few weeks' service. Richard understood from his own experience in the wars against Scotland that gathering a force together was not easily done with speed: when in March 1481 York agreed to send 120 soldiers to serve in Scotland, they had still not left the city by September.

Richard might be able to mobilise men through the commissions of array, but there was no guarantee how effective this assembled force might be. In spite of the civil wars, England had not been at war in France for nearly three decades. An entire generation of men had gone without the experience of fighting on a protracted scale or the knowledge of siege warfare; in consequence they were desperately short of military experience. It was a problem that alarmed those who believed that the English now lacked the capabilities of their Continental neighbours. When the printer William Caxton dedicated his translation of Raymond Lull's *Order of Chivalry* to Richard in 1484, he took the opportunity to lament 'where is the custom and usage of noble chivalry that was used in those days?' Instead of practising military exercises, knights now instead 'go to the baths and play at dice'. How many knights, Caxton asked, would know how to ride a horse in armour? He asserted that if 'a due search' were performed, 'there should be many found that lack. The more pity is.' Twice or three times each year, Caxton suggested, there should be a tournament of knights to encourage each knight to take up their training, with a 'diamond or jewel' as a prize, to 'cause gentlemen to resort to the ancient customs of chivalry to great fame and renown'. Caxton hoped that every knight would read Lull's book in order to 'come to the noble order of chivalry' and ended by urging Richard, his 'redoubted, natural and most dread sovereign lord', to 'command this book to be had and read unto other young lords, knights and gentlemen within this realm, that the noble order of chivalry be hereafter better used and honoured than it hath been in late days passed. And herein he shall do a noble and virtuous deed. And I shall pray almighty God for his long life and prosperous welfare, and that he may have victory of all his enemies.'

Caxton's fears were no exaggeration: in May 1485 Richard had been forced to write to the bailiff and constables at Ware, complaining that he had discovered that the inhabitants of the town had shunned their archery practice, 'necessarily requiste to be exercised for the defence of this our realm', preferring instead to 'to use carding, dicing, bowling, playing at the tennis, coyting and picking and other unlawful and inhibited disports' – as well as poaching the king's game. The activities of the town could hardly have left Richard with much confidence that he would have at his disposal a fearsome army ready to combat his enemy.

As the king's letters reached the appointed commissioners of array across the country, men gathered their weapons and made their way to the muster points, in preparation for a battle still on an unknown horizon. Not knowing when they would be required to leave their homes and families and depart within the hour for a punishing march to an unknown field, some decided to make other preparations. The commissioner for Buckinghamshire, John Iwardby, made his will on 22 June, the same day as the instructions sent out by Richard for his troops to be ready at an hour's notice. Iwardby knew that when the final call came, he might never return alive. With his own mortality in mind, he requested that he be buried in *loco sacro ubi complacebit* – 'in a sacred place where it shall please God'.

On 24 July Richard sent letters to his chancellor John Russell, Bishop of Lincoln, demanding 'for certain reasons' that he hand over the Great Seal to the keeper of the rolls Thomas Barowe, so that it could be taken immediately to Nottingham. There could be no clearer sign that Richard expected that an invasion was imminent. If he hoped to raise an army against Henry, he would need to have this ultimate instrument of royal authority in his possession; the impression of the king's Great Seal, on one side displaying the king seated upon his throne wearing the regalia of state, on the reverse, a knight in armour, charging with his sword borne aloft, was not merely a symbol of the king's royal authority, it possessed real authority of its own. Without it, Richard knew his commissions of array or signet letters drawing men to his side would have little force. A Norfolk gentleman, Sir Edmund Bedingfield, would later have difficultly persuading his neighbours to obey a commission of array he had been tasked to execute, since it had not been sealed 'under wax, wherein hath been great argument'; 'it was thought I ought not to obey no copy of the commission' unless it was appended with the Great Seal.

Richard had learnt this lesson during Buckingham's rebellion, when he had found himself almost powerless to act for days without possession of the Great Seal. Then he had written to Bishop Russell requesting that in light of the bishop's ill health the seal be sent to him; however Russell had delayed acting on Richard's instruction until four days later, and Richard was not to receive the seal until a week after he had requested it. While he looked to restore order throughout his kingdom, Richard barely allowed the seal to leave his sight, when from 19 October until 26 November he personally retained its control.

On 29 July, in the lower oratory of the Inner Temple, Russell delivered the seal to Barowe 'at the eighth hour'. Three days later, on 1 August, Barowe arrived at Nottingham Castle, carrying the Great Seal in a white leather bag, sealed with Bishop Russell's signet, bearing the image of an eagle. At seven o'clock in the evening, in the oratory of the chapel of the castle, and in the presence of the Archbishop of York, John, Earl of Lincoln, Thomas, Lord Scrope, George, Lord Strange and the king's secretary, John Kendall, Barowe delivered the seal to Richard, 'whereupon the king, for causes and considerations him moving', returned the seal into Barowe's hands, appointing him keeper of the Great Seal 'then and there'.

The same day, Henry Tudor, having made his final prayers, 'praying to God that his undertaking should be fortunate and successful', ordered his fleet to raise their anchors from the small harbour at Harfleur, and aided by 'a favourable wind', to set sail across the Channel for England. The preparation of the fleet had taken months, while negotiations had continued with Charles VIII and his council as to what aid Henry might be able to secure from the French. As late as 29 June, he had remained in Rouen, where the register of the cathedral records that 'the King of England, Prince of Richmond' offered a gold ecu from Aquitaine when he worshipped in the Chapel of the Virgin Mary there.

Henry had waited anxiously to launch his invasion, while a fleet was prepared on the Normandy coast. Denis Beton, a merchant from Barfleur who helped to fit out Henry's fleet would later be remembered by Henry for his 'various services and kindnesses' and 'certain other causes specially moving'. For the invasion to be a success, however, Henry desperately needed money and men from Charles VIII and the French government. At first, it seemed as if no financial support would be forthcoming; according to one account, the 'Ballad of Lady Bessie', when Henry arrived at Paris, in the company of Lord Lisle, the Earl of Oxford and Humphrey Brereton, pleading for help from Charles, the French king refused any support, 'no ships to bring him over the seas; men nor money bringeth he none'.

Charles had ordered that Henry should be granted 40,000 livre tournois in preparation for his invasion and the expenses of his army. However, the grant was not quite what it appeared. The account roll registered by Jean Lallement, the receiver-general of Normandy, reveal that while Charles had promised a grant of 40,000 livre tournois, this was to be paid in instalments, of which only 10,000 livre tournois was paid up front, 'for his passage to England'. This would be enough for

Henry to begin his preparations, but it would also allow the Beaujeu regime to keep him where they wanted him. Dependent on any future sums of money, Henry would remain securely in France as he planned for military invasion. But at the same time the regime could monitor the situation and any chance of English intervention in Brittany. Henry continued to be a diplomatic pawn, tied by the purse strings of his French backers.

While France had been threatened by Richard's allied involvement with Brittany, Henry had been a valuable diplomatic counter, acting as a threat which they might unleash at any moment. The hostile environment had remained even as late as 25 June 1485, when Richard had promised to send a force of 1,000 archers to aid Brittany; the same day the French government warned its subjects that the English were preparing to invade their realm. Yet suddenly all this changed. Dissident Breton rebels who had been sheltered by the Beaujeus launched an invasion on the duchy on 24 June. The army that Landais had raised against them refused to resist. By the end of the month his regime had collapsed. A warrant for his arrest was issued on 3 July. After being interrogated, Landais was summarily executed. In an instant, the threat that Landais' hostility had posed evaporated, and with it the need for the Beaujeu government to countenance giving further financial backing to Henry's enterprise.

Just as the grant had been agreed, so there was no guarantee that it would be honoured. With the diplomatic situation between France and Brittany substantially altered with Landais' capture, the French had begun to have second thoughts about the need for Henry's invasion, and whether it was worth backing at all. Indeed it seems that the first instalment of 10,000 livre tournois was all that Henry ever received: the French receiver-general's accounts for 1484–5 confirm Lallement's initial quarter payment to Henry, but it also suggests that this was the only money granted to him. There is no sign that the rest of the 30,000 livre tournois ever arrived.

With only 10,000 livre tournois and unable to pay for the cost of his invasion, Henry needed cash as soon as possible. He would need to look elsewhere to finance his expedition. In desperation, he would need to borrow money. He turned to Phillippe Lullier, Seigneur de Saint-Jean-le-Blanc, one of Charles VIII's councillors and captain of the

Bastille. Pleading with Lullier of his 'besoigné et necessité' – great need and necessity – on 13 July 1485, at the office of the notary Pierre Pichon on Rue Saint-Antoine, Paris, a private contract was drawn up between Henry and Lullier, who agreed to lend Henry 20,000 ecus d'or, the equivalent of 30,000 livre tournois.

As surety for the loan, Henry was to surrender all his personal goods and possessions. But even this was not enough. As pledges for the loan he agreed to leave behind Thomas Grey, Marquess of Dorset and the teenage John Bourgchier, Lord FitzWarin, promising to reimburse the additional costs for their captivity in the Bastille Saint-Antoine. Dorset swore a chivalric oath, that as a knight of the Order of the Garter and 'noble personne' he would honour the agreement.

Luillier must have known that the possession of the only two York-ist lords would have increased his chances of getting his money back, regardless of the outcome of Henry's campaign. But the absence of Dorset and FitzWarin from the campaign would mean that Henry would have been unable to rely on landing his army in the West Country, where both nobles had considerable support. Instead he would have to rely on disembarking in Wales.

He had also been waiting to learn of the support that he had hoped to secure in Wales upon his landing. This finally came when John Morgan, sent by his mother Margaret, intercepted him on his journey from Rouen to Harfleur, with Morgan confirming that Sir Rhys ap Thomas and John Savage were prepared to lend their support to his enterprise and would be 'strong supporters' of his cause. Morgan also informed Henry that Reginald Bray had managed to secure 'not an inconsiderable sum' of money to pay for his soldiers' wages, and urged Henry to 'make straight for Wales as soon as possible'.

'Overjoyed' by the news, Henry 'hastened his journey', realising that any further delay could only leave his supporters and friends 'in suspense between hope and fear'. At Harfleur, his men had begun to gather a large force in readiness for embarking across the Channel. While this included the 500 Englishmen who had joined Henry in exile, it is likely that there was also a substantial number of Scottish mercenaries, led by Sir Alexander Bruce. The Scottish chronicler Pitscottie, writing in the late sixteenth century, stated that there were 1,000 men-at-arms 'called the Scottish company which had to their captain a noble knight which was called Sir Alexander Bruce of Ershall' and 'a born man of Haddington'. Pitscottie's source for this information seems to have been the history of John Major, published in 1521, which recorded how, 'inasmuch as the Earl of Richmond had been long a dweller in France, Charles VIII granted him an aid of 5,000 men of whom 1,000 were Scots, but John, son of Robert of Haddington, was chief and leader of the Scots'. The English sources make no mention of any Scottish support at Bosworth; this must have been because the Scots were in the service of the French king. Nevertheless, Sir Alexander Bruce was later given an annuity of £20 by Henry 'in gracious renumeration of his good, faithful, and approved services, and his great labours in various ways heretofore, and lately done in person'.

Another Scotsman with close links to the French who seems to have taken part in Henry's invasion was Bernard Stewart or 'Bernard de Stuart, le seigneur d'Aubigny' as he was known to the French. An expatriate Scot who had joined the French royal household; described by Commynes as 'bon chevalier et saige et honnourable', Stewart had served as a man-at-arms in France since 1469, and in 1483 had been given command of over a hundred lances. In 1484 he was sent by Charles VIII to renew the alliance between France and Scotland. On 13 March James III confirmed the alliance in Stewart's presence, and the treaty was ratified by the French king on 9 July 1484. As part of the agreement, James sent to France eighteen companies of Scottish footmen led by Stewart. It was probably these men who were now to be sent across the sea to take part in the invasion. Later, Stewart would write his own military manual on how to fight battles, and it is perhaps from his experiences during his campaign with Henry's forces that he reflected upon how 'the English have a good way of doing things' since 'from the first day they get into battle he who is the warring party's master has all of it under his command, and this is a very good disposition and practice for the good of the people'.

The bulk of Henry's contingent was to be supplied from French forces, recently demobilised from fighting on the front at Flanders. The exact number of French troops supplied by Charles VIII can be debated, but they must have totalled over half of Henry's armed fleet that departed from Harfleur. Polydore Vergil was later keen to downplay the French contribution to Henry's force, commenting only that Henry received a 'slender supply' from Charles VIII, 'with 2,000 only of armed men and a few ships', though his observation, made in the manuscript copy of his work, that the force was 'partly English and partly French' was later judiciously removed. Perhaps equally intent to increase the level of the French contribution to Henry's enterprise, Molinet wrote that Charles VIII had given Henry 1,800 troops together with artillery and ships for his invasion; Commynes increased this to 4,000 men, with 'a large sum of money and some artillery'. Yet it is notable that the Crowland Chronicler recorded how Henry's troops were 'as much French' as English.

There can be no doubt that Henry's force included a substantial number of French troops, yet while mentioning Charles VIII's order that 1,800 troops be sent to Henry, Molinet described how none of these was actually from 'his own house'. Instead Henry was forced to enlist men from elsewhere; as Commynes recorded, he did so with 'some three thousand of the most unruly men that could be found and enlisted in Normandy'.

It seems likely that many of the French mercenaries who were recruited to serve in Henry's army came from a military garrison commanded by the aged Marshal of France, Philippe de Crevecoeur, lord of Esquerdes, or 'Cordes' as he was better known in England. Esquerdes had long been a thorn in Richard's side. Shortly after Edward IV's death, he had launched a naval campaign, 'to the great hurt and prejudice of certain English merchants', under the pretext that he had been unable to be recompensed for ships and goods seized from him during the previous reign. When he sent messengers to England, he felt they had been 'insultingly treated by the English, or at least derided'. One commentator believed that this was merely a distraction from Esquerdes' true intent: 'under colour of avenging a private wrong', he 'was supposed to have made the beginning of a war between these most unfriendly nations'. Esquerdes was certainly in no mood to compromise. 'When our ships, losses, and injuries are restored to me,' he wrote uncompromisingly to Lord Dynham in May 1483, 'I shall be ready to remove my hand from all the arrests that I have caused to be made.' Described as an 'extremely active commander', Esquerdes' chief ambition was to recover Calais, which he 'sore longed' to recapture from the English, so much so that it was reported that 'he would commonly say that he would gladly live vii years in hell, so that Calais were in possession of the Frenchmen'.

By 1485 Cordes had become commander of a large military base in the valley of the Seine at Pont de l'Arche. At the height of his military activity following the death of Charles the Bold in 1477, Louis XI had sought to establish a military camp there to house a settled garrison for a standing army of 'gendarmerie', a permanent military army to be commanded by Esquerdes. Louis purchased 2,100 horses, 700 tents and 700 carts stamped with the royal arms for the camp, but almost as soon as it had been established, the king had begun to have second thoughts about the viability of such a massive military operation. After the peace of Arras in 1482, its enormous costs, financed by 'cruel and excessive tallies' on the surrounding neighbourhoods, seemed unnecessary; the permanent infantry force of franc-archers was ordered to be slowly disbanded, after costing 288,000 livre tournois in pay alone and the force itself being widely criticised for its indiscipline. The entire camp itself had been threatened with closure, with Pierre-Louis de Valtan having been appointed 'capitaine generale de la closure', yet the garrison remained under the command of Esquerdes, with payments surviving for a company of 4,000 men in 1482 and 1483, in spite of costs of the garrison at Pont-de-l'Arche rising to unsustainable proportions, with wages alone increasing from 700,000 livre tournois in 1482 to 827,660 livre tournois in 1483. Neither could the camp shake off its reputation for being 'as cowardly as they were merciless'. Nevertheless, Valtan was still in position in 1485, suggesting that the camp remained operational in some form when Henry was recruiting a force for his expedition.

It was at Pont-de-l'Arche that soldiers were hastily mustered by Esquerdes to join Henry's army, on the promise of pay and possible military glory. The camp was divided into four separate divisions of men: the 'archers du camp', the professional group of French archers, crossbowmen ('abaletiers'), halberdiers ('voulgiers') and later a band of pikemen (referred to as 'lanciers' or 'piquiers'), though the only evidence of the type of soldier sent to fight with Henry comes from a letter by one 'archer du camp', Colinet Leboeuf, who had been present in 'du camp sous M. D'Esquerdes' when he was enlisted to join Henry's enterprise, which Leboeuf himself referred to as the 'voyage d'anglettere'.

When approached for men from his garrison to join Henry's army against Richard, Esquerdes must have felt it was yet another opportunity to cause division and disarray among the English nation whom he hated. Esquerdes would later be credited for transforming Henry's fortunes from a 'fugitive of his own country', with Esquerdes' own epitaph stating how 'by me had Richmond revived in French land . . . I was ordained judge settler of the tournament', while another French poem addressed to Esquerdes recalled how 'You were made the Lord to take away one's right, for another as well awaited his own right, so to make his name . . . you were made judge thereof, for you supported him'. For the moment, it is likely that Esquerdes simply saw in Henry Tudor the chance to cause maximum discomfort to an English king who, once more bogged down in civil war, might one day loosen his grip upon Esquerdes' precious territory of Calais.

Esquerdes himself chose not to lead his forces across the sea; instead command of the French troops was given to Philibert de Chandée, a young nobleman from Savoy, who had recently joined the French court following the death of Louis XI, under the household of Philippe de Savoy, Count of Bresse. Henry would later refer to Chandée as being 'our dear kinsman, both of spirit and blood', suggesting that Tudor himself believed that they were both descended in kinship through the French royal family.

With a fleet of around thirty ships in place, Guillaume de Casenove, known by his nickname 'Coulon', a notorious naval captain whose expertise was recognised at the French court, was chosen as commander of the fleet for the journey, commanding his flagship, the *Poulain of Dieppe*. Everything was now in place. Leaving Thomas, Marquess of Dorset and John Bourgchier behind them, Henry made his final preparations before embarking on his voyage. On 1 August, around the same time as Richard received the Great Seal in the solemn ceremony in the sanctuary of Nottingham castle, Henry Tudor and his flotilla of French troops and English exiles left the shelter of the Seine at Harfleur and made their journey out towards the Channel on a soft southerly breeze, determined to claim the Crown of England and its Great Seal as his own.

PART THREE:

'THIS OUR ENTERPRISE'

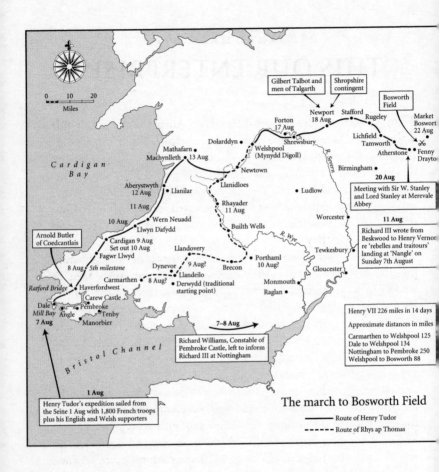

The march to Bosworth Field

Route of Henry Tudor

- - - - Route of Rhys ap Thomas

Gilbert Talbot and men of Talgarth

Shropshire contingent

Bosworth Field

Newport 18 Aug

Stafford

Rugeley

Market Bosworth 22 Aug

Forton 17 Aug

Shrewsbury

Lichfield

Tamworth

Atherstone

Fenny Drayton

Dolarddyn

Welshpool (Mynydd Digoll)

Mathafarn 13 Aug

Machynlleth

Newtown

Birmingham

20 Aug

Cardigan Bay

Aberystwyth 12 Aug

Llanilar

Llanidloes

Ludlow

Meeting with Sir W. Stanley and Lord Stanley at Merevale Abbey

11 Aug

Rhayader 11 Aug

Worcester

11 Aug

Wern Neuadd

Builth Wells

R. Wye

Richard III wrote from Beskwood to Henry Vernon re 'rebels and traitours' landing at 'Nangle' on Sunday 7th August

Llwyn Dafydd

Cardigan 9 Aug Set out 10 Aug

Arnold Butler of Coedcantlais

Llandovery

Tewkesbury

Fagwr Llwyd

8 Aug *5th milestone*

Dynevor

9 Aug?

Porthaml 10 Aug?

Gloucester

Carmarthen

Brecon

8 Aug?

Ratford Bridge

Llandeilo

Derwydd (traditional starting point)

Monmouth

Haverfordwest

Dale

Carew Castle

Mill Bay

Pembroke

Tenby

Raglan

Angle

Manorbier

7 Aug

7–8 Aug

Henry VII 226 miles in 14 days

Approximate distances in miles

Carmarthen to Welshpool 125
Dale to Welshpool 134
Nottingham to Pembroke 250
Welshpool to Bosworth 88

Bristol Channel

Richard Williams, Constable of Pembroke Castle, left to inform Richard III at Nottingham

1 Aug

Henry Tudor's expedition sailed from the Seine 1 Aug with 1,800 French troops plus his English and Welsh supporters

0 10 20
Miles

9

MARCH TO WAR

◆◆

It was shortly before sunset on Sunday 7 August when at half-tide and under a clear sky, the fleet of thirty ships led by Guillaume de Casenove's flagship, the *Poulain of Dieppe*, turned inwards into the mouth of Milford Haven. The fleet had been at sea for seven days, though a 'favourable wind' had eased their journey. Sailing past the sheer-faced red sandstone cliffs several hundred feet high, hidden from view to the left was their intended destination, the small rocky inlet that formed Mill Bay.

Shielded by two large promontories, the bay was out of sight from the village of Dale and its castle a mile and a half away, where Henry's landing went unnoticed. Henry had learnt that the previous winter, Richard had sent a 'cohort' of men to be stationed there, in order to 'turn him away from the shore', yet arriving onshore, there was no sight of armed resistance, no troops shadowing the cliffs or boats skirting the haven, as Henry must have feared, remembering his experiences in Plymouth nearly two years previously.

Henry's immediate sense of relief was obvious. According to the chronicler Robert Fabyan, 'when he was come unto the land he incontinently kneeled down upon the earth, and with meek countenance and pure devotion began this Psalm: *Judica me deus, & discern causam meam*' (Psalm 43: 'Judge me, O God, and distinguish my cause'). When Henry had finished reciting the psalm 'to the end', he 'kissed the ground meekly, and reverently made the sign of the cross upon him'. Afterwards, he commanded those around him to 'boldly in the name of God and Saint George to set forward'. In spite of Henry's Welsh ancestry, and the location of his landing, it would be the English saint and chivalric hero that Henry would seek to emulate. As the ships were unloaded, one of the principal banners unfurled was one of 'the image

231

of St George', though Henry's Welsh descent was also represented with a second banner of a 'red fiery dragon beaten upon white and green sarcenet'. Following traditional chivalric precedents, Henry also decided upon landing to knight eight of his most prominent followers – Edward Courtenay, Philibert de Chandée, John, Lord Welles, John Cheyney, David Owen, Edward Poynings, John Fort and James Blount, men who would then have been expected to take up roles as commanders within the army. It was a significant moment, the implications of which everyone watching the ceremonies being performed would have understood: Henry was formally asserting his claim to be the fount of virtue, something only a king could legitimately claim. In knighting his men, Henry was staking out his own claim to be king.

A fragment of the jubilant landing scene is preserved in a eulogy to a Carmarthenshire squire who was present at the landing: 'You conducted . . . your king from the water once when chieftains landed and mustered . . . There were seen our gallant ones and a throng like York fair and the host of France, a large and heavy host by the sea-shore, and many a trumpet by the strand, and guns around a red banner, and mighty tracks where you passed.' Its mention of the strength of French troops indicates their importance to Henry's overall military campaign. Numbering in their thousands, in spite of a disagreement over the exact figures, it was clear, as Vergil stated in his manuscript history, Henry's army was very much 'partim Anglorum, partim Francorum'.

One report stated that French troops remained aboard while Henry landed at Dale, reluctant to disembark. When finally they were persuaded, they were 'marvellously well and kindly received' and given fresh provisions of food and drink to cheer them up. As soon as all the soldiers had disembarked, the French commander of the fleet Guillaume de Casenove was quick to depart for adventures new. On 20 August 1485 he was already to be found near Cape St Vincent in southern Portugal where he was involved in an attack on four Venetian galleys sailing to Flanders, before returning to England where he divided up his booty, 'a great quantity of merchandise belonging to Spanish subjects', causing the Spanish monarchs Ferdinand and Isabella to write to England in protest. With Casenove's ships disappearing around the edge of the Milford Sound and out into the Atlantic, Henry was now on his own. There could be no turning back.

Once both men and munitions had been unloaded from the boats, the first task was to reach the village of Dale and to secure its castle. At half-tide, reaching twenty feet above the water level at low tide, the landing spot would have been cut off from the path out of the bay. The only route was to climb up through the steep incline rising 200 feet to Brunt Farm, a third of a mile away. The farm is said to have been named after a comment supposedly made by Henry, struggling up the hill, that 'This is Brunt' – 'brunt' meaning difficult or hard. The village proved somewhat less difficult to subdue, though Vergil hints that it had to be 'occupied', suggesting some brief resistance.

As the skies darkened and night fell, Henry ordered that his army set up camp at Dale, possibly on the stretch of land near the castle. Possibly with his French troops in mind, whom Commynes had after all described as being 'the most unruly men that could be found', Henry addressed his troops, according to Bernard André, telling them 'not to commit any wrong on the common folk either to gain sustenance or to turn a profit, nor to take any property from any inhabitant without paying him recompense. And if you require money, behold, men are here to pay you a proper salary. Do not do anything to other men, either by word or by deed, that you would not wish to have done to yourselves. If you conduct yourself thus, God will be propitious to us, since a thieving lawbreaker does not long rejoice in other men's property.' If Henry was to ensure a swift and safe journey through Wales, he would only be able to enlist support if his troops maintained discipline and did not take it upon themselves to pillage the surrounding neighbourhoods. Henry would later draw up a series of ordinances of war, which must have reflected his own rules set out during the campaign. These outlined the powers of the king's harbinger, whose responsibility was to purvey lodgings for the king's camp. 'Also that no manner of person or persons, whatsoever they be, take upon them to lodge themself nor take no manner of lodging nor harborage but such as shall be assigned unto him or them by the King's harbinger, nor dislodge no man, nor change no lodging after that to be assigned, without advice and assent of the said harbinger, upon pain of imprisonment and to be punished at the said will of our said sovereign lord'. Ordinances of war were essential if discipline were to be kept. Henry would later issue strict instructions 'ordained by his proclamations, for the good rule of his host'. No soldier was to 'take nor presume to take any manner of victual, horse meat, or man's meat, without paying therefore the reasonable price thereof assigned by the clerk of the market or other the king's officer therefore ordained, upon pain of death'. Henry would later comment to the Earl of Oxford that 'blessed be God', the English army 'hath among themselves kept such love and accord that no manner of fray or debate hath been between them since the time of their departing'.

Oxford and Pembroke were also ordered to muster the French troops in order to 'take a view of their defects' and to understand what equipment and weapons they lacked. It was not an encouraging sight. 'They were very raw and ignorant in shooting, handling of their weapons, and discharging the ordinary duty of soldiers; men, as it seemed, raised out of the refuse of the people'. According to the account of his life, Sir Rhys Ap Thomas, who retained a life-long distain for the French, revealing his own personal desire 'soundly to cudgel those French dogs', later found himself having to equip them with as much equipment as he could spare, though in his heart he wished he could send them back to France, 'there being not one man of quality among them'. It was perhaps the mutual hostility between the French and the Welsh soldiers that forced Henry to decide to separate his troops, agreeing that they be 'kept asunder, to prevent such jarres and quarrels, as commonly arise between strangers'.

As the first light of dawn broke on the morning of Monday 8 August, Henry began his march from Dale to the town of Haverfordwest. Speed was essential if Henry was to make progress and gather momentum before Richard discovered news of his landing. Haverfordwest was around twelve miles away, along a route which passed near Merlas and crossed a tributary of the Western Cleddau river at Radford Bridge, yet the army marched so fast and without delay that the town had hardly been notified of Henry's landing, with it being 'announced that he was present at the same time as it was announced that he was on his way'. There Henry and his army were received 'with the utmost goodwill of all'.

This encouragement was soon shattered by the disappointing news brought by John Morgan that, contrary to what Henry had been informed in Normandy, 'nothing had come of the help which he had previously indicated' and that Rhys ap Thomas and John Savage were not prepared to defect and join his forces, with Morgan reporting that they were apparently still 'in arms for King Richard'. Worse still, the funds that had been promised by Reginald Bray to pay for his troops' wages had not materialised.

If Henry was distraught at the news, he was quickly cheered by the arrival of the Welshman Arnold Butler, whom Henry had last seen during his exile in Brittany; Butler had accompanied Henry when he had fled to Brittany in 1471, but had been removed from Henry's service by Duke Francis II and forced to return home. According to Vergil, Butler 'came to him and told him that the entire nobility of the County of Pembroke was prepared to serve him, provided that he would grant pardon for and wipe out the memory of anything they had done against him and against Earl Jasper during the time when both had gone to Brittany'. Henry, 'in accordance with his nature and for the benefit of his enterprise, with Jasper easily forgave them. At which they came voluntarily to him and bound themselves by the military oath.' Vergil, in his printed work, makes clear that Jasper's own position as the region's traditional lord must have been influential in their decision to support Henry, stating that 'they were prepared to help their Earl Jasper'.

The defection of Arnold Butler was significant, not just for bringing the support of Pembroke with him, which 'cheered the troubled minds of all'. Butler himself was a close friend and long-time acquaintance of Sir Rhys ap Thomas who, recognising Butler's renowned skills as a soldier, had employed him to train young gentlemen, 'according to the true military discipline of those times, in which they employed much labour, accustoming them daily (as if they had been in field) to the hardest duties of a soldier'. Could Butler's defection be taken as a sign that Rhys remained sympathetic to Henry's cause? Henry was uncertain of Rhys ap Thomas's motives; having promised his support, remaining in the Tywi Valley, Rhys had decided to remain cautious. Richard's servants Richard Williams and Sir James Tyrell continued to hold a strong grip on the region; in any case Rhys may have wished to pursue a deliberate policy of tracing Henry's progress, shadowing him as he moved northwards in order to decide at a later stage whether to support or crush him.

It was in this atmosphere of extreme uncertainty and nervousness that Henry departed from Haverfordwest that same afternoon, setting out for Cardigan, twenty-six miles away. Five miles into the journey, Henry decided to pitch camp 'at the fifth milestone' towards Cardigan so that his soldiers might rest. Suddenly a rumour broke out and spread throughout the camp that Sir Walter Herbert, the Earl of Huntingdon's younger brother, and Rhys ap Thomas had encamped near Carmarthen and 'were not far away with a huge band of armed men'. Uproar immediately ensued, and in the panic 'each man began to get ready his arms and test and prepare his weapons' as 'a certain degree of fear seized them all'. The fear that was evidently latent among Henry's followers is understandable: not only had Herbert and Rhys ap Thomas been tasked with crushing any rebellion, but the entire region of South Wales remained both in Richard's control and his pay. During Buckingham's rebellion, if the act of attainder against the duke's ninety-seven supporters is considered comprehensive, not a single Welshman rose in support, while twenty-two men residing in South Wales were rewarded with annuities. Among them was Sir Thomas Vaughan of Tretower, whose father had been executed by Jasper Tudor at Chepstow in 1471. Vaughan had ensured that a watch was sent into the surrounding countryside, and was instrumental in the capture of the Duke's castle at Brecon. To many marching through the hostile countryside, victory must have at that moment seemed against all odds.

Henry decided to send a party of scouts on horseback to discover the true situation. When they reported back that 'all was quiet', nerves were calmed. In fact, the rumours were likely to have been caused by the sight of the arrival of Gruffydd Rede, whose family had been prominent in Carmarthen for generations, who having left Walter Herbert and Rhys ap Thomas's camp had journeyed to join Henry, bringing with him a band of soldiers, 'although few were properly equipped'. Rede was accompanied by John Morgan of Tredegar in Gwent, described as a man 'of no mean authority among the Welsh', who had been a royal officer in Carmarthenshire and Cardiganshire during the 1470s. The defection of the two men 'greatly heartened the spirits of all', while their presence in Henry's camp perhaps gave Rhys ap Thomas an effective line of communication to Henry, allowing him to negotiate terms for his possible desertion.

With three defections in the course of the day, momentum seemed to be gathering. It seems likely that, after a seventeen-mile journey and several delays both at Haverfordwest and in the temporary panic that Gruffydd Rede's arrival had caused, there was little time in the day for any further march, and the army would have remained encamped at the fifth milestone.

They would need their rest; by the following morning of Tuesday 9 August Henry felt confident enough to begin the next and most difficult part of the march, leading his army up over the craggy Preseli Hills, the highest point of the journey where, several hundred metres above sea level, clouds can often descend over its highest point. It would be a lonely and punishing journey; the slow climb at times must have seemed endless as fields and pasture gave way to a desolate bracken-covered landscape. Crossing the ridge of the Preseli hills at Bwlch-y-Gwynt, 'the Pass of the Wind', Henry intended to reach Fagwr Llwyd, south of Cilgwyn, a seventeen-mile journey. The site lies a mile from the Cardigan road. Abandoned in the early twentieth century, the ruins of the farmstead remain marked by a clump of beech trees, yet the shape and size of the building is clearly discernible, overlooking the valley of the river Nevern, above the haven of Newport, which must have provided a good campsite for his army. Across the valley, Henry could view his next intended destination: Cardigan, where crossing the river Teifi, he would enter the Principality of Wales.

Resuming his march the next day on Wednesday 10 August, after a journey of nine miles, Henry and his army crossed the river Teifi at Cardigan, reaching the walled town where little resistance seems to have come from the castle there. Tradition records that Henry stopped at the Three Mariners Inn; despite the short journey, Henry decided that he would need to pause to gather further support from the Welsh gentry in the north. Now that he had entered the Principality of Wales, Henry felt able to formally set out his claim to the throne. Letters were written, to be sent out across the region. A copy of one of these letters survives, addressed to John ap Meredith ap Jevan ap Meredith, an influential squire who lived in the Eifionydd area of south Caernarfonshire:

By the King.

Right trusty and wellbeloved, we greet you well. And where it is so that through the help of Almighty God, the assistance of our loving friends and true subjects, and the great confidence that we have to the nobles and commons of this our Principality of Wales, we be entered into the same, purposing by the help above rehearsed in all haste possible to descend into our realm of England not only for the adeption [recovery] of the crown unto us of right appertaining, but also for the oppression of that odious tyrant Richard late Duke of Gloucester, usurper of our said right, and moreover to reduce as well our said realm of England into his ancient estate, honour and prosperity, as this our said Principality of Wales, and the people of the same to their erst [original] liberties, delivering them of such miserable servitudes as they have piteously long stand in. We desire and pray you and upon your allegiance straitly charge and command you that immediately upon the sight hereof, with all such power as ye may make defensibly arrayed for the war, ye address you towards us without any tarrying upon the way, unto such time as ye be with us wheresoever we shall be to our aid for the effect above rehearsed, wherein ye shall cause us in time to come to be your singular good lord and that ye fail not hereof as ye will avoid our grevious displeasure and answer unto at your peril. Given under our signet.

There is no personal comment in the letter, suggesting that it may have been a standard missive, but it remains a fascinating insight into Henry's own mind during his campaign to claim the throne. What is most striking is its tone of authority. Beginning with the traditional formula of royal letters, 'By the King. Right trusty and wellbeloved, we greet you well' and sealed under Henry's own 'royal' signet, the letter outlined Henry's clear intention to seize the reins of monarchy, speaking of 'our subjects' and 'our realm of England'. The letter had also been carefully crafted to appeal to its Welsh readers. Not only was Henry setting out his claim as King of England, refusing to even acknowledge Richard's title, he was positioning himself as the liberator of the Welsh, playing upon Welsh nationalism by claiming that he had come to restore their liberties, promising to deliver them from 'such miserable servitudes as they have piteously long [stood] in'. It was a convincing and powerful elucidation of Henry's intentions, of which anyone reading the letter could have been in no doubt. Equally powerful was Henry's royal assertion and threat that if men failed to come to his aid, they would face his 'grievous displeasure and answer unto at your peril'. To those reading the letter, the message was obvious: no longer could they avoid taking sides. The time had come to make their decision.

As messengers hastened ahead of him with copies of his declaration, Henry's forces left Cardigan, moving northwards, hugging the route along the coast. Stopping for water at Ffynnondewi at the fourteenth milestone north-east of Cardigan, Henry reached the country mansion of Llwyn Dafydd in the parish of Llandysillio-gogo. Henry's resting place after a total journey of twenty-three miles may have been a house called Neuadd, belonging to Dafydd ab Ieuan. Standing over a narrow and secluded valley which runs down to Cardigan Bay at Cwmtydu, two miles south of Newquay, it is worth considering that the cove nestled there is the only viable location where ships might be safely landed on the Cardigan Bay, raising the question of whether Henry's entire army had journeyed with him on land, or whether a small fleet may have traced the Welsh coastline, allowing more troops to disembark once Henry's advance party had reached this next location. The resting place clearly had significance for Henry, who would later reward Dafydd ab Ieuan for his pains with a gift known as the Hirlas Horn, a drinking horn mounted on a silver stand, decorated with the Welsh dragon and a greyhound, the insignia of the Woodville family as well as being a Breton Celtic symbol, linked to the honour of Richmond, and with images of roses and the portcullis, the traditional insignia of the Beaufort family, engraved on a silver covering around the rim of the horn.

Earlier in the year, after it had seemed that Henry was too unprepared to launch an invasion of any significance, Richard had decided to withdraw some of the ships that he had placed in defensive positions guarding the Welsh coastline, including those based in the Milford Sound. Still he remained cautious. 'Lest he might be found altogether unready', he had ordered members of the nobility and gentry 'dwelling about the sea coast, and chiefly the Welsh men, to keep watch by course after their country manner, to the intent that his adversaries should not have ready recovery of the shore and come a land'. Polydore Vergil described how in time of war, on nearby hills lamps would be 'fastened upon frames of timber'; 'when any great or notable matter happeneth, by reason of the approach of enemies, they suddenly light the lamps, and with shouts through town and field give notice thereof; from thence others afterwards receive and utter to their neighbours notice after the same sort. Thus is the same thereof carried speedily to all villages, and both country and town arm themselves against the enemy.' If Henry were to slip through his net, Richard was determined that he should know as soon as possible where his enemy had landed.

At Dale, the ideal position for such a beacon would have been at St Ann's Head, at the top of the cliff face on the north side of the Milford Sound, which today remains the site of the coastguard and lighthouse. Located on the site in 1595 was an 'old chapel decayed having a round tower builded like a windmill or pigeon house of stone', twenty feet high and used by sailors as a navigation landmark. Though the beacon could be seen from the opposite side of the bay to the south, due to a rise in the land on Dale Peninsula, St Ann's chapel would have been invisible inland on its own side. This helps to explain why, even if a beacon had been lit there, knowledge of Henry's landing did not reach Haverfordwest in time before his arrival. The burning torch would however have been clearly visible four miles away across the mouth of the Haven, in the neighbourhood near Angle.

As a chain reaction of beacons were lit on the south side of Milford Haven, news soon reached the constable and steward of Pembroke Castle, Richard Williams, who had succeeded in the office from the Duke of Buckingham in January 1484. He had previously only been an usher of Richard's chamber, but Richard's trust in Williams was demonstrated by his substantial land grants to him in December 1484, when he was granted the lordship of the castle of Manorbier and the manor of Penally. Under his stewardship, the castle was put in a state of defence, with £113 14s 6d spent on fortifying the castle; the woods around the nearby town of Narberth were felled to supply fuel and wood for beacons. Realising that the first beacon must have been lit at Angle, indicating that Henry had finally landed there, Williams knew that he had no time to waste. He decided to ride the journey of 210 miles to Nottingham, managing an average speed of fifty-two miles a day, a considerable feat considering that the expected distance covered by a mounted messenger was around thirty to thirty-five miles. To achieve such a distance, Williams would have had to ride through the night, making use of the king's post-horses that were stationed every twenty miles which would allow him to maintain his breakneck speed.

When he arrived, Williams found Richard not at Nottingham Castle but at his hunting lodge at Bestwood Park. Lying to the north of Nottingham in Sherwood Forest, Bestwood Park had been a royal hunting ground since at least the twelfth century, where it remained well stocked. Covering 3,000 acres, a survey of 1607 reported that 'there are in the park at least three hundred fallow-deer, and four and twenty red deer'. The park had been completely enclosed by Edward III in the 1360s; at the same time a timber-framed hunting lodge was constructed on the most attractive part of the estate. In 1593 it was reported to have contained thirty-eight rooms, built of lath and plaster, with a tiled roof. It was here that, according to the Crowland chronicler, news of his adversary's landing was broken to the king.

Richard's initial reaction was one of delight and rejoicing – 'or at least he pretended to rejoice', as the Crowland chronicler noted. According to Vergil, Richard believed that Henry's forces would be 'unprepared and weak' compared to his own troops who he had stationed in Wales. He was confident that Henry 'because of the small number of his men, was destined to have a bad end when he would either be compelled to fight against his will or be taken alive by Walter Herbert and Richard Thomas'.

Richard's confidence was reflected in his own military experience. In contrast to Henry, he had a formidable reputation as a successful soldier and general, and must have believed that, given his previous experience, he would have the upper hand in any forthcoming battle. From an early age, Richard had demonstrated his abilities to command men under his standard. In June 1469, aged seventeen, he had managed to recruit men to fight under his banner against a rebellion led by Robin of Redesdale in the north, by 'waging' them to fight. Two years later, he had fought at the battle of Barnet, where he was close enough to the action to be wounded, and again at Tewkesbury weeks later, where leading the vanguard he had crushed the Lancastrian forces, with one chronicler describing how he bore the brunt of the struggle alongside his brothers. Later, Richard would remember his fellow companions who had died under his standard. When in 1477 Richard granted a Lordship to Queen's College, Cambridge, in return for the establishment of a chantry foundation in its chapel, he requested that four priests pray for, among the other family members both living and dead, 'the souls of . . . all other gentlemen and yeoman servants and lovers of the said Duke of Gloucester, the which were slain in his service at the battles of Barnet, Tewkesbury or at any other fields or journeys'.

Richard's service at Barnet won him unique praise, being compared in one literary panegyric to one of the greatest chivalric warriors, Hector of Troy:

> The Duke of Gloucester, that noble prince
> Young of age and victorious in battle,
> To the honour of Hector that he might come,
> Grace him followeth, fortune, and good speed . . .

Richard would have known of Hector's bravery; in the manuscript copy of the story of Troy which he owned, Hector is described as 'a knight of unheard valour . . . there was none who was distinguished by as great a spirit as Hector . . . he surpassed all other in courage'. In the same copy, in a passage describing the advantages of fighting among friends and relatives to protect one's home, a fifteenth-century hand has written in the margin, 'note well the fair words' as well as the words 'note the crow and its vigour', a reference to the image of the weaker crow defending its nest from attack by a stronger falcon. It was just one of the influential military works that Richard was well-read in; works that the king even sought to educate his own son with, ordering a copy of the classic textbook, Vegetius' *De Re Militari*, to be made for his education.

After Tewkesbury, however, the opportunity for Richard to extend his military reputation had been limited. When Edward IV had stated his intent to invade France in 1475, drawing up plans for over 11,000 troops to sail across the Channel, Richard threw himself into the preparations, relishing the opportunity to win military glory abroad. At Picquigny he had taken the opportunity to survey his opposing French army, and was bitterly disappointed when the subsequent peace treaty denied him the chance of battle, refusing to be present during the signing ceremony since, according to one French chronicler, he was 'mal content' with the treaty.

War in Scotland finally had allowed Richard to partly fulfil his ambitions of leading an army into battle: having been appointed lieutenant-general in 1480, Richard sought to take an active role in crushing the Scots, launching his first raid across the border in September 1480. The following year, together with the Earl of Northumberland, Richard attempted to recapture the stronghold of Berwick. The town finally fell in 1482, after an energetic campaign which had seen Richard reach the gates of Edinburgh without resistance. The recovery of Berwick marked a symbolic milestone for the Yorkist cause: it had been given up by the Lancastrians under Henry VI to secure Scottish backing. Richard himself marked its capture with a major new rebuilding programme, repairing the castle and the town's walls together with the construction of 120 houses. Such was the success of Richard's campaign, Parliament officially declared its gratitude to him, while Dominic Mancini wrote that 'such was his renown in warfare, that whenever a difficult and dangerous policy had to be undertaken, it would be entrusted to his discretion and generalship'.

Perhaps Richard's bellicose attitude is best summed up in his choice of emblem, that of the white sanglier or boar. William Worcester in his *Boke of Noblesse* had urged Edward IV to wage war on France and follow 'the example of the boar', 'advancing your courageous heart to war . . . furious, eager . . . against all those nations that . . . would put you from your . . . rightful inheritance'. The sanglier was considered the most dangerous animal in the forest, whose ferocity and power made it one of the most difficult animals to hunt – its killer was greatly honoured. The boar was also admired in literature, including in Geoffrey of Monmouth's *History of the Kings of Britain*, which makes mention of the 'fierce Boar, which will try the sharpness of its tusks in the forests of Gaul; for it will lop down all larger oak trees, taking care however to protect the smaller ones. The Arabs shall dread the Boar and so shall the Africans.'

Like many knights of his day, Richard was drawn by the idea of crusade, demonstrating sympathy with crusading warriors engaged in wars of religion against the Turks. His own book of hours contains a litany beseeching God to destroy 'the peoples of the heathen'. Richard's own interest in crusading can also be witnessed in his patronage of the chapel of All Hallows, Barking, where it was believed that the heart of Richard I was buried, and in his appointment of John Kendale, an officer of the Order of the Knights of St John, to present his obedience to Pope Innocent VIII. According to a visitor at his court, Nicolas Von Poppelau, when his conversation with Richard turned to the Turks, who had recently been defeated in battle by the Hungarians, Richard grew enlivened, replying that 'I would like my kingdom and land to lie where the land and kingdom of the King of Hungary lies, on the Turkish frontier itself. Then I would certainly, with my own people alone, without the help of other kings, princes or lords, properly drive away not only the Turks, but all my enemies and opponents.' Richard's words may have been an expression of hope rather than intent, but it is worthwhile noting that one of the coronation regalia used in the king's coronation, the Holy Oil of St Thomas of Canterbury, was believed to have mystical properties, and when 'carried in the breast' its small ampulla would ensure certain victory over the king's enemies; its carrier would also supposedly recover Normandy and Aquitaine, and 'build churches in the holy land and chase all the heathen from Babylon'. Richard gave the oil to Westminster Abbey for safe keeping, but only on the specific condition that it would be returned 'whensoever it shall please him to ask it'.

In Henry Tudor, Richard finally had his own crusade to win: according to one ballad, when confronted with the news of Henry's invasion and its gathering support, he swept aside the threat, stating: 'By Jesus full of might, when they are assembled with their powers all, I would I had the great Turk against me to fight, or Prester John in his armour bright, the Sultan of Syria with them to bring.' According to the chronicler Jean Molinet, his first reaction on hearing the news of Henry's arrival was to counter his march immediately, only to be dissuaded by those nobles around him who replied: 'Do not move, we shall do well.'

Preparations would need to be made to ensure that the royal army was gathered together at Nottingham in order to march on the enemy. Richard immediately ordered that letters were to be sent 'everywhere to say that the day he had longed for had now arrived when he would easily triumph over such a wretched company'. The time had come, he believed, that he could finally 'restore the strength of his subjects with the blessings of certain peace'. At the same time, the threat could not be underestimated. Richard 'sent out terrifying orders in manifold letters to all the counties of the kingdom'. No man, 'at least none of those who were born to any inheritances within the said kingdom, should withdraw themselves from the coming battle, with the threat that, after the victory had been gained, anyone who might be found, in any part of the kingdom not to have been present in person with him on the battlefield could hope for nothing but the loss of all his goods, his possessions and his life'. Letters were dispatched across the country; opened and read, many of them had the desired effect. It was later claimed that Geoffrey St Germyn had been been 'so manashed' by Richard's letters, that he believed he had no choice but to come to the king's aid, or else 'he should lose his life, lands and goods; for dread whereof' he travelled to the king 'full sore against his will'. Roger Wake also later explained that he had journeyed to aid the king 'against his will and mind', quoting from Richard's letters which commanded him to fight 'upon pain of forfeiture of life, land, and asmuch as he might forfeit'.

One of Richard's letters survives, written from Bestwood on 11 August to one of the esquires of his body, Henry Vernon. It must have been dictated by the king, fresh from discovering that Henry had landed, as Williams had told him from his own knowledge of the lit beacons, at 'Nangle':

> Trusty and wellbeloved, we greet you well. And forasmuch as our rebels and traitors accompanied with our ancient enemies of France and other strange nations departed out of the water of Seine the first day of this present month making their course westwards, been landed at Nangle besides Milford Haven in Wales on Sunday last passed, as we be credibly informed, intending our utter destruction, the extreme subversion of this our realm and disinheriting of our true subjects of the same, towards whose re-countering, God being our guide, we be utterly determined in our own person to remove in all haste goodly that we can or may. Wherefore we will and straightly charge you that ye in your person with such number as ye have promised unto us sufficiently horsed and harnessed be with us in all

haste to you possible, to give unto us your attendance without failing, all manner [of] excuses set apart, upon pain of forfeiture unto us of all that ye may forfeit and lose. . .

There is no evidence that Vernon responded to the letter by mobilising for the king. Richard's letter to Vernon survives in a collection of summonses, the first dating back to March 1471, when Henry Vernon, then an officer in the household of the Duke of Clarence, was required by the duke to 'see that as well all your tenants and servants as ours in those parts be ready upon an hour's warning to wait upon us in defensible array whensoever we send for you and them'. Several other letters followed, but Vernon failed to obey them; he was not present at the battle of Tewkesbury, prompting Clarence to write for the fourth time, threatening that 'we desire and for your weal advise you, and also in my said lord's name charge you, to dispose you to come and attend upon us'. It seems that, just as fourteen years before, Henry Vernon chose the course of least resistance.

In addition to leading members of the gentry and officers of the crown, Richard intended to summon members of his nobility to Nottingham, commanding them to bring with them their own retinues that would help to bolster the commissions of array. Letters were sent to John Howard, Duke of Norfolk and his son, Thomas, Earl of Surrey to muster their troops at Bury. The king also commanded Henry Percy, Earl of Northumberland and other 'friendly' nobles in the north to conduct musters immediately, travelling to him with their equipped soldiers. Messengers carrying the king's letters were also sent to Robert Brackenbury, the constable of the Tower of London, 'to come to him as soon as possible' bringing with him Thomas Bourchier, Walter Hungerford and several other knights 'as if they would be participating in the war, for he held them in suspicion'. Further letters were sent out, according to the 'Ballad of Bosworth Field', 'throughout England far and near' and 'to every man in his degree'. Even as far south as Exeter, the city had received letters from the king, and duly prepared to send sixteen men to any forthcoming battle. Few records of the musters that were taking place across the country survive, though one letter from the Duke of Norfolk, Thomas Howard, writing from his castle at Framlingham to a member of the Norfolk gentry, Sir John Paston, indicates that

Richard's letters had prompted those supportive members of the nobility to take swift action. Norfolk wrote to Paston, urging him to muster his men at Bury, where he intended to wait on Tuesday 16 August ready to head towards the king's army at Nottingham:

> To my wellbeloved friend, John Paston, be this bill delivered in haste.
>
> Wellbeloved friend, I command me to you, letting you to understand that the King's enemies be a land, and that the King would have set forth as upon Monday but only for Our Lady Day, but for certain he goeth forward as upon Tuesday, for a servant of mine brought me to the certainty.
>
> Wherefore, I pray you that ye meet with me at Bury, for, be the grace of God, I purpose to lie at Bury as upon Tuesday night, and that ye bring with you such company of tall men as ye may goodly make at my cost and charge, be said that ye have promised the King; and I pray you ordain them jackets of my livery, and I shall content you at your meeting with me.
>
> Your lover,
>
> J. NORFOLK

Reading the text of the duke's letter, Sir John Paston must have felt a sense of déjà vu. Only two years earlier, Norfolk had written an almost identical letter, when he requested that Paston bring a company of 'six tall fellows in harness' to help crush Buckingham's rebellion. Then, Paston had ignored the duke: what chance was there that he would decide to act any differently now? And even if John Paston had been at the battle, could Norfolk be entirely confident that he would be fighting on his side? Paston had long been a Lancastrian sympathiser; his patron had traditionally been the Earl of Oxford, whom he had fought for and been wounded fighting against Norfolk at the battle of Barnet.

Paston's loyalties were probably the least of Norfolk's worries: he had promised previously that he would be able to muster 1,000 men at his own cost for the king. Now with Richard demanding that he deliver, Norfolk searched desperately through his tenants, servants and retainers to make up the numbers he had pledged. A list of the 'names of the men that my Lord hath granted the king' survives in his household books, and includes his household servants, tenants, and estate officers who were to bring two or three men each. James Hobart had promised Norfolk at least three men, in addition 'he hath promised my Lord to get him as many men as he can get'. Sir Harry Rosse, Thomas Hoo and Richard Lewknor undertook to 'get my Lord's grace of his servants and tenants, beside them before named . . . out of Sussex and Surrey, well horsed and harnessed'. Whether they did so at Bosworth is debatable: only Thomas Hoo received a minor rebuke when he was removed from the commission of the peace for a year, while James Hobart was promoted to attorney-general in 1486, making it unlikely that he personally fought alongside the duke.

While John Paston or Thomas Hoo may have chosen to absent themselves from any forthcoming conflict, evidence survives for those who chose perhaps a braver course of action. The recent rediscovery of the will of Thomas Longe of Ashwellthorpe gives an indication of the kind of ordinary retainer whom Norfolk could rely upon to follow their lord blindly into battle. On the same day that Norfolk had informed John Paston in his letter that he would be departing Bury for Richard's army at Nottingham, Thomas Longe drew up his will in a nuncupative, or spoken, form, suggesting that Longe had dictated the will himself, as he was about to depart on the long march northwards:

> In the name of God, Amen. The Tuesday after the feast of the Assumption of our Lady, the 16th day of August in the year of our Lord 1485, Thomas Longe of Ashwellthorpe, whole of his body and of a good mind, willing to die as a child of the Church, the said day and time, going forth unto the king's host at Nottingham to battle, made his nuncupative testament in this form.
>
> First he commended his soul to almighty God, [the] king of bliss, and his body to be buried amongst Christian people, in such place as God would dispose for him . . .

The will makes no mention of land, only of chattels. This may be because it was nuncupative but it could also be indicative that Longe was not a man of great substance and that his position in the manor may have been as a retainer within the household of the Earl of Surrey. A Norfolk manor situated some 3½ miles south-east of Wymondham and 12½ miles south-west of Norwich, Thomas Longe's village of Ashwellthorpe had a long Yorkist pedigree – Norfolk's son the Earl of Surrey owned the lordship of the manor. One can imagine Longe, commanded to meet at Bury on 16 August to march under his lord's the Earl of Surrey's banner, to have hastily drawn up his will; knowing that he was to join 'the king's host' at Nottingham and then 'to battle', Longe would have been typical of the unnamed soldiers who would form the backbone of battle. Departing from his home village, the drawing up of his will indicates that Longe himself was uncertain whether he would ever return home, a sense of doubt highlighted by the ambiguous phrase that his body might be buried 'in such a place as God might dispose for him'.

If ordinary men such as Thomas Longe were prepared to fight for their king, it seemed that there were others who were less than certain. Rumours began to spread that many nobles were preparing to delay their arrival, in the hope that they might avoid taking any part in the impending conflict. According to the chronicler Molinet, the nobility was unwilling to prepare for war, with some deciding to 'turn their backs'. Others prepared for war, 'not in the least to come to the help of the king, but to settle their debts with him, and to avenge the bad deeds he had done'. Of all the members of the nobility, it was Thomas Stanley's response Richard most feared, being suspicious over his wife Margaret Beaufort's influence, that she 'might induce her husband to support her son's party'.

According to Vergil, earlier in the summer Stanley had requested permission to 'have gone into his country, for his pleasure as he said, but indeed that he might be ready to receive earl Henry as a friend at his coming'. Richard refused Stanley's request, 'and would not suffer him to depart before he had left George Lord Strange his son as a pledge in the court'. On the other hand, the Crowland Chronicler related that 'a little before the landing' of Henry's army, Thomas Stanley had received permission from Richard to go into Lancashire to visit his family 'from whom he had long been separated', yet he had only been permitted to leave 'on no other condition than that of sending his eldest son, George Lord Strange, to the king at Nottingham in his stead; which he accordingly did'. It seems that rather than leave his son at court before he departed, Thomas Stanley and Lord Strange had journeyed together into Lancashire, where the records reveal that they jointly signed a legal document in Lancashire on 18 July. By 1 August, however, Lord Strange had returned to the king's court at Nottingham Castle, where he was present when the Great Seal was delivered to the king.

Richard's worst fears were confirmed when, after sending orders to Stanley to present himself at Nottingham 'without any delay', he refused. According to 'Bosworth Field', Stanley had left to visit Richard at court but 'fell sick at Manchester by the way', claiming to be suffering from 'sweating sickness'. Lord Strange continued on to Nottingham, where he was arrested. Attempting secretly to escape from his prison cell, he was 'discovered by a snare and seized'. Upon his re-arrest, Strange revealed, possibly under torture, that there was a conspiracy between himself, his uncle Sir William Stanley and Sir John Savage 'to support the party of the Earl of Richmond'. He begged for forgiveness and promised that 'his father would come to the king's aid, as fast as possible, with all his power'. Strange wrote to his father making clear his own precarious situation and the 'danger he was in' together with a plea for urgent support.

It seems that Lord Strange was not alone in being singled out for arrest. A Welsh poem dedicated to William Gruffudd, a nephew of Thomas Stanley by marriage who had been appointed chamberlain of Gwynedd in late 1483, suggests that Gruffudd was arrested and taken to Nottingham at the same time as Lord Strange: 'manifestly by deceit he was put unwillingly somewhere out of his own country . . . the arrest and the taking away of Lord Strange . . . was a double misfortune'. Another poem mentioned that his arrest was due to his office, and that Gruffudd was 'under God's care while at the mercy of King Richard, a man who is cruel to a prisoner'.

According to a version of the 'Ballad of Bosworth Field', Richard sent a messenger to Thomas Stanley who told him he 'must raise up under your banner to maintain Richard our king, for yonder cometh Richmond over the flood with many an alyannt [foreigner] out of far country, to challenge the crown of England; you must raise that under your banner be with the noble power that you may bring, or else the Lord Strange you must never see, that is in danger of our king'. If the ballad is correct, news of Strange's imprisonment came as a surprise to Stanley, who is supposed to have remarked that he had never dealt 'with traitory'. Both Thomas Stanley and his younger brother

Sir William had previously benefited from Richard's patronage, with the king showing his gratitude for their support during Buckingham's rebellion, granting Thomas Stanley the lordship of Kimbolton and Sir William Stanley Buckingham's manor of Thornbury in Gloucestershire. Other grants to the family followed, 'for the singular and faithful service which they have hitherto done to us not only in favouring our right and title . . . but also in repressing the treason and malice of our traitors and rebels'. In the context of the Stanleys' previous support, Richard's arrest of Lord Strange seems to have been a political miscalculation that would backfire spectacularly. The ballad suggests that Stanley only became involved against Richard and joined Henry's cause after the arrest of Lord Strange, alleging that Richard was advised by 'wicked councell' that Stanley and Strange had been in conspiracy with the Earl of Oxford, organising that 'they may show upon a day a band such as may no Lord in Christianity' and urged him to order their arrest, 'or else short while continue shall ye in England to be our King'.

For now, despite the king's dire threats, Thomas Stanley chose to remain uncommitted to either side. Stanley's caution was understandable. With his son in captivity, to demonstrate any sign of revolt would have inevitably resulted in Strange's execution. As long as Richard remained uncertain about Stanley's actions, and which side he might take in the forthcoming battle, Stanley could have reasonably surmised that his son would be safe: possession of Lord Strange was all that Richard had to influence his father's actions. Polydore Vergil believed this was why Thomas Stanley had refused to commit to Henry's cause sooner, knowing that to do so would have placed his son's life at risk.

His brother Sir William Stanley's reply to Richard's messenger was more peremptory. 'I marvel of our king', he is reported to have said, discovering news of Lord Strange's arrest, 'he hath my nephew, my brother's heir; a truer knight is not in Christianity: he shall repent . . . for all the power that he can bring, he shall either fight or flee, or lose his life. I will make a vow, I shall give him such a breakfast on a day as never knight gave king.' Perhaps Sir William Stanley felt that he had nothing to lose: he had always been more hot-headed than his elder brother, being attainted for his participation at the battle of Ludlow in the Parliament of 1459, whereas Thomas Stanley had more sensibly avoided punishment. In the summer of 1485, there was perhaps another reason behind William Stanley's fatalism: on 12 August, his sixteen-year-old stepson Edward, the Earl of Worcester, died. Stanley had married the boy's mother, Elizabeth Hopton, sometime after the death of the previous earl, John Tiptoft, who had been executed in October 1470; Stanley and his wife had been awarded the joint guardianship of the estates of the earldom, ensuring that Sir William was able to live the life of a nobleman with wealth independent of the king's favour. All this changed in August 1485, when the death of the young earl meant that the title lapsed, with the estates passing to the remaining sisters of the family.

Sir William Stanley was probably comforting his wife Elizabeth on her young son's death when news reached him that Richard had issued a proclamation at Coventry and other towns publicly denouncing him and Sir John Savage as 'traitors to the King'. Suddenly he was left with nothing: and with nothing to lose, neither lands nor offices, he must have considered that he had no other choice than to declare his hand, throwing his lot in with Henry Tudor.

The Crowland Chronicler was in little doubt that Henry's journey, 'along wild and twisting tracks', was aiming for North Wales, 'where William Stanley . . . was in sole command'. Continuing his march northwards on 11 August, according to tradition Henry stopped at Wern Newydd, four miles from Llwyndafydd. It seems unlikely that, only four miles away from Llwyndafydd, Henry would have made an overnight stop, but this does not preclude his enjoying some kind of hospitality. Travelling across the low-lying plains, he finally spent the night at St Hilary's church at Llanilar, four miles south of Aberystwyth, where Henry is supposed to have slept at the old mansion of Llidiardau, which overlooks the Ystwyth valley.

The following day, on Friday 12 August, Henry and his forces continued their march towards Aberystwyth. According to Vergil, Henry made almost uninterrupted progress, 'delaying almost nowhere'. There were, however, he wrote, 'several enemy districts which had been strengthened by garrisons' that had to be overcome, but he 'took them with almost no trouble'. In his printed work, Vergil did not specify which locations exactly had caused Henry's army difficulty, but in his manuscript he revealed that when Henry reached Aberystwyth castle, 'held by his opponents with a not very strong garrison', he was forced to attack it 'and took [it]without much trouble'. The castle had been under the control of the Duke of Buckingham before it had been granted to Walter Devereux, Lord Ferrers, a stalwart supporter of the king's. If Richard needed any evidence that Henry's invasion, which he had at first dismissed as being of little consequence, was picking up momentum, the news that Aberystwyth had fallen to his enemies must have been a significant blow.

For Henry, the absence of any effective opposing army was proving unsettling. It was almost as if his uninterrupted journey was too easy. He remained especially nervous about the movements of Walter Herbert and Rhys ap Thomas; he had hoped that Rhys would have joined him at his landing in Milford Haven, but instead had to make do with a trickle of defections from Rhys's camp while Rhys himself remained frustratingly elusive. The later 'Life of Rhys ap Thomas' claimed that the defections had been deliberate, 'so to strengthen his party, if occasion were offered; to direct and convoy him over those uncouth ways and fastnesses; to call in for such provisions, as the country could afford, for the relief of their army; and lastly, to inform the people as they went along, what side Rhys ap Thomas meant to stick to'. Nevertheless Henry remained 'much appalled and troubled in mind, not knowing well what to think', since rumours that had spread through his army suggested that Rhys 'meant to side with Richard, and for that purpose was ready to give him battle and interrupt his passage'. According to the Tudor chronicler Edward Hall, Sir Walter Herbert and Rhys ap Thomas intended 'to encounter' with Henry's army and 'to stop their passage', while another stated how they were both 'in a readiness to give him battle'. Rhys had his own reasons for remaining ambivalent. The account of his life later claimed that Richard had written Rhys a letter demanding his loyalty and an oath of allegiance that he was to use his 'best endeavours for the conservation of your royal authority in these parts, and to apply likewise my soundest forces for the safe guarding of Milford Haven from all foreign invasion; especially to impeach and stop the passage of the Earl of Richmond, if so by any treacherous means he should attempt our coasts', at the same time as sending his young son as a hostage. Rhys refused to send his son, but may have been bought with further financial inducements: Jean

Molinet suggested that Richard had given £700 to 'a rich man named Thomas to raise an army, and they had to gather together with Lord Herbert'.

Rhys's 'Life' would later claim that his hesitancy to commit to Henry's cause was a deliberate ploy on his part in order to 'hoodwink' Richard into believing that he intended to give battle. Even if this convenient story were the case, Henry could not afford to gamble on Rhys's equivocation. After he had taken Aberystwyth, possibly spending the night there, he paused to send out scouts to discover where Rhys and Walter Herbert's armies were encamped. Since Henry's landing, both armies had been shadowing his progress through Wales; Rhys ap Thomas had commanded that beacons across the region be set on fire, 'thereby to give notice to all the countries adjacent, of his landing, and withal to summon his friends and kinsmen from all parts'. He now had at his disposal a significant force, estimated at 1,500 men. Having travelled to Carmarthen, he then journeyed to Llandovery and then to Brecon in the Usk valley. By the time Rhys came to Brecon, his train had grown so long that he needed to reduce its number, 'the company that followed him growing cumbersome'. Finding that women and children were apparently offering themselves to fight, Rhys decided to examine his troops and selected the best 2,000 men fully armed on horseback, who supposedly 'drew with a kind of ravishing delight, the eyes of all beholders'. At the same time, Rhys decided to make provision for his own fortunes, and how to 'make a safe retreat in case of extremity'. In doing so, he chose an additional 500 men whom he placed in the charge of his two brothers, David and John, and his only son Griffiths Rhys, commanding them not to take to arms 'until his pleasure were further signified'. They were also to ensure that those who had rallied to support him were to be protected from injury. Those who were left behind went back to their homes, not without an 'abundance of tears' while Rhys continued to move northwards across the mountainous terrain of Wales.

Henry's scouts returned, informing him that though Rhys and Herbert 'were before him in arms' they 'were keeping to their camp'. Henry could no longer avoid confrontation: he had pushed as far north as he was able, and now needed to turn inland, making his way to the English border. After a 'speedy consultation with his people' Henry decided that he would continue to 'march towards them' and 'set out for England as soon as possible'. The following morning on 13 August, Henry continued his march into the Dyfi estuary and on to Machynlleth, a distance of twenty-three miles, arriving at the town by the evening where tradition records that he lodged in a house still surviving in the town.

Henry's arrival at Machynlleth was laden with significance. The former capital of Wales, it was here that Owain Glyn Dwr had declared himself Prince of Wales and had held his own parliament during the rebellion that had drawn Henry's ancestors into combat with Henry IV. Nearly eighty years later, once more it provided the focus of yet another assault upon the crown. Henry used his time there to send out another round of letters in preparation for the next stage of his journey. During his march along the Welsh coast, letters sent out in advance to the nearby Welsh gentry along the route had ensured that his forces had swelled with new recruits to his cause. In this next stage of his journey, across particularly difficult terrain, Henry hoped that as he approached the English border, he might maximise the potential number of his troops, or at least ensure that he would receive a welcome passage without the inconvenience of any hostility.

One of Henry's letters written from Machynlleth on 14 August survives. As was becoming common practice for Henry by now, the letter begins with the common formula of the royal signet: 'By the King. Trusty and wellbeloved, we greet you well'. It is addressed to Sir Roger Kynaston, a Shropshire knight and the uncle by marriage of John Lord Grey of Powys; Grey was an important and powerful local magnate, who held the surrounding lordship of Merioneth and the constableship of the impregnable Harlech Castle, the former bastion of Lancastrian dissent that had served Jasper Tudor so well during his renegade years. Grey was also considered one of Richard's allies: a member of the king's council, for which he received £100, the previous year he had been placed in command of the thousand archers sent by Richard to Brittany to serve under Duke Francis II.

Yet Henry had discovered that Grey was currently absent from Wales. With Kynaston placed in charge of his estates, he hoped instead that he might be able to persuade him to support his cause. In order to achieve this, Henry was prepared to make some remarkable claims. He wrote to Kynaston that he had been 'credibly informed that our trusty and wellbeloved cousin the Lord Powis hath in the time passed be of that mind and disposition that at this our coming in to these parts he had fully concluded and determined to have do us service'. It is worth considering here the timing of Grey's mission to Brittany with the English archers. The archers had departed shortly after 26 June 1484, while Grey was back in England by September, where he was a witness to the peace treaty with Scotland. At the same time, Henry appears to have remained in Brittany until mid-September. Did Grey meet Henry during his mission, secretly giving him his allegiance? Henry certainly believed he did; if so, it is testament to the detail and time that had gone into planning the invasion. Henry continued:

> Now we understand that he is absent and ye have the rule of his lands and folks, we will and pray you and upon your allegiance straightly charge and command you that in all haste possible ye assemble his said folks and servants and with them so assembled and defensibly arrayed for the war ye come to us for our aid and assistance in this our enterprise for the recovery of the crown of our realm of England to us of right appertaining. And that this be not failed as ye will that we be your good lord in time to come and avoid our grievest displeasure and answer to us at your peril. Given under our signet beside our town of Machynlleth the xiiii of August.

For others, Henry was prepared to trade threats for other means to secure support. By the time he reached Machynlleth, Henry understood that Rhys ap Thomas was driving a hard bargain. In particular, it was clear that his support would come at a price: according to Vergil, it was a price Henry was willing to pay, promising Rhys either in letters or through messengers 'the perpetual governorship of Wales if he came over to his side'. It must have been at Machynlleth that Henry planned the final course of his route, deciding that he would enter England through the town of Shrewsbury. There he would need to cross the river Severn, the Rubicon between Wales and England. To do so, some significant obstacles needed to be overcome: firstly, without Rhys ap Thomas's support, it was likely that he would be cut off at the pass; secondly, Henry desperately needed the Stanleys to show their hand and join his cause. Hoping that whatever previous agreements had been made would now be honoured, Henry sent his chaplain Christopher Urswick with instructions to Thomas Stanley and his mother Margaret, residing at Lathom, 'so that the friends whom he trusted should know in what district to meet him'. Letters were also sent to Sir William Stanley at Holt Castle, Gilbert Talbot 'and some others'. According to Vergil: 'This was the gist of his instructions: he had decided, relying on the help of his friends, to cross into England through Shropshire, [and] accordingly to ask them to meet him and he would tell them more about his plans in a suitable place and at a suitable time.'

After a march of ninety-two miles in seven days, Henry was about to embark on the last and most perilous stage of his journey. He looked to gather strength from wherever he might find it. While at Machynlleth, tradition records that Henry paid a visit to the home of one of his most devoted supporters, the Welsh bard Dafydd Llwyd at Mathafarn, six miles east of the town. One story relates how Henry asked Dafydd, a noted prophesier, whether he would be victorious in his campaign. Dafydd was too nervous to give an immediate answer in case he gave the wrong reply, promising instead that he would return a verdict the following morning. Retiring to his bed somewhat dejected, his wife asked Dafydd the reason for his sudden melancholy. When the poet explained, she retorted incredulously that the answer was simple: it was obvious that he should tell Henry that he should succeed to the throne. If that proved to be the case, she argued, Dafydd could only be rewarded; 'if not, you need not fear that he will return here to reproach you for being a false prophet'. One can assume the answer Dafydd gave to Henry on his return; whether Henry truly believed him is impossible to say.

On 15 August Henry resumed his march knowing that as he made his way inland, there could be no quick escape or turning back. The next stage of his journey would be both a bleak and difficult one. Leading his army across the divide between the Dyfi and Severn rivers, down the Severn valley into Newtown, without halting, the army moved northwards away from the Severn, continuing across the hills, following the desolate divide between the Dyfi valley and the valley of the Upper Banwy known as the pass of Bwlchyfedwen. It was a punishing thirty-mile journey; twenty-four miles was considered a good day's march by the standards of the day, without taking into account the narrow and twisting unpaved tracks which made fast progress impossible. It was evening before Henry reached his intended destination, the mansion of Dolarddyn near Castle Caereinion, a few miles west of Welshpool.

The following morning on Tuesday 16 August, the army travelled the six-mile journey to Welshpool. Without stopping in the town, Henry led the troops several miles outside its walls to climb up to the top of a hill nearby. Long Mountain, known in Wales as the Mynydd Digoll, was a well-known site, with a vast plain at its summit across which traversed a Roman road, leading to Shrewsbury and on to Watling Street. With views stretching into the horizon and the Severn below, Henry could see England within his grasp.

Long Mountain had not been chosen as Henry's destination for the night simply because of its views or strategic importance. It was here that, after setting up camp for the night, Henry could first hear, then witness, the arrival of Rhys ap Thomas, his banners displaying his insignia of the black raven heralding the arrival of his 'battle' described as 'a goodly number of soldiers', estimated at between 1,000 and 2,000 men. It had taken some bargaining to convince Rhys to join with Henry, but the offer of making Rhys the chamberlain of South Wales, made at Machynlleth two days before, had its desired effect. On Long Mountain, Rhys formally pledged his loyalty to Henry and 'submitted to his authority'.

Rhys ap Thomas was not the only Welshman to commit to Henry's cause that evening. Throughout the night, other members of the Welsh gentry arrived to join Henry's assembled army on Long Mountain, including William Griffith of Penrhyn near Bangor and Richard ap Howell of Mostyn in Flint and Rhys Fawr ap Meredudd of Plas Iolyn in the upper Conwy valley. With them they brought not only men and arms, but provisions such as fattened oxen to refresh Henry's exhausted troops.

The rendezvous point at Long Mountain had been carefully planned, with its location chosen in advance, probably at Machynlleth two days earlier when Henry had sent messengers to Rhys and the surrounding gentry in a final appeal for their support. After Henry's offer had been relayed to him by messengers, Rhys ap Thomas had decided that the moment to finally defect from Walter Herbert's forces had come. Nevertheless, Rhys could not be entirely sure whether he was making the right decision. Marching northwards from Brecon, he decided to leave a contingent of 500 cavalry commanded by his two brothers to act as a rearguard in case he changed his mind. Travelling across the Eppynt hills to Builth, Rhys journeyed along the upper Wye valley to Rhayader then to the upper Severn valley at Llanidloes before making the short final march to Henry at Long Mountain.

The impact of Rhys ap Thomas's decision to join Henry at Long Mountain could not be underestimated. The author of the ballad 'The Rose of England' wrote how Rhys's defection had drawn 'Wales with him, a worthy sight it was to see, how the Welshmen rose wholly with him'. The following morning, on Wednesday 17 August, his confidence bolstered by Rhys's support, Henry decided to advance upon Shrewsbury in the Severn valley below. It was essential that he enter the town in order to cross the Severn across its Welsh bridge. He could not afford a repeat of what had taken place at Gloucester in 1471, when the city refused to allow Margaret of Anjou and the Duke of Somerset's Lancastrian troops to enter, delaying their crossing of the Severn and forcing them to embark upon an exhausting march to their fateful end at Tewkesbury.

Yet the prospect of history repeating itself was exactly the nightmare Henry faced when he arrived at the town's gates. When he requested entry to the town, in spite of his insistence that the town would remain unharmed, its gates remained locked. According to the town's chronicle, Henry arrived to find the town's gates shut against him with the portcullis let down. When Henry's messenger came to the gate, 'commanding them to open the gates to their right King', the head bailiff Thomas Mitton refused outright, swearing that he 'knew no king but only King Richard to whom he was sworn, whose life tenants he and his fellows were, and before he should enter there he should go over his belly'.

Thomas Mitton, whom Richard considered 'our trusty and wellbeloved squire', had served twice as town bailiff, once before in 1480. After Buckingham's rebellion, Richard had granted Mitton 'in consideration of his good and acceptable service' the castle and lordship of Cawes in the Welsh Marches, together with lands worth £50. It is hardly surprising that Mitton remained steadfastly loyal to a king in whose service he had already been well rewarded. Mitton's insistence that he would not break the oath he had taken was so vehement – he declared to the messenger that he would need to be 'slain to the ground and so to "roon ov'hym" before he entered' – that Henry decided to withdraw his forces to the nearby village of Forton, three miles away, where his men spent the night on the heath, with Henry himself staying at a certain Hugh of Forton's house in the village. The Hugh in question was likely to have been Hugh Fortune, described in a taxation return as owing 20s, yet in the margin of the document it was recorded how Henry 'lay in his house one night in the journey of his arrival'.

The following morning, Thursday 18 August, Henry sent his messengers once more to entreat with Mitton, insisting that his forces wished only to 'pass quietly' and that 'the Earl their master did not mean to hurt the town nor none therein but to go to try his right'. Further, they were to promise that Henry would protect Mitton's oath. Henry had devised an ingenious plan. Returning from Forton to the town, Henry summoned Mitton and explained that he wanted him to lie on his back. The town's chronicler recorded the extraordinary scene: 'upon this they entered and in passing through the said Mitton lay along the ground and his belly upward and so the said Earl stepped over him and saved his oath'.

The image of Thomas Mitton lying down so that Henry might step over him in order to preserve his oath may have been apocryphal; an identical and unlikely story is recorded in the seventeenth-century 'Life of Sir Rhys ap Thomas' that Rhys too lay on the ground and 'suffered the earl to pass over him, so to make good his promise to King Richard, that none should enter in at Milford, unless he came first over his belly'. Alternatively, it may have been an acknowledged method of avoiding the implications of breaking an oath before God, perhaps influenced by biblical and classical examples.

In any case, something, or more importantly, someone had persuaded Mitton to change his stance overnight. What had caused the bailiff to quite literally roll over? The arrival at Shrewsbury of several influential local gentry from the surrounding region strengthened Henry's forces: William Megheyn joined Henry 'toward the town of Shrewsbury', while it would later be remembered how Richard Crompe 'by his means and diligent labour caused the town of Shrewsbury to be delivered' to Henry 'at your coming by that way'. The most significant arrival to join Henry's army, however, was Sir Richard Corbet, who later wrote how he 'was one of the first, to his poor power, that took your part, and first came unto your Grace at the Town of Shrewsbury, and there was sworn your liegeman'. Corbet brought with him a company of 800 men, 'gentlemen and others his friends that came with him'. Corbet's influence arose not only from the number of men he had brought with him, but also from the fact that he was Lord Thomas Stanley's son-in-law.

Important clues are also to be found in Polydore Vergil's manuscript history. It was, Vergil notes, on the same day that Henry arrived at the gates of Shrewsbury, that Christopher Urswick returned 'laden with money' from 'the individuals to whom he had been sent'. Urswick was also to inform Henry that 'all was safe with his friends', and that they 'were prepared to do their duty at the right time'.

It must have been Stanley's influence that had caused the gates of Shrewsbury to be lifted to Henry. The ballad traditions, which must be treated with caution given their origin within the Stanley household and the subsequent degree of importance they place upon the Stanley involvement in Henry's enterprise, provide a detailed insight into the nature of that influence. The 'Ballad of Lady Bessie' records that it was Sir William Stanley, rather than Thomas Stanley, who had sent his messenger Rowland Warburton to Shrewsbury, together with letters signed by his own hand, ordering that the citizens there admit Henry and his army. When Warburton arrived, he found the portcullis down and the citizens and bailiffs 'in full great scorn' refusing to allow anyone inside the city, especially Henry who they claimed 'in England he should wear no crown'. Only when Warburton decided to tie Sir William Stanley's instructions to a stone and threw it over the city walls, asking that the bailiffs read them, did the town open its gates and allow Henry's troops to proceed through its streets, though the ballad states that Henry did not stay overnight there, hearing that Richard was preparing his forces. Another ballad, 'The Rose of England', indicated that through a garret on the city walls, Thomas Mitton had shouted out: 'At these gates no man enter shall', and kept Henry waiting outside the town for the night and the following day, until letters arrived from Sir William

Stanley, whereupon 'the gates were opened presently'. The ballad adds the additional flourish that when the troops entered the town, the Earl of Oxford was so furious at Mitton's initial refusal to open the gates that he threatened to cut his head off with his sword, being only prevented from doing so by Henry, who suggested that 'if we begin to head so soon, in England we shall bear no degree'.

With the town's gates finally opened, Henry and his troops were led through Shrewsbury escorted by the bailiffs, with Henry riding in the middle of the columns of his forces. The 'Life of Rhys ap Thomas' recorded that Henry was received with a hero's welcome, 'the streets being strewed with herbs and flowers, and their doors adorned with green boughs, in testimony of a true hearty reception'. Clearly the town's citizens felt that they had much ground to make up after their initial frosty refusal to admit the earl: the bailiff accounts for the town, signed off by Thomas Mitton and Roger Knight, record that £4 4s 10d was 'paid for divers costs incurred by the town at the time of the coming of King Henry VII against King Richard, and for wages of divers soldiers hired by the king himself'.

10

SECRET FRIENDS

•◆•

S ince his discovery of Henry's landing in Wales, Richard had remained calm, confident that he would be able to deal with the invasion. When reports had reached him that Henry was 'utterly unfurnished and feeble in all things', the king believed that Henry had 'proceeded rashly, considering his small company' and would 'surely have an evil end'. Lord Strange's arrest, bringing with it news of a plot involving Sir William Stanley, had left him unsettled, but still Richard was prepared to wait at Nottingham. He decided to delay his departure from the city until Tuesday 16 August, since the Monday was the religious festival of the Assumption of the Virgin, a public holiday that had special significance in Nottingham, where the borough church had been dedicated to the Virgin Mary. When Tuesday arrived, however, Richard had still not made up his mind to leave, and instead returned to his hunting lodge at Bestwood where he stayed the night.

Richard remained at Bestwood for the rest of the next day. It was here that the king was greeted by two men, John Sponer, the sergeant of the mace of the city of York, and another messenger, John Nicholson. They had ridden through the night for an audience with him, having been sent by the mayor and citizens of York, who had met the previous morning in their council chamber, having heard the news that the king's rebels, led by Henry Tudor, had landed. Yet, somewhat alarmingly, the citizens had still not received any instructions from the king to assemble an armed force. That summer the plague had raged though the city, and they were understandably anxious as to what demands needed to be placed upon them. 'It was determined,' the recorder of the minutes of the meeting wrote, 'that John Sponer . . . should ride to Nottingham to the king's grace to understand his pleasure as in sending up any of his subjects within this city to his said grace for the subduing of his enemies late arrived in the parties of Wales.' Meanwhile, the city had sent out proclamations of their own, ordering that every citizen should be 'ready in their most defensible array to attend upon the mayor, for the welfare of this City, within an hour's warning, upon pain of imprisonment'.

Hearing this news related to him in his chamber at Bestwood by the two messengers, Richard must have been puzzled. Commissions of array had already been ordered to muster in preparation. Letters had been sent out to commissioners ordering them to prepare their forces: for York, the Earl of Northumberland, as commissioner for the East Riding, should have given them warning. If Richard mused on the reasons why the earl had not yet sent out summonses to York, he kept his thoughts to himself. He thanked Sponer and Nicholson for the city's loyalty, asking them to inform the mayor that he would require 400 men to be sent to him as soon as possible. John Nicholson immediately set off to return to York with the king's message, while John Sponer chose to remain in Richard's household, accompanying him back to Nottingham.

When Richard returned to the city, the king was greeted by further bad news. Henry Tudor had managed to enter Shrewsbury and cross the Severn. Richard was overwhelmed with anger. 'Suffering no inconvenience', his confident mask began to peel. 'He began to burn with chagrin', one chronicler wrote, railing at those he had trusted, no doubt men such as Rhys ap Thomas, whom he believed had broken their oaths. How had Henry's march been able to progress through Wales and into Shrewsbury unchallenged? Threatening retribution, according to one ballad he promised to kill any Lancashire knight or squire 'from the town of Lancaster to Shrewsbury', leaving 'none alive'. He was equally furious that Wales had succumbed to Tudor's march, pledging to lay waste 'from the holy-head to St David's Land / where now be towers & castles high', reducing them to 'parks & plain fields'. In singling out men from Lancashire in his outburst, Richard must have suspected that Henry's success in entering Shrewsbury had been aided by Stanley support. He had already condemned Sir William Stanley as a traitor, but Thomas Stanley's suspected treachery was more difficult to prove: while Lord Strange remained in his custody, Richard calculated, Stanley could hardly gamble with own his son's life.

For now, it was clear to Richard that he would have to confront Henry as soon as he possibly could. In order to 'espy what route' Henry's forces were taking, he sent out his own men, known commonly as 'scurriers', to track the oncoming march of his enemy. In the records of the borough of Nottingham, there is reference to Thomas Hall being paid 6s 8d 'by the Mayor's commandment' on Thursday 18 August, 'riding forth to aspye for the town before the field'. Slowly, the city was filling with thousands of armed men as the commissions of array creaked into action, the Crowland chronicler remarking that 'there was a greater number of fighting men than there had ever been seen before, on one side, in England'. As soon as Richard could discover what his enemy's next moves were, he would be ready to face him in battle.

Once news of Henry's progress through Wales and his intended destination through Shrewsbury had reached Thomas Stanley at his castle at Lathom, he decided to mobilise his own forces. Leaving Lathom Castle with his retinue, Thomas Stanley intended to keep a separate course from his brother William: if his brother had been condemned as a traitor by Richard at Coventry, Stanley's caution was understandable. He could hardly have been prepared to jeopardise his son's life by openly joining forces with his brother.

According to the 'Ballad of Lady Bessie', Thomas Stanley set out from Lathom on Monday 15 August, travelling through Warrington where he was joined by other retainers, both knights and squires who had assembled with 'their banners in the sun glittering', before heading for Newcastle under Lyme. There exists an undated letter from Stanley, requesting James Scarisbrick to meet him with twenty-four horsemen at Warrington to ride with him to London.

Meanwhile Sir William Stanley rode from Holt, just thirty miles to the north of Shrewsbury, to Nantwich, where he met 'all the North Wales for the most part, the flower of Cheshire, with him he did bring'. Richard had issued a commission to all the knights and gentlemen of Chester on 13 January 1485 signalling that he had granted Lord Stanley, Lord Strange and Sir William Stanley 'to have the rule and leading of all persons appointed to do the king service when they be warned against the king's rebels . . . and if any rebels arrive in those parts that then all the power that they can make be ready to assist the said lords and knight'. Sir William had been given the power to muster their entire county, ordering that its men obey his every command; now Stanley took the opportunity to raise the forces against Richard. Henry himself would later acknowledge the 'good and faithful service' that the sheriffs at Chester, John Norys and Hugh Hurleton, together with 'other of the said city', had committed to his cause. According to the ballad, on Tuesday morning 16 August, Sir William continued his journey from Nantwich to Stone.

Henry's hopes had been 'raised' by the news that the Stanleys intended to come to his aid. Just as welcome was the additional funds he had been given, with Christopher Urswick returning to his camp 'laden with money which he had received from the individuals to whom he had been sent'. Departing Shrewsbury, Henry and his army crossed over the Severn at the town's Welsh bridge, making the journey to Newport, where he pitched camp on the nearest hill for the night.

Already his army had benefited from some significant recruits over the past few days. In addition to the 1,500 men brought by Sir Rhys ap Thomas, a large number of gentry from nearby surrounding counties had begun to join Henry's standard. Sir Richard Corbet, whose stepfather was Sir William Stanley, had led a force of 800 men from Shropshire. Thomas Croft, a former Yorkist who had been brought up with Edward IV, arrived from Herefordshire; from Worcestershire, John Hanley, a former servant of the Duke of Clarence, while in Gloucestershire, Robert Pointz had set out to join the army. There was further good news when that same evening after they had passed through Shrewsbury, as Henry's camp settled down for the night outside Newport, Gilbert Talbot came to him in the evening 'with 500 and more armed men'.

An uncle of the young Earl of Shrewsbury, Talbot also commanded significant influence among the Shropshire gentry. Talbot's defection had not come as a surprise; he had been in contact with Henry in exile since 1484, but it is likely that he brought with him news of the Stanleys' initial movements. It is perhaps for this reason that the following morning, Friday 19 August, Henry advanced his army northwards to Stafford, where it had been arranged for him to meet Sir William Stanley, who had ridden from Stone for the meeting. Polydore Vergil is tantalisingly brief about the nature of the discussions between Sir William

ll Bay, near Dale on the Milford Peninsula: scene of Henry Tudor's landing on the ning of 7 August 1485.

Rhys ap Thomas, whose eventual support for Henry Tudor in his march through Wales gave a welcome boost to the campaign.

revale Church, Atherstone, originally Gate Chapel of the Cistercian Merevale bey, where Henry Tudor met with the nleys shortly before engaging battle at sworth.

Welsh Gate, Shrewsbury, where Thomas tton initially refused Henry Tudor entry the town.

The Blue Boar Inn, Leicester. Tradition records that Richard lodged in the town before travelling to Ambion Hill ready for battle. Originally named the White Boar, its name was altered on Henry's accession.

Sir Gervase Clifton, a former Esquire of the Body to Edward IV, who fought on Richard's side at Bosworth, yet survived and was later pardoned by Henry VII.

Roger Wake of Blisworth, Northamptonsh[ire], brother-in-law to William Catesby. Wake survived the battle and petitioned against his attainder claiming he had fought under duress. He was later pardoned by Henry V[II].

Simon Digby, who defected to Henry Tudor's side shortly before the battle.

Sir John Cheyney, reportedly six feet eight inches tall, who was unhorsed by Richard I[II] in the final moments of the battle.

...oking out across the fields where Richard's final last stand may have taken place, and where ...haeological investigations in 2012 discovered significant numbers of cannon balls and vital ...es, such as a silver gilt badge of a boar, Richard III's insignia.

The battle of Bosworth from an early sixteenth-century relief carving, originally commissioned for the Earl of Oxford's residence at Castle Hedingham. In the centre, Henry rides over Richard III, who is clutching his crown.

...anoramic view of the battlefield at Bosworth, known by contemporaries as Redemore, ...en from the top of the tower at St Margaret's Church, Stoke Golding.

A gold signet ring depicting Richard's insignia of the boar found near the battlefield.

The collection of thirty-four cannon balls discovere at the battlefield site.

The Bosworth Crucifix. Discovered in the eighteenth century, its roundels are emblazoned with the Yorkist sun.

Evidence of Richard's forces at Bosworth: th silver gilt boar badge would have been worn a gentleman in the king's army. Could it hav been lost in the fighting or in flight?

A broken sword handle, discovered in 2012: clear evidence that hand-to-hand combat took place in the Redemore plain.

Richard III's prayer book, which the king took to the battle with him. Henry later gave the manuscript to his mother Margaret.

A lead badge representing the Yorkist sun, which was probably worn by an ordinary soldier in Richard's army.

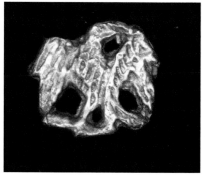

The golden badge of an eagle with a snake in its mouth, discovered at a separate location, possibly near the windmill where the Duke of Norfolk was captured and Richard's vanguard was defeated.

The gravesite of Richard III, discovered in August 2012 under a carpark on the site of Greyfriars Church. The hands of the skeleton have been tied.

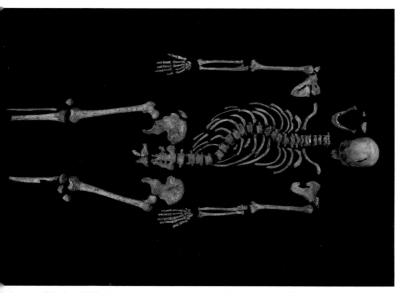

e bones of Richard III clearly demonstrate a noticeable curvature of the spine known as
liosis.

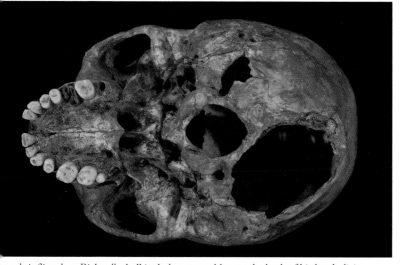

ounds inflicted on Richard's skull include a severe blow to the back of his head, slicing
ough the bone that would have certainly proved fatal and a puncture wound at the top of
skull. In total, ten wounds to the skeleton have been identified.

St James' Church, Dadlington, where the 'bones and bodies' of the Bosworth dead were buried. In 1511, Henry VIII signed a warrant allowing the churchwardens to fundraise for a battlefield chapel.

A terracotta bust o Henry VII by Piet Torrigiano.

and Henry, observing only that 'while he stayed in that district, William Stanley came to him with a few companions, had a brief discussion with him, and returned to his soldiers whom he had collected.'

What exact words were spoken between Henry and Sir William, or what agreement may have been reached, is unknown. Without Thomas, Lord Stanley's tacit approval, William must have remained circumspect as to the precise support the Stanley family could promise Henry, although William himself, free from any restraint, could easily have committed himself to his cause. According to the ballads originating from the Stanley household, when Sir William arrived in Henry's presence he knelt in front of him, and taking Henry by the hand, said: 'I am full glad of thee. Through the help of my Lord thy brother & thee, I trust in England to continue King'. The poem places the following words in the mouth of Sir William:

Welcome my sovereign King Henry!
challenge thy Heritage & thy Land
that thine own is, & thine shall be
be eager to fight, & loath to flee!
let manhood be bred thy breast within!
& remember another day who doth for thee
all of England when thou art King.

After the meeting, Stanley returned to Stone 'by light of the day'. Stanley was not prepared to compromise his brother by joining forces with Henry quite yet; nevertheless it is significant that, after his meeting with Sir William Stanley at Stafford, Henry changed the direction of his march, deciding to move in a south-easterly direction to Lichfield and on towards Watling Street. Once he joined the Roman road, he would be able to make swift progress into the capital, where he might proclaim himself as king, leaving Richard stranded at Nottingham. Henry arrived at Lichfield that evening, deciding to remain outside the city overnight. His entry into Lichfield early the following morning of Saturday 20 August must have given him confidence that his plan to aim for London would be possible: the 'Ballad of Bosworth Field' paints a picture of joyous crowds, 'both old and young' crowding together to watch Henry's army pass into the city over Woosley bridge, so that they might 'had they a sight of our King'. Meanwhile, guns 'cracken on high' in what was 'a goodly sight to see'. Polydore Vergil wrote in his history that Henry had been 'received honourably' by the city's inhabitants, though in his original manuscript he was clearer as to what had taken place, describing how Henry, upon entering the town, had been 'received by the clergy as King, with entreaties'. If some kind of unofficial ceremony had taken place, recognising Henry as king, it was a significant moment.

It is not difficult to envisage who may have been involved in planning the elaborate ceremony, treating Henry's arrival at Lichfield as if it were some kind of coronation triumph. Three days previously, Thomas, Lord Stanley had arrived at the city with an entourage of about 5,000 armed men. Leaving Lichfield before Henry had the chance to make an entry into the city, Stanley journeyed instead to Atherstone, on the edge of the Roman road at Watling Street, where he intended to wait for Henry's army to arrive. For several days, Thomas Stanley had appeared to withdraw each time Henry's army had advanced, shadowing his movement. In doing so, Stanley would be able to defend his actions to the king, by blocking the road to London his forces were preventing the rebel advance. 'This he did,' Vergil observed, 'to avoid suspicion, fearing if before they should come to hand strokes he should overtly show himself to stand and hold with earl Henry, least that King Richard, who as yet did not utterly mistrust his loyalty, might kill his son George.' Stanley may have been certain of his own tactics, yet for Henry the prevarication was nailbiting. At any time, Stanley could turn against him, destroying Henry's cause, if it meant saving his own son's life.

When scouts sent out by the king returned, they informed Richard that Henry Tudor had entered Lichfield to great fanfare. The king knew that he could not afford to delay a confrontation any longer. Henry's army was advancing fast towards Watling Street. If he did not act now to stop Henry's march, he risked being overtaken, leaving Tudor with an open road into the capital.

Richard would need to move his troops out of Nottingham, towards Leicester, as soon as he possibly could. According to Vergil, the city thronged with 'a huge number of men in arms' that were assembled there, 'his soldiers being brought forth into good array'. Yet Richard still believed that his army remained unprepared. Henry's haste, the Crowland chronicler recorded, 'moving by day and night towards a direct confrontation', had forced the king to move his troops in spite of the army being 'not yet fully assembled'.

With letters having been sent out just eight days before on 11 August, it had taken time for levies of armies to be prepared. Soldiers from the north were slow in making up the distance, though their own delays and uncertainty in sending men to Richard had not helped. After the citizens of York had sent John Nicholson and John Sponer to Richard to clarify how many troops were needed, news of the king's instructions did not reach York until 19 August, after Nicholson had made a round trip of over 140 miles. When the city authorities assembled in the council chamber on Friday morning, they listened to Nicholson's report listing Richard's demand for 400 men. 'It was determined upon the report . . . which was commen home from the king's grace,' the council register recorded, 'that iiiixx [80] men of the city defensibly arrayed, John Hastings gentleman to the mace being captain, should in all haste possible depart towards the king's grace for the subduing of his enemies.' The council resolved to meet again at two o'clock to muster their troops: each soldier was to receive 10 shillings for ten days, with 12 pence a day thereafter. Even if the troops departed straight away at 2 p.m., it would not have been possible for men to arrive until 22 August if they rode on horseback, or more likely 23 August if they marched on foot. Complicit delays such as these meant that even as many began to set off towards Nottingham, they would find that the king had already departed and would miss the battle. Robert Morton of Bawtry, county York, a kinsman of John, Bishop of Ely and a son-in-law of a former retainer of Lord Hastings who had been taken into Richard's service, made his will on 20 August, 'going to maintain our most excellent King Richard III against the rebellion raised against him in this land'. In fact Morton may have made his preparations, but left too late to arrive at the battle in time.

In particular, two noblemen on whom Richard had hoped to depend were missing. The Great Chronicle of London infers that both Thomas Stanley and the Earl of Northumberland, despite each having 'great companies', 'made slow speed' towards Richard, and had yet to arrive, forcing the king to leave Nottingham without them.

By every account, Richard's departure from Nottingham was a spectacular occasion. In spite of the fact, one chronicler wrote, that 'its numbers were not yet fully made up', the size of the army that Richard had amassed was staggering. 'Here was found ready to fight for the king a greater number of soldiers than had ever been seen before in England'. It seems that most of Richard's army would have been on horseback. According to Mancini, troops brought horsemen with them: 'Not that they are accustomed to fight from horseback, but because they use horses to carry them to the scene of the engagement, so as to arrive faster and not tired by the fatigue of the journey: therefore they will ride any sort of horse, even pack horses. On reaching the field of battle the horses are abandoned, they all fight under the same conditions so that no one should retain any hope of fleeing.' In his letter of 11 August, Richard had also demanded from Henry Vernon that he attend 'ye in your person with such number as ye have promised unto us sufficiently horsed and harnessed be with us in all haste to you possible'.

Riding along the road from Nottingham to Leicester, Richard ordered his entire army into a defensive formation, commanding his troops 'to march forward in square battle that way by the which they understood their enemies would come'. In the middle of the square formation, all 'impediments' were 'gathered into the midst of the army'. This included 'a great mass of treasure', which one observer described as 'all the king's treasure', along with Richard himself, mounted on 'a great white courser' accompanied 'with his guard' by his side. On either side of the army 'did follow the wings of horsemen ranging on both sides', keeping the army in its tight formation. The army arrived at Leicester shortly before sunset, where Richard was joined by the army gathered by the Duke of Norfolk, who was already quartered in the city. Tradition suggests that Richard spent the night at Leicester at an inn named the White Boar on Northgate Street, a timbered building that upstairs had 'a large gloomy chamber' set with beams carved with images of 'vine tendrils executed in vermillion', setting up his own bed that had been brought from Nottingham Castle with his baggage train. Robert Brackenbury had still to arrive from the Tower with its ordnance, while the Earl of Northumberland was yet to reach the city on his journey from the north, though Richard expected both to reach Leicester by the morning. That evening he sent out further scouts to discover 'where the enemy were likely to rest the following night', as Richard prepared for sleep and the final march to the battlefield where he hoped to finally destroy his rival.

Departing from Lichfield, Henry had moved seven miles south-east towards Tamworth. Although Henry gave the impression of 'noble courage' as his forces increased in number 'wherever he went', privately he remained anxious, his thoughts being subsumed by 'a great fear'. Still unsure of Thomas Stanley's commitment, he had been informed by his spies of the alarming size of the army that Richard had gathered: 'nothing was stronger . . . nothing more ready'. When he discovered that Richard 'with a host innumerable, was at hand', he began to question his own ability to defeat the king, having second thoughts about the entire enterprise. Needing time to think and assess his position, Henry allowed his troops to continue their march while he remained behind with twenty armed men, 'so as to deliberate what to do' as he followed 'gloomily' at a distance. As night fell, Henry somehow became detached from his army, and 'lost sight of its tracks'. According to Vergil,

After he had wandered about a long while and could not find it, he fearfully came to a certain hamlet more than three miles from his camp. So not to fall into a trap, he did not dare ask the way of anybody, and he spent his night there, not so afraid of his present danger as of that yet to come. For he feared this was an omen of some future disaster. His army was no less distraught over the sudden absence of its commander, and then on the next day, as the sky grew light, Henry returned to the army, offering the excuse that this had happened on purpose rather than by his mistake, for he had been outside the camp to receive some welcome news from certain secret friends.

The episode, related only by Vergil, remains shrouded in mystery. Henry's own thoughts during these dark moments of uncertainty can only be guessed at, though a stroke of fortune would allow him to hide the real reasons behind what seemed a temporary desertion of his forces. Who were these 'secret friends'?

The answer may lie in an episode told by the Great Chronicle of London. As Sir Robert Brackenbury travelled up from London to meet Richard at Leicester, around Stony Stratford he had been deserted by Walter Hungerford, Thomas Bourgchier 'and many other' who then intended to make their way towards Henry. A former Lancastrian, Hungerford had become a loyal servant of Edward IV, and was later to join the household of Edward V. Both men had been involved in Buckingham's rebellion, Hungerford in the Wiltshire rebellion, and Bourgchier in Kent. Richard had chosen to pardon Hungerford, restoring to him his lands. Yet Richard remained wary of his loyalty, ordering that Brackenbury bring both men with him to the battlefield together with other gentlemen 'whom he had in suspicion'. Understanding that Richard 'had them in jealousy, because they would not be brought to their enemy against their wills', Vergil relates how they forsook Brackenbury, travelling towards Henry's camp 'in the night season'. The Great Chronicle infers that Brackenbury, who 'held good countenance' with them and 'had for many of them done right kindly', did little to prevent their departure, with Hungerford and his men 'giving to him thanks for his kindness before showed, and exhorted him to go with them, for they feared not to show unto him that they would go unto that other party, and so departed, leaving him almost alone'.

Late in the evening of 20 August, with their leader having mysteriously disappeared, Henry's troops decided to camp on the river plain in the shadow of Tamworth Castle, where they were joined by Hungerford and Bourgchier who 'yielded themselves to his obeisance'. They were not the only ones who were attempting to make contact with Henry that evening. According to the Great Chronicle of London, 'many of the knights and esquires of this land, they gathered much people in the king's name and straight sped them unto that other party, by mean whereof his power hugely increased', while Vergil wrote how 'there flocked to him also many other noble men of war, who from day to day hated King Richard worse than all men living'.

It seems that, with several bands of armed men making their way across Watling Street to join Henry, Thomas Stanley's own preparations were thrown into confusion. According to the 'Ballad of Bosworth Field', Stanley's camp, having settled at Atherstone 'in a dale cold', discovered news that an armed band of men was fast approaching.

Stanley himself believed that it was Richard's army: he would be forced to declare his hand, and confront the king's troops before Henry arrived from Lichfield. Spending the night at Atherstone, in the early hours of Sunday 21 August, after hearing Mass they moved 'toward the field', arranging their troops in array with Thomas Stanley taking the vanguard, Sir William Stanley the rearguard, with Thomas Stanley's fifth son Edward taking a wing, where they remained waiting for Richard's attack. It seems that there may have been some kind of skirmish during the night, according to the 'Ballad of Bosworth Field':

> Then in their host there did fall affray
> A little time before the night;
> You never saw men so soon in their array
> With fell weapons fierce for to fight.

There may be some truth behind there being some kind of initial skirmish, if not several, taking place during the night of 20 August and the early morning of the 21st. If later inquisitions post mortem are taken at face value, Richard Boughton, the sheriff of Warwickshire and Leicestershire, is recorded as having died on 20 August, John Kebell of Rearsby in Leicestershire on the 21st; both were prominent Leicestershire figures who had been retainers of Lord Hastings, but had continued to serve Richard as JPs. A separate group of men, from around the Essex area, are also recorded as having died on 20 or 21 August, including John Cock of Chadwell St Mary in Essex, who died on the 20th, William Curson of Brightwell in Suffolk, who died on the 21st, Thomas Hampden of Great Hampden in Buckinghamshire but who also owned lands at Theydon Mount in Essex died on the same day, as did William Joyce, who may have been the same person as William Joys of Halesworth in Suffolk. None of these men held any office under Richard, but they did all live near to Castle Hedingham in Essex, the ancestral home of John, Earl of Oxford. Could these men, making their way to join Oxford in Henry's camp, have been intercepted by loyal enforcers of Richard's regime along the way? If the Essex men had travelled from the location of Castle Hedingham, they would have taken the Roman road from Cambridge to Leicester, before joining Watling Street at its junction at Mancetter. It may have been possible, that in doing so, they had been forced to confront Richard's men or had become caught up in a battle with the Stanleys.

The following morning, hearing the sound of 'trumpets and tabors tempered on high' from a 'forest side', Stanley's men prepared themselves for Richard's attack. They were surprised to find that it was in fact Henry arriving from Tamworth, riding on a 'bay courser'.

It was at the Cistercian abbey at Merevale near Atherstone where Henry finally met Thomas Stanley. Henry's relief at making contact with the man whose intentions he had remained unsure of until just hours before was shared by many who were present. 'It was a goodly sight to see the meeting of them', one observer later remarked. According to Vergil, Henry and Stanley took each other 'by the hand, and yielding mutual salutation', both were 'moved to great joy', after which 'they entered in counsel in what sort to arraigne battle with King Richard, if the matter should come to strokes, whom they heard to be not far off'. After planning the disposition of both armies for battle, the meeting ended with further good news for Henry, with more defections arriving at his camp, including John Savage, Brian Sandford and Simon Digby, together with 'many others, revolting from King Richard'. They brought with them 'a choice band of armed men' which cheered Henry's spirits further, 'and greatly replenished him with good hope'.

Henry and his troops departed from Stanley, leaving the main Roman road of Watling Street, intending to settle his camp for the night 'nearer the enemy'. The exact location of his camp was decided by men on Henry's own side with local knowledge of the terrain. John de Hardwicke was lord of the nearby manor of Lindley. He had joined Henry that day with men and horses, and apparently served as a guide on the morning of the battle. The camp must have been situated within the location of the neighbouring villages of Witherley, Atterton and Fenny Drayton just outside Atherstone. It was at 'Wryth', which must be Witherley, that Henry knighted several of his key supporters including Sir Richard Guilford, whom Henry had appointed master of his ordnance on 8 August, Sir John Hastoy, Sir John Risley, Sir William Brandon, Sir John Trenzy, Sir William Tyler and Sir Thomas Milborn.

Evidence that the camp was established near the villages also comes from payments Henry later made to reimburse local residents in compensation for the grain and pasture that they had lost when his troops had settled for the night, camping on the nearby fields. Henry issued a warrant to reimburse the abbot of Merevale with 100 marks sterling, writing that 'we understand that the abbot of the monastery of Merevale had sustained great hurts, charges and losses, by occasion of the great repair and resort that our people coming towards our late field made, as well unto the house of Merevale aforesaid as in going over his ground, to the destruction of his corns and pastures'. The abbot was later given a separate reward of 10 marks. John Fox, the parson at Witherley, was also given £12 2s 'for divers damages of the towns and boroughs in his grain'. A sense of the damage to the crops that Henry's army had caused in each township can be gathered from reimbursements Henry made 'to certain townships, which sustained losses of their corns and grains by us and our company': Atherston received a total of £24 20s 4d, Fenny Drayton £20, Witherley £13, Atterton £8 10s and Mancetter £5 19s.

From surviving records of expenses that Henry later paid, we can also guess at the state of his own personal military preparations including the equipment he intended to use. William Bret, a draper in London, was reimbursed for purchasing six complete cuirasses 'called harneys' and twelve pairs of brigandines, twenty-four sallettes for £37 which were sent to Henry in France, 'by our commandment . . . and to our use'. Having largely been sheltered or imprisoned away for most of his adult life, the inexperienced Henry Tudor, who had probably never even needed to wear armour before, now found himself preparing for his first battle.

On the morning of Sunday 21 August, Richard's scouts returned, reporting back the location of Henry Tudor's position near Atherstone. By now, both the Earl of Northumberland had arrived from the north and Sir Robert Brackenbury from London, breaking to Richard the news of Hungerford's defection from his force. The king's disappointment was soon forgotten when, donning his surcoat of arms over his full plated armour and placing a 'diadem' on his head, he rode out to inspect his assembled army.

It was an impressive sight. The Crowland Chronicler described how there assembled at Leicester 'great lords, knights and esquires and a countless number of commoners'; 'you never heard tell of such a company', the 'Ballad of Bosworth Field' reported, giving a list of the members of the nobility and gentry who had joined Richard's army. In the higher ranks of the peerage, eight names are mentioned, including the Duke of Norfolk, the Earl of Surrey, the Earls of Kent, Shrewsbury, Lincoln, Northumberland, Westmorland and Viscount Lovell, who was 'sad at assay'. Of the peerage, the poem names sixteen other lords, though the list is both factually incorrect and at times somewhat confused: the list included Lord Maltravers, the Lord Arundell, Lord Wells, Lord Grey of Codnor 'in his armour bright', the unknown 'Lord Bowes', surely a case of mistaken identity, Lord Audley 'fierce to fight', Lord Berkeley 'stern on a steed', Lord Ferrers of Chartley, Lord Ferrers of Groby, Lord 'Bartley' 'Chamberlain of England that day was he', Lord Fitzhugh, Lord Scrope of Upsal, Lord Scrope of Bolton, and Lord Dacre who had 'raised all the North country', Lord Lumley and Lord Greystoke who 'brought with him a noble company'. An earlier prose version of the ballad, however, does not include in its list Lincoln, Arundell, Welles, Grey of Codnor or Lord Bowes. At the same time there are several alterations to the ballad's inaccuracies. Lord 'Bartley' is replaced by Lovell, while Arundell is instead Lord Ogle. The 'Ballad of Lady Bessie' suggests that the Bishop of Durham was present at the battle, as well as the Earl of Kent and Lord Scrope.

Of the members of the gentry who assembled for Richard, sixty-seven names are listed in the ballad, while the prose version names sixty; however, both lists should be treated with a degree of caution. There are significant differences between the two lists: only thirty names appear in both, while there are stanzas in one version that are missing in the other, with four stanzas in 'Bosworth Field', naming knights from the Midlands including Gervaise Clifton, Henry Pierpoint, John Babington and Humphrey Stafford, who are absent from the prose version. On the other hand, three stanzas in the prose version naming Yorkshiremen such as Sir Robert Plumpton, Sir William Gascoigne, Sir Thomas Markenfield and Sir John Pudsey, are missing from the ballad. Nevertheless, both lists highlight Richard's dependence upon the northern members of the gentry, from Yorkshire, the East Riding and Durham, in constituting the bulk of his forces.

There were other members of Richard's forces assembled at Leicester that morning who had come from much further afield. Juan de Salazar was a Spanish soldier who had been a prominent commander in the army of Charles the Bold and later for the Emperor Maximilian; he had been given his epithet of 'little Salazar' to distinguish him from the 'Grand Chevalier' Jean de Salazar, a fellow knight from the Biscay area, and possibly his father, who fought in the French armies of Charles VII and Louis XI. As captain of a band of Spanish mercenaries in Flanders, his campaigns against the French were recorded by the chronicler Jean Molinet who described him impressively 'as bold as Hector, as subtle as Ulysses and as fortunate as Caesar'. In 1480 Salazar married Beatrice de Portugal, a wealthy widow, and at the wedding feast, perhaps to his new bride's surprise, he wagered that he could spend six nights in enemy territory undetected. He did and won the bet. He was present at the successful siege of Utrecht in 1483, but then disappears from record in any Continental accounts until 1486.

Instead Salazar is to be found in England, employed in Richard's service. The king's own signet docquet book indicates that Salazar must have been present in England from at least 1484: on 26 September 1484, payment is made for £51 6s 4d 'by the King's commandment' for a ship to be rigged out to 'convey Saluzard' to Brittany. The following March, passports for Salazar's servants to travel to Flanders and Brabant were issued, as well as 'a passport for Henry Delphant, servant of the Captain Salasar with ii servants in his company and as many horses . . . to go unto the Duc of Ostriche [the Duke of Austria, Emperor Maximilian]'. Three more of Salazar's servants were granted similar permission, the last being given by Richard at Nottingham on 16 June 1485.

Now he was back in England, accompanying the king into battle. Salazar's involvement places Richard's confrontation with Henry in the European context it should be seen, particularly in the growing tensions between Maximilian, who had recently been victorious in Flanders, and Charles VIII. Salazar had presumably been given permission by Maximillian to travel to England to aid the king, though it is unknown whether he brought any significant force of Burgundian soldiers with him.

As Richard prepared to lead out his force to embark on his final journey towards Atherstone, Richard knew that one man was missing: in spite of his promises to attend the king, Thomas Stanley had failed to show, possibly still claiming that he was preventing Henry

Tudor's march down Watling Street towards London. Whether Richard believed him was another matter; the king would soon find out whether Stanley would be true to his word.

Commanding the front of his army, Richard rode out of Leicester 'amid the greatest pomp, and wearing the crown upon his head', flanked by Norfolk and Northumberland. Richard understood the need for ceremony and the importance of his own leadership to enthuse his men. Before his coronation, according to Mancini, Richard had summoned 6,000 troops to muster on Finsbury Fields; the king 'himself went out to meet the soldiers before they entered the city; and, when they were drawn up in a circle on a very great field, he passed them with bared head around their ranks and thanked them'.

Richard's glittering armour, together with the crown upon his head, must have made a formidable impression. Only the wealthiest and most important commanders would after all be dressed in full plate armour. The average soldier would be dressed more plainly, though according to Mancini, who observed Richard's troops in 1483,

There is hardly any without a helmet, and none without bows and arrows: their bows and arrows are thicker and longer than those used by other nations, just as their bodies are stronger than other peoples', for they seem to have hands and arms of iron. The range of their bows is no less than that of our arbalests; their hands by the side of each a sword no less long than ours, but heavy and thick as well. The sword is always accompanied by an iron shield; it is the particular delight of this race that on holidays their youths should fight up and down the streets clashing on their shields with blunted swords or stout staves in place of swords. When they are older they go out into the fields with bows and arrows, and even the women are not inexperienced at hunting with these weapons. They do not wear any metal armour on their breast or any other part of the body, except for the better sort who have breastplates and suits of armour. Indeed the common soldiery have more comfortable tunics that reach down below the loins and are stuffed with tow or some other soft material. They say that the softer the tunics the better they do withstand the blows of arrows and swords, and besides that in summer they are lighter and in the winter more serviceable than iron.

Richard led his army out through Leicester's west gate and over Bow Bridge, perhaps across the water meadows near to the Augustinian priory and towards Leicester Forest where he travelled through its open chase towards Earl Shilton. With a complete absence of sources describing the journey, the exact route of Richard's journey can only be guessed at. In any case, the direction of his army could have altered significantly depending upon local hazards met along the route. The medieval idea of a road was not an exact and defined carriageway upon which people might travel freely, but rather that of a route, a right of way between two points, which might change according to seasonal variations in the weather, particularly across marshy terrain. In such a situation, a journey might take several routes across higher ground, especially if carrying heavy equipment such as artillery. At the western edge of the forest, Richard would have faced a choice of moving southwest onto Watling Street, but with his 'scurriers' informing him that Henry was camped at Atherstone, he would turn westwards along an ancient track that seems to have crossed the country from east to west, leading to the village of Sutton Cheney, Ambion Hill. Alternatively, Richard could have taken the Roman road that led directly to Mancetter, passing Kirby Muxloe, where towards his right he would have caught sight of the unfinished red-brick country residence that had been built by William, Lord Hastings, abandoned by his workers who had downed their tools shortly after their master's execution. Partially deserted, the imposing unfinished ruin stood as a memorial to the man who had unwittingly helped to place Richard on the throne and for his reward had gone to his death.

After making the eight-mile journey, Richard chose to pitch his camp west of Sutton Cheney, in the vicinity of Ambion Hill. Rising to 400 feet above sea level, the hill had been the site of the early medieval village of Anebein, abandoned in the fourteenth century. Now the area was covered with 'furze and heath'. Looking down across the landscape, to the left of his view Richard would have seen the track of the Roman road leading to Mancetter and Atherstone, as well as the village of Dadlington up on higher ground; tracing the road along its route, in the distance he would have been able to make out the spire of St Margaret's church in Stoke. To his right was the village of Shenton, while looking northwards, the square tower of the church at Market Bosworth could be seen. In between these settlements, made purposefully upon the higher firmer ground, the gentle western slope of Ambion Hill gave way to a wide plain, its only notable feature being a windmill that had been recently built in the 1470s. Beneath him lay the marshy terrain of a plain around the Sence river, known locally as Redemore, its grasses still green in high summer.

As he surveyed the land that he had chosen for the site of battle, Richard would have been satisfied with his position. He understood well the need to occupy the most advantageous terrain for battle, as set down by the precepts of Vegetius, translated by Christine de Pizan in the early fifteenth century. 'The wise commander will decide to be the first to take advantage of the terrain,' Pizan had written. 'There are therefore three points to consider: the first is to take the high place; the second is to make sure that at the hour of combat the sun will be in the enemy's eyes; the third, that the wind should be against them. If these three things can be arranged, he will profit as there is no doubt that the one in the highest place has an advantage of strength over the one below.'

Richard ordered his men to set up camp upon the hill itself or nearer the village of Sutton Cheney; with nearly 15,000 men in his army, the royal camp would have encompassed several fields stretching across the area. Richard himself prepared to spend the night in his royal tent. While the tent may have been constructed of canvas and wood, the splendour of the royal court was imitated as best possible with tapestries, brought especially with the king's train, being hung from the inside walls, along with the king's camp bed. The bed itself was far from being of simple construction: when the German visitor Nicholas Von Poppelau was invited into the king's tent at Pontefract in 1484, he found 'the king's bed decorated from top to bottom with red samite and a gold piece which the Lombards call altabass and which also decorates His Imperial Majesty's bed. In the king's tent there was also a table set up next to the bed, covered all around with silk cloths of gold embroidered with gold.'

That night, as the skies darkened across Redemore plain below, Richard would have seen the flickering of his enemies' campfires, pitched several miles away towards the villages of Fenny Drayton, Witherley and Atterton. His mind turning towards the next morning, having ensured that his men were fed and 'refreshed' 'from their exertions', he chose to make 'a lengthy speech to encourage them for the coming battle'.

As the king's camp settled down for the night, filled with the restless sleep and muttering prayers of men uncertain whether the following morning might be their last day upon the earth, a sense of unease was palpable in the air. Perhaps some drowned their fears in drink, which might help to explain the Scottish chronicler Pitscottie's tale of how, the night before the battle, a highlander named Macgregor, a servant of the Bishop of Dunkeld who having been present at Richard's court at Nottingham had somehow managed to find himself swept up in the campaign, stole the royal crown from Richard's tent. Having been seized, he was brought to the king who asked why he had attempted the theft. Macgregor replied that his mother had once prophesised that he would one day be hanged, and that he thought if this were the case, he should be at least hanged for something memorable. Amused by his explanation, Richard supposedly granted the Scotsman an immediate pardon.

Other pranks were considered less welcome. According to the Tudor chronicler Edward Hall, during the night an anonymous message was pinned to the gate of the Duke of Norfolk's tent. It read:

Jack of Norfolk be not too bold
For Dicken thy master is bought and sold.

The anonymous writer who urged the duke not to place his faith in the king, believing that Richard's fate had already been sealed, was perhaps attempting to warn Norfolk of what, under the cover of darkness, was already taking place. Several men managed to slip away, either in retreat or to join Tudor's camp. One of the royal commissioners of array, John Biconnell of Somerset, in spite of his family ties with Lord Zouche, took his forces to Henry.

That night Richard struggled to rest. The following morning he spoke of how in his fitful sleep he had 'a terrible dream', imagining that 'he was surrounded by evil demons, who did not let him rest'. Rather than being refreshed from sleep, he awoke feeling 'sick at mind' and filled with 'anxious cares'. Richard always had a countenance, the

Crowland Chronicler observed, 'which was always drawn', but by the morning he appeared 'even more pale and deathly'. Vergil, who claimed that in the morning Richard 'related his dream to many men' so that his men did not think that he displayed any 'melancholy because he feared the enemy', believed that 'from this apparition he foresaw the evil outcome of the battle, and he did not prepare himself for the fight with his usual eager expression'.

11

THE BATTLE

•—•—•

At around quarter past five, the sun began to rise across the horizon. After waking and leaving his tent, Richard requested to hear Mass. Even though Sunday Mass would have been observed upon the army's arrival at Ambion, Richard was determined to receive one final divine blessing before he entered battle. He had brought with him his book of hours, an illustrated manuscript in which Richard's own birth date had been entered in its calendar. At some stage during his reign, Richard had commissioned a personal devotional prayer inserted into the book. Perhaps now, Richard turned its pages to recite the passage that reflected his own desperate predicament, hoping that he might be spiritually armed against the challenge he faced:

And you Lord, who reconciled the race of man and the Father, who purchased with your own precious blood the confiscated inheritance of paradise and who made peace between men and the angels, deign to make and keep concord between me and my enemies. Show me and pour over me your grace and glory. Deign to assuage, turn aside, destroy, and bring to nothing the hatred they bear towards me . . . Stretch out your arm to me and spread your grace over me, and deign to deliver me from all the perplexities and sorrows in which I find myself . . . Therefore, Lord Jesus Christ, son of the living God, deign to free me, thy servant King Richard from every tribulation, sorrow and trouble in which I am placed and from all the plots of my enemies, and deign to send Michael the Archangel to my aid against them, and deign, Lord Jesus Christ, to bring to nothing the evil plans that they are making or wish to make against me . . . By all these things, I ask you, most gentle Lord Jesus Christ to keep me, thy servant King Richard, and defend me from all evil, from the devil and from all peril present, past and to come, and deliver me from all the tribulations, sorrows and troubles in which I am placed, and deign to console me . . .

Yet when Richard ordered 'Mass to be said before him' before he armed himself for battle, his chaplains were unprepared and 'not ready to celebrate Mass'. According to one account, taken by surprise, the chaplains struggled to find the bread and wine, since 'ever one thing was missing'. It seems that the king, possibly kept awake by his nightmares, had risen before dawn in an unsettled state, taking his chaplains unaware. Richard's early awakening had left his cooks equally unprepared, for according to the Crowland chronicler, 'nor was any breakfast ready with which to revive the king's flagging spirit'.

The sense of disorganisation in Richard's camp, suggesting that the king never managed to hear Mass before departing for battle, together with his unsettled dream, has been viewed by later writers as some kind of divine judgement. Polydore Vergil was quick to give his own interpretation of events, stating that Richard's nightmare 'was no dream, but a conscience guilty of heinous offences, a conscience I say so much the more grevious as the offences were more great, which . . . in the last day of our life is wont to represent us to the memory of our sins committed, and withal to show unto us the pains imminent for the same'. The image of a ruler facing battle unable to hear Mass due to the disappearance of the host was a familiar example used by authors to suggest that God was not on their side. Even if Richard had faced delays in hearing Mass, it is unlikely that some form of ceremony would not have taken place, probably performed by his confessor John Roby, a Franciscan friar whom Richard had rewarded with preferment.

There survives a powerful reminder of the central role that faith would play in the conflict for Richard in the form of one of the most striking battlefield relics, the 'Bosworth Crucifix'. Discovered at or near the site of the battle in 1778, the cross is 23 inches tall and 11 inches wide, made of bronze alloy and would have been originally overlaid with gold. At its centre is the figure of a crucified Christ, cast in bronze alloy. Each arm of the crucifix ends with a roundel, decorated on its front with the symbols of the four evangelists, likely to have been covered with enamel. On their backs, the roundels are engraved with what appear to be suns or stars, with rays streaming from them, the familiar emblem of the Yorkist sun. There would have been additional branches carrying the figures of Mary the Virgin and St John, since attachments for the branches spring from the base of the cross, although these are missing. The cross could have been mounted either for use on the altar in a private chapel, or on a stave for processional use. Maybe the crucifix itself had been used during Richard's private Mass, positioned upon a portable altar in the royal tent; after the king had heard Mass, it would have been taken off its base and mounted upon a tall wooden stave, fastened into place by a hinged ring of iron, to be led out into the fields of battle.

There was another reason why Richard's camp was in disarray. According to a later account related by Ralph Bigod, who was present at the camp on Ambion Hill, it was the unexpected sight of Henry's advance 'coming on apace' which had suddenly left Richard's camp unprepared, being 'constrained to go into battle'.

Early that morning, as the sky was 'barely growing light', Henry sent a messenger to Thomas Stanley. Stanley had moved his own forces forward, so that having approached 'the place of the fight' he was now 'midway between the two armies', in the fields between Stoke and Dadlington, south of the Roman road running through the country-side. Henry requested that Stanley should allow his men to join with his own troops, allowing him to place his army into formation, with Stanley being asked to personally lead the vanguard. Stanley's reply was not what Henry had expected. 'He would lead his men into the line', he replied, but only when Henry 'was there with his army drawn up'. It was clear that Stanley was not prepared to join the battle until Henry himself was about to engage. Whereas Henry had planned for Stanley's participation in advance, joining with his army into one single force, Stanley would only commit to 'be at hand with his army in proper array', located in 'the battle area midway'. Meanwhile, his brother Sir William Stanley remained to the side of his brother's forces, perhaps closer to Stoke, being described as 'hindmost at the outsetting'. Nevertheless, the Stanleys arranged for their forces to be prepared in a state of military readiness, remaining drawn up into two 'battles', totalling 6,000 men. The ballads suggest that Stanley did provide Henry with at least some help: recognising that Henry's forces were too small to combat Richard's army, he sent Sir Robert Tunstall, Sir John Savage, Sir Hugh Percivall and Sir Humphrey Stanley to join Henry's vanguard.

This was hardly the aid that Henry expected to receive. With time running out, and knowing 'the greatness of the cause', Henry became 'anxious and began to lose heart'. He had little choice: he would have to fight without the Stanleys. Henry had no other option but to draw up a 'single battle line' as far as he was able, on account that he had too few men. It was 'making a virtue of necessity', Vergil wrote, though it seems that Henry was carefully advised by his generals as to what his battle formation should take.

The Earl of Oxford played a central role in devising how Henry's forces should be drawn up for battle. Having been given the command of the vanguard after Thomas Stanley's refusal to take up the post, the earl had in effect been placed in charge of the military leadership of Henry's army. According to André, it was Oxford – 'not inexpert at arms' – who 'urged a strategy on the prince'. At the front of the line Oxford placed the available archers, with himself in command. He ordered Gilbert Talbot to take the right wing to 'defend' the archers and in order 'to keep an eye' on the battle line, while on the left wing he placed John Savage. Behind this line Henry, still hoping to rely on Stanley's aid, placed himself 'surrounded by scarcely one squadron of cavalry and a few infantry', including his standard bearer, Sir William Brandon. Some of the French mercenaries were also placed alongside Henry. According to one French report, written by a participant in the battle, Henry remained on foot, surrounded by Frenchmen, claiming that 'he wanted to be on foot in the midst of us'. Curiously, there is no mention of Jasper Tudor's involvement in the battle, or where Henry's uncle was positioned as the armies came to face each other. Perhaps he remained close by to his nephew, ready to prepare for a possible escape if the outcome of the battle turned against them.

As for the rest of the French mercenaries in Henry's army who made up a significant number of the force, having been kept separate from the English and Welsh troops overnight, setting up their own forces 'a quarter league from the camp' they now 'similarly held their preparations' and joined Oxford's men, with the Crowland Chronicler noting that the earl's army now consisted 'of a large body of French and English troops'. Placed in charge of these 'sturdy soldiers', Bernard André noted, was Philibert de Chandée, 'a man endowed with a military education'. Vergil believed that the total number of Henry's soldiers 'was not more than 5,000' compared to Richard's army which 'was about 15,000'.

Oxford's decision to draw his limited forces up into a single battle line with two wings, rather than the traditional formation of a vanguard, a middle army and a rearguard, reflected the fact that Henry's army was numerically inferior to Richard's own forces. Yet the precise layout of the troops seems to have been based on advice in Christine of Pizan's work, the *Fais d'armes et de chevalerie*, itself based largely on the classical work by the Roman author Flavius Vegetius Renatus, the *De Re Militari*. In her work, Pizan advised that if there were not enough men available to form the traditional formation of a vanguard, a main army otherwise known as the 'great battle' or forward followed by a rearguard, 'some that be expert in arms do counsel that when men have no great quantity of commons but have for the most part all men of arms, that all the whole assembly be put together only in one battle without none other forward or a rearguard but only the wings of the front of the battle, and say that more surely they fight'. To prove her point, Pizan recalled the victory of the French king Charles VI who, despite being vastly outnumbered by 40,000 Flemings at the Battle of Roosebeke in 1382, had managed to obtain victory against the odds by employing a similar single formation, as had John the Fearless, Duke of Burgundy against the might of 25,000 rebel citizens at Liège in 1408.

Pizan's influence on the arrangement of Henry's forces may have come from the French influence of Chandée, but it seems that Oxford himself was a keen follower of Pizan's work, having most likely read it in the original French: the earl could speak both English and French – a later inventory records that he owned 'a chest full of French and English books' worth £3 6s 8d. William Caxton would later translate *The Four Sons of Aymon* 'out of French at the request and comandment of ye right noble and virtuous Earl, John Earl of Oxford, my good, singular and especial lord'.

More revealing, however, is the fact that Caxton would also later be asked by Henry to translate the *Fais d'armes et de chevalerie* into English. According to his epilogue to his translation, *The Book of Faytes of Armes*, Caxton recalled how Henry had personally invited him to Westminster in January 1489, where he asked the printer 'to translate this said book and reduce it in to our English and natural tongue and to put it enprint to the end that every gentleman born to arms and all manner men of war captains, soldiers, victuallers and all other should have knowledge how they ought to behave them in the feats of war and of battles'. It was Oxford, who was standing next to Caxton, who then handed him a copy of Christine's work. This seems to be a telling clue that the earl himself had full knowledge of Pizan's work. Maybe during his years of imprisonment at Hammes Castle, living on a hardly insubstantial allowance of £50 a year, Oxford was able to spend his time reading military treatises such as Pizan, absorbing their advice, at the same time reflecting on the reasons for his catastrophic defeat at the battle of Barnet, when a lack of military discipline had allowed his forces to become separated from the standards, ending in disaster. If this was the case, the lessons Oxford had learnt from Pizan would be employed with devastating effect on the battlefield.

If Richard's initial preparations that morning had been thrown into confusion by Henry's sudden advance, the king quickly seized the momentum as his forces were hastily drawn up into battle order. In preparation, Richard ordered his standards to be unfurled: they included his own insignia of the white boar, though previously Richard had ordered one 'banner of sarcenet of our lady', 'one banner of the Trinity' together with banners depicting St George, St Edward and St Cuthbert, four standards 'of sarcenet with boars' and 'one of our own arms all sarcenet' with 'three coats of arms beaten fine gold' which may have been present on the battlefield.

Cartloads of guns and cannon that had been brought from the Tower by Sir Robert Brackenbury were wheeled into their positions. Artillery remained close to Richard's heart, with the king taking a keen interest in the latest military technology. In June 1480, as Duke of Gloucester, Richard had written to the French king Louis XI thanking him for 'the great bombard which you caused to be presented to me', acknowledging that 'for as I have always taken and still [take] great pleasure in artillery I assure you it will be a special treasure to me'. Upon his accession as king, Richard had ensured that his own arsenal would match that of any Continental monarch. John Donne had been appointed as Master of the Armory at the Tower of London, on a wage of 12d a day. Under his charge, Henry Wydeboke was appointed yeoman and keeper of the armory and 'habiliments of war' at 6d a day. William Clowte 'of Gelderland' had been employed as a 'gunmaker' along with William Nele, while the king's official armourer was Vincent Tetulior, paid a salary of £20. In March 1484 Thomas Rogers was sent to Southampton to purchase twenty new guns and two serpentines for £24.

The artillery that Richard now had ranged against his enemy was a memorable sight, with the 'Ballad of Bosworth Field' describing how 'They had 7 scores Serpentines without doubt / that were locked & chained upon a row / as many bombards that were stout.' Molinet, who may have received his information from the French mercenaries facing opposite on Henry Tudor's side, described how the king had a 'great quantity' of range artillery – described as '*engiens volants*', translated literally as 'flying objects'.

Even this impressive range of firepower could not detract from the sheer number of men gathering under the king's standard. 'You never heard tell of such a company, at sowte, seige, nor no gathering', the author of the 'Ballad of Bosworth Field' remarked. According to the ballad, Sir William Stanley looked down upon Richard's army from his vantage point near Stoke, to witness the battle line stretched out for five miles, across which no ground could be seen 'for armed men & trapped steeds', their armour glittering as bright 'as any gleed' – a burning coal. 'To tell the array it were hard for me', the poem's author recalled. Estimates of the exact number of the king's forces vary wildly from an implausible 70,000 to 40,000, and 20,000 men, though perhaps more realistically Vergil indicates that Richard's forces numbered around 15,000 in total.

Richard led out his entire army or 'host' from their camp, drawing it into an extended single line. According to Vergil, Richard's force, 'well furnished in all things', was extended to 'such a wonderful length' with both footmen and horsemen packed together 'in such a way that the mass of the armed men struck terror in the hearts of the distant onlookers'.

This was exactly the effect that Richard had hoped to achieve. The king's decision to form his army into a 'remarkably extensive line of battle, close-packed with infantry and cavalry', seems remarkably similar to the textbook military advice given by Christine de Pizan, who wrote how the vanguard should be 'of considerable length, with men-at-arms arranged close together, so that one should not pass another, the best and most select being in the fore-front, the marshals with them, following their standards and banners'. On the wings at their sides should be placed 'the firepower, cannoneers along with crossbowmen and archers similarly arranged'. Behind this first line of the army, the 'principal battle formation' composed of a 'great mass of men-at-arms' with their captains in their midst, 'their banners and standards raised'.

Despite the impressive size of his army, the sheer mass of soldiers in itself presented a problem. Many of the men gathering under the king's standard had been recruited by the commissions of array, like Thomas Longe from Ashwellthorpe, ordinary men whose military expertise and experience would have been limited. The Crowland chronicler observed that, leaving Leicester, Richard's army had been made up of a 'countless multitude of commoners'. To solve the problem of having a large number of troops without any military expertise, Christine de Pizan suggested that while the ranks lined up and were arranged, ordered by the constable of the army so that 'none are to get out of order', if there were a 'considerable number of common people' in the army, they should be 'used to reinforce the wings in well ordered ranks behind the firepower' and commanded by experienced captains. Pizan also wrote how they should be placed 'in front of the major part of the formation, so that if they should be tempted to flee, the men-at-arms behind them would prevent it'. To ensure discipline within his amateur ranks, Vergil in his printed work, though omitting the detail from his original manuscript, described how Richard went further, ordering that his 'scouts' should patrol along the ranks, 'flying hither and thither' to ensure that his men remained committed to the battle.

Pizan suggested that in the middle of the formation should be placed the 'commanding prince', his principal banner held by 'one of the best and important men in the army' in front of him, 'on which the formation keeps its eyes'. Behind the main battle formation or 'principle battle' should be arranged the rearguard. These were to be organised in order to 'support those in front'; the rearguard should be composed of yeomen on horseback, 'who can aid the others if they have need of it', holding the horses of their masters, while at the same time 'forming an obstacle so that no one can attack the army from the rear'. If there were enough men in the rearguard, Christine de Pizan advised, another battalion could be formed, composed of 'those who are most eager to fight, and are expert in their skill with arms' who might have their backs turned to both the vanguard and the 'principle battle', in case the army came to be attacked from behind by the enemy.

Following Pizan's advice, at the front of his army Richard placed his archers in a vanguard led by the Duke of Norfolk and Sir Robert Brackenbury, formed into 'a most strong bulwark'. At the rear of the extended battle line was the king himself, accompanied by a 'select force' of soldiers. Richard was surrounded by his most loyal servants, his personal guard otherwise known as the 'knights of the body', including Richard's household men, esquires of the body and household knights, described by Vergil as a 'chosen strength of soldiers'. To Richard's left and nearly three-quarters of a mile behind according to one account, a rearguard was to be commanded by the Earl of Northumberland, apparently accompanied by 10,000 men; according to the bailiff of one of the earl's sixteenth-century successors, the earldom was able to raise at least 9,000 men from its Yorkshire and Cumberland estates alone, including 3,000 horse.

As Richard arranged his forces spread across the lower slopes of Ambion Hill, probably on an elevated position around the 300-foot contour line of Ambion, the exact position and direction of his men would be crucial. The 'Ballad of Bosworth Field' relates that, after raising his banners, Norfolk arranged the position of Richard's vanguard and archers 'speedily', keeping 'to the sun and wind right'.

The duke, by now in his sixties, was an experienced military commander, who had seen service in the French wars during the 1450s, where he had reportedly been wounded and taken prisoner at the English defeat at the battle of Castillion in 1453. He had fought at Towton, in several military campaigns in the north during the 1460s, and had been at Barnet in 1471, where he had clashed with the Earl of Oxford's forces. Vergil, who would have met men who had known the duke, describes him as 'a man very politic and skilfull in wars'. Norfolk also spoke French fluently, acting as Edward IV's lead envoy during the negotiations at Picquigny in 1475; he owned a number of French books, including the military treatise *The Tree of Battles* by Honoré Bouvet. It is likely that the duke would have been familiar with Christine de Pizan's work. As he drew up his vanguard, placing the archers in the front rows of his men, with the morning sun rising in the east to the left of his position, and in the early morning still behind him, the duke was deliberately following the standard military practice set out by Pizan, who recommended that, in drawing up a line of troops, a commander should 'set thy troops in so large a place that thou may move and turn all times of the day with the sun and have the sun and the wind on thy back and in thine enemy's visage'. By these means, Pizan wrote, 'the sun shining in one's face troubleth his sight full sore, and likewise doth the wind that filleth them with sand'. The arrow's flight would also be helped by the wind, and 'alighteth more sore and beareth a greater strength'.

With their armies drawn up, both Richard and Henry made their final battle preparations by addressing in person their assembled armies, even if only a few would be close enough to hear them. In doing so, both men followed a long tradition of leaders attempting to inspire their forces before battle. Christine de Pizan had urged every military leader to do so, observing that 'the good admonition of the valiant leader increases determinations, courage, and strength. For this reason he should often and firmly show his men the rightness of their cause and the enemy's errors, and how they are obligated to the prince and the country, admonishing them to do well, to be valiant – promising offices and great gifts to those who do so – and, in fact, to give an example to the others.' Richard's speech was filled less with optimism than an abject sense of fear, telling his assembled troops 'that the outcome of this day's battle, to whichever side the victory was granted would totally destroy the Kingdom of England. For he also declared that he would ruin all the partisans of the other side, if he emerged the victor, predicting that his adversary would do exactly the same' to his own supporters 'if the victory fell to him'. A later sixteenth-century account by the chronicler Edward Hall, although embellished with details of the battle that cannot be substantiated, giving as it does the official version of history as the Tudors wished it to be written, nevertheless captures well the final moments before battle. Hall highlighted how

Richard's oration focused on Henry the 'unknown Welshman, whose father I never knew, nor him personally saw', who intended to 'overcome and oppress' the country with 'a number of beggarly Bretons and fainthearted Frenchmen'.

According to Hall, when Henry 'knew by his foreriders that the king was so near embattled, he rode about his army, from rank to rank from wing to wing, giving comfortable words to all men, and that finished (being armed in all pieces saving his helmet) mounted on a little hill, so that all his people might see and behold him perfectly to their great rejoicing'. While most of Henry's speech, related by Hall nearly seventy years later, must have been placed in his mouth for literary effect, one line in the speech stands out, reflecting Henry's own uncertain predicament: 'Backward we cannot fly: so that here we stand like a sheep in a fold circumcepted and compassed between our enemies and doubtful friends'.

No doubt Henry's passing comment referred to Thomas Stanley who, despite his promises the day before, now refused to join his army, only making the cryptic comment, to be interpreted either way, that 'he would lead his men into the line' when Henry himself 'was there with his army drawn up'. Still, as battle approached and Henry had moved his men into position, Stanley remained stationary, his army positioned between both forces. The ballads, which suggest that the battle was fought in a 'vale' surrounded by hills, depict both Sir William Stanley and Lord Thomas Stanley camped on the same side of the battlefield to Henry's right, watching from hilltops where they would have been afforded an excellent view of both armies marching towards one another. According to one ballad, Sir William Stanley 'removed to a mountain full high', possibly around the hills sloping towards Stoke, where he looked down 'into a dale full dread' to witness the sight of Richard's army; shortly afterwards Richard himself 'looked on the mountains high' where he spotted Lord Stanley's banner, possibly the same ones that Stanley had ordered to be fashioned out of crimson and blue sarcenet for the French expedition ten years earlier.

Henry could not know what decision Thomas Stanley would take, or ultimately to which side he would choose to commit. For Stanley, whose son Lord Strange remained imprisoned in Richard's camp, it remained crucial to be seen as being able to commit to either side. In drawing up his forces midway and overlooking the battlefield, he had positioned himself close enough to Richard's forces to be considered a kind of additional vanguard or wing on the king's left-hand side. This suggests that he had taken up his position, ranged on the brow of the gentle hills around Dadlington, with his brother Sir William Stanley, commanding a force of 3,000 men, assembled on the line of the hill further along towards Stoke. As the Stanleys looked down upon the battlefield, their armies twice the number of Henry's own forces, Henry understood his fate would be entirely in their hands.

With the battle lines drawn up on either side, as Henry's forces advanced towards Redemore plain, for the first time both sides caught sight of one another 'in the distance'. The soldiers made their final preparations for battle, equipping themselves with helmets, and 'awaiting the signal to advance with ears pricked up'. Edward Hall, though writing in the sixteenth century with his own imagined perspective, nonetheless gives a vivid depiction of the tension palpable in the air: 'how hastily the soldiers buckled their helms, how quickly the archers bent their bows and frushed their feathers, how readily the billmen shook their bills and proved their staves, ready to approach and join, when the terrible trumpet should sound the bloody blast to victory or death'. Before the armies could engage, they would need to come within a sufficient distance for their arrows and artillery to be effective. Meanwhile, as Henry's forces advanced, they took care to navigate around a marsh which, according to Vergil, Henry had 'on purpose left to his right so that it should be a protection to his men'. By now, with the low lying morning sun having risen higher in the sky, by turning leftwards towards the north, he also hoped to have 'the sun in his rear'. It is uncertain who gave the first cry for battle to commence; Vergil states that it was Richard, witnessing 'that the enemy had passed the marsh . . . ordered his men to attack them', though at the same time, once Henry's vanguard had passed the marsh, he too 'gave his men the signal for battle'.

The first sounds of battle after Norfolk had raised 'a sudden shout' were the whistling of arrows as both sides began to fire at each other as the archers 'let sharp arrows fly', the bowmen being able to fire at a rate of around twelve arrows a minute. At Tewkesbury, Edward's archers, placed in the vanguard, had 'so sore oppressed' the Lancastrians 'with shot of arrow, at they gave them right-a-sharp shower'. The onslaught of arrow and gunshot had provoked the Lancastrians into panic, launching their vanguard into battle early, with fatal consequences. Yet the initial trading of firepower seems to have been inconclusive, with both sides holding their positions. Next came the deafening sound of Richard's artillery being unleashed. Recent archaeological investigations have revealed the extent of this awesome firepower, with over thirty lead cannon shot, often containing cubes of iron or pebbles encased in lead, littered across the battlefield, ranging from 30mm in diameter to 94mm. This indicates that there would have been a significant number of guns of different size and range firing that day, with the largest cannonball being comparable to the shot fired from some of the most powerful weapons of the day. According to Molinet, it was Henry's French mercenaries, who would have had considerable experience of Continental warfare and how to counter artillery fire, who now revealed their crucial expertise. Studying the 'lie of the land' by the direction and power of 'the king's shot', as well as 'the order of his battle', they informed Henry that 'in order to avoid the fire', he should 'mass their troops against the flank rather than the front of the king's battle'. With Richard's left flank facing the marsh, it would have been the king's right flank, where his vanguard was located, that the French believed the attack should be focused, moving Henry's men out of the line of fire and strengthening Oxford's forces as they approached Norfolk's troops.

Meanwhile, as Oxford's vanguard neared Norfolk's forces, on both sides the archers downed their bows and as 'they came to close quarters' began to fight 'with swords', as the ballad described how the sound of 'brands rang on basinets high, battle axes fast on helms did light'. The initial clash of the vanguards was fast and furious, reflecting the personal animosity that must have existed between the two commanders. Norfolk and Oxford were old rivals, who jostled for the leadership of their East Anglian region. They had fought against one another before, at Barnet fourteen years before, when Norfolk had defeated the earl, if only as a result of Oxford's own military failures that day. While Oxford remained imprisoned, it was Norfolk who had benefited from the distribution of his lands. Fourteen years later, the earl now had his chance of revenge.

It was not long before Oxford believed that his men had pushed too far into Norfolk's ranks. Fearing that they might be subsumed and 'completely encircled' by the greater numbers of Richard's long battle line, the earl sent out an order through the ranks 'that no soldier was to advance four feet from the standards', though in relating the detail of the manoeuvre, Vergil later changed the distance to ten feet. The earl's orders were once again classic textbook advice, with Christine of Pizan advising that troops should keep within a set 'interval or distance' so that 'men ought to see by great care that they overpress not each other' nor drift too far away; to allow either, she warned, would either 'lose their strokes and their fighting for lack of more room and space' or 'give to their enemies an entry through themself, and so were they in peril to be broken'.

For Oxford, there was perhaps a more personal reason for making his order. The earl had learnt from his bitter experience fourteen years before at Barnet the need to maintain a tight formation among his forces. There his troops had lost the battle through becoming too detached from the main army; when the battle had turned ninety degrees upon itself, in the confusion and the poor visibility, the earl had ended up attacking his own Lancastrian side. It had been a painful lesson that Oxford was not going to repeat this time. As a result, when the earl's men received the command, they 'crowded together and withdrew a short way from the battle'. The decision seems to have caused a brief impasse in the fighting, and Norfolk's vanguard, 'if terrified and suspecting a trick because of this, also stopped fighting for a short time'.

As Richard studied the opening salvoes of the battle, there were other issues pressing on his mind. Catching sight of Thomas Stanley's banner fluttering in the distance, with Stanley's own forces remaining motionless, the king regarded his inaction as nothing short of betrayal. Furious, he was determined to reassert his authority, demonstrating to his own men the price that would be paid for desertion and disobedience. The temporary lull in the fighting gave Richard the chance to order the imprisoned Lord Strange to be brought to him immediately to pay the ultimate price for his father and uncle's actions. Informing Strange that he was to face his death 'for thy uncle's sake', Strange took the news patiently. He called upon a Lancashire gentleman named

Latham, whom he gave a ring from his finger, asking that it be sent to his wife. If Henry were to 'lose the field', then she was to be sent a message to flee in exile abroad together with his eldest son, in the hope that one day he might be able to exact revenge against Richard.

Sir William Harrington urged Richard to delay Strange's execution until both Lord Stanley and Sir William Stanley were captured: 'we shall have them soon on the field, the father, the uncle and the son, all three; then you may deem them with your mouth, what kind of death that they shall die'. The tradition is upheld in all of the ballads, and is revealing about the time of the order, which seems to have come just as Richard's vanguard began their engagement: 'Then came a knight to King Richard, and said, "It is high time to look about; look how your vanguard beginneth to fight. When ye have the father and the son . . . look you what death they shall die: ye may head all at your own will"'.

The story is given credence by the Crowland chronicler, who recorded that as the battle had progressed, Richard ordered that Lord Strange 'should be beheaded on the spot'. 'However, to whom this task was given, seeing that the matter in hand was at a very critical stage and that it was more important than the elimination of one man, failed to carry out' the command, 'and on their own judgement, let the man go and returned to the heart of battle'. It seems that Strange was allowed to go free, perhaps even to join the battle; his fellow prisoner William Gruffudd certainly seems to have been able to do so, for one Welsh poem considered that he was 'the most important Knight on Henry's field, and Sir Rhys was there by your side'. It is a telling sign of the breakdown of authority in Richard's own ranks that the king failed to have his commands obeyed, in stark contrast to Edward IV's summary execution of Lord Welles before his troops had engaged the Lincolnshire rebellion in 1470. Richard's kingship, it seems, was already collapsing around him.

Of course there could have been other reasons why Richard was forced to delay Lord Strange's execution. The incident seems to have chimed with another critical moment in the battle. Having withdrawn temporarily from the fray and drawn his troops closer together, the Earl of Oxford now renewed his attack on Norfolk's vanguard. Vergil relates how the earl 'collected his squadrons together and attacked the enemy on one side', a manoeuvre that seems to chime with Molinet's description of how the French forces on Henry's side advised how to avoid Richard's cannon fire 'by assembling on the side of the king rather than facing him'. In effect, Oxford was placing all of Henry's strength on his left wing. In making this formation, Oxford once again followed Christine de Pizan's advice, who had urged in her work that commanders should 'take most heed of that whether thou fight with thy right wing, or thy left wing or thy centre' and to 'set thy strongest and mightiest and wisest fighters that thou hast, both horsemen, footmen and archers, there where the burden and brunt of the battle will be'.

Yet this strengthened attack on Richard's right hand side was not the only manoeuvre that Oxford had planned. At the same time, the earl ordered that 'others on the other side made a wedge and simultaneously pressed on and renewed the battle'. The use of a wedge formation, or '*cuneo*' in Vergil's account, exactly the same Latin word deployed by Vegetius, to describe a tight column of men charging forward, was used to break through the ranks of an extended battle line such as Richard had deployed. The timing of the renewed charge of the wedge into Richard's main army at the same time as Oxford pressed forward onto the right flank of Norfolk's vanguard came just as Richard was giving his orders for Lord Strange's execution. According to the 'Ballad of Lady Bessie', Strange's execution was only delayed by Sir William Harrington's insistence that 'our ray breaketh on every side', believing that any delay 'put our folk in jeopardy'. The ballad suggests that it was Rhys ap Thomas's men, wearing their recognisable liveries of a black gown who were part of this wedge formation that broke 'the ray' of Richard's men, causing Northumberland on Richard's left flank to be isolated.

In fact, what Oxford hoped to achieve by this pincer movement was far more complex than this. The combined effect of his own attack around the side of Richard's right flank at the same time as sending a wedge of soldiers to break through the king's battle line, was not only to attempt to separate Richard's forces, detaching Northumberland's rearguard from the fighting, but to turn the entire battle round so that Oxford's forces would now be attacking Norfolk's from behind, thereby ensuring that the sun was now in their faces when they faced Oxford's attack. With the fighting now having swung round on its axis, fighting Norfolk's vanguard from their extreme right-hand side and rear,

Oxford had also managed to secure another advantage by ensuring that the sun was facing directly into the eyes of Norfolk's men; one ballad, 'The Rose of England', states that Oxford managed to take Norfolk's right hand, so that 'the sun and wind of them to get'. The position of the morning sun across the battlefield is crucial here: the actual date of the battle in our modern calendar would have been 31 August, when early in the morning, the sun rises from an easterly direction, moving across the sky at approximately fifteen degrees each hour. At the beginning stage of the battle, from where Richard's forces were positioned along the brow of Ambion Hill and Sutton Cheney, the sun would have been roughly behind them. As the hours passed, and the sun rose in the sky, its position would have moved to in between the two forces. As the battle went on and the sun rose in the sky and swung round to a more midway point in the sky, the advantage that Norfolk would have had at the beginning of the battle was being slowly lost. It seems the only move Oxford could have made to gain the sun's position behind him was if he were able not only to attack the right flank of Norfolk's vanguard, but to move completely round these opposing troops and turning round, begin to attack Norfolk's troops from behind.

Once again, the movement itself had been set out by Christine de Pizan, as a means by which a small army facing an opposing force of far greater number, might be able to inflict defeat in spite of their size. Pizan suggested that:

If you can draw up a small number of brave and very experienced men in the proper position, you may be victorious even supposing that your adversary has more men. When the formations come to assemble, you will move your left wing from its position to another, so that you have a long view of the right wing of your enemy, and so that they can neither shoot nor throw missiles there. Your right wing joins their left, and there you begin a rough and strong battle with the best of your men, and the left wing with which you have made contact is so thoroughly invaded by cavalry and infantry that you can go about striking and outflanking in such a way that you can reach the enemy's rear.

The only problem with this version of events is that Oxford's military judgements seem to follow Pizan's textbook to the letter, as if Bosworth was itself a perfect exemplar of the principles of battle set down by Vegetius and translated by Pizan. The only source that describes Oxford's complicated manoeuvre is Polydore Vergil, who having arrived in England in 1502 did not begin his work until around 1508, by which time most of the main participants of the battle were dead, with the exception of the Earl of Oxford. Since Oxford had a clear interest in Pizan's teachings, handing the work to William Caxton to translate in 1489, could it be possible that the earl himself wished for Vergil's own account of the battle to depict him in the role of the classical military general, executing textbook manoeuvres? It is worth considering that the earl may have been one of the principal sources for Vergil's account; in relating his own version of the battle to the Italian, could Oxford have created, for the purposes of his own legacy, an imagined battle that belonged more in the pages of Pizan and Vegetius than on the marshy plain of Redemore? Ultimately, we cannot know: yet it is worth reflecting that as captives of their sources and contemporary accounts, we must remain wary of accepting the exactitude of their accounts of military manoeuvres as incontrovertible fact.

With the conditions now ranged against him, and isolated from Richard's main battle, it was not long before 'after a brief fight' the Duke of Norfolk's vanguard had been 'completely routed and dispersed, with many others being killed in the flight itself'. Molinet noted how there had been 'several feats of arms on both sides', while the 'Ballad of Bosworth Field' describes the efforts of Sir Gilbert Talbot, who being on Oxford's right-hand side may have been involved with the formation of the wedge that attempted to drive through Richard's line, splitting his forces and causing confusion in the ranks as Oxford himself attempted his manoeuvre. Talbot, who was apparently 'sore hurt' in the battle, 'stoutly stirred' causing 'his enemies low to light'. Sir John Savage also, together with his men wearing their livery jackets with a white hood, is described in the ballad as a 'hardy knight' who dealt 'death's dints' during the attack. In the most extreme and obviously imagined account, the seventeenth-century poet John Beaumont described the titanic clash of the vanguards in vivid detail. In Beaumont's poem, the opposing forces met with a clash of spears, with 'shiver'd pieces' flying into the air, before taking hold of their swords. Norfolk took aim at

Oxford's head, landing a direct blow upon his helmet, which slid down striking Oxford on the arm, 'biting through the steel' and inflicting a wound. As both men continued to fight in hand-to-hand combat, the earl managed to split Norfolk's helmet open, leaving his face exposed when suddenly he was killed by an arrow through his eye.

While this entertaining story can hardly be accepted as truth, there is however another version of Norfolk's death, related in one of the ballads, that is worth considering. The 'Ballad of Lady Bessie' describes how, after the battle had begun to turn in Oxford's favour, Norfolk 'would have fled', but retreating to a windmill that stood 'upon a hill so high' he was encountered by Sir John Savage. Noticing Norfolk's retreat to the windmill, Savage managed to capture the duke, taking both Norfolk and his son the Earl of Surrey prisoner. The ballad's account of Norfolk's final demise seems to be given some credence by Molinet, who believed that the duke, having been taken prisoner with his son Surrey, was brought to Henry, 'who sent him on to the Earl of Oxford who had him dispatched'.

The destruction of Richard's vanguard, with 'a great number killed in the flight itself', having been 'put to flight' and apparently 'picked off by Lord Stanley', caused panic in Richard's army. One ballad observed that after witnessing the rout of Norfolk's forces, Lord Dacre 'began to flee, so did many others more'.

Other sources record that even before Norfolk's forces had been crushed, many 'fled even before coming to blows to the enemy'. 'Many more, who had followed Richard against their will,' Polydore Vergil believed, 'easily abstained from fighting and slipped secretly away, inasmuch as they were not desiring the safety, but rather the destruction, of their king, whom they hated.' Robert Fabyan explained how while the fighting raged on, Richard had looked for further reinforcements, but 'many toward the field refused him, and went unto that other party. And some stood hoving afar off till they saw to which party the victory fell.'

Other accounts of the battle are more specific as to who on Richard's side refused to come to their king's aid. According to the Crowland chronicler, the deserters came from the ranks composed of 'many northerners, in whom, especially, King Richard placed so much trust'.

In particular, Northumberland's troops on Richard's left flank remained unmoved. 'Where the Earl of Northumberland stood,' the chronicler observed, 'with a troop of a size and quality befitting his rank, no opposing force was visible, and no blows were exchanged in anger.' Molinet claimed that the earl 'ought to have charged the French, but did nothing except to flee, both he and his company, to abandon his King Richard'. It may have been that with a marsh in front of him, blocking any visible passage to cross to come to the king's aid, further advance was impossible: pinioned in by the difficult and marshy terrain, Northumberland had little other choice but to remain stationary. Most accounts of the battle agree, however, that the decision to remove himself from the battle was entirely of the earl's own choosing.

Even before the battle had begun, it seems, treachery was in the air. According to Molinet, while many members of the nobility had been unwilling to prepare for war, deciding to 'turn their backs', some had decided to join the king's forces and prepare for war, 'not in the least to come to the help of the king, but to settle their debts with him, and to avenge the bad deeds he had done'. For Molinet, the Earl of Northumberland had an 'understanding' with Henry, 'as had various other who left him wanting'. Could some secret agreement have been reached between Northumberland and Henry in advance of the battle?

These thoughts may have crossed the earl's mind on the day of the battle, but it might have been possible that, in his refusal to come to Richard's aid, Northumberland may have had far grander designs in mind. The Spanish account of the battle written by de Valera suggested that Henry was later told that Northumberland, 'in spite of the assistance rendered him during the battle . . . had not really intended this Henry to be king, but had rather arranged for a son of the Duke of Clarence to become king and to marry a daughter of his'. In his hesitancy, had Northumberland been waiting to discover the final outcome of the battle, hoping that he might be able to take advantage of the result? The only evidence of the earl's state of mind at the time comes from his will, made on 27 July 1485, less than a month before the battle. In it, Northumberland made generous provision for both his daughters Eleanor and Anne, with a dowry of 3,000 marks being given to his elder daughter Eleanor. The date of his will, together with the earl's request that his body be buried at Beverley, but only 'if it fortune me to depart from this present life within the county of York', and the fact that the will makes financial provision for any of his servants subsequently 'maymed' in his service, all suggest that Northumberland certainly understood the uncertainty of the times; whatever part he chose to play in deciding both Richard's and Henry's fate that day, he did so knowing that he had the opportunity of becoming a kingmaker. And it seems likely that he chose the opportunity to seize it.

Several accounts of the battle suggest that rather than merely withdraw his forces from the battle as the fighting continued, Northumberland actively turned on Richard's men, joining in the battle not with the king, but against him. The Spanish account asserts that the earl 'left his position and passed in front of the King's vanguard with ten thousand men, then, turning his back on Earl Henry, he began to fight fiercely against the King's van, and so did all the others who had plighted their faith to Earl Henry'. This sudden manoeuvre was also testified by the Scottish chronicler Pittscottie, who claimed that part of Richard's forces 'that should have opposed' Henry's army, instead 'gave them place and let them go by' while others on Richard's side 'themselves turned around and faced King Richard as if they had been his enemies'. Of course, if the battle had turned around, with the Earl of Oxford's troops now managing to attack Norfolk's vanguard from behind, in the confusion, and with the sun now in their eyes, it may have been possible that the fighting that was taking place could have been mistaken for Richard's troops attacking their own side from behind.

Molinet describes how, when Richard noticed Northumberland's desertion and 'found himself alone on the field he thought to run after the others'. One ballad has Richard in 'full woe' calling out to his men, praying them not to flee and pledging to die 'like a man free' rather than face being captured by the Stanleys. It was at this point that some in Richard's army believed the best course of action was to encourage their king to flee. According to Polydore Vergil, 'Richard could (as they say) have found safety for himself in flight. For when those who were round him saw the troops wielding their arms languidly and lazily, and others secretly leaving the battle, they suspected treachery and urged him to flee.' Believing it was obvious that 'the battle had manifestly turned against him, they procured a fast horse' for Richard.

'But Richard, who knew that the people were hostile to him, cast aside all hope for the future that would come after this, and is said to have replied that on that day he would make an end either of wars or of his life, such was the great boldness and great force of spirit in him'.

Vergil's account seems to be confirmed by other accounts of the battle. The Spanish account written shortly after the battle related that it was this sight of men deserting the battlefield and others on Richard's side turning against their own men that prompted Juan de Salazar, a witness to the treason 'of the King's people', to urge Richard to depart, telling him: 'Sire, take steps to put your person in safety, without expecting to have the victory in today's battle, owing to the manifest treason of your following'.

'Salazar,' Richard replied, 'God forbid I yield one step. This day I will die as a king or win.'

The story of Richard being confronted and urged to flee is mentioned in several ballads of the battle, with the 'Ballad of Lady Bessie' suggesting that it was Sir William Harrington who exhorted the king to escape, urging him that 'another day you may your worship win, and to reign with royalty, and wear your crown and be our king'. Richard refused: 'Bring me my battle axe in my hand', the ballad has the king insisting, 'and set the crown of gold on my head so high; for by him that shape both sea and sand, King of England this day will I die.'

It was at this point, the Spanish account records, that Richard, having donned his cote d'armes, then placed over his helmet 'the crown royal, which they declare to be worth one hundred and twenty thousand crowns'. The image of Richard placing the royal crown upon his head, over his helmet, before charging into the final battle is a striking detail observed by every source: the Crowland chronicler describes it as the *pretiosissima corona*, the 'priceless' crown, while John Rous indicates it was 'the crown itself' that the king had brought with him to the battlefield, 'together with great quantities of treasure'. For Vergil, Richard's motive for doing so was clear:

> Because he knew for certain that that day would either give him his kingdom at peace again, or take it away for ever, he went into the battle wearing the royal crown on his helmet, so that, indeed, if he was victorious wearing his crown, that would be the day which would

give him an end of his troubles. But if indeed he was defeated, he would fall more honourably with the insignia of royalty.

Richard's decision to throw himself fully into the battle seems to have coincided with the news that Henry Tudor's standard, indicating his presence on the battlefield, had been spotted. While the vanguards had been engaged in fighting, Richard had been informed by his scouts that 'Henry was in the distance with a few armed men gathered round him'. Now, 'with Henry now nearer, he recognised him more surely from his standards'. Richard, enraged with anger, 'spurred his horse and made an onslaught on him from the other side, beyond the battle-lines'.

As the battle had progressed, Henry had remained in the rearguard, surrounded by 'a few armed men', described as 'scarcely one squadron of cavalry and a few infantry'. According to a French archer who was present at the battle, Henry had chosen to remain unmounted, surrounded by his men, since he 'wanted to be on foot in the midst of us'.

As Oxford's vanguard had pushed forward, a gap had opened up between the two battles, which Richard was now determined to exploit. In a mounted cavalry charge, he charged to his left, around the fighting of the vanguards that was taking place to his right. Witnessing Richard's charge towards him, Henry must have feared the worst. Isolated and with only a small band of men huddled around him, he was too far detached from Oxford's troops for the earl to come to his aid. Contrary to the promise he had received from Thomas Stanley that morning, the Stanleys had not joined his forces, remaining disengaged from the battle, watching from the nearby higher ground. Henry had no other choice but to prepare for battle; knowing that 'all hope of safety lay in weapons, he eagerly faced the struggle'.

In the king's 'first onslaught', Richard crashed into the first ranks of Henry's men who had huddled around their leader, managing to penetrate through the line of defence, one account describing how he made 'a way everywhere for himself with his sword', while another recounted how the king went into the fray with his battle axe in his hand. Richard fought with so 'much vigour' that 'putting heart into those that remained loyal', it seemed that there might be a chance of turning the battle round.

Richard had aimed straight for the one recognisable sign of Henry's location, his standards of St George, the Red Dragon, and the Dun Cow. Reaching one banner, held by Henry's standard-bearer Sir William Brandon, Richard struck out at Brandon, killing him as Henry's standard was 'thrown to the ground'. According to the ballads, Brandon 'hevyd on high' Henry's standard, 'and vamisyd it, tyll with deathe's dent he was stryken downe'. The force of Richard's blow was a powerful one. In the eighteenth century, the antiquarian John Nichols recalled speaking with a lady who had read a manuscript account of the battle which had subsequently been destroyed, which stated that Richard had cleaved William Brandon 'down the head at one blow'.

Richard then 'joined battle' with John Cheyney, at 6 foot 8 inches possibly one of Henry's tallest supporters, who 'met him as he came'; it is testament to Richard's strength that he thrust Cheyney to the ground, 'with great force'. Tradition recalls that Cheyney rode in to retrieve the standard, yet Richard managed to unhorse him by striking him around the head with a broken lance. This struck the crest from his helm and, when he fell unconscious to the ground, his head was laid completely bare. Stunned, he recovered to find that he had lost his helmet. Taking his sword, he cut the skull and horns from a bull's carcass, which happened to be lying nearby, and placed them on his head as a makeshift helmet in order to rejoin the battle. While the story seems somewhat unlikely if not practically impossible, this did not get in the way of a good tale of honour in battle, and Cheyney would be later granted the bull's scalp as his family crest.

At such close quarters, the battle around the two standards was fiercely fought. Richard's standard-bearer, Sir Percival Thirwall, finding himself under attack, held on to Richard's standard 'till both his legs were cut from him, yet to the ground he would not let go, while breath was in his breast'. Of those who were not killed, many must have been maimed or injured. Roger Acton later petitioned, 'in consideration of the true and faithful service that your humble subject Roger Acton hath done unto your highness, now in your victorious field and under your standard and there sore hurt'.

As Richard continued to cut his way through Henry's ranks, it was becoming clear that Henry himself was at serious risk. With his men 'very unsure of victory', Vergil claimed that Henry himself 'withstood the attack longer than even his soldiers thought possible'. As later writers added further colour to Richard's final charge, the story of Richard's confrontation with Henry would later come to be distorted, so that it appeared more like hand-to-hand combat. According to the later sixteenth-century chronicler Hollinshed, Henry, seeing Richard charging towards him like a 'hungry lion', 'gladly preferred to encounter him body to body, and man to man', managing to keep Richard 'at the swords point' while the late-sixteenth-century poet Michael Drayton would later claim that Richard was 'scare a lance's length' from Henry. It has been suggested that Richard's attack was held off by a number of French 'pikemen' from among the mercenaries collected from the Pont-de-l'Arche, who may have formed a hedgehog-like bristle of pikes in a square formation by which to defend Henry. One French source, supposedly a fragment of a letter written by a French participant in the battle, the day after the conflict, stated how Richard had attacked 'with all his division, which was estimated at more than 15,000 men, crying, "These French traitors are today the cause of our realm's ruin".' Was this a reaction to a sudden manoeuvre that caught the king by surprise as he charged, as rows of pikes facing him were assembled, by which means the French mercenaries defended Henry, preventing Richard from breaking through the line? According to the fragmentary evidence of the French letter, which has never been verified as an original source, it stated how 'in part we were the reason why the battle was won'. The deployment of such a manoeuvre, which the Swiss had used so effectively at the battle of Grandson in 1476, seems unlikely, however: rather than professional soldiers, the French mercenaries were clealy *archers du camp*, in other words professional archers, rather than pikemen. None of the sources makes any mention of pikes, eighteen-foot-long wooden spears, being in use at the battle, which surely would have been spotted. Moreover, Richard had his own expert in Continental warfare in Jean de Salazar, who having been in communication with the king as the battle progressed, would have been able to warn Richard about the threat he faced. And if Richard had faced a bristling wall of pikes which would have countered his cavalry charge, how then had he been able to break through its ranks to kill Sir William Brandon and unhorse Sir John Cheyney?

Whether Henry Tudor himself, lacking any military experience, would have proved an effective match for Richard seems to have been ignored by the later Tudor writers; all agree, however, that he was in desperate trouble. The writer of the 'Life of Sir Rhys ap Thomas' relates a story that Rhys, witnessing Henry 'beginning to quail', 'took this occasion to send unto Sir William Stanley, giving him to understand the danger they were in, and entreating him to join his forces for the disengaging the Earl, who was not only in despair of victory, but almost of his life'. Sir William Stanley, who had apparently 'understood not the danger before' joined the battle, and joining with Rhys, 'both together rushed in upon their adversaries and routed them'. According to Vergil, it was only when Henry's life was 'in immediate danger' that Stanley arrived, 'bearing quick and very timely aid' that rescued Henry 'safe and sound from a slaughter'. In fact, Sir William was not acting alone, with Vergil believing that the 'strong band of soldiers' under Sir William's charge had been sent 'by his brother Thomas, who had been sitting idle not far from the battlefield'. This raises the question why Thomas Stanley decided to take action so late in the battle. The timing of Stanley's movement against Richard seems mysterious. He could not be sure that at the precise moment, with Richard so close to Henry Tudor, that the king might not easily defeat Henry, in which case his late charge into the battle would have been taken as treason. Perhaps it was also at this moment when Stanley must have assumed that Lord Strange had been killed, leaving him with nothing else to lose but to order Sir William Stanley to charge into battle. Alternatively, Stanley could have discovered that Strange had been freed during the battle, thereby removing the one cause for constraint that had prevented Stanley from declaring his support for Henry Tudor.

Sir William Stanley's charge seems to have taken Richard entirely by surprise. Leading a force of 3,000 men, Stanley swept into the battle 'down at a bank' to set upon Richard and his men, smashing into the king's left side, while Thomas Stanley remained motionless, deciding to 'hove on this hill / That fair battle for to see'. William Stanley's forces aimed straight for the king's standard, upon which 'fast did they light'. 'The Rose of England' described the image of how William Stanley's men, wearing their jackets 'of white and red', 'laid about them lustily', adding 'a worthy sight it was to see'.

Vergil believed that Richard 'was killed at the selfsame moment', describing how, witnessing Sir William Stanley's sudden charge, the rest of the king's men were 'thrown into flight'. Nevertheless, Richard remained committed to battle and it was only 'while fighting in the thickest press of the enemy' that he was 'struck through'. It seems that as Stanley's men pushed forward, Richard was swept towards the marsh that Henry had intended to act as his defence. The details of Richard's final moments remain elusive, though the prose version of the 'Ballad of Bosworth Field' recorded that Richard was 'in a marris' while Molinet believed he 'ended his days iniquitously and filthily in the dirt and the mire', adding that the king had died after 'his horse leapt into a marsh from which it could not retrieve itself. One of the Welshmen then came after him, and struck him dead with a halberd.' Even once Richard had been killed, the rain of blows upon his battered body continued as his crown was 'hewyd' from his head 'with dowtfull dents'. The 'Ballad of Lady Bessie' adds further lurid detail, suggesting that Richard's head was battered to the point that his basinet was driven into his head, 'until his brains came out with blood'.

Later there would be many who would claim the credit for delivering the final fatal blow that had killed the king. Molinet recorded that Richard had been killed by a 'Welsh halberd': according to Welsh tradition, it was Rhys ap Maredudd, known also as Rhys Fawr, 'Rhys the Mighty', who having immediately picked up Henry's Red Dragon standard after Brandon's death, had managed to kill Richard. Yet those same traditions, told by various Welsh bards, told that it was Sir Rhys ap Thomas who killed the king, 'manfully fighting with him hand to hand', and that in gratitude Henry honoured Sir Rhys with the quaint epithet of 'Father Rice'. The Welsh poet Guto'r Glyn, addressing a poem to Rhys after the battle, implied that he had delivered the fatal blow himself, and 'killed the boar, destroyed his head'. Another poet, Tudur Penllyn, also gifts Richard's killing to Rhys.

While in the confusion and heat of battle, it was perhaps impossible for even those men who were present to say who exactly had killed Richard. Nevertheless, another tale worth considering is the story told in 1610 by James Ley, who claimed that his great-grandfather, Henry Ley, had been 'a man of arms' on Henry's side, 'and was near about the earl's person, at such time the king was slain by one Thomas Woodshawe'. Henry Ley had accompanied his lord Sir Robert Willoughby to the battle, yet it is notable that one 'Thomas Woodshawe', a tenant on the Middleton Hall estate also owned by the Willoughby family, was rewarded by Henry on 20 September with the office of bailiff of the lordship of Berkeswell in Warwickshire and made keeper of the park there 'during pleasure'.

There can be little doubt that Richard had fought, whether in determination or desperation, to the last. By his 'sole effort', one chronicler wrote, he had 'upheld the battle for a long time'. Despite being no fan of Richard, whom he compared to the Antichrist, John Rous of Warwick wrote how 'if I may say the truth to his credit, though small in body and feeble of limb, he bore himself like a gallant knight and acted with distinction as his own champion until his last breath'. The Crowland chronicler praised Richard's bravery, 'for in the thick of the fight, and not in the act of flight, King Richard fell in the field, struck by many mortal wounds, as a bold and most valiant prince'. And even Polydore Vergil, intent upon presenting the king in the worst possible light, had to admit that Richard had demonstrated 'a proud, fierce spirit, which did not desert him even in death, which, abandoned by his men, he preferred to meet rather than to save his life by shameful flight'.

It was an almost unbelievable victory: for the Crowland chronicler, Henry's crown had been 'remarkably won'. Not since the Norman Conquest had an invasion resulted in a king's death on the battlefield, the passing of one dynasty and the birth of another. 'I observe from the chronicles that no such end for a King of England (being killed that is on a battlefield in his own kingdom) has been heard of since the time of King Harold, who was a usurper and was defeated in battle by William the Conqueror coming from Normandy whence also these men had come.'

Upon the sight of his death, Richard's army melted away in flight. 'The rearguard,' Molinet wrote, 'seeing King Richard dead, turned in flight.' Immediately those in the field 'threw down their arms and willingly surrendered into Henry's power' to be taken prisoner. As a result, the Crowland chronicler added almost crestfallen, 'there was left no part of the opposing army of sufficient significance or substance for the glorious victor Henry VII to engage, and so add to his experience in battle'.

The battle had lasted little more than two hours. According to Robert

Fabyan, a 'sharp battle' had been fought, 'and sharper it should have been, if the king's party had been fast to him'. For many, the end of the battle had come as a relief. Many of Richard's men would have surrendered earlier, Vergil wrote, 'of their own accord even when Richard was alive, assuming it could have been done without danger'.

According to Vergil, when Henry learnt of Richard's death he was 'amazingly overjoyed'; only in the later printed edition of his work did he note that Henry 'immediately gave thanks to Almighty God with many prayers for receiving the victory he had won'. Henry 'betook himself to the nearest hill', described somewhat optimistically in one of the ballads as a 'mountain high', located south of where the battle had taken place, near to the village of Stoke, from which its inhabitants had watched the battle unfold from the tower of St Margaret's church. Henry's reasons for heading for the hill may also have been to reach Thomas Stanley, who in Vergil's account was 'encamped with his troops not far from the battlefield'. From this location, overlooking the carnage of the dead and wounded in the marshy ground below, Henry first addressed his victorious army, praising his soldiers and ordering that the wounded should be looked after and that the dead be buried. According to Bernard André, Henry spoke of his grief 'when I behold the deaths of so many brave men, whom I would like to commit to a decent burial. In particular, I am of the opinion that the body of King Richard should be buried . . . with all due reverence.' Vergil noted how Henry took especial care to give his 'everlasting thanks' to his 'leading men', promising that he 'would remember their good deeds'. As he ended his speech, his soldiers began to hail him 'in a great shout', cheering 'with very willing hearts': the ballads record that 'with a voice they cried King Henry'.

According to Vergil, Thomas Stanley, witnessing this, took Richard's crown, which 'had been found in the meantime among the spoils . . . then, with all acclaiming him in this way, Thomas Stanley placed the crown on his head'. Later, in his printed work, Vergil took the unofficial crowning ceremony to be an official sign of Henry's legitimacy to the throne, having been declared by the 'vox populi', 'just as if he had been hailed as king by the will of the people in accordance with ancestral custom; and this was the first omen of happiness'. André also provides details of how 'all the churchmen who had come along with the most fortunate Earl of Richmond offered up heartfelt and most pious prayers to heaven', including the Franciscan friar Michael Deacon, the Bishop of Asaph, the sometime confessor to the king, and Christopher Urswick.

It was the perfect culmination to Henry's victory; too perfect perhaps. Bernard André idealised the scene of victory, complete with the 'blare of bugles and bray of trumpets' that 'assaulted the stars'. But there is another story. The Great Chronicle recorded that it was Sir William Stanley, 'as it was said', who having 'won the possession of King Richard's helmet with the crown being upon it' came straight to King Henry and set it upon his head saying, "Sir, here I make you King of England"'. Could Sir William Stanley, rather than his brother, have been the official kingmaker, as his actions on the battlefield had won the day? It seems unlikely that Thomas Stanley, as the senior nobleman of the two brothers, would not have been given the honours of crowning Henry. If Henry had climbed what was to become Crown Hill in order to reach Thomas Stanley's camp, seeking his approval for his victory, it would seem natural for Stanley himself to perform the unofficial ceremony. Sir William Stanley, having retrieved Richard's crown, could of course have passed the crown to his brother; the ballads suggest that the crown was delivered to Lord Stanley who 'unto king Henry then went he, and delivered it, as to the most worthy to wear the crown and be their king'.

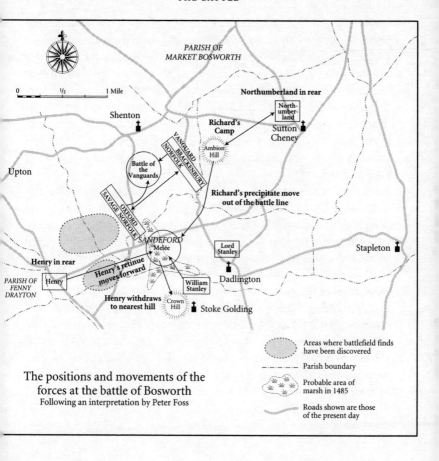

The positions and movements of the
forces at the battle of Bosworth
Following an interpretation by Peter Foss

PART FOUR:
AFTERMATH

12

OUR VICTORIOUS FIELD

◦•◦

According to the Crowland chronicler, Richard's corpse had been discovered '*inter alios mortuos*' – among the other dead. It is likely that Richard's body would have at first been unrecognisable, as one chronicler described, 'so all besprung with mire and filth'. Molinet suggested that Richard had been killed by a Welsh halberd, while another account described how Richard's helmet had been beaten into his skull and 'destroyed the head'. If this were the case, it is hardly surprising that the king's body may have at first gone unnoticed among the scattered bodies of the dead covered in the mud of the marshy land on Redemore plain where they had fallen. At the Battle of Nancy eight years earlier, Richard's brother-in-law Charles the Bold, Duke of Burgundy, was killed: 'refusing to fly, and fighting desperately to cover the retreat of his scattered forces, [he] was surrounded and was cleft through helmet and skull by the tremendous blow of a Swiss halberd'. It took two days to find Charles's body, by now frozen. As a result of the 'mighty blow', his face was 'one gash from temple to teeth', leaving him 'totally unrecognisable except to his Italian valet who knew him by his long fingernails, and to his Portugese doctor who identified him by the old battle scars on his stripped and frozen corpse'. When the first Earl of Shrewsbury was killed at the battle of Castillon, after his body had been stripped of its armour, he was only later identified by his missing left molar.

Once Richard's body had been identified, the Crowland chronicler noted, 'many other insults were heaped on it, and, not very humanely, a halter was thrown around the neck'. It was likely that rather than Richard's body being stripped naked as part of a deliberate humiliation of the dead king, his body 'besprinkled with mire and blood' had only been identified after his armour had been removed. Polydore Vergil gave more precise details about the fate of the corpse: 'stripped of all he was wearing and put on its back', Richard's body was placed on the back of a horse and brought to Leicester 'with his head and arms hanging down on one side of the horse and his legs on the other, a wretched sight indeed, but very worthy of the man's life'. Trussed up like a 'hog or another vile beast', his entrance into the town was followed by a lone herald, 'the pursuivant called Norroy'. The chronicler could not help but observe with pathos that 'as gloriously as he by the morning departed from that town, so as irreverently was he that afternoon brought into that town'.

Henry had ordered that Richard's body, almost naked, should be placed on public display for two days in Leicester, 'for all men to wonder upon'. In doing so, it was clear that Henry intended to prove that Richard had died in battle, to prevent any rumours to the contrary. After the battle of Barnet, Edward IV had done the same with Warwick's body, which had been displayed at St Paul's laid out almost naked in a wooden coffin. Men flocked to get a sight of the dead king, 'with everyone wishing to look at him', 'naked and despoiled to the very skin, and nothing left about him, not so much as a clout to cover his privy parts'. Richard's bloodied and near-naked corpse had been trussed up in the collegiate church of St Mary-in-the-Newarke. The decision to display his mortal remains there appears to have been entirely deliberate: not only was the church a Lancastrian foundation, Richard's body would suffer the further indignity of being displayed among the tombs of Henry, Earl of Lancaster, Henry, Duke of Lancaster and Mary de Bohun, the grandmother of Henry VI, who had all been buried there. The message could not be clearer: Henry, the inheritor of the Lancastrian dynasty, had finally ensured that vengeance had been secured. When Richard's corpse was cut down, Henry chose not to have the Yorkist king buried among his Lancastrian ancestors, but rather in the plainer Greyfriars church, part of the Franciscan Friary, 'irreverently buried' without any funeral ceremony in the choir of the Franciscan Friars Minor in Leicester.

It was not until ten years later, in September 1495, that Henry would give thought to providing the dead king with any tombstone to mark his grave, ordering that James Keyley be paid £10 1s for making 'King Richard's tomb'. Even in the grave, it seems, Richard would continue to cause controversy, with the payment for the alabaster monument becoming the subject of a lawsuit between two stonemasons. There are no contemporary descriptions of the monument, but a manuscript copy of its epitaph survives. It reads:

I, here, whom the earth encloses under ostentatious marble,
Was justly called Richard the Third.
I was Protector of my country, an uncle ruling on behalf of his
    nephew.
I held the British kingdoms in trust, although they were disunited.
Then for just sixty days less two,
And two summers, I held my sceptres.
Fighting bravely in war, deserted by the English,
I succumbed to you, King Henry VII.
But you yourself, piteously, at your expense, thus honoured my
    bones
And caused a former king to be revered with the honour of a king
When in twice five years less four
Three hundred five-year periods of our salvation had passed.
And eleven days before the Kalends of September
I surrendered to the red rose the power it desired.
Whoever you are, pray for my offences,
That my punishment may be lessened by your prayers.

Richard's tomb did not survive the Dissolution of the Monasteries, which brought an end to his final resting place at Greyfriars. John Speed, in his *History of Great Britian*, published in 1611, stated that at the suppression of Greyfriars' monastery, Richard's tomb was 'pulled down and utterly defaced, since when the grave overgrown with nettles and weeds is very obscure and not to be found.' According to one tradition, after the monastery had been dissolved during the reformation, the tomb was broken into and the bones of the dead king were carried through the town accompanied by jeers, finally to be thrown from Bow Bridge into the river Soar below. Richard's supposed coffin was apparently placed outside the White Horse Inn in the city, where it served a new purpose as a watering-trough for horses. John Evelyn wrote in his diary in 1654 that Leicester, that 'old and ragged city', was famous only 'for the tomb of the tyrant Richard III, which is now converted into a cistern, at which (I think) cattle drink'. The trough was eventually broken up during the reign of George I, to be used as steps into a cellar. Christopher Wren, Dean of Windsor and father of the great architect, told a different tale: after Richard had been slain, he wrote, 'his body was begged by the Nuns of Leicester, and buried in their chapel there; at the dissolution whereof the place of his burial happened to fall into the bounds of a citizen's garden, which being after purchased by Mr. Robert Herrick was by him covered with a handsome stone pillar, three foot high, with this inscription, "Here lies the body of Richard III, some time King of England." This he showed me walking in his garden, Anno 1612.'

For centuries, in spite of the location of Richard's final resting place being well known, the king's body was forgotten by history. Robert Herrick's house was eventually demolished, to be replaced in the eighteenth century by a row of houses; eventually the site of Richard's burial would become a council car park, with the king's remains lying somewhere beneath its tarmac.*

Henry and his victorious army eventually arrived at Leicester, where he was received 'with all honour and gladness'. He remained there for two days, allowing his soldiers to refresh themselves and prepare for his march to London to claim the crown. In the aftermath of the battle, several important tasks faced the new king. In his victory speech upon Crown Hill, Henry had spoken of his grief at beholding the sight of the deaths 'of so many brave men'. He had witnessed his own standard-bearer William Brandon being cut down and killed by Richard during his final ill-fated charge; according to Polydore Vergil, Brandon was 'the only one from the nobility' who had fallen on Henry's side, which had seen 'scarcely 100' soldiers killed in the battle. Estimates of the number of men killed during the two hours of fighting varies wildly between different sources, with one even suggesting that over 10,000 died on both sides. The number of bodies scattered across the battlefield was undoubtedly fewer than this: a more realistic total comes from Vergil, who estimated that in addition to the hundred men lost on Henry's side, 'on Richard's side about a thousand men fell in this battle' while Molinet believed that there were 'only 300 dead on both sides'.

* See Postscript, p.390

Casualties had been heaviest on Richard's side where the engagement of the vanguards or 'in the first battle line' had taken place. Led by the Duke of Norfolk, according to Vergil, 'a very great number were killed in the flight' following their rout by Oxford's troops. Once identified, Norfolk's body was taken from the battlefield to be buried in his family tomb in Thetford priory. Later it would be moved to Framlingham following the priory's dissolution, and in 1841 the sheet lead coffin was opened, where the skull of an old man, judging by the state of its teeth, was discovered still with its hair, 'of a fair or sandy colour' intact. At the front of the skull there was 'a large hole . . . as if the head must have had some severe blow at some time or other'. No epitaph for the tomb survives, yet the chronicler Edward Hall gave perhaps the most fitting tribute for a man who had fought his first battle in the French wars during the 1440s, who had witnessed the tribulations of battle throughout the tumult of the civil wars of the 1450s and 1460s, who had been present at Barnet, and who finally went loyally to his death over forty years later: 'he regarded his oath, his honour and promise made to King Richard; like a gentleman and faithful subject to his prince he absented himself not from his master, but as he faithfully lived under him, so he manfully died with him to his great fame and laud'.

Among the dead were also Richard's dedicated supporters who must have joined the king on or near to his final charge. Richard's close companion Sir Richard Ratcliffe, Sir Robert Brackenbury, the keeper of the Tower of London, John Kendal, the king's secretary, Sir Robert Percy, controller of the king's household and Walter Devereux, Lord Ferrers all perished. Of the commissioners of array who assembled for Richard, ten were likely to have been killed at the battle: in Buckinghamshire, Thomas Hampden of Kimble and Thomas Straunge, William Allington in Cambridgeshire, John Coke in Essex, John Kebyll in Leicestershire, Richard Boughton and Humphrey Beaufort in Warwickshire, Sir Thomas Gower and Sir Robert Percy in Yorkshire all are listed among the inquisitions post mortem as having died around the date of the battle. Other commissioners are known to have died in late 1485, perhaps from injuries sustained in battle, though this cannot be confirmed. Those who died with only young children as their heirs indicates that their deaths were probably unexpected, though sudden death from the sweating sickness that swept England in the autumn of 1485 cannot be discounted. They included Thomas Pygot in Cambridgeshire, John Harlyng, John Grene, William Gate and John Wrytell in Essex, John Twynyho and John Wykes in Gloucestershire, William Druell in Hertfordshire, Sir Thomas Frowyk and Thomas Windsor in Middlesex, Henry le Strange in Norfolk, Sir William Stokes in Northamptonshire, John Cawardyne in Staffordshire, John Wode junior in Sussex, John Hugford in Warwickshire and Sir John Stourton in Wiltshire.

At least forty of the nobility and gentry who fought for Richard and were killed can be traced, men from at least sixteen counties, with eight arriving at the battle from the southern counties of Cambridgeshire, Buckinghamshire and Oxfordshire. Nevertheless, the large number of northern gentry who were among the battle dead is testament to the support that many northerners had given their king, in spite of Northumberland's inaction and Stanley's defection. Henry was well aware of the contribution that northerners had played in the battle, issuing a proclamation the following month stating how 'many and diverse persons of the north parts of this our land, knights, esquires, gentlemen and other have done us now of late great displeasure being against us in the field with the adversary of us'.

The Yorkshire knights Sir Thomas Gower, Ralph Danby and Sir Robert Percy were among the dead, while from Durham, Robert Brackenbury, William Gilpin, Gilbert Swinburne of Chopwell and Robert Claxton were named as having died on the king's side. Other evidence survives of the names of those who must have lost their lives in the battle from the inquisitions post mortem taken the following year: Alan Fulthorpe, the constable of Middleham Castle, had died on the Vigil of St Bartholomew (23 August), while Robert Brackenbury's inquisition has the date left blank. Four of the men named held the constableships of six of Richard's castles, while two were sheriffs in 1484–5.

Regardless of whether they had fallen fighting for or against his standard, Henry ordered that every man should be given 'a decent burial'. The ballads recall how the noble dead of the Duke of Norfolk, Lord Ferrers 'and many other more' were carried from the field 'boldly' on biers. Many were buried near the parish church of St James at nearby Dadlington, whose churchwardens over twenty-five years later petitioned Henry VIII to recognise the significance of its location 'standing upon a parcel of the ground where Bosworth feld, otherwise called Dadlyngton feld, in our county of Leicester was done', requesting that a battlefield chapel might be constructed where 'the bodies or bones of the men slain in the said field be brought and buried'.

As the armour was pulled from the lifeless carcasses and bodies placed on carts to be taken to Dadlington, there were also the wounded to tend to. Some were so severely injured that they had little chance of survival: John Mynde, a Shropshire gentleman who had survived the battle, had received 'such grevious hurts and bresurs' during the fighting that he died soon after. He had fought alongside his son John and six others, several of whom had been 'right grievously hurt, and some of them maimed for ever'. Many who had been injured in the battle survived, even if they were maimed. Peter Peirse of Bedale lost a leg, but lived 'long after' while Gilbert Talbot, who was knighted shortly after the battle by Henry along with Sir John Mortimer, Sir Rhys ap Thomas, Sir Robert Poyntz and Sir Humphrey Stanley, according to John Leland, had been 'sore wounded at Bosworth'. Roger Acton later petitioned Henry how he had fought 'in your victorious field and under your standard and there sore hurt'. Ralph Bigod was injured during the battle, and would have 'likely to have been slain' had not the battle ended so suddenly.

Many of the wounded must have been taken to Leicester for treatment. Three years after the battle, Henry granted to the mayor and burgesses of Leicester an annuity of £20 for seven years, noting 'the great costs and charges that they have sustained and borne by our commandment in our journeys, fields, and battles, and of the costs they did and made upon our servants wounded and maimed in our first field', to a total of £180. It is also noteworthy that the office of 'principal surgeon for the king's body' was granted to William Altoftes, who came from the nearby town of Atherston.

An example of the type of injuries faced by some participants in the battle can be found in a surviving medical textbook that describes how 'a gentleman that was shot at Barnard or Bosard felde' had been hit from behind in the thigh by shot from a 'hackebush' or arquebus; wearing a coat of mail which had protected him, three rings of mail were 'left in his left buttock . . . by ignorance of the surgeon'. Twenty years later, with pains in his ankle, the man 'met with an old surgeon' who, examining him, asked 'what armour he wore at that time'. Discovering that he had been wearing a coat of mail, the surgeon deduced that the pieces of mail had worked their way down towards his patient's ankle; cutting it open, he 'found the three mails as bright as could be and so he healed him where as a plaster could not have and he lived long after'.

As the battle had ended, in the confusion many participants on Richard's side who had 'easily abstained from fighting' had 'slipped secretly away' and 'without incurring any loss'. Among those who had been able to flee the battlefield unnoticed were Francis, Lord Lovell, together with John de la Pole, Earl of Lincoln, Humphrey Stafford and his brother Thomas, who 'with a good number of companions' rode through the day and night across the country to reach sanctuary in the monastery of St John at Colchester, on the Essex coast.

Still the number of prisoners captured after the battle had finished 'was very great, since after Richard was killed men threw down their arms and willingly surrendered into Henry's power'. Many would have done so earlier, Vergil observed, 'of their own accord even when Richard was alive, assuming it could have been done without danger'; he would later add in his printed work that 'the majority would have done from the beginning if it had been possible with Richard's scouts flying about hither and thither'.

The most prominent captives were Henry, Earl of Northumberland and the duke of Norfolk's son, Thomas, Earl of Surrey, and Richard's councillor and close confidant William Catesby. Vergil suggests that Surrey was 'pardoned at once', though this clearly did not happen before the earl was taken to Queenborough castle on the Isle of Sheppey until October before being removed to the Tower, where he was still present in December. Northumberland's surrender was a far more complex matter. Through his inaction, the earl had helped to ensure that victory fell to Henry. Yet Henry remained suspicious over Northumberland's precise motives and had him 'seized and held in prison until he handed over that son of the Duke of Clarence and did him homage together with two Earls his relatives, promising to serve him always like loyal vassals'.

There is no evidence that Northumberland had any control over Edward Earl of Warwick, but Henry was taking no chances. One of the first actions after the battle was to send Robert Willoughby to

Yorkshire to seize the fifteen-year-old, whom Richard had placed in Sheriff Hutton. According to Vergil, Henry, 'not unaware of the mob's natural tendency always to seek changes', was concerned that 'if the boy should escape and given any alteration in circumstances, he might stir up civil discord'. On Willoughby's arrival, Edward was handed over by the castle governor and brought to London where he was imprisoned in the Tower. Northumberland soon joined him, though he seems to have been released shortly before 6 December, before being restored to favour as the warden general of the East and Middle Marches in January the following year.

Since most of Richard's inner circle had either been killed or fled the battle, few reprisals seem to have been considered necessary. Most men who had fought for Richard who were taken captive were later released, with the Crowland chronicler recording that only two men 'from the western parts', named Bracher, who had fallen into 'the hands of the victors' were later hanged on the gallows. Their deaths may have in any case been part of some private vendetta: William Bracher was a yeoman of the crown who in March 1484 had been rewarded with the manors of Cheddar and Barrow Gurney that had belonged to Sir William Berkeley 'for his good service against the rebels'. With battle came the legitimate opportunity to settle old scores; it was on the field that private and public grievances could be settled as one.

For Thomas Stanley, who for several decades had conducted a campaign of violence and intimidation upon a neighbouring gentry family, the Harringtons, over a land dispute, the battle provided the opportunity he had been waiting for to ensure that his local rival was all but destroyed for taking Richard's side. After the battle, Harrington was left with 'no livelihood' and in 'great poverty' as a result of his attainder. Harrington's nephew later claimed that the attainder had only been passed at Stanley's insistence, 'for old malice and grudge that he had'. Years later, one of the family's ancestors went so far as to declare that Stanley had 'caused' Sir James Harrington to be attainted, 'where in for a truth the said James was never against the King in no field'. In the heat of battle, however, not all private vengeances were exacted as successfully: one north Midlands squire, John Babington of Dethick, was allegedly killed by James Blount, motivated by the chance to increase his inheritance. But Blount got the wrong man. His intended target had been John Babington of Chilwell.

Battle and its aftermath also gave men the perfect opportunity to exploit the instability of the new regime to their own advantage. Humphrey Stafford quickly moved to occupy the lands of Sir Robert Willoughby, whose residents later complained to Henry that he had 'within two days next after your most victorious journey, entered, and yet be in possession of the same accordingly'. Robert Throckmorton, having been appointed sheriff for Warwickshire and Leicestershire after the battle, having failed to bring the counties to order, sought pardon from Henry since having been appointed to his office for a month he had found himself 'incontinent' with the surrounding countryside in 'such rebellion and trouble, and your laws not established' that he 'neither might nor could execute his said office of sherrifwick to any profit of your said highness'.

Recognising the need to swiftly restore order and stability to the realm, Henry issued his first proclamation from Leicester:

Henry, by the grace of God, King of England and France, prince of Wales and lord of Ireland, strictly chargeth and commandeth, upon pain of death, that no manner of man rob or spoil no manner of commons coming from the field; but suffer them to pass home to their countries and dwelling places, with their horses and harness. And moreover, that no manner of man take upon him to go to no gentleman's place, neither in the county, nor within cities nor boroughs, nor pick no quarrels for old or new matters; but keep the king's peace, upon pain of hanging.

And moreover, if there be any man offered to be robbed and spoiled of his goods, let him come to master Richard Borrow, the king's serjeant here, and he shall have a warrant for his body and his goods, until the time the king's pleasure be known.

And moreover, the king ascertaineth you, that Richard Duke of Gloucester, lately called King Richard, was lately slain at a place called Sandeford, within the shire of Leicester, and there was lain openly, that every man might see and look upon him. And also there was slain upon the same field John, late Duke of Norfolk, John, late Earl of Lincoln, Thomas, late Earl of Surrey, Francis, Viscount Lovel, Sir Walter Devereux, Lord Ferrers, Richard Ratcliffe, knight, Robert

Brackenbury, knight, with many other knights, squires, and gentle-men: on whose souls God have mercy.

It did not matter that the Earl of Surrey, the Earl of Lincoln and Lovell had not been killed, preferring to flee rather than face death in battle. The statement was not intended to reflect the precise details of what had taken place on the battlefield, although the claim that the victory had resulted in the deaths of most of the nobility who had fought for Richard's cause was probably deliberate, aimed at preventing any further uprisings from disaffected Yorksists.

Equally important for Henry was that he should be viewed as a king who intended to draw a line under the past. He wanted to send out the message that he would not be prepared to tolerate any attacks on men who had taken arms up against him, a clear break from the vicious reprisals that had followed previous battles such as Tewkesbury or Towton, when the defeated side had been pursued ruthlessly to their deaths. Henry knew that the situation was too delicate, and his own position still uncertain, to provoke possible reprisals. He must also have been mindful that his narrow victory had been won not by his own valour, having come close to death as a result of Richard's final charge, but by Sir William Stanley's final show of strength, crashing through the battle to defeat Richard at the very moment it seemed that the late king might have destroyed Henry. Henry must have understood that victory had been obtained not just by the acts of engagement during the battle of a few, but by the abstention of the many from joining the fray altogether.

He owed them his crown too: Northumberland's desertion ensured that Richard's rearguard had stood still, refusing to come to their king's aid; as the Crowland Chronicler remarked, 'where the Earl of Northumberland stood, with a troop of a size and quality befitting his rank, no opposing force was visible, and no blows were exchanged in anger'. Molinet made clear that Northumberland was expected to charge upon the French, but instead 'did nothing, and left him and his suit, and abandoned King Richard'. Molinet wrote later that he believed Northumberland had an 'understanding' with Henry, 'as had various other who left him wanting', but was the earl alone responsible for ensuring that his men did not take part in the battle?

Northumberland had faced the spectre of battle and the consequences of defeat before. Previous to Edward IV's ascendancy, his
family loyalties had traditionally rested with the Lancastrians. For this
they had paid the price: the earl's father had died from wounds received
fighting on behalf of Henry VI at Towton in 1461, while Northumberland himself was captured, attainted and imprisoned. He was released
eight years later and his attainder reversed. Yet the memories of that
bloody battle, in which tens of thousands from the Yorkshire region
had died, did not affect Northumberland alone. In 1471, when Edward
returned from exile to reclaim his crown, Northumberland should have
prevented his landing and opposed his march, but he did not. Instead,
landing at Ravenspur and travelling southwards, Edward commanded
Northumberland to provide him with an armed force. Northumberland sought to encourage his men to fight for Edward IV, yet according to one report, the memory of the Yorkist victory at Towton was too
painful for many to commit to Edward's cause, and 'many gentlemen,
and other, which have been arrayed by him, would not so fully and
extremely have determined them self in the King's right and quarrel as
the Earl would have done himself'. Unable to command his own men
to take Edward's side, Northumberland had no other choice but to do
nothing. Nevertheless, one chronicler reported, the earl's decision at
least prevented some in the north from rising up against Edward: 'his
sitting still caused the city of York to do as they did, and no worse, and
every man in all those north parts to sit still also'. Could the same situation possibly have repeated itself at Bosworth, where the earl's inaction
at least prevented his men from turning against Richard?

According to the Crowland chronicler, it was 'for the most part those
northerners in whom King Richard had so trusted, took flight before
it came to hand-to-hand fighting'. It remains particularly striking that
all the northern magnates were not later attainted for their possible
attendance in Richard's army: Northumberland, Westmorland, the two
Lord Scropes, Lord Greystoke, Lord Dacre, Lord Fitzhugh and Lord
Lumley. In considering why separate noblemen may have decided to
sit on their hands and refuse to join in battle, it is worth studying their
own individual ambitions. Westmorland, for example, had hoped to
have been rewarded for his support for the king; in June 1483 Richard
had written to him, appealing to Westmorland to 'do me good service

as you have always done, and I trust now so to remember you as shall be the making of you and yours'. What did Westmorland hope to achieve, or more likely gain, from his support for Richard? He certainly must have hoped to claim a share of the inheritance of his maternal uncle Henry Holland, Duke of Exeter, of whom Westmorland was the male heir. Edward IV had instead passed the inheritance to the Woodvilles in 1483 – Westmorland expected, with a change of regime, that he would retrieve his rightful lands. He was to be disappointed; Richard stripped the inheritance from the Woodvilles, only to keep the Exeter lands for himself in the crown's possession. Westmorland might have also hoped for the lucrative wardenship of the West Marches, now that the office had been vacated by Richard's accession as king: it was an office that had previously 'belonged' to his great-grandfather. Yet again, he was denied it, with Richard choosing to retain possession of the office, appointing Humphrey, Lord Dacre as his lieutenant. Instead, rather than advancing his power, Westmorland found his influence in his own region curtailed by Richard's showering of patronage upon Sir Richard Ratcliffe, and by July 1484 even the revenue from the Neville family seat at Raby Castle was assigned to support the Council of the North. The earl must have thought that there was little reason to place his own life at risk, fighting for a king who had not provided him with what he expected was his by right. Westmorland was likely to have been at Bosworth, yet this does not mean that he actually fought on Richard's behalf. Like so many of his fellow northern men, he stood watching and waiting. After the battle had ended, he joined Northumberland and Surrey in custody, having been captured. He entered into several bonds for his good behaviour on 1 December 1485 totalling £400 and 400 marks, to be paid at Christmas 1486, the feast of the Purification of the Virgin Mary and Michaelmas 1487. On 5 December 1485 he granted Henry the wardship of his eldest son Ralph.

The Earl of Westmorland was not alone in his decision: in their absence and prevarication, the nobility settled Richard's fate at Bosworth. The Scottish chronicler Pittscottie wrote that 'some others of King Richard's army stood and looked on while they saw who had the victory'. Robert Fabyan's Chronicle remarked that the battle should have been 'sharper' if only Richard's forces had remained loyal to the King; instead they 'refused him', some surrendering to the opposing forces while others 'stood hoving' from a distance until the outcome of the battle and which way 'victory fell' was certain.

The attitude of William Berkeley, the Earl of Nottingham, is perhaps typical of the approach that many of the nobility must have had towards the uncertain outcome of the battle. Berkeley may have been present in the field, but whether he actually engaged is another matter. He must have had divided loyalties: Berkeley, thirty years older than Tudor, seems to have known him from his time when he was resident at the Herbert household at Raglan between 1462 and 1469, since he testified in January 1486 that he had known Henry 'well for twenty years and more'. A family history written in the seventeenth century attests to the earl's decision to neither declare for one side nor the other, stating that while he had sent men to the king's side, he had sent money to Tudor, and 'neither of both with his person' so that 'he preserved the favour of both, at least lost neither of them'.

Four-fifths of the nobility, twenty-eight men, decided it best to remove themselves from the conflict altogether. Of those who chose to fight, two abstained from joining the fray, and only two attainted earls, Oxford and his uncle Jasper, fought for Henry. Only six can be proved to have joined Richard and fought for his cause. Norfolk and Lord Ferrers gave their lives during the battle, yet both were elderly men. Norfolk's son and heir, Thomas Howard, Earl of Surrey, Francis, Viscount Lovell, Lord Scrope of Bolton and John, Lord Zouche also fought, yet most, it seems, did so because they owed their livelihoods to the king. Francis Lovell, for instance, the king's closest friend, had been rewarded with grants of land estimated at £400. Lord Scrope of Bolton had been given lands in Devon and Cornwall worth over £200 annually, and had been given an annuity of £156 as well as a salary as the king's councillor.

It was in this atmosphere of uncertainty and uncommitted loyalty that Henry's clemency and decision not to wreak revenge would prove a wise one. 'And since it was not heard nor read nor committed to memory that any others who had withdrawn from the battle had been afterwards cut down by such punishments, but rather that he had shown clemency to all,' the Crowland chronicler observed, 'the new prince began to receive praise from everyone as though he was an angel sent from the kingdom through whom God deigned to visit his people and to free them from the evils which had hitherto afflicted them beyond measure.'

Not even Henry's leniency could extend as far as to save the life of Richard's most notorious and closest councillor, William Catesby. Captured on the battlefield and taken to Leicester, Catesby must have known that death was inevitable. It was his treachery that had ensured his patron Lord Hastings' execution, and paved the way to Richard's seizing the crown. Thomas More later wrote that it had been 'the dissimulation of this one man that stirred up that whole plague of evils that followed'. Ambition had led Catesby to collude in the downfall of his former master; his reward had been to supplant Hastings as the major landowner in the East Midlands and a meteoric rise at court with his appointment first as Chancellor of the Exchequer and later Speaker of the House of Commons. His influence and power over Richard was almost mesmeric, with the Crowland chronicler believing that the king 'hardly ever dared offer any opposition' to his opinion. His position as the king's most trusted councillor seemingly unassailable, even the nobility had to grovel before him, with Thomas Stanley paying him an annuity 'for his good will and counsel past and to come'. Catesby used his position at court to ruthless effect, building up a landed estate around Northamptonshire, Warwickshire and Leicestershire fit for a nobleman. If Richard had been victorious, perhaps Catesby, hopeful of further promotion, might have even hoped to establish his own noble dynasty. With defeat and the death of his king, his dynastic ambitions lay in tatters.

Catesby had gone into battle alongside his friends and kinsmen; now they were either dead or had escaped. Isolated and deserted, he must have known that the wheel of fortune had come full circle. On 25 August at Leicester he dictated his final will and testament. With no other friends or associates to rely upon, he requested that his wife Margaret, 'my dear and well-beloved wife, to whom I have ever been true of my body', act as his sole executor. Leaving a list of bequests, including that he be buried at the church in Ashby St Ledgers, Northamptonshire, 'and to do such memorials as I have appointed for', he asked that 'all lands that I have wrongfully purchased' be restored to their rightful owners; those that he had obtained legally, he hoped that his children might inherit 'as she thinketh good after her discretion'. 'I doubt not the King will be a good and gracious Lord to them,' he reassured her, 'for he is called a full gracious prince', adding somewhat disingenuously, 'I never offended him by my good and Free Will; for God I take to my judge I have ever loved him'.

Another bequest was of £100 to the Duke of Buckingham's widow (of whose late husband's estates he had been given charge after his execution) 'to help her children' and to have Buckingham's outstanding debts paid. Catesby concluded his testament with an emotionally charged plea to his wife: 'my especial trust is in you mistress Margaret, and I heartily cry you mercy if I have dealed uncourteously with you. And ever pray you to live sole and all the days of your life to do for my soul . . . I pray you in every place see clearness in my soul, and pray fast and I shall for you, and Jesus have mercy upon my soul Amen.'

Then, almost as an afterthought, Catesby decided to add a final post-script, recognising that his last moments on earth were drawing near. Uncertain as to the whereabouts of his colleagues who had fled the battlefield, including Francis, Lord Lovell, he hoped that if 'my Lord Lovell come to grace, then that ye show to him that he pray for me'. He asked his 'uncle John', Sir John Catesby, to 'remember my soul as ye have done my body, and better'. These last words, however, were to be marked with a streak of bitterness, aimed at those whose disloyalty, in his eyes, had led to his downfall: 'My Lords Stanley, Strange and all that blood, help and pray for my soul for ye have not for my body as I trusted in you.' Hours later, Catesby was beheaded in the market square. His execution, the Crowland chronicler remarked, barely containing his delight, had been 'a last reward for his excellent service'.

As William Catesby's headless corpse was being placed upon a cart to be wheeled out of the marketplace at Leicester, Henry had begun to make his preparations for his triumphal journey to the capital. He had been received enthusiastically by the inhabitants at Leicester, who had been quick to repudiate any connection they had previously had with the dead king. Even the innkeeper at the White Boar, the supposed location of Richard's final night's accommodation before he had marched out of the town, found an ingenious solution to his dilemma of displaying the dead king's badge from his walls by hastily painting the boar on his sign, renaming the inn the Blue Boar, an entirely appropriate change since the blue boar was a badge of John, Earl of Oxford.

After departing Leicester, Henry travelled down Watling Street, the present A5, through the towns of Northampton and St Albans where he was welcomed along the way 'like a triumphing general' being 'greeted with the greatest joy by all' along the route and in each town and village he passed. 'Far and wide the people hastened to assemble by the roadside,' Vergil observed, 'saluting him as king and filling the length of his journey with laden tables and overflowing goblets, so that the weary victors might refresh themselves.'

Such liberality was on display as Henry passed through Coventry, where the city annals record how the city gave him £100, raised hurriedly from loans given by local merchants, and a gold cup. Henry spent the night at the house of the city's mayor Robert Onley. It was to be a costly visit for the city authorities, who could hardly refuse their new king their hospitality, in spite of their evident displeasure that Richard had been 'shamefully carried' to Leicester. The city annals reveal the extent of the celebrations the night before, with 512 penny loaves of bread costing 42s 8d, washed down with 110 gallons of red wine worth £6 and 41s 4d spent on twenty-seven casks of ale, each containing four and a half gallons.

Not everyone was as elated by Henry's victory. John Sponer, having been sent by the citizens of York only days before to discover Richard's wishes, had been outpaced by the speed of events. He had probably only just reached Nottingham when he discovered that the king had been killed during battle. Turning back without delay, he returned to York on 23 August and rushed straight into the council chamber where the citizens were gathered. There, according to the council minutes, Sponer, perhaps not himself entirely sure of the exact details of the battle that had taken place at 'the field of Redemore', broke the news that 'King Richard late mercifully reigning upon us was through great treason of the Duke of Norfolk and many other that turned against him, with many other lords and nobles of this north parts was piteously slain and murdered'. As the reality of Richard's death reverberated around the council chamber, the minutes recorded how the news was met by a 'great heaviness'. Both stunned and uncertain for their future, the council resolved that a letter should be sent to the Earl of

Northumberland, 'beseeching him to give unto them his best advice how to dispose them at this woeful season both to his honour and worship and well profit of this city'. In the confusion of the aftermath of battle, receiving John Sponer's equally confused report of what had occurred, the citizens could not have realised the bitter irony that it had been their patron Northumberland who had turned against the king, and was now imprisoned, just as they could not have known that their traitor, the Duke of Norfolk, had gone to his death fighting loyally for Richard's cause. All they could know for certain was that *their* king was dead: as if to emphasise the point, in the minute book, following the date of the meeting, the clerk added the words '*vacatione regalis potestatis*' – 'the throne being vacant'.

The following day, Henry's messenger Sir Robert Coton arrived in York with a copy of the new king's proclamation. Coton must have guessed how unpopular his arrival would be since 'for fear of death' he refused to travel through the city unguarded, choosing instead to meet the mayor and aldermen at an inn somewhat unsuitably named the 'Boar' within the protection of the castle. The proclamation was duly recorded in the council minutes, but still the council refused to acknowledge Henry to be their legitimate new king, preferring instead to record how 'on the 22nd day of August Anno Domini 1485 at Redemore near Leicester there was fought a battle between *our Lord* King Richard III and others of his nobles on the one part, and Harry Earl of Richmond and others of his followers on the other part'. It was not until 22 October that the city authorities at York could bring themselves to date their minutes by the reign of Henry VII.

Meanwhile in the capital, as the outcome of the battle became known, there remained a heightened sense of uncertainty and nervousness. A proclamation was sent out by the mayor on 26 August ordering all vagabonds, 'idle people which have no masters to wait upon' and soldiers to depart from the city within three hours of the announcement being made. A curfew was placed on all citizens between 9 p.m. and 5 a.m., with watches being ordered to patrol the city. The city began to make preparations for the triumphant arrival of their new king, an unknown exile whom most of the city authorities had never met. Four hundred and thirty-five citizens, each wearing cloaks of 'bright murrey' were chosen to ride to meet him, led by the mayor and aldermen. On 3

September Henry was received by the curious Londoners at Shoreditch where he was led in procession through the city; the sound of trumpeters 'thundering forth martial sounds' announcing Henry's arrival was soon followed by carts laden with spoils from the battle trundling along the streets. Among the crowds was Bernard André, the blind poet who would later join Henry's court and be commissioned to write a biography of the king, who was so moved by the occasion that he took to publicly reciting verses celebrating the triumph.

The procession made its way through the streets to St Paul's, where at the rood of the north door, on which William Collingborne had pinned his ill-fated doggerel lambasting the dead king Richard, Henry offered up three ragged standards from the battle. The presentation of the standards was nothing less than a statement of Henry's divine right to rule and kingship, proven by his victory in battle; Edward IV had performed the same ceremony after Barnet. What is striking, however, is Henry's choice of standards to lay at the foot of the altar: the arms of St George, a red 'fiery dragon painted upon white and green sarcenet' and lastly, a 'banner of Tarteron' beaten with an image of 'a Dun Cowe'; the Cow had likely been used by Henry as an assertion of his claim to the Beaufort line, since the Beauforts had claimed descent from Guy of Warwick, the legendary slayer of the fearsome Dun Cow of Warwick. Already Henry intended to make obvious to all that he was not going to forget his Lancastrian roots.

After prayers had been said and the *Te Deum* sung, Henry removed to the palace of the Bishop of London, while for several days 'plays, pastimes and pleasures' were performed across a jubilant city, perhaps more than anything through relief that a bloody civil war seemed to have been avoided. After spending the following fortnight at Baynard's Castle, Henry chose to move south to Guildford, where he remained until 11 October. It was here that he spent his days in the company of his mother Margaret, at her manor house at Woking. It was the first time that mother and son had been reunited since the autumn of 1470, when Henry, aged just fourteen, had been entrusted to his uncle Jasper, soon to flee abroad to the shores of Brittany. From now on, Margaret would rarely leave her son's sight, her rooms specially prepared at court to be adjoining to the king's own. It was later observed how 'the king is much influenced by his mother', and it must have been in these early days of reconciliation that Henry came to depend upon the woman who had been so determined to set her son upon the throne. In a letter to her, Henry declared that he was 'as glad to please you as your heart can desire it', since 'I know well that I am as much bounden so to do as any creature living, for the great singular motherly love and affection that it hath pleased you at all times to bear towards me'. For Margaret, writing to her son on a separate occasion, Henry was 'my dearest, and only desired joy in this world'. For now, it was likely that it was here that Henry offered up to his mother a present that had been discovered in Richard's tent after the battle, the dead king's illuminated book of hours, that Margaret would keep safely preserved for the rest of her life.

In one of his earliest grants as king, Henry ordered a London residence, the magnificent house of Coldharbour, overlooking the Thames, to be prepared for his mother; carpenters and workmen worked incessantly to prepare and renovate the building, with a stained glass escutcheon of Margaret's arms set into the window overlooking the banks of the river. At the house, Margaret was to be entrusted with looking after Henry's intended bride, Elizabeth of York, who was taken from Sheriff Hutton to London, where rooms were specially prepared at Coldharbour for her, along with the ten-year-old Edward Plantagenet, the Earl of Warwick, who was to be placed in Margaret's secure custody. Accommodation was also prepared for the eight-year-old son of the late Duke of Buckingham, Edward Stafford, whose wardship, worth over £1,000, was eventually granted to Margaret. Like Warwick, Stafford had a viable claim to the throne; it was best to keep both close to the new regime, with Margaret acting in effect as their informal gaoler.

There was another reason for Henry's decision to depart from the capital so soon after making his triumphal entrance. The citizens of London had welcomed his army of Frenchmen and 'beggarly Bretons' into the city walls, though they were soon to regret it. Of the city dignitaries who rode to meet the new king at Shoreditch, two mayors, six aldermen and scores of citizens would be dead within weeks. The cause of death was the terrifying disease known commonly as the 'sweating sickness', most likely some variant form of influenza that had struck the country in periodic bouts. It was feared as much as the plague: those who became infected burned with an uncontrollable temperature and thirst, forcing men to tear their clothes from their bodies in even the coldest climes. Within twenty-four hours, most had succumbed to the illness. The most detailed account of the outbreak comes from the Fellows of Merton College, Oxford who recorded in their Register that:

> About the end of August and the beginning of September, a strange and unprecedented occurrence began in the university, which coming with sudden sweating, has abruptly taken the lives of many. At length, about the end of September, the affliction spread just as suddenly throughout the whole realm. In the City of London, three mayors died within ten days and thus, spreading from east through the south and into the west, the extraordinary scourge smote almost all the nobles both spiritual and temporal short of the very highest. Within twenty-four hours all either died or recovered. Such a sudden and cruel massacre, as it were, of the wise and good men among us has not been heard for centuries. Apart from a few cases, the epidemic did not last beyond a month or six weeks. At length a remedy has been found against this extraordinary pestilence in that the infected person should be promptly covered by blankets for twenty-four hours, not to excess but in moderation (many in fact had been suffocated by covering with excess blankets), he should drink warm beer and not take any air.

It may have been that the disease had already appeared during the summer; according to the Crowland Chronicler, Thomas Stanley claimed to be suffering from the disease as an excuse not to travel to Richard's court at Nottingham, while at York a 'plague of pestilence' had broken out by June 1485. Nevertheless, it was hard for many not to draw their own conclusions that the French and Breton mercenaries in Henry's army had brought the disease with them. It was hardly a good omen for the new king whose arrival seemed to bring upon the capital the divine retribution of pestilence and death.

Away from London, Henry waited patiently for the arrival of his official coronation as king, set for 30 October, with a new Parliament being summoned on 15 September to meet on 7 November. In the meantime, Henry's first priority was to make full use of his new-found powers of patronage, rewarding his close supporters and those who had accompanied him in exile and into battle. Throughout September 1485 his accounts are filled with grants of land, office and annuities, each signed at the top by the grateful king as he constructed his new regime from his loyal men who had served him in exile 'beyond the sea'. Aside from his most obvious and noteworthy supporters, the records reveal at least seventy-four persons who were granted office, land or annuity for joining Henry in exile, with another forty-eight being rewarded for either taking part in his 'victorious journey' or serving on his 'victorious field'. While it is unlikely that every single exile at Henry's unofficial court in Brittany then France will be known, the names mentioned in the grants total almost a quarter of the 400 estimated to have been at Vannes.

Some of the earliest grants made by the new king reward those towering figures of influence to whom Henry knew he owed the crown: his stepfather Lord Thomas Stanley, described by Henry as his 'right entirely beloved father', was granted several manors in Flint, Chester and Warwick, as well as being appointed master forester and steward of the king's game north of the Trent and chief steward of the Duchy of Lancaster 'in consideration of the good and praiseworthy services performed by him before now with great personal exertions and costs, in many ways and on divers occasions, and now lately in the king's conflict within the realm of England, and which services he ceases not to continue'. They were to be the first of many grants that would place Thomas Stanley as one of the pre-eminent nobles within the kingdom.

As promised, Sir Rhys ap Thomas was rewarded for his services with his anticipated appointment as chamberlain of South Wales. Henry was not prepared to make the same mistakes as his predecessor; instead of allowing Rhys to recreate the Duke of Buckingham's position as an overlord in Wales, his power was to be carefully bridled, with Jasper Tudor being appointed to the office of chief justice in South Wales, while Adam ap Jevan ap Jenkin was made the king's attorney in Carmarthen and Cardigan 'in consideration of the true service that our well-beloved subject hath done unto our noble progenitors of long time passed, and to us now late in our victorious journey and field, to his great costs and damages'. Other Welshmen who had joined Henry on his march through Wales were rewarded for their loyalty, including Morris Lloyd whose 'service in our late triumph' was acknowledged with grants of office while Owen Lloyd was granted the constableship of Cardigan castle. The Stanleys' influence in maintaining order in Wales was further acknowledged, with their kinsman William Griffith, who had been previously placed under arrest with Lord Strange, being appointed chamberlain of North Wales, with Sir William Stanley being granted the office of chief justice of the region, as well as the constableship of Caernarfon castle and the captaincy of the town there.

As Henry pondered his chosen rewards, he had cause to remember those who had served himself, his family and the Lancastrian dynasty throughout the long dark decades of civil strife. John Denton was rewarded with the keepership of Framlingham Castle 'for the true and faithful service done unto the king and unto his right dear and most beloved lady and mother'. John Pylton was rewarded 'in consideration of the good service done to Henry VI, the king's most dear predecessor'. John Robinson was given the bailiwick of Boston in Lincolnshire 'for services done in many ways heretofore to the king's most dear father' Edmund. Henry's former guardian Anne Devereux, the Countess of Pembroke, was ordered to visit the king at court, with Henry granting to his 'most dear cousin' safe passage. One of Henry's former tutors, Andrew Oterborne, was granted an annuity of 20 marks 'for services rendered to us from our youth', as was Sir Hugh John, provided with a reward of £10 'in consideration of the good service' which he 'did unto us in our tender age'.

Then there were those who had risked their lives and safety for Henry's own security during his exile. Stephen Calmady, whose boat had been used to assist exiles fleeing after Buckingham's rebellion in their escape to Brittany, was given a new ship 'with all tackle' 'in recompence of the great jeopardies, tribulation and losses sustained by him heretofore including his service to the king when he was in the parts beyond the sea'. Christopher Urswick, named as Henry's 'wellbeloved chaplain', was appointed as the king's almoner and granted the prebend of St Stephen's chapel in Westminster. Lewis Carleon, Margaret Beaufort's physician who had passed messages between her and Elizabeth Woodville in sanctuary, was given an annuity of £40 a year. Sir John Risley, who had organised a rebellion in Essex in late 1484 before escaping into exile, was given the constableship of Pleshey Castle and the keepership of Dunmow in Essex 'in consederation of the true heart and service . . . borne and done unto us in sundry wise herebefore, as well beyond the sea as at our late victorious field . . . to his great charge, labour and jeopardy'. Piers Curteys, Richard's Master of the Wardrobe who had fled into sanctuary in the summer, was rewarded with the office of keeper of the king's privy palace and wardrobe, as well as the honour of the lordship of Leicester for his 'great heaviness, pain and fear, abiding our coming', as well as the 'great persecution, jeopardies, and pains, robberies and losses of his goods' that he had suffered in the aftermath of his defection. Curteys's reappointment to his former office was indicative of the continuity that Henry sought to achieve in several offices at court: William Misterton, who had served in the great wardrobe under Henry VI, Edward IV and Richard III, was to find his services retained.

Other defectors who had joined Henry shortly before the battle were also rewarded such as Simon Digby with the lieutenancy of Sherwood and Beskwood forest, worth £20 a year. Walter Hungerford, who had defected from Robert Brackenbury's army at Stony Stratford on the journey towards Bosworth, was granted several manors 'in consideration of the great jeopardies, losses, costs and charges sustained in the king's service'. John Fogge, who had finally joined Henry in exile despite being pardoned twice by Richard III, was, together with John Heyron, appointed to the office of keeper of the rolls of Common Pleas, 'the king with certain knowledge bearing in mind the praiseworthy and gratuitous services done by them in times past, as also their losses and the dangers to their persons which they have in many ways undergone by reason of such services'.

The events of recent memory, of his journey through Wales and into England, loomed large in the king's mind. The Welshmen who had joined his service along the route were remembered and appropriately rewarded for their support, receiving gifts of land and office, including Retherth ap Rhys and Owen Lloyd, who received the constableship of Cardigan Castle with an annuity of £10, Maurice ap Owen and Richard Owen, who became steward and receiver of the lordship of Kidwelly 'for services to the king at his last victorious journey to resist his great enemy', and Rees ap Llewellen ap Hulkyn who was awarded the legal status of an Englishman 'in consideration of the true service done to the king as well in his last victorious field'. Robert Crompe, rewarded by Henry with a position at court as one of the marshals of his hall, was granted the additional office of feodary of the honour of Wallingford and position of clerk of Sherwood forest, for 'jeopardising his life, lands and all his goods' by joining Henry's forces, 'in your late victorious field and journey at his proper cost and charge, and also by his means and diligent labour caused the town of Shrewsbury to be delivered unto your hands and your coming by that way'. The town that had finally opened its gates was itself to be rewarded with an exemption for fifty years of ten marks' payment in tax, since Henry had for himself witnessed the 'ruin, poverty and decay of their town'. Crossing the English border, Henry had been grateful for the support that the sheriffs of Chester, John Norys and Hugh Hurletone, had provided him, rewarding them for 'the good and faithful service that the said sheriffs and other of our said city hath done unto us in this our victorious journey for the repressing of our great enemy the late Duke of Gloucester, and his adherents'.

From the rewards, glimpses of individual episodes and dramas in battle can almost be formed. The Savage family must have played an important role in the action. Henry rewarded John Savage the younger with land forfeited by the attainders of Lord Zouche and Lord Lovell, in addition to all castles, lordships and manors in the High Peak, 'in consideration of his having largely exposed himself, with a crowd of his kinsmen, servants and friends, as volunteers in the king's service in the battle'. Henry also rewarded John's sons Christopher and James for their service, 'as well as for the repressing of our rebels and traitors'. John Savage senior was also rewarded for his 'good and faithful services in the king's last victorious battle'. Thomas Bevercotes, in being awarded the office of the king's sergeant-at-arms, mentioned his true and humble service, but marked out his conduct 'in especial in our victorious field, for the subduing of our enemies'. Roger Acton petitioned Henry shortly after the battle, 'in consideration of the true and faithful service that your humble subject Roger Acton hath done unto your highness, now in your victorious field and under your standard and there sore hurt'. Others were to receive reward and honour in what was almost a roll call of those worthy to be mentioned in dispatches. Hugh Browne was granted the office of forester of Lothewode, Salop, for his service 'in our late victorious journey, to the jeopardy of his life'. John Browne was rewarded with the office of bailiff of Greteham, Rutland for his service 'to his great costs and jeopardies'. Ralph Vernon was given the bailiwick of Hoton Paynell in York in consideration of his service 'at our victorious journey to his great cost and charge'. Thomas Morton was granted an annuity of 40 marks, 'in compensation for goods and friends lost in the king's just cause'. John Farrington fought 'to his great hurts and costs' while Henry remembered William Sommaster 'late deceased' who had 'died in our homage'.

The warrants also provide us with a hint of the additional help that Henry had received during the conflict. The Scots commander Alexander Bruce who had accompanied Henry from France was rewarded with an annuity of £20, for his 'good, faithful and approved services heretofore done by him with great trouble and recent personal service . . . he sustaining therein great losses'. He was granted safe conduct and special protection for himself and a retinue of twenty persons, with a licence to make 'whatever stay he pleases in England, and to go to and fro as often as he likes during this protection'.

The Earl of Oxford was to play a crucial role in the early days of Henry's new administration. As the Great Chronicle observed, the earl was recognised as almost an agent to the new king, 'to whom was then made great suit and labour as well for matters concerning himself as for causes touching soliciting of causes unto the king, for then such persons as had occupied his lands by gift of King Edward or by purchase were fain to restore it, with all such profits'. Desperate in the hope of securing the support of the new regime, the University of Oxford wrote to the earl, flattering him with warm words: 'during your long exile, in the many changes of this life and the cruelty of fortune, your unswerving loyalty and noble character have caused you to be regretted by the people as few have been; so that we may venture to say that, though none dared to praise, yet none ceased to love you. So marvellous have been your escapes from snares and perils that we must attribute them to a special interference of providence, which has brought you back to your country not only in safety but in honour; to be the chief buttress of the throne and defender of the realm.'

A sign of his influence in the new regime, Oxford was appointed to the hereditary office of great chamberlain, an honour which his ancestors had held from 1133 to 1388. He was further granted the office of Admiral of England, 'in consideration of the sincere and inward affection which the king bears him', and appointed constable of the Tower of London on a salary of £50, his prisoners including the Earls of Northumberland and Surrey as well as accommodation for seven Frenchmen and two Scotsmen who may have been participants in the battle. Oxford's appointment as constable highlights Henry's own preoccupation with immediately securing the defence of the capital, with other offices in the Tower going to loyal men such as Henry's 'faithful servant' Robert Jay, who was made keeper of the 'New Bulwark' at the Tower for his 'true service . . . as well beyond the sea as within this our realm, at our victorious field'. Almost immediately, Henry ordered for the Tower to be restocked with supplies, with Sir Richard Guildford confirmed in his post as master of the ordnance and master of the armoury with a salary of 2s a day, with 'divers allowances for persons employed under him', and sergeant of the master of armour in the Tower with a salary of 12d a day. The appointment was dated from 8 August 1485, 'when he was appointed by the king to this office'. Mindful of the value of having skilled craftsmen working there, and perhaps even impressed at the sight of the dead king's own armour and weaponry in battle, Henry also reappointed Richard III's armourer Vincencio Tutolez as his official armourer with a salary of £20 a year. He was soon busy re-equipping the royal supplies, ordering 1,000 bowstaves at a cost of £42 10s. William Nele, 'gunfounder', was paid £10 for making weights, while William Meryk, a merchant from Bristol, was paid £16 13 4d for gunpowder. William Lovell was appointed master and keeper of arrows as 'bowyer' in the Tower, Thomas Walsh the sergeant of 'the king's tents and pavillions'. Others who no doubt helped to play a critical role in the campaign and battle were further rewarded: John Rygby, an 'archer of the king's guard', was granted the bailiwick of Rye while John Harpere, the 'yeoman harbinger' for Henry's household, was appointed the sergeant of the Mace in Parliament, with a daily salary of 12d, for his service 'in Brittany and France during two years and in this our noble realm at our victorious field in subduing our enemies'.

Other key strategic defence posts throughout the country would be rapidly filled with trustworthy captains who could secure the coast and Marches against invasion. Nearly all the new officeholders had both accompanied Henry from exile through his 'victorious journey' and fought at Bosworth; for their services they would now be amply rewarded. Sir Edward Woodville was rewarded with the captaincies of Carisbrooke Castle on the Isle of Wight and Porchester Castle, as well as the 'government of the town of Portsmouth', while Giles Daubeney was made constable of Bristol Castle. Sir James Blount was regranted the possession of Hammes Castle. Thomas Idem was rewarded for his 'good and gratuitous service' abroad 'as on this side of the sea, now lately in the conflict which has lately taken place between the king and his mortal enemies, sustaining thereby for a long time excessive losses in his goods and possessions' the keepership of Rochester Castle. In granting him the keepership of Sandwich Castle in Kent, Henry acknowledged that William Frost sustained 'for a long time excessive losses in his goods and possessions' as a result of his 'good and continuous service which he performed, as well beyond the sea in those parts where the king was before he returned, with the help of God, to this kingdom, as on this side of the sea, now lately in the conflict which has lately taken place between the king and his deadly enemies'. John Turbevill 'for good and faithful service done at his great costs and charges' was made constable and keeper of Corfe Castle. John Spicer was appointed porter of Hertford Castle for his 'service beyond the sea and within this realm'. Jevan Lloyd Vaughan was made constable of Neath Castle in Glamorgan for his 'true and faithful service to us late done in our late triumph and victory'. Thomas Gaywode was rewarded with the office of porter of Stafford Castle for his service 'in our most victorious journey'.

Many of Henry's companions in exile were appointed as yeomen to the king's guard, a personal bodyguard that would be employed to defend the king, similar to what Henry had witnessed at the French court. According to Polydore Vergil, 'they should never leave his side, in this he imitated the French kings so that he might thereafter be better protected from treachery'. The guard, numbering 200 men who were each paid 6d a day and under the command of the captain of the guard, Sir Charles Somerset, the illegitimate son of Henry, Duke of Somerset, and arguably one of Henry's closest male relatives after his uncle Jasper, were composed of men who had followed Henry into exile and had fought at Bosworth, proving their military capabilities to the full. They included John Edwards, Henry's 'wellbeloved servant' who had performed 'true and faithful service . . . in Brittany and

France', Robert Bagger, John Rothercomme, Owen ap Griffith, Thomas Leche, William Brown for his good service 'beyond the sea as at our victorious journey', Richard Nanfan, Richard Selman, Richard Pigot, Henry Carre 'in consideration of good and true service, as well beyond the sea as within the realm of England', William Cheeseman, Stephen John, Thomas Kingman, Robert Jay, Thomas Westby and Thomas Gaywode, among others. Many of these yeomen were also granted local offices to keep law and order, for instance Thomas Kingman and Stephen John being made bailiffs of Somerton and gaolers of Ilchester in Somerset.

While the new regime had quickly made peace with France, the flight of Richard's supporters, including the Harringtons, the Huddlestons, the Middletons and the Frankes, together with Lord Lovell remaining in sanctuary, posed a significant challenge for the fledgling authority of Henry's kingship, breeding uncertainty. As the fellows of Oxford University wrote to Thomas Stanley, 'everything is new to us, and though we hope the present order may prove firmly established, it is but in its infancy'. Order struggled to be established, as Robert Throckmorton, the new sheriff of Warwickshire and Leicestershire, had noted in his petition to the king that there was 'within your realm such rebellion and trouble, and your laws not established'. Henry's greatest challenge lay in the north, Richard III's home territory, which remained fiercely loyal to the dead king and the Yorkist memory. Henry himself was fully aware of the contribution that northerners had played in the battle, issuing a proclamation on 24 September which stated how 'many and diverse persons of the north parts of this our land, knights, esquires, gentlemen and other have done us now of late great displeasure being against us in the field with the adversary of us'. While some had sought pardon to be reconciled to their new king, others flatly refused to obey Henry's authority. When Henry issued a separate proclamation on 8 October excluding certain of Richard's Yorkshire supporters from pardon, including the city of York's recorder Miles Metcalfe, a prominent supporter of the dead king who it was claimed 'hath done much against us which disables him to exercise things of authority . . . which his seditious means might . . . and fall to divers inconvenients'. But still York refused to replace Metcalfe, though any possibility of a stand-off with the new king was resolved when Metcalfe died early in 1486; even then, the authorities replaced him not with Henry's own nominee, but one of Richard's supporters, John Vavasour. In this febrile atmosphere, there was every possibility that the country might once again become divided upon regional loyalties as Richard's memory burned bright; worse still, if the northern rebels were able to join up with the Scots leading to an invasion across the border, Henry's kingship threatened to become the shortest in living memory.

On 25 September Henry issued commissions of array in case of a possible Scottish invasion; in a telling display of either trust or of his own vulnerability, he deputed Thomas Stanley to raise the whole of Lancashire on his behalf. On 17 October Henry wrote to Henry Vernon, explaining 'that certain our rebels and traitors being of little honour or substance' had made contact 'with our ancient enemies the Scots' and had 'made insurrection and assemblies in the north portions of our realm, taking Robin of Reddesdale, Jack St Thomalyn at Lath, and Master Mendall for their captains, intending if they be of power the final and abversion . . . of our realm'. It was a fragile time filled with uncertainty, but before Henry could deal with suppressing rebellion within his realm, he needed to be officially crowned and recognised as King of England.

13

REWARD, RETRIBUTION
AND RECONCILIATION

❖

After Parliament was summoned on 15 September to meet at Westminster on 7 November, preparations began in earnest for the coronation that had been arranged for Sunday 30 October. On 19 October a commission to prepare for the coronation met, headed by Sir Edward Courtenay and the Earl of Oxford, with the new steward of the royal household, Robert Willoughby, being placed in charge of ordering supplies for the spectacle. Immediately work started on crafting the extravagant display, with twenty-one tailors and fourteen skinners specially employed to fashion the robes of the new king, his nobles, including a robe for the Earl of Oxford cut from forty-one yards of crimson velvet at a cost of £61 10s. Throughout the symbols of St George – with a banner of the saint's cross being made from six yards of crimson velvet costing £4 11s – the red rose of Lancaster and the Welsh dragon were ever visible. Two cartloads of clothing and hangings were taken from Richard's royal castle at Nottingham. In total, £1,506 18s 10d would be spent on the ceremony, preparing garments and attire from the finest silks that could be found from whatever tailor or silk woman that was prepared to sell them.

Before the coronation would take place, Henry had already decided that other ceremonies should take precedence. First, he had resolved, there were further rewards to be made. On Thursday 27 October, on the eve of the feast of St Simon and St Jude, Henry dined with the Archbishop of Canterbury at Lambeth before going to the Tower, 'riding after the guise of France with all other of his nobility upon small hackneys, two and two upon a horse'. The next morning, after attending Mass, the king returned to his presence chamber where, under his cloth of estate, he sat as his uncle Jasper, already appointed as Lieutenant of Ireland, was presented before him, this time 'in the habit of estate of a Duke'. Jasper was led by the Duke of Suffolk and the Earl of Lincoln, having recently been released from prison, a clear sign of Henry's determination that members of the Yorkist royal household serve the new regime, with William, Viscount Berkeley carrying his cap of estate, and the Earl of Shrewsbury bearing his sword, the pommel facing upwards. 'In the entering of the chamber door he did his first obeisance, and in the midst of the chamber the second, and in the king's presence the third'. The Garter King of Arms, John Writhe, delivered the letters patent to the Earl of Oxford who, as great chamberlain, in turn delivered the patent to the king. Henry handed over the letters to his secretary, commanding that they be read openly. As they were read out, Henry placed a girdle around his uncle's neck, and a cap upon his head. After the patent had been read, 'the king received it, and delivered the said patent of the creation of the annuity of the Duchy of Bedford to his said uncle the Duke of Bedford'.

From that day, as the legends of his seal and the opening sentence of his letters patent bear witness, whenever his name was cried out in public by heralds, Jasper was styled 'The high and mighty prince, Jasper, brother and uncle of kings, Duke of Bedford and Earl of Pembroke'. The choice of titles could hardly have been more prestigious. There had only been two previous Dukes of Bedford, and while the second holder of the title, George Neville, the son of John Neville, the Earl of Northumberland, was relatively unknown, it was the first Duke of Bedford, Henry V's younger brother John, whom Henry must have had in mind when seeking a title for his uncle. The link signalled Henry's conscious desire to reflect the continuity between the house of Tudor and the house of Lancaster. It also reflected Henry's gratitude to a man without whom his kingship would have been impossible. Whereas the first Duke of Bedford had been a pillar of the house of Lancaster, establishing a formidable reputation as a soldier and statesman, Jasper too had dedicated his life in exile to securing his nephew's future. In doing so, he had sacrificed his own personal life, being without a wife or an heir. With his new ducal title, in his fifties, Jasper now turned to resolving the problem; by 7 November he had found himself a bride in Katherine Woodville, the widow of the Duke of Buckingham and the sister of the dowager Queen Elizabeth. She was twenty-seven, half Jasper's age. Jasper could have been forgiven for thinking that, over twenty-five years after he had pledged to avenge the death of his father and the fall of the house of Lancaster, in which he had given up years of exile and imprisonment for the sake of the welfare of his young nephew, only now had he only just begun to live a life for himself.

Jasper's new title was not the only peerage that Henry decided to bestow upon his supporters over the next few months. The most unexpected promotion came for Henry's French commander Philibert de Chandée, who had led his French mercenaries at the battle to devastating effect. Despite having no connection to the local area, Chandée was created Earl of Bath on 6 January 1486, 'in consideration of his laudable service to us done heretofore', and was awarded an annuity of 100 marks. He entertained the French ambassadors at Greenwich the same year, at a cost of £26, and was then conducted by one of the king's councillors to Dover, stopping off at Braynford and racking up further expenses of £23 6s 8d, before heading back to France. We hear little more of him after, and his name disappears from record.

Sir Giles Daubeney, one of Henry's most trusted councillors and described by Bernard André as 'a good man, prudent, just and loved by all', was to be created Lord Daubeney in March 1486, on the grounds that he had been a descendant of a baron from the fourteenth century, and his impeccable Yorkist credentials – he was an esquire of Edward IV's body before deserting Richard to join Henry in exile – helped to reassure those who may have considered that Henry would reward only his Lancastrian supporters.

On the same day as Jasper's elevation to the dukedom of Bedford, Henry further restored Edward Courtenay to the earldom of Devon, a long-cherished ambition of Courtenay's, whose calculated gamble in supporting Henry's cause during Buckingham's rebellion had finally paid off. Henry also chose to reward one of his longstanding supporters, granting an earldom to Thomas, Lord Stanley, ensuring that his mother Margaret would be raised to the status of countess. Like Jasper Tudor's dukedom, Lord Stanley's new title of Earl of Derby had strong Lancastrian connections, since the title had last belonged to Henry of

Bolingbroke, the founder of the house of Lancaster. Though Thomas Stanley would continue to insist that he had played little part in the battle, stating in a confession concerned with Henry's papal dispensation to marry Elizabeth of York that he had known Henry 'well' only since 24 August, two days after the battle, the patent creating him an earl clearly acknowledged his role in the fighting and the action on the day, referring to 'his distinguished services to us and indeed the great armed support recently accorded us in battle, both by himself and by all his kinsmen, not without great hazard to life and position'.

Thomas Stanley's earldom was not the only reward that Henry was prepared to bestow upon the man he referred to in his grants as his 'right entirely beloved father'. Within weeks of the battle, Stanley was rewarded with several manors and royal offices such as master forester and steward of all the king's game north of the Trent for 'the good and praiseworthy services performed by him before now with great personal exertions and costs, in many ways and on divers occasions, and now lately in the king's conflict within the realm of England', though the most significant of all Stanley's rewards came with the position of Constable of England, together with its salary of £100. Henry was also notably generous to Stanley's son and his brother-in-law George, Lord Strange, who was addressed at court as 'the king's brother' and lavishly rewarded with constableships of castles in Ireland, 'in consideration of the good and laudable service which our right trusty and entirely beloved brother hath done unto us in manifold wise to our singular pleasure'.

With his brother's elevation, Sir William Stanley must have believed that in reward for his actions on the battlefield, he would have a strong chance of a peerage, if not more: he personally coveted the Earldom of Chester. Yet no reward was forthcoming. After what must have seemed to Stanley as a deliberate snub, he was eventually forced to take the humiliating step of petitioning the king in person to confirm the manors and castles granted to him by Richard, 'which said grant he feareth is not sure and sufficient in law', requesting the king confirm the grant 'in consideration of the true and faithful service of him'. Eventually, Henry reconfirmed his position of justiciar of North Wales and constable of Caernarfon Castle and captain of the town there, though any further rewards were limited to an annuity of £20 from the rent of a manor formerly belonging to Lord Lovell. For the man whose actions on the battlefield had effectively saved Henry's own life and placed him on the throne, this was hardly the reward he could have expected as kingmaker.

After the ceremonies were complete, the newly created nobles took their place around the dining table in the king's great chamber in celebration. After the second course, Henry proclaimed seven new knights, among them Reginald Bray, Edward Stafford, the young Duke of Buckingham and Lord Fitzwalter, and that evening Henry himself visited them to read the 'advertisement of the order of knighthood'. The following day, on Saturday 29 October, they were formally received by the king under his cloth of estate, with a new herald also being created, with a new name, Rougedragon, no doubt reflecting Henry's Welsh origins, before the new knights together with the king attended chapel and returned to the hall, where they dined at a single table. That same afternoon, the customary procession from the Tower to Westminster Hall in preparation for the coronation the following day took place. Riding bare-headed, as tradition dictated, Henry was dressed in a long gown of purple velvet furred with ermines as he rode on a horse trapped with cloth of gold, a royal canopy held above his head by four knights marching on foot. Ahead of his procession rode Thomas Stanley, Oxford and the Earls of Nottingham and Lincoln, behind came Jasper, now Duke of Bedford, and the Duke of Suffolk, followed by six henchmen. Finally, Sir John Cheyney, as the knight for the king's body, led the riderless horse trapped in cloth of gold and embroidered with the king's arms, the courser of estate.

The next day, Sunday 30 October, the stage was set for the king's coronation at Westminster abbey. Scaffolds had been specially prepared for the crowds to witness the public ceremony. In procession, Jasper, as Duke of Bedford, bore the crown before the king; Stanley as Earl of Derby held the sword of State, Oxford bore the king's train. As prominent Yorkist supporters, the Bishops of Durham and Bath and Wells were excluded, while the Archbishop of Canterbury, Thomas Bourgchier, was by now considered so frail that his role in the coronation formalities was limited, though he did perform the anointing and crowning ceremony; in his place, the Bishop of Exeter asked 'the will of the people' while the Bishop of London sang the Mass. The entire ceremony had a makeshift quality to it, and was hardly aided by the noise of a collapsing scaffold, overcrowded with eager onlookers, though one observer noted that no one was killed 'blessed be God'. Perhaps a sign of the speed at which the coronation had been prepared, with most of the attention, and costs, being paid to the splendour of the occasion, little thought had been given to the text of the coronation ceremony itself. The official format that the coronation was expected to follow was usually taken from the fourteenth century *Liber Regalis*; however, since it was obvious that Henry would not be able to marry Elizabeth of York in time for the ceremony, the usual text that had been prepared for a coronation of a king and his queen would need to be shelved. In its place, a copy of the coronation text that had been used for Richard's anointing ceremony in July 1483 was hastily altered, even though it failed to remove the dead king's name from critical moments during the ceremony, and retained key roles reserved for the Duke of Norfolk, in spite of his death on the battlefield, and Viscount Lovell, who had fled into hiding.

Still, in the moment of the occasion, all this mattered little. The significance of Henry's coronation as king, in many ways unfathomable to those officiating and watching from the galleries, must have left most in stunned silence. Yet as the crown was placed upon his head, the sound of one woman weeping 'marvellously' could be heard; it was the king's mother, Margaret, whose tears were not of joy but rather fear. She understood only too well the responsibility that the weight of the crown bore, and the danger that it could bring to her son. If it had been a long and dangerous journey to this moment; the path ahead lay uncharted, uncertain, terrifying.

After the ceremonies had concluded, Henry returned to the Tower in preparation for the coronation banquet. At his feet, under the table, two esquires of his body, Thomas Newton and Davy Philip were placed, as if to act as bodyguards for the monarch's personal protection. Once again Jasper took chief place as steward of the feast, riding on a horse trapped with cloth of gold trimmed with ermine. After Henry and the hall had been served the first course, the king's champion Sir Robert Dymmock entered the hall on a horse and issued his customary challenge, demanding if there was anyone who would challenge him as defender of the king's right to the throne. The theatrical nature of the occasion must have been mused upon by some present, who had witnessed Dymmock performing the identical ceremony two years before for Richard III, the only noticeable difference being that then his horse had been trapped with red and white silk; now, with obvious reference to the new king's Welsh origins, it proudly displayed a 'rich trapper of Cadwaller's arms'.

The final part of the ceremonies, the traditional coronation jousts were originally scheduled for the Sunday following the coronation ceremony, but were postponed to Sunday 13 November, with Sir Richard Guilford spending £50 2s 2d over the hundred marks he had been granted in preparation for the competition. It seems that the Frenchmen and Bretons who remained in the capital were drafted in for one final battle, the 'jousts of peace': a challenge was formally issued by 'six gentlemen of name and of arms' who had come from 'beyond the sea with the king's grace' to be 'disposed for the king's pleasure and sport and the Ladies to challenge and hold Justes against all men'. For the victor who broke the most spears, just as William Caxton had urged Richard III the previous year in an attempt to restore to a nation its sense of chivalric pride, a prize of a large diamond would be awarded.

News of Richard's death at Bosworth had reached the courts of Europe slowly. On 30 September Cadinal Sforza wrote to his nephew, the Duke of Milan, from Rome: 'this very evening news has reached the Ambassador of the King of England that the people have cut in pieces that King'. The Bishop of Imola, wrote to Pope Innocent VIII on 20 October, still uncertain of the outcome: 'According to common report as heard by me on the way, the King of England has been killed in battle. Here some people tell me he is alive and reigning, but others deny it'. Even when the Spanish monarchs Ferdinand and Isabella wrote complaining of the piracy of Henry's French naval captain Guillaume de Casenove or 'Coulon' who, after leaving Milford Haven, had headed south to Cape St Vincent in southern Portugal, attacking ships and seizing 'a great quantity of merchandise belonging to Spanish subjects', they addressed their letter to the English king yet purposely left the name blank. Elsewhere, as news of Henry's victory leaked out, in Danzig one chronicler recorded that Richard had been replaced by a new king called 'Ritzmund'.

Henry's coronation had seen him acclaimed as king. He now needed to affirm his title in law, stamping his authority on his new kingdom. On Monday 7 November the newly crowned king took to his throne in the painted chamber of Parliament, the assembled lords and bishops seated before him. Henry's chosen candidate for chancellor, replacing Thomas Rotherham, was Bishop Alcock, who in his new office gave the traditional opening sermon, on the theme of 'To strain, to prosper, to go forward and reign', exhorting members of both houses in a speech filled with classical references to pursue the public and common good. The following day, the commons were instructed to assemble to choose their speaker, Henry's favoured candidate Thomas Lovell, whose attainder under Richard for his participation in Buckingham's rebellion seems to have been conveniently ignored – it would, as many probably predicted, soon be reversed.

Henry's first priority was to have his title affirmed by Parliament in the form of a bill presented by the commons, to be approved by the lords and the king. Without any reference to what had taken place during the decades of civil strife and competing claims between the houses of Lancaster and York, the bill simply declared that

> To the pleasure of Almighty God, the wealth, prosperity, and surety of this realm of England, to the singular comfort of all the king's subjects of the same, and in avoiding all ambiguities and questions, be it ordained, established, and enacted, by the authority of the present Parliament, that the inheritance of the crowns of the realms of England and of France, with all the pre-eminence and dignity royal of the same pertaining , and all other seignories to the king belonging beyond the sea, with the appurtenances thereto in any due wise or pertaining, be, rest, remain, and abide in the most royal person of our now sovereign lord King Harry the VIIth, and in the heirs of his body lawfully coming, perpetually with the grace of God so to endure, and in none others.

After the bill had been presented, Henry himself spoke to the assembled audience, accepting its contents and going further than the bill by insisting that he had gained the crown by just hereditary title as well as by God's own word, revealed through his victory in battle.

The Crowland chronicler noted how Henry claimed his kingship 'not by one but by many titles so that he may be considered to rule rightfully over the English people not only by right of blood but of victory in battle and conquest'. This was dangerous ground, especially given that many Yorkists would have still considered Elizabeth of York to have a stronger claim to the throne. Henry himself recognised the inadequacy of his Beaufort ancestry by bolstering its legitimacy, re-enacting the statute of 1397 that had declared the Beaufort family legitimate, yet consciously ignoring the 1407 statute that had added the provision that the Beauforts should never succeed to the throne, thereby removing any stigma of bastardy. Henry himself would adopt the Beaufort emblem of the portcullis, a symbol that would feature more prominently, along with the red rose of Lancaster, than the double Tudor rose, in future commissions of stained glass and carvings. In contrast, the Yorkist claim to the throne was further undermined by statements littered throughout bills passed in the Parliament that Richard was a usurper, with no formal claim to the throne, being 'king in deed but not in right'. Later, the formula was quietly dropped in 1495, with the dead king being termed 'Richard, late Duke of Gloucester, otherwise called King Richard III' or even 'the said King Richard'.

It was hardly an encouraging sign for those Yorkists who had thrown in their lot with Henry against Richard, convinced by the Welshman's promises that he would marry Elizabeth of York, thereby reconciling both competing claims. Yet with no date set for a wedding, it seemed that Henry was once again pressing his right to rule through his own Lancastrian ancestry alone, something that was hardly part of the bargain. The Crowland chronicler recorded the sense of disenchantment at Henry's actions, revealing that 'there were those who, more wisely thought that such words should rather have been kept silent than committed to proclamation, particularly because, in that same Parliament, and with the king's consent, there was discussion about the marriage to the lady Elizabeth, King Edward's eldest daughter, in whose person, it seemed to all, there could be found whatever appeared to be missing in the king's title elsewhere'.

If Henry were to marry Elizabeth, he would first need to remove the legal taint of illegitimacy that Richard's infamous *Titulus Regius* had cast upon Edward IV's children. The scandalous act was deemed by the judges impossible to recite in public in case it perpetuated its terms; instead, it was rehearsed somewhat obliquely that 'afore this time Richard, late Duke of Gloucester, and after in deed and not of right, king of England, called Richard the IIIrd, caused a false and seditious bill of false and malicious imaginations, against all good and true disposition, to be put to him'. The bill was now to be 'void, annulled, repelled . . . and of no force nor effect'; it was to be removed from the Parliament roll 'and burnt and utterly destroyed'. Anyone possessing a copy of the act was to destroy it or return it to the chancellor, 'upon pain of imprisonment'. The slow dismantlement of Richard's regime had begun.

With his own title confirmed in law, Henry moved to establish his new regime as soon as possible. An Act of Resumption was passed that restored to the crown all lands that had previously been granted out since 1455, albeit with a substantial list of exemptions and provisos. At the same time, Henry's supporters who had suffered confiscations or penalties as a result of their service in the rebellion of 1483 or beyond had their titles restored: even the dead were remembered, with Henry VI, Margaret of Anjou, their son Prince Edward and Henry Beaufort, Duke of Somerset, having all acts passed against them reversed. Margaret Beaufort was restored to whole possession of her lands, as was Edward Stafford, Buckingham's heir, and Elizabeth Woodville, who in spite of her miscalculation of returning to Richard's side, was also restored to all her properties.

What the new king might give, he was also prepared to take away. On 9 November he announced his intention to punish those who had offended him 'in the court of the present parliament according to their deserts'. An Act of Attainder was passed, setting out how the king, 'not oblivious nor putting out of his godly mind the unnatural, mischievous and great perjuries, treasons, homicides and murders, in shedding of Infants' blood, with many other wrongs, odious offences and abominations against God and Man, and in especial our said Sovereign Lord, committed and done by Richard, late Duke of Gloucester'. The act stated specifically how on 21 August, 'the first year of the reign of our Sovereign lord', there had assembled at Leicester in the county of Leicestershire a great host, traitorously intending, imagining, and conspiring, the destruction of the King's royal person, our Sovereign Liege lord. And they, with the same host, with banners spread, mightily armed and defenced with all manner arms, as guns, bows, arrows, spears, gleves, axes, and all other manner articles apt or needful to give and cause mighty battle against our said Sovereign Lord, kept together from the said 22nd day of the said month then next following, and then conducted to a field within the said shire of Leicester, there be great and continued deliberation, traitorously levied war against our said Sovereign Lord, and his true subjects there being in his service and assistance under a banner of our said Sovereign Lord, to the subversion of this realm, and common weal of the same.

What was most striking, and controversial, about the Act of Attainder was its dating of Henry's reign from 21 August, the day before the battle of Bosworth had actually taken place. In doing so, Henry claimed that Richard and his forces, in assembling at Leicester and marching into battle, had rebelled against their lawful king. As rebels, each was to have his property forfeit and his titles removed. On the face of it, the redating made little difference, since those who were attainted had fought against Henry the following day. Yet the legal consequences of such an arbitrary decision, when it was clear to all that thousands of men, summoned by commissions of array with little choice in the matter, had followed a king they considered to be the lawful monarch, crowned and acclaimed by Parliament, into battle against the then pretender. According to the Crowland chronicler, this deliberate redating of the reign provoked 'much argument or, to be more truthful, rebuke'. As the chronicler well understood, there were profound potential consequences to the decision: 'Oh God! What assurance will our kings have, henceforth, that on the day of battle they will not be deprived of the presence of their subjects who, summoned by the dreaded command of the king, are well aware that, if the royal cause should happen to decline, as has often been known, they will lose life, goods and inheritance complete?' The chronicler was not alone in his criticism of the Attainder, which provoked stormy debates and bad feeling at Westminster; one observer wrote that 'there is much runyng amongst the lords . . . it is said it is not well amongst them'. And even though the Act would stand, Henry himself had second thoughts on the provision, making amends a decade later when he allowed Parliament to pass 'a bill that no man going to battle with the prince should be attainted'.

The actual number of men attainted was in fact far modest than could have been expected. Only twenty-eight men had sentence passed against them, of whom eight were already dead. The Act of Attainder was, the Crowland Chronicler observed, 'far more moderate than anything of the sort which had been seen in the days of King Richard or King Edward'. Most were the familiar names of Richard's closest supporters, including William Catesby, Sir Robert Brackenbury, Richard's secretary John Kendall and Richard Ratcliffe. It is tempting to read into the Attainder a complete collapse in support for Richard's cause on the day of battle: of the thirty-eight English peers that had been summoned to Parliament in 1484, only five were to be attainted. Of these, Norfolk and Ferrers gave their lives during the battle; the other three were Nofolk's son and heir, Thomas Howard, Earl of Surrey, currently imprisoned, Francis, Lord Lovell and John, Lord Zouche, both of whom remained at large having been able to escape the battlefield. Only one southerner, Sir Richard Charlton, was to be attainted. It is far more likely, however, that in passing only a limited Act of Attainder, Henry was continuing his policy of reconciliation rather than retribution. It remains particularly striking that all the northern magnates were not attainted: Northumberland, Westmorland, the two Lord Scropes, Lord Greystoke, Lord Dacre, Lord Fitzhugh and Lord Lumley.

Henry understood how vulnerable his own position in the north remained; while he struggled to maintain order on the borders with Scotland and fearing possible invasion, rumours had begun to circulate of a renewed attack by Richard's supporters, with one commentator noting that 'here is much speech that we shall have aschip again, and no many can say of whom, but they deem of Northernmen'. To counter this, in issuing a curtailed attainder, Henry may have been hoping to persuade some of Richard's supporters in the north to reconcile themselves with his succession, delaying any recrimination in the hope that some might fall upon his mercy; a sign of how far the new king was prepared to make allowances is hinted at in the fact that three of the eight men who had been specifically excluded from a royal pardon of

11 October, it being suggested that their offences against the king were too great, were not included in the Act of Attainder. There may have been an element of deception in this, since there were others who were treated as attainted men who were not mentioned in the Act. Nicholas Spicer, a Bristol merchant and prominent supporter of Richard's, was not included in the list of men attainted and recorded on the Parliament roll; however, an inquisition conducted on 31 October into men who had fought for Richard and consequently had their lands confiscated included 'Nicholas Spycer late of Bristol, "merchant"'.

Still there was every sign that Henry was prepared to be as good as his word. Pardons were granted to prominent members of the old regime, including many local sheriffs as Henry calculated he would need to retain their support to restore law and order. Thomas Fulford, the former sheriff of Somerset and Dorset was pardoned and released. Ralph Willoughby, the former sheriff of Norfolk and Suffolk, was pardoned for 'all offences committed previously to date'. Meanwhile, John Paston, whose support the Duke of Norfolk had hoped to attract on his journey to Bosworth, had been awarded the office in Willoughby's place, being a reward of £160 in addition to his £80 salary. Henry also demonstrated a degree of kindness to those caught in a situation hardly of their own making, with the king granting an annual pension of £10 to Jean, Lady Zouche, 'towards the sustenation of her and her children', which was later increased to 100 marks in consideration of her 'poverty and wretchedness', though this may have been because Jean was the sister of Katherine Arundell, the widow of Sir Thomas Arundell who had been in exile with Henry. Richard's illegitimate son John was also given an annuity of £20. The Earl of Oxford was equally magnanimous in victory. Sir James Tyrell, a squire of the body to Edward IV who had been appointed Richard's Master of the Horse in 1483, became one of Oxford's closest retainers. He was one of the earl's retinue who was knighted at the battle of Stoke in 1487 and by 1492 had a permanent chamber at Castle Hedingham and was paid a fee of £6 13s 4d for life by 1509. Another of Richard's supporters, Sir William Say, who had been knighted by the king and granted the manor of Sawbridgeworth, Hertfordshire in 1484, brought twelve men to Oxford in 1487. The former Lancastrian Sir Henry Wentworth was a squire in Richard's household by 1484 and received a £5 pension as the 'king's servant'; the year after Bosworth he was witnessing property transactions for the earl and may have mustered for the earl in 1487. The Earl of Surrey's wife, the Countess of Surrey, who perhaps had most to fear from the earl whose authority in Essex lay in direct competition with her family's, told John Paston that 'him I dread most and yet as hither to I find him best'.

Certainly some of Richard's former supporters who had faced attainder were encouraged enough to appeal against the decision, throwing themselves upon the new king's mercy. Less than a week after the Act had passed, Roger Wake petitioned Henry to overturn his attainder. He explained how he had fought at Bosworth 'against his will and mind', quoting from Richard's letters which commanded him to fight 'upon pain of forfeiture of life, land, and asmuch as he might forfeit'. He went on to explain how he had a wife and eight children 'of tender age, which without your especial grace unto them should be like to perish for default of sustenance: the children be of so tender age they can be put to no one else to relieve themselves, and their mother can full simply apply her to ask alms for them it is so contrarious to her bringing up'. Wake pleaded for Henry's 'gracious and merciful disposition with which God of his great grace hath excellently and abundantly endowed you' and asked him to pardon his life and spare his personal possessions, 'whereby he, his said wife, and children may have some living unto the time that he at your other leisure sue further to your good grace for their more relief'. Though he had died in battle, Geoffrey St Germyn was one of those attainted, yet his daughter Margaret petitioned Henry that, although she admitted her father had fought for Richard 'in the last field', he had done so under duress, having been 'so manashed by the letters of the same late Duke, that unless he came to the said field he should lose his life, lands and goods; for dread whereof, he was in the same field, full sore against his will'.

The experiences of Roger Wake and Geoffrey St Germyn, together with the fates of other attainted men, highlight the thousands of individual consequences and tragedies that had occurred on the day of battle, leading to divided loyalties between king and family, country and community. There were difficult choices to be made, often cutting through traditional family relations. Sir Gervase Clifton and John Byron were friends and neighbours, but chose to fight on opposite sides of the field. Clifton was a royal servant active in the Duchy of Lancaster and an esquire of the king's body as well as a prominent Nottinghamshire landowner; there would have been no chance of his not committing to the king. Byron on the other hand decided to back Henry. Tradition recalls that they made a pact on the battlefield that whoever survived would protect the interests and inheritance of the other. Richard's own supporters, perhaps through close family ties, also managed to help the relatives of the fallen. John Kendal was attainted after the battle, though survived to marry Elizabeth, the widow of Sir Richard Charlton, who had died fighting for Richard. Sir Richard Charlton's death on the battlefield must have left his sister Agnes distraught, not least because her husband was Sir Thomas Bourgchier, who had defected to Henry's side. Perhaps her grief was alleviated when her brother's lands were granted to Bourgchier in reward for his service.

Other families torn by the battle included the Berkeley family, revealing very different attitudes between generations. Sir William Berkeley of Uley in Gloucestershire, aged forty-nine, fought for Richard, while his younger cousin, Sir William Berkeley of Beverstone, aged thirty-five, had chosen to take Henry's side; Berkeley of Beverstone had been a household knight of Edward IV and had taken part in Buckingham's uprising, later fleeing abroad into exile in Brittany and France. Sir William Berkeley of Uley lost his lands, suffering attainder for his support for Richard. On the other side of fortune's wheel, his cousin Berkeley of Beverstone had been appointed a king's councillor. The turn of the wheel could be fast: three months later, Berkeley of Beverstone was dead, with his elder cousin outliving him by fifteen years. Eleven years after the battle, Sir William Berkeley's attainder was eventually reversed, though his family never recovered its property, and were still pursuing their lands in vain in 1531.

If there was a general anticipation during the winter of 1485 that the new king would issue pardons to those attainted, Henry was not so fast to act. 'These lords and gentlemen that was attainted', one London merchant wrote in surprise in February 1486, 'they get no grace, as it is said'. Restoration to the king's favour would clearly be a slow process, a form of probation that would necessarily have to be drawn out over a long period – long enough to win back the king's limited trust. Roger

Wake's attainder was annulled in the following Parliament, and by the time of his death in 1503, he had nearly recovered all the lands that he had lost fighting at Bosworth.

With the lands of the attainted being parcelled out to his own supporters, the balance between reward, retribution and reconciliation was a delicate one. Henry understood the precarious financial position that the realm stood in. Forfeited lands that were not used to reward his followers were an invaluable source of income for the crown. In an early sign of the king's determination to exploit the machinery of government to strengthen his authority, Henry set out to ensure that he received all the forfeitures that he was entitled to. In August 1486 a commission was established to oversee the collection of revenues still outstanding. No amount was too small: the crown even recovered plate which Sir Robert Brackenbury had sold to a London chaplain a week before Bosworth in order to pay off his debts, but which the chaplain had failed to hand over.

Parliament ended its first session on 16 December with a petition being handed to the king by the speaker Thomas Lovell, on behalf of the commons, urging that Henry should now take Elizabeth of York as his wife. The language of the petition made it clear that Henry's own title should in no way depend upon the legitimacy of the Yorkist heiress. As its text tacitly hinted, Henry was king in his own right, but the marriage could only bring further union between the houses of Lancaster and York. Already preparations had begun to obtain from Innocent VIII a formal papal dispensation for the marriage , with a list of eight witnesses, including Thomas Stanley, testifying in January that the match had long been considered. A draft oration intended to be delivered to Innocent VIII further explained how 'the king of England, who had been tossed on the waves and exposed to innumerable dangers, like another Aeneas, having been nearly fifteen years an exile, acknowledged that it was by divine aid and beyond all human expectation that he had recovered in so brief space the throne of his ancestors. To put an end to civil war, he had, at the request of all the lords of the kingdom, consented to marry Elizabeth, daughter of Edward IV.' The papal dispensation was finally granted in a Bull from Innocent VIII on 27 March 1486. An English version of the letter was swiftly sent off to printing presses for circulation, to be distributed across the realm. The value of papal support for Henry's kingship was too great not to go unnoticed; it would now be used to highlight the emotional significance of the marriage:

> Our Holy Father, the Pope Innocent the VIII . . . Understanding of the long and grievous variance, contentions, and debates that hath been in this Realm of England between the house of the Duchy of Lancaster on the one party, and the house of the Duchy of York on that other party. Willing all such divisions . . . following to be put apart . . . approveth, confirmeth and establisheth the matrimony and conjunction made between our sovereign lord King Henry the Seventh of the house of Lancaster of that one party and the noble Princess Elizabeth of the house of York of that other, with all their Issue lawfully borne between the same.

In fact, Henry had already taken matters into his own hands, and on 18 January had married Elizabeth in a ceremony somewhat shrouded in secrecy. Perhaps he had little choice but to do so sooner rather than later; eight months later, on 19 September, a male heir, Arthur, was born to the couple. Nevertheless, Elizabeth's official coronation as queen was delayed for almost two years, with the ceremony taking place finally on 25 November 1487.

For the moment, there were other matters clearly weighing down the new king's mind, not least the prospect of renewed opposition in the north, 'whence all Evil spreads', the Crowland chronicler observed menacingly. Recognising the limitations of his own power and authority in the region, Henry had chosen to tread carefully in his appointments there, retaining most of Richard's officers in their posts: noblemen such as John, Lord Scrope of Bolton and Thomas, Lord Scrope of Masham, in spite of their actions fighting for Richard at Bosworth were to be reappointed as commissioners of array to the north in September 1485. Sir John Conyers of Hornby, a member of Richard's ducal council and appointed a knight of the garter, similarly appears on the commission of array and by February 1486, on account of his 'good and faithful service' to Henry, was granted several offices in Richmondshire and appointed a knight of the king's body. Sir Thomas Markenfield, a knight of Richard's body who had been rewarded with an annuity of 100 marks and appointed sheriff of Yorkshire in November 1484, despite his fighting on Richard's side at Bosworth, was allowed to remain in the post as sheriff there. For Marmaduke Constable, Bosworth was to be but a temporary setback to his career. In the aftermath of the battle, he was stripped of his Duchy of Lancaster offices in Staffordshire, Derbyshire and Leicestershire, yet by 18 November he had secured a pardon and by May 1486 was restored to his position as a knight of the body. In the same year he rode alongside Henry during his first progress into Yorkshire. Like Richard, Henry would need the support that northern gentlemen such as Constable could offer: unlike Richard, who had planted Constable in the south, Henry wanted him exactly where he lacked support, in the north. He was soon to be appointed sheriff of his native county of Yorkshire, supplemented with an unusually generous reward of £340.

After first appointing another prominent Ricardian, Lord Fitzhugh, to the office of warden of the East and Middle Marches, Henry soon came to realise that he needed the weightier support that the Earl of Northumberland's Percy connections brought; in December the earl was released from prison and restored to his former office as warden of the Marches held by Fitzhugh. Northumberland's rehabilitation was a limited one: the earl was appointed warden of the East and Middle Marches on the border with Scotland, but was not granted the security of tenure his family had previously enjoyed, while Henry preferred to retain Thomas, Lord Dacre as warden of the important Western March.

By mid-February, Henry had resolved to make a personal journey to the north. 'It is said he purposes to do execution quickly there on such as have offended against him', wrote one commentator. On his journey towards York in early April 1486, the king was 'struck by a great fear' when he discovered that Viscount Lovell and Humphrey Stafford, having fled their sanctuary at Colchester, were planning on raising the standard of revolt in Yorkshire and Worcestershire. Undeterred, Henry continued on his journey, arriving at York to be welcomed by Northumberland. In the event, Henry had less cause for concern than he imagined. Lovell managed to raise a large army around Richard's former stronghold at Middleham, but he had underestimated the success of

Henry's policy of rapprochement with many of Richard's former supporters, who were unwilling to indulge in yet more bloody fighting. When Jasper Tudor was sent ahead, offering the rebels pardon if they threw down their arms, it was enough for Lovell to realise that his efforts were doomed to failure; slipping away in the middle of the night, he escaped to the north where a band of the most diehard Ricardians held out in the wilderness, camped out on the Furness Fells. One by one, the group led by Sir Thomas Broughton and Sir John Huddlestone were prised out by promises of pardon.

As his support eventually melted away, Lovell fled abroad to Flanders, where he sought the protection of Richard's influential sister Margaret, Duchess of Burgundy, who was determined to seek revenge upon Henry for her brother's death, pursuing him 'with insatiable hatred and with fiery wrath'. Humphrey Stafford meanwhile desperately sought sanctuary again near Abingdon, with little success: he was dragged out forcibly, and in July 1486, after it had been formally decreed that sanctuary could not be pleaded in treason cases, went to the block.

Henry's visit to York was not without incident; it was reported that there was an attempt on the king's life on St George's Day, thwarted only by the actions of Northumberland. There had also been other worrying signs of underlying discontent, with Richard's nephew, John, Earl of Lincoln, making a failed attempt to escape the city 'over the walls' to join the rebels. It would soon become clear that Henry would continue to face further resistance to his regime, this time coming in the remarkable episode of Lambert Simnel, a joiner from Oxford, who was persuaded by a priest to impersonate Richard's nephew, Clarence's son, Edward, Earl of Warwick. When rumours spread that the young man pretending to be Warwick was free, Henry took them seriously enough to have the real earl, until now imprisoned in the Tower, paraded around the streets of London in February 1487.

It was not enough to prevent several prominent Yorkists, who had previously submitted themselves to Henry, choosing to throw in their lot on this bizarre last throw of the dice, John, Earl of Lincoln among them, who fled across to the Low Countries to join the court of Margaret of Burgundy, where Viscount Lovell had fled. Irreconcilable to the new regime, Lovell had remained undeterred by his previous defeat.

With his latest venture, he believed he had the means to oust the Tudor pretender. Margaret of Burgundy provided the resources to finance 2,000 German mercenaries led by the experienced Swiss captain Martin Schwartz, who landed in Ireland on 5 May 1487, with Lambert Simnel being crowned 'Edward VI' there several weeks later. Schwartz's forces, bolstered by 6,000 Irish levies who, in spite of being severely ill-equipped, landed at Furness in Lancashire on 4 June. From the start it was obvious that the resources he had been promised by Richard's supporters were not going to be forthcoming. When the opposing forces clashed at Stoke in Nottinghamshire on 16 June, Henry placed the command of his troops once more in the trusty hands of the redoubtable Earl of Oxford while the king remained, as at Bosworth, sensibly positioned at the very back of the field. There was little chance that Schwartz was ever going to replicate the success of Philibert de Chandée and his French mercenaries at Bosworth: completely outnumbered by the royal army twice his army's size, Schwartz, together with Lincoln and Lovell, chose to mass their forces into a single unit. Even then, they struggled to face the force of the king's vanguard and the fire of its archers, so much so that the battle was over before most of Henry's army even had the chance to engage in the fighting. Four thousand Irishmen were slaughtered on the field; Lincoln's body lay strewn among them. Lovell escaped, never to be seen again, though his disappearance may have been solved by the discovery of a sealed underground chamber at Minster Lovell, Lovell's family residence, when workmen were laying a new chimney in the building in 1728, 'in which was the entire skeleton of a man' sat at a table, 'with a book, paper, pen' 'which the family and others judged this to be lord Lovell, whose exit hath hitherto been so uncertain'.

Lambert Simnel himself was captured. Rather than face execution, Henry decided to show his mercy by employing the boy in the royal household, first as a kitchen spit turner and later as a falconer. Rather than exact revenge upon the Yorkists who had turned against him in spite of his previous promises of pardon, he would offer clemency but only at a price. Both Lords Scrope, who seemed to have been reconciled to Henry's rule before turning against him in June 1487, bought their lives with bonds of £3,000.

If Henry was looking for encouragement, he could point to the fact that Richard's designated successor, the Earl of Lincoln, was dead. He could also take heart that if a few disaffected Yorkists had chosen the path of rebellion, most had not, deciding to remain loyal to his new regime. Lord Dacre, who had previously 'raised all the north country' for Richard at Bosworth, sat on his hands, as did Thomas, Earl of Surrey, who reportedly refused the chance to escape from the Tower during Simnel's rebellion. The Earl of Northumberland stuck loyally by the king's side, mopping up outbreaks of revolt and keeping the city of York in obedience. If Henry had forgiven the Earl of Northumberland for his role at Bosworth, it would prove that others would not. Two years later the earl was doing his duty as one of the king's officers, collecting an unpopular income tax, when he was attacked by a mob of protesters at South Kilvington, just outside Thirsk, on 28 April 1489. According to the Earl of Oxford, relating news of the earl's death, Northumberland, hearing that the men were unarmed, had approached them not wearing any harness, hoping to address them 'in peaceful manner, trusting to have appeased them': 'How be it, as it is said, that he is distressed and that they have taken him or slain him, which the King intendeth to punish'.

What was most striking for contemporaries was that as the earl was struck down and attacked, his retinue stood around him in silence, refusing to come to his aid. In the poet John Skelton's words: 'Barons, knights, squires, one and all . . . Turned their backs and let their master fall.' Henry issued a proclamation against the 'rebels' who had 'against all humanity cruelly murdered and destroyed his most dear cousin', though the author of the Great Chronicle of London remarked that he had died for reason of the 'deadly malice for the disappointing of king Richard at Bosworth field'. When in York, a year after Northumberland's death, in a drunken conversation 'distempered either with wine or ale', John Painter believed that the earl 'died a traitor to our sovereign the lord the king', he did not mean Henry VII, but that the earl 'was a traitor and betrayed King Richard'.

Henry remained dogged by challenges to his authority for years to come, with Yorkists remaining sheltered by Margaret of Burgundy who provided them with their own exiled court. It was apparent to Vergil that the king would remain 'harassed by the treachery of his opponents and assaulted frequently thereafter by the forces of his enemies and the insurrections of his own subjects'. A fresh pretender to the throne arrived in the figure of the imposter Perkin Warbeck, who became a puppet in the hands of neighbouring foreign rulers, yet failed to win a strong enough following in England to mount a serious challenge to Henry's reign. Ironically one of the few men who chose to desert the king was the man who had done so much to place him on the throne, Sir William Stanley. The days of Henry's impromptu coronation on Crown Hill in the moments after the battle at Bosworth long behind him, Stanley's disappointment at not receiving what he considered his due reward had slowly transformed itself into bitterness and resentment. According to Vergil, 'William, although he held a great place of friendship with the king, was more mindful of the favour he had conferred than that he received, and he still hoped, as the Gospel verse has it, to have more abundance, so that he put a low value on the rewards given him by the king. When Henry perceived these were cheap in his eyes, he began to be so angry that the both of them, their minds provoked, lost the fruit of their grace.' Ten years after he had turned the tide of the battle, placing Henry on the throne and maybe even placing the crown on his head, Sir William Stanley decided to throw his lot in with Perkin Warbeck. Arrested, he was convicted for treason and executed in 1495, though Henry felt remorse enough to contribute to the costs of his funeral. After his death, Stanley's castle at Holt was surveyed, with an inventory of its contents made: among his possessions was a gold collar, emblazoned with the livery of Yorkist suns.

For those who considered loyalty the best policy, the aftermath of Bosworth was soon to become a distant memory. Sir Ralph Bigod, who had recalled the disorganisation of Richard's camp on the morning of the battle, was soon restored to favour, being made a knight of the new king's body; the following year he was granted the royal offices of constable and porter of Sheriff Hutton, as well as the bailiff of the town and keeper of the park there. He continued to be a loyal servant of the crown, being placed on commissions of the peace and array, and in 1492 served in the invasion of France. In 1503 he accompanied Henry's daughter Princess Margaret to Scotland on her journey to marry James IV. Bigod continued to serve under Henry VIII with equal distinction: in 1513 he was ordered to seize the Yorkshire properties of the Scottish king, who by then was at war with England. When he died in 1515, his grandson and heir became a ward of Thomas, Cardinal Wolsey.

Now firmly a member of the Tudor establishment, in 1492 Sir Marmaduke Constable accompanied Henry VII on his expedition to France, just as he had done with Edward IV in 1475; Constable was himself involved with the negotiations that resulted in the Treaty of Étaples in November 1492. He continued to serve unstintingly in various offices, including a third term as sheriff of Yorkshire, the local MP and justice of the peace in the East Riding, until late in life came his greatest triumph, when at the age of seventy, he was to captain the left flank of the English forces at the battle of Flodden in 1513. The epitaph on his tomb, written at his death five years later, carved out how Constable wished to be remembered, serving both Edward IV, 'that noble knight', and 'noble King Henry', making 'adventure into France', being 'at Berwick at the winning of the same, and by King Edward chosen captain there first of any one', and his service at Flodden, where 'then being of the age of threescore and ten . . . courageously advanced himself among other there and then . . . he nothing heeding his age. Any mention of Bosworth and Richard III had been conveniently erased from memory.

Others remained proud of their actions that day. John Sacheverell, son of Ralph Sacheverell of Switterton and Hopwell in Derbyshire, who fought and died on Richard's side, was remembered with a memorial brass at his local church forty years later, stating that 'he died in the war of Richard the third near Bosworth'. William Sheldon's tomb in St Leonard's church in Beoley, Worcestershire also attests to the fact that he fought for Richard at Bosworth; however, Sheldon survived the battle, and with his lands eventually restored to him, died in 1517.

Henry too, could hardly have been prepared to forget his past. He never forgot his fondness for Brittany, despite the fact that Duke Francis's death in 1488, coming months after the disastrous battle of St Aubin du Comier, that had seen another Bosworth veteran Sir Edward Woodville killed fighting as a mercenary on the battlefield, had brought the collapse of Brittany as an independent state, with his daughter Anne marrying Charles VIII in 1491, thereby bringing a union between France and the last independent duchy. Seventeen years after his victory at Bosworth, in January 1502 Henry sent an envoy to the cathedral at Vannes to deliver a chasuble of crimson velvet, decorated with the royal arms of England in gold leaf and the words *Regis Henrici Septimi* on the back, along with two crimson velvet altar cloths, woven with gold leaf, intended for the altar of St Vincent Ferrier, the town's patron saint. When Henry commissioned his own tomb to be built in Westminster Abbey, he personally ordered one of the gilt medallions to be reserved for St Vincent.

There was another Breton saint whom Henry was minded to remember, believing that he had provided him with personal protection during his trials. According to legend, in the sixth century St Armel had founded a Breton monastery after defeating a dragon that had terrorised the surrounding region. He had bound the dragon to his religious vestment, before commanding the beast to drown itself in a nearby river. Armel's relics were preserved in the small church at Ploermel in southern Brittany, less than five miles away from the castle at Josselin, where Jasper Tudor had been imprisoned. Tradition recalls that both Jasper and Henry had prayed to the saint during their time in Brittany, and that they believed St Armel's intercession had saved their small fleet from shipwreck during their aborted journey to England in November 1483, when during a gale the stormy seas had tossed their ships throughout the night, leaving them in fear of their lives. From then on, Henry had kept the saint close to his heart; in the chapel he had built at Westminster Abbey, Henry ordered that not one but two separate statues of St Armel be placed there, depicting the saint as a bearded man with a dragon at his feet, tied to a stole that Armel holds in his right hand covered by an armoured glove. Notably, a similar carved statue of Armel appears in the memorial to John Morton, the Bishop of Ely, who had been instrumental in helping to organise Buckingham's rebellion and assisting Henry in exile.

There is another location where St Armel's image is to be found: in the stained glass of Merevale church, the former gatehouse of Merevale Abbey where Henry had met with the Stanleys before the battle. For the Crowland chronicler, revealing his ecclesiastical bias, Merevale Abbey was central to the battle's location: Richard set up camp 'near the abbey of Merevale' and the battle is later referred to as 'this battle of Merevale'. Yet recognising the debt that he owed to the abbey, not least in providing his army with food and sustenance as they camped on the abbey's lands, crushing its crops at the height of harvest season, on 7

December 1485 Henry granted 100 marks to the abbot of Merevale in compensation for 'right great hurts, charges and losses by the occasion of the great repair and resort that our people coming toward our late field made, as well unto the house of Merevale aforesaid as in going over his ground, to the destruction of his corns and pastures'. With the battle still fresh in the king's mind, the abbot decided to take his chances and press Henry for even greater reward for the assistance the abbey had given him, 'meeking beseeching' the new king to grant the abbey the lordship of Atherstone, 'which if ye so do shall be to your avail, as here before ye have been informed and in perfect and perpetual remembrance of your late victorious field and journey at the reverence of god, to whom he shall specially pray for the prosperous continuance of your most noble and royal estate'.

There is no evidence that Henry responded to the abbot's audacious letter, let alone granted him his request, but eighteen years after the battle, with his kingdom secured and the uncertain early years of revolt and rebellion firmly behind him, in September 1503 Henry decided to return to the place of his triumph, visiting the abbey, where he gave money for a stained glass window. In the south aisle of the church, the window remains there to this day. There is St Armel, his open cape revealing a full suit of armour, a breast plate with mail beneath, with his legs and feet also covered in metal plate. He carries in his right hand a bible and a bag, from which protrudes a dragon, its eyes peering out from a slit-like opening. Perhaps Henry believed that the saint had been with him during the uncertainty of battle, when with the Stanleys refusing to commit to join his side, it seemed for a moment that all had been lost as he faced Richard's final desperate charge.

It was not the last time that a Tudor king would pay homage to the site of Henry's 'victorious triumph'. In August 1511 the young king Henry VIII passed through Leicester where he travelled to Coventry, staying at Merevale Abbey. With the occasion of the battle, the anniversary of which had only just passed, very much in his own mind at the time, Henry decided to mark the battle with its own official memorial, a chapel dedicated to those who had fallen on the field. At Nottingham, on 24 August, two days after the battle's anniversary, Henry VIII issued a signet warrant authorising the churchwardens of Dadlington to appeal for funds throughout four midland dioceses for a period of seven years, 'towards the building of a chapel of Saint James standing upon a parcel of the ground where Bosworth field, *otherwise called Dadlington field*, in our county of Leicester was done, and towards the salary of a priest by the said churchwardens provided to sing in the said chapel principally for the souls of all such persons as were slain in the said field'.

In doing so, Henry was following the long tradition of establishing battlefield chapels. The earliest dates from the Saxon period, erected on the site of King Oswald's victory at Hefenfeld in 634; perhaps the most famous is Battle Abbey, founded by William the Conqueror to commemorate 1066, with its high altar on the spot where King Harold's standard had fallen. The tradition had been renewed with vigour in the fifteenth century, with the greatest example being All Souls College, Oxford, which had been founded in 1438 as a place to pray for 'all Christian souls' who had died during the French wars; the civil wars between the houses of Lancaster and York saw further smaller chantries founded in memory of the battle dead, close to the site of the battle itself: in 1458, when Richard of York was reconciled to Henry VI at their 'Loveday', he agreed to endow a chantry at the abbey of St Albans for the souls of those killed in the battle fought there three years before. Henry VII chose to found a chantry at Tewkesbury Abbey in 1500 that included prayers to be said for those slain in the battle within the abbey's shadow. A small mortuary chapel known as the 'hermitage' was built to commemorate the fighting at Barnet, while at Towton Edward IV had planned to enlarge an existing chapel where many of the dead had been buried, going so far as to obtain a papal indulgence to attract contributions. The plans were left to Richard to complete, with the king himself heading a list of donors to the proposed chapel there with the donation of £40. Even then Towton's memorial remained incomplete, with the Tudors hardly prepared to countenance a memorial towards the greatest single defeat of their Lancastrian forebears; instead, the location of their victory at Bosworth Field, or 'Dadlington Field' as Henry VIII had noted significantly, would be the focus of attention.

As soon as the royal warrant had been granted, the churchwardens at Dadlington hurried to publish a printed appeal, known as a letter of confraternity, urging parishioners throughout the dioceses of Lincoln,

Chester, Worcester and Norwich to grant alms for the building of a new battlefield chapel, its text containing a blank space for the name of the relevant donor who would be 'declared to be a partner and partaker of all the indulgence, pardon, masses, prayers, good deeds and meritorious works as is afore rehearsed both in life and death for evermore'. Its initial letter formed by a woodcut depiction of St James, the chapel's patron, the appeal letter declared:

> Charity hath caused our Sovereign Lord the King to consider how gracious how meritorious and how pleasant a deed it is to Almighty God and what great reward they shall have of God for it that prayeth for ye souls of them that were slain at Bosworth field and therefore he hath given out his letters patent under his broad seal desiring all his subjects and lovers favourably to receive the messengers of St James' chapel to the which the bodies or bones of the men slain in the said field be brought and buried and to give or send something to the same chapel for the building and maintenance of it and of the priests and ministers that be found there to sing and read and pray and for the said souls and all Christians.

The amount raised was enough to pay for Dadlington church, which had previously shared a resident curate with the nearby village of Stoke, to employ for the first time its own priest, Roger Normanton, with the substantial salary of £4 until at least 1526.

Henry VII had preferred to make his own memorial a more personal one. In 1509, as he lay on his deathbed surrounded by his anxious courtiers, he devoted his final energies to drawing up his lengthy final will and testament. Among his many bequests, he would not forget those who had dedicated and sacrificed their lives to placing him upon the throne, remembering those 'lords as well of our blood as other, and also knights, squires, and divers our true loving subjects and servants' who had 'faithfully assisted us, and divers of them put themselves in extreme jeopardy of their lives, and losses of their lands and goods, in serving and assisting us, as well about the recovery of our Right and Realm of England'. And in one final tribute to his victory in battle twenty-four years before, the dying king requested that a wooden image, wrought with plate of fine gold, should be made, 'representing our own person

... in the manner of an armed man', to be equipped with an enamelled coat of the arms of England and France, together with a sword and spurs. The statue was to be placed kneeling on a silver table, 'holding betwixt his hands the crown which it pleased God to give us, with the victory over our enemy at our first field'. The statue was to be dedicated to St Edward the Confessor, and set in the middle of his shrine, with detailed instructions as to the exact measurements of the statue, so that it would seem as if Henry was almost offering up his crown to St Edward in thanks.

Of those surrounding the frail king as he languished in his bed, Henry would have recognised few faces who would have been at his side on the fateful day of his 'victorious field'. By then, most of his old comrades in arms were dead: Sir Edward Woodville had been killed in 1488; Sir John Savage had also died in action in Bolougne in 1492; his uncle Jasper had died in 1495, the same year Sir William Stanley had been beheaded for treason; his queen Elizabeth had died in 1503, followed by Thomas Stanley the next year; Sir Richard Guildford had passed away while on pilgrimage to the Holy Land in 1506; Giles Daubeney had died in his bed in 1508. In their place came a fresh-faced generation of new men who had little experience of the tribulations that their king had faced during the decades of civil war that were fading fast into distant memory.

It was a very different world to the one George Neville had described in 1461, when he had written that the English were 'a race deserving of pity even from the French' due to their 'intestine' civil wars. Even if the tenacious king, paranoid to the last, may not have believed it himself, Henry had healed a nation, laying the foundations for the future stability of the Tudor dynasty that would remain on the throne until 1603.

While previous assertions that 1485 had marked the birth of the early modern period and the death of the medieval age are both anachronistic and unsubstantiated, Richard's death at Bosworth had brought with it the end of the Plantagenet dynasty. Henry's accession had heralded the self-conscious image of a new monarchy that brought with it the idea of a country reconciled and harmony restored. As the decades wore on and the Tudors became more entrenched, strengthening their power and authority upon their subjects, they wove their own official history of events, best typified in Edward Hall's *The Union of the Two Noble Families of Lancaster and York*, asserting that Henry's ascent to the throne was an act of providence, bringing with it 'the union of the two noble and illustrious families of Lancaster and York, being long in continual dissension for the crown of this noble realm, with all the acts done in both the times of the princes, both of one lineage and of the other, beginning at the time of Henry IV, the first author of this division, and so successively proceeding to the reign of the high and prudent prince King Henry VIII, the indubitable flower and very heir of both the said lineages'. The events of the fifteenth century were to be fashioned into drama, with Hall's chapter on Richard's own reign being titled 'The Tragical Doings of King Richard the Third'. It was a compelling tale of the Tudor's inexorable rise, contrasted against the downfall of the houses of Lancaster and York, inspiring William Shakespeare to transform it into blank verse for popular audiences who devoured his history plays, the power of which defined for generations the wider view of what became known in Sir Walter Scott's famously invented phrase, 'the Wars of the Roses'.

The reality of Henry Tudor's ascent to the throne – his narrow escapes from death, his failures and anxieties, complete with constant uncertainty of his situation and the compromises that he had been forced to make, including the support from France and his former Yorkist enemies in gaining the crown – was a far less welcome tale. It remains nonetheless just as remarkable; against all the odds, at Bosworth Henry achieved a victory that he should not have won. For Philippe de Commynes, who had met Henry as a fourteen-year-old when he arrived as an exile at Duke Francis's court in Brittany in 1471, knowing exactly how Henry, who had told Commynes to his face how he had been a prisoner all his life since the age of five, had 'suffered much' having 'neither money, nor rights, so I believe, to the crown of England, nor any reputation except what his own person and honesty brought him', there could be no other explanation. Writing his memoirs, Commynes wrote simply, 'A battle was fought. King Richard was killed on the battlefield and the Earl of Richmond was crowned king of England on the field with Richard's crown. Should one describe this as Fortune? Surely it was God's judgement.'

14

BOSWORTH REDISCOVERED

◦—◦

When the blind French poet Bernard André came to describe the events of the Battle of Bosworth in his life of Henry VII, the *Vita Henrici Septimi*, he quite literally drew a blank. Writing that 'although I have heard of this battle with my ears' from men at Henry's court, he believed that when it came to detailing exactly what had happened, in 'this business the eye is a surer witness than the ear'. Joking that if this was the case he was hardly best placed to pass comment given his blindness, he declared that he 'would not be so bold as to affirm the day, the place, and the order of battle, and so I pass this by'. In the place of his description of the battlefield, at least 'until I am better informed', André resolved to 'leave a large blank field on this paper'.

Fortunately for the historian of Bosworth, several fuller accounts of the battle do exist, allowing for a conjectural history of the events of 22 August to be pieced together. The most comprehensive description of the battle comes from Polydore Vergil's *Historia Anglia*, first published in print at Basle in 1534, yet Vergil had written his history in manuscript form thirty years before when he was a visitor at Henry's court, noting how when writing his history, 'on approaching our own times, I could find no such annals' so he 'betook myself to every man of age who was pointed out to me as having been formerly occupied in important and public affairs, and from all such I obtained information about events up to the year 1500'. For the first time this book has returned to this original manuscript, still surviving in the Vatican Library in Rome, to add fresh details to the story.

Vergil can be supplemented by other fifteenth-century narratives such as the 'Spanish Account' of the battle, written on 1 March 1486 by Mosen Diego de Valera, in a letter to the Spanish monarchs, Ferdinand

and Isabella. Valera was writing from Puerto de Santa Maria, a port inland from the Bay of Cadiz, but he had been inspired to write following the arrival of 'trustworthy merchants who were in England at the time of the battle'. The identity of the Crowland chronicler, who wrote his account of events in the same year, has been hotly debated; however, it is clear that the author must have had a first-hand view of Richard's court. Other accounts of the battle can be found in the Great Chronicle of London, written in the late 1490s, as was the Burgundian chronicler Jean Molinet's description, though this relies heavily on the experience of the French mercenaries fighting on Henry's side, while two ballads, the 'Battle of Bosworth Field' and the 'Ballad of Lady Bessie', were likely to have been composed by members of the Stanley affinity, probably before Sir William Stanley's execution in 1495. These accounts do not provide a definitive detailed version of events; indeed, it can be difficult to reconcile these disparate sources into a single narrative, with each providing their own separate, often conflicting, version of events. The history of what actually happened that day must therefore remain in the hands of the historian's own judgement, balancing competing claims surrounding the timings of the battle, the movements of both armies, and most controversially, the location of where both sides clashed and victory was won.

How did the battle become known as the Battle of Bosworth? The first mention of the battle as being named as 'Bosworth' was not until twenty-five years after the event, mentioned in the manuscript edition of Vergil's *Anglia Historia* as being at a place near Leicester 'Bosworth'. The manuscript of the Great Chronicle of London also observed how Richard 'came unto a village called Bosworth where in the fields adjoining both hosts met'. But the name Bosworth was first printed in the 1516 edition of Robert Fayban's New Chronicles; Fabyan, who is thought also to be the author of the Great Chronicle, indicated that the battle had taken place 'near unto a village in Leicestershire named Bosworth'. Yet in one edition of the work, discovered in the National Library of Scotland by Peter Foss, in the margins next to the account of the battle, a sixteenth century hand has corrected: 'the battay[le] of Redesmore heath was bytwene K.R. & K.H. th[e] viith'. The anonymous reader of the Chronicle, taking his pen to the margins of the printed work, was only reflecting what had long been common knowledge. Indeed it was 'the field of Redemore' that was first identified by the city of York as where their king Richard had been 'murdered', with the name in various forms appearing in nearly all other contemporary accounts. It was Redemore that contemporaries recognised as the location where the battle had been fought: but what or more importantly where was the field of Redemore?

For most of the past century, especially since Leicestershire County Council established an official Battlefield Centre near the village of Sutton Cheney, it had been assumed that the battle had been fought near Ambion Hill. Over time, successive generations of antiquarians and historians managed to convince themselves that, with topographical features such as 'King Richard's Well' nearby, the fighting had occurred around this location. Yet the first mention of Ambion comes as late as 1577, when the chronicler Raphael Hollinshed stated that Richard had 'pitched his field on a hill called Anne Beame, refreshed his soldiers, and took his rest'. If Ambion Hill had played a part in the battle, it was clear from the beginning that it was never actually where the battle had been fought.

But if the primary accounts of the battle are not forthcoming in detail as to where the battle was fought, it was evident from some of the earliest attempts to piece together the location of the battlefield that Bosworth was not fought upon Ambion Hill, but rather upon a plain. The notion that the battle was fought on a 'plain' comes not from Vergil, but is first found in Hall's Chronicle, who stated how 'King Richard, being furnished with men and all habiliments of war, bringing all his men out of their camp into ye plain'. The poet Michael Drayton, born in 1563 at Hartshill, not far from the battle, stated that the armies had fought 'on a spacious Moore, lying southward from the Towne', while Sir George Buck, in his *History of the Life and Reign of King Richard III*, written in 1619 has Richard's death occurring 'upon the plain'. But it was the seventeenth-century Leicestershire historian William Burton, who in his *Description of Leicestershire* published in 1622, was to give the earliest detailed description of where the battle took place. Burton was born in Lindley in 1575 and his family owned the manor of Dadlington from 1585. He wrote that as a child he had heard accounts of actual eyewitnesses to the battle second hand. While the likelihood of this remains slim, Burton must have been able to draw upon local tradition of where the battle was fought, stating how he had constructed his history 'by relation of the inhabitants, who have many occurrences and passages, yet fresh in memory; by reason, that some persons thereabouts, who saw the battle fought were living within less than forty years: of which persons myself have seen some, and have heard their discourses, though related by second hand'. Burton claimed that the battle had been 'fought in a large, flat, plain, and spacious ground, three miles distant from this Towne [Market Bosworth], between the Towne of Shenton, Sutton, Dadlington, and Stoke'.

Burton's own words, depicted as they are with distances in miles in mind, sound like those of someone who had studied a map of the area. Yet the emergence of cartography was to play an important part in shifting perceptions of the battle's location away from its accepted site at Redemore and instead to up on Ambion Hill. Through subtle, almost unnoticeable changes, Redemore was to become divorced from the battle site, known as 'King Richard's Field'. In 1576 Christopher Saxon published the first map of Leicestershire and Warwickshire that showed 'Kinge Richards feild' as a pear-shaped area; the map lacks any further detail, yet this was supplied in 1602, when a map of Leicestershire and Rutland was drawn up, with Burton's assistance, which drew a pear-shaped boundary around what it described as 'K. Ric: feild', in the precise location that Burton describes. The field in question is bisected by a tributary of the river Sence, a branch of the Tweed which has its source near Stapleton. Eight years later, however, John Speed's map of the county made significant changes, separating the area known as 'Red More' from 'Kinge Richards field', on a separate orientation. Speed clearly shows 'Redmore' as taking up only a part of the field, to the north-east of the river, nearer the area around Sutton Cheney.

These subtle changes were to have a significant impact on the ideas of future historians, not least William Hutton, who published his *Battle of Bosworth Field*, the first book dedicated solely to the battle, in 1788. It was Hutton's supposedly comprehensive account which would influence historians for centuries to believe that Bosworth had been fought around Ambion, with Hutton himself publishing a plan of the battle that went much further than Speed's map and pushed the battle site entirely north of the river Sence, imagining the confrontation to take place on Ambion Hill itself, with Hutton himself discounting any evidence that seemed not to fit in with his own designs, declaiming that 'there neither is, nor ever was' a marsh, in spite of its almost universal feature in all early accounts of the battle.

For Hutton, describing in detail the terrain as it existed in the late eighteenth century, 'Redmore Plain', where the battle had been fought, was to be placed a mile from Market Bosworth, with its name derived 'from the colour of the soil'. In believing Redmore had been named after its red soil, Hutton was following in a tradition stretching back to the sixteenth-century poet Michael Drayton who used the analogy in his poem 'Poly-Olbion' to lament how 'then it seemed, thy name was not in vain, when with a thousands blood, the earth was coloured red'. Hutton placed Redmore in the parish of Sutton Cheney, with the village lying to its east.

> It is rather an oval form, about two miles long, and one broad, and is nearly in a line between Bosworth and Atherstone. The superficial contents may be 1,500 acres, inclosed in a ring fence. Part is waste land, part is grass, and part in tillage. The whole field is uneven. The south end, where Henry approached, is three miles from Bosworth, now a wood of 4 or 500 acres, and is bounded by the above rivulet. About thirty yards above the wood is a spring, called at this day King Richard's Well. A small discharge of water flows from the well, directly down the hill, through the wood, into the rivulet; but, having no channel cut for its passage, it penetrates through the soil, and forms that morass which Henry is said to have left on his right. Richard left his tents standing, and commanded the troops to rendezvous in Sutton field, about the mid-way to Amyon Hill.

Hutton's depiction of the battle being fought in the area was embellished further by John Nichols in his *Description of Leicestershire*, published in 1811, with another detailed map of the formations of Henry and Richard's battles opposing one another on Ambion Hill, supposedly synonymous with Redmore Plain.

The recent researches of Peter Foss have comprehensively unpicked Hutton's theory: to begin with, the name Redmore has nothing to do with it being a 'Red Moor'; instead, the etymology of the word comes from the Anglo-Saxon word for 'reed', and is used to describe an area adjacent to wetland. There are references in the thirteenth and fourteenth centuries to 'Redelondes' and 'le Redehull' in the parish of Market Bosworth, yet to locate precisely where Redemore is, we need to go back several centuries to an agreement concerning the allocation of tithes made in the parish of Hinckley, dated 1283. This document refers to 'six roods of meadow in Redemor in the fields of Dadlington'.

If Redemore should be placed near Dadlington, then we might expect evidence for the battle having been fought around the fields near the village. In particular, an important clue to where the battle took place can often be found in the location where the bodies of the battle dead are buried. Unlike at Towton, no identifiable grave-pits have been discovered, though successive historians have been keen to identify various surrounding tumuli or raised earth as signs of mass graves. Where are the Bosworth dead? Putting aside the most exaggerated claims that 10,000 men were killed, Vergil's estimate that a thousand were slain on Richard's side and a hundred on Henry's seems the most realistic. Nevertheless, the number is sizeable enough that a mark or sign of their burial might have been noted. Some of the more illustrious victims of the battle, such as John, Duke of Norfolk, would have been taken away from the site to be buried in their family chapels and churches. But the majority would have been buried near the battle itself. Henry gave orders that they should be buried 'with honour' at the field itself, with the tradition that the dead should be buried in the parish in which they fell persisting. It is here that the rediscovery of Henry VIII's signet letter of 1511 and the printed letter of confraternity by the churchwardens of St James' chapel at Dadlington by Colin Richmond in 1985, provided the crucial evidence that it was at Dadlington that the dead were buried. Henry VIII's signet letter reveals that St James' chapel stood 'upon a parcel of the ground where Bosworth field, otherwise called Dadlington field, in our county of Leicester was done', while the printed letter of confraternity is insistent that it was at St James' chapel where 'the bodies or bones of the men slain in the said field be brought and buried'. Yet whereas Henry VIII had stated that Bosworth Field was known also as 'Dadlington Field', the churchwardens seem to have taken little interest in having the battle renamed for their own benefit, preferring instead to keep the battle's name of Bosworth Field in their letter appealing for alms. Perhaps by 1511 Bosworth had already become the accepted name for the battle.

Though unsubstantiated by modern archaeological investigation, there is a wealth of anecdotal evidence of discoveries of the remains of those killed in battle being unearthed around Dadlington over the centuries. William Burton described how it was 'in the churchyard whereof many of the dead bodies (slain in the said battle) were buried'. In his history of Leicestershire, published in 1811, John Nichols further noted that 'indented spaces of ground, probably the graves of victims in this bloody battle, are visible in several spots' around Dadlington. A succession of finds seem to suggest a number of mass burials being found in its churchyard. In 1868, when a grave was being prepared to the right of the entrance gate in the churchyard of the chapel, 'a quantity of human bones' was uncovered two feet beneath the ground, 'many of which were of full size and in a good state of preservation. 'Amongst them were counted as many as 20 skulls', with another account of the find describing how the layer of bones 'was a yard thick'. When a carpenter was employed in the restoration of Dadlington church in 1889, a compact mass of bones was discovered in the north-eastern end of the churchyard. In 1950, the sexton at Dadlington chapel uncovered layers of compacted skeletons when digging a grave on the right of the church path just inside the gate, the same location of the 1868 finds. Reports of other burial finds in the local area were noted by John Nichols in his history of Hinckley, published in 1782, that recorded in the field known as Crown Hill 'whence gravel is sometimes fetched to repair the highways . . . there have been dug up many skeletons, which are said to be very common on breaking fresh ground'. Other local testimonies, unfortunately unproven and now lacking comprehensive evidence, include a 'man in armour' being unearthed two feet below ground on land belonging to Stoke Lodge in Stoke Golding around 1900, which was reported to have 'crumbled to dust' soon after.

If the battle was fought around the surrounding area of Dadlington, it seems also clear that the tradition that Henry was crowned at nearby Stoke Golding on 'Crown Hill' suitably fits this assertion. Tradition records that villagers scaled the tower of St Margaret's church to watch the battle; the fields below, lying off Fenn Lanes and stretching across to Dadlington towards the right, are clearly visible, unlike the fields surrounding Ambion Hill. The evidence of place names is of central importance to understanding where exactly Henry may have been crowned after the battle. The village was called Stoke in the fifteenth century, with its name being changed to 'Stoke Manfield' in a subsidy roll of 1505, finally settling upon its present name sometime between 1563 and 1576, when 'Golding', the term itself suggestive of a crowning, was added. The name 'Crown Hill' can be traced back in local records to the early seventeenth century, with one field being called 'Crown Hill Field' and another 'Le Gulden' in a document detailing the sale of the lordship in 1605. The recent discovery of a list of lands and field names from the 1480s indicates that the same piece of land, an open field jutting out in a triangular shape, was known as 'Garbrodfelde', revealing that its name had been deliberately changed to reflect its role in the battle. The same document also mentions, in the western end of the parish, an area of land known as 'the brown heath' that Peter Foss has suggested local records accurately locate nearby Foxcover Farm; it is perhaps telling that one of the earliest mentions of the battle, contained in a genealogy, records Henry as defeating Richard 'super brownehethe'.

The document also contains numerous mentions of another significant feature, a quagmire or fen hole known as the 'Holow', located in the valley below Crown Hill on the boundary of Stoke Golding and Dadlington. Foss's exhaustive researches into the local documentary records and topography of the area have revealed references to several 'fen holes' around the boundaries of Shenton, Dadlington, Stoke and Upton in an area one and a half miles from Dadlington, stemming from tributaries of the Sence river, including an area of wetland on the Shenton and Upton parishes area known as 'Foomeers', which Foss suggests derived from the word 'foul mere' – it was known as 'fowlismeres' in 1307, also indicating that it was a permanent feature on the landscape. Evidence of wetland terrain and fen holes in the area brings with it proof that, as most of the contemporary sources of the battle agree, the battle had been fought alongside a marsh.

The problem of locating the exact site of the marsh is that so much of the landscape has subsequently changed in the intervening centuries. While the landscape would have been open countryside in the fifteenth century, the ground has since been divided into fields with fences and hedgerows, with woods having grown up across the area surrounding Ambion Hill. The construction of the Ashby-de-la-Zouche canal in the late eighteenth century, bisecting straight across the land, together with the construction of the Nuneaton to Ashby-de-la-Zouche railway line, with its cuttings and embankments, have radically altered the appearance of the battle site. Yet dramatic changes to the land began as early as the sixteenth century, with its marshy landscape being drained, to the extent that by 1577 the chronicler Raphael Hollinshed stated that the once marshy site of the battle 'is grown to be firm ground by reason of ditches cast'. This had taken place as early as 1530, when the Dadlington Court Roll records that 'Redmore dyke should be scoured before All Saints on pain of 12d'. While the testing of soil samples in the area has detected where alluvium and peat, signs of former areas of marshland, had gathered, creating a virtual map of the appearance of the landscape's original medieval appearance, once again the surviving documentary evidence points to the fact that there must have been a marsh and fen lands in the area known as Redemore, its plain located west of Dadlington and north of Stoke Golding. In particular, the surviving manorial records for Dadlington, surviving only in a transcript made by William Burton in the seventeenth century, make clear that 'le Fenmore', which must have been one of the names for the site of the marshy Fen hole, was located between 'Dadlington, Upton and Shenton'.

One source also mentions another notable feature that marked out the landscape at the time of the battle. According to the 'Ballad of Lady Bessie', the Duke of Norfolk retreated during the battle of the vanguards, and 'went up to a wind-mill and stood upon a hill so high' where he was confronted by Sir John Savage who killed him on the spot. Standing out across the plain, this windmill would have been the most visible feature on the landscape as the armies confronted each other. The windmill is mentioned in an agreement concerning tithes in Dadlington made in 1479, six years before the battle, where it is described as a 'new windmill in the same Lordship'. It seems that the windmill was demolished in the sixteenth century, with a later chancery document dating from the reign of Elizabeth I revealing that by the 1570s the mill had been 'taken down and sold unto divers persons unknown the timber and stones of the said mill' by Robert Holte of Mancetter and his wife Katherine. It is worth noting that the owner of the windmill and surrounding land was Lord Ferrers of Chartley. One of his ancestors, an earlier Lord Ferrers, had fought and died on Richard's side, and there is evidence in the stained glass at Merevale church of his coat of arms, possibly a memorial to Ferrers' death in the battle. It raises the question of whether Richard had been guided by Ferrers himself to pitch his tents around Ambion, thanks to Ferrers' unique local knowledge of the area.

To the varied evidence supplied by the surviving archives and local documentation, recent archaeological finds uncovered by the latest battlefield survey undertaken by the Battlefields Trust and led by Professor Glenn Foard supply significant new information that confirms Bosworth was fought not at Ambion Hill, but in fact nearly two miles south-west, around the location first suggested by Peter Foss in his groundbreaking work. In March 2009 the first cannon shot, a 30mm lead ball, was discovered in a field off Fenn Lanes; soon the surrounding area yielded up over thirty similar projectiles. The discovery of so many cannon shot, more than has ever been found on any European fifteenth-century battlefield, provides new insights into the methods of warfare used at Bosworth. Most of the lead round shot unearthed at Bosworth ranges in diameter from less than 30mm up to 94mm. Some of the cannon shot are of solid lead, though others contain an iron cube or pebble or large pieces of flint at their core. It remains uncertain whether this was done to save lead or in an attempt to reduce the weight of the shot, allowing it to travel further, or perhaps to reduce the pressures placed on the gun barrel of the cannon, fashioned as they were at the time from wrought iron rather than cast iron or bronze as casting technology did not develop until the sixteenth century. From the finds uncovered so far, there are enough different diameters present that there must have been at least ten pieces of artillery and two hand cannons at the battlefield. The largest shot would have been fired from the largest field artillery piece in common use in the following centuries, while some of the cannon balls show evidence of having been fired from an octagonal rather than a round barrel, with flat edges having been scored onto the lead as they were fired from the cannon.

While the scatter of cannon balls evidently indicates that action was spread around the fields either side of Fenn Lanes, until more detailed analysis is conducted into which shot can be matched up with the type of guns that fired them, they cannot reveal exactly the positions of both armies. The fact that both sides employed the use of artillery has long been apparent from the written sources, with Henry's Act of Attainder against Richard's supporters detailing how the king's army was 'mightily armed and defenced with all manner of arms, as guns, bows, arrows, spears, glaives, axes, and all other manner of articles apt or needful to give and cause mighty battle'. The 'Ballad of Bosworth Field' reveals how Richard's army had at least 140 'serpentines' chained together in a row, with as many bombards. Commynes also provides evidence that Henry also had been given artillery by Charles VIII, while he would have had the opportunity to obtain ordnance along his journey from castles in Wales and at Stafford, Tamworth and Lichfield, where, as the 'Ballad of Bosworth Field' recorded, he had been greeted by a volley of cannon fire. The fact that Sir Richard Guildford had been appointed as Henry's master of the ordnance on 8 August, a day after landing in Dale, suggests that Henry's forces brought artillery with them.

With both sides firing upon each other, the cannon balls could have been fired from either direction along Fenn Lanes; recent experiments in firing similar sized weapons has demonstrated that cannon shot could travel over a kilometre, bouncing for a significant distance from their first impact on the ground. Added to this, the fields where the finds were discovered have been extensively ploughed over the centuries, bringing with it the prospect that the shot would have been moved from where they originally came to rest at the battle. While this does not diminish the importance of the discovery of these remarkable archaeological finds in reassessing how medieval warfare was fought, a sensible note of caution should also be applied when using the cannon shot to pinpoint the exact site of the battle, even if they do correspond closely with all the evidence that pinpoints 'Redemore' to the fields surrounding Fenn Lanes beneath Stoke Golding and Dadlington.

The most celebrated find of the recent investigations find has been the silver-gilt livery badge depicting a boar, roughly two centimetres in length and a centimetre in width, that has been heralded as 'a vital clue' 'as to the exact spot where Richard III died'. The figure of the boar was certainly Richard's personal device which most likely would have been worn by a member of his retinue. On the back of the badge is evidence of its fastening in a figure of eight design, suggesting that it may have been held in place by a pin. The boar badge was discovered in a field close to a footpath off Fenn Lanes Farm. Nearby is a ditch and evidence of the possible 'Fen Hole', lying in the parish of Dadlington. Whether we should be confident enough to suggest that the discovery of the boar badge 'has helped to pinpoint the likely site of King Richard's death', however, is to place upon the archaeological evidence a weight of expectation that cannot necessarily be sustained. Though the fact that the badge is fashioned from silver gilt suggests that it must have been worn by a soldier of substance, possibly from the gentry class and one of the 'choice' men with whom Richard had decided to surround himself, it is entirely possible that the badge could have come loose as he fled the battle. The discovery of a broken sword-pommel nearby, however, does suggest that this must have been an area in which hand-to-hand combat took place, in addition to the greatest concentration of cannon shot being found in the neighbouring fields.

This note of caution is highlighted by an equally significant find, a lead badge clearly depicting a blazing sun, the Yorkist badge of the sun in splendour that also features on the back of the Bosworth crucifix, that was discovered in an entirely separate location to the boar badge, between Mill Lane and a field known formerly as Mill Field, the likely site of the Dadlington windmill. It was here also that a silver gilt heraldic badge of an eagle grasping a snake in its beak was discovered. Other artefacts that have come to light in the archaeological investigations include a double petard of Charles the Bold of Burgundy (1467–77), was discovered near the Fenn Lanes ford. Tantalisingly, the find is suggestive of the presence of Burgundian troops at the battle; after all, Maximilian's agent Juan de Salazar had been present at the battle. Yet again, the assumption is not so clear cut: Burgundian coins were legal tender in England, so the coin itself does not prove that it belonged to a Burgundian solider, although two other Burgundian coins were also recovered, both from the Ambion Hill area, which suggests that they may have come from Richard's camp.

The recent archaeological investigations have nevertheless wielded a wealth of new information about the battle, adding to what has already been a ferocious debate about where the battle was fought. No doubt it will last for decades to come, as new finds are uncovered and future investigative technology develops. If anything, it proves that the debate around Bosworth or 'Redesmore' remains alive and well. Long may it continue. Over 500 years since the battle was fought, in many ways Bosworth remains so close but yet so far from our own imaginations. Part of the responsibility for this remains with the paucity of original documentary evidence, and what there is remains open to interpretation.

There is, however, one last clue to the battle's location that has puzzled historians for centuries. When Henry's victory was proclaimed in York by the Windsor herald three days after the battle, Richard was described as having been slain at a 'place named Sandeford'. The proclamation was not known for its accuracy, issued in the confusion of what had actually occurred: it wrongly included Thomas, Earl of Surrey in the roll call of the dead. The citizens of York certainly ignored the location, knowing as they did that the fighting had occurred at 'the field of Redemore'. Subsequently historians have sought to locate where this 'sandy ford' might be, whether it represents a sandy area of ground in the area of 'redemore'. Yet medieval battles could be named not only by their geographic location, but also by their iconic significance. One of the first mentions of the battle of Towton, for instance, recorded it as being Northfield or Palm Sunday battle. The herald's proclamation was not just second-hand news, but an official statement of the new king's will and intent and how, importantly, he wanted his victory to be recognised. Sandeford need not necessarily be a place, rather a representation of how Henry wished his 'victorious field' to be viewed. In fact, Sandeford was a long-established name for a battle, made popular through prophecies associated with Thomas the Rhymer of Erceldoun from the thirteenth century. In one, it was described how there would be a terrible battle at Sandeford, which is described as the 'last battle'. There is a strong link between prophecy and Henry's expected arrival, particularly from Welsh Bards. Is it possible that in using 'Sandeford' in his proclamation, Henry was using bardic traditions to reinforce his new kingship? Ultimately, we cannot know. Perhaps Bernard André was right; in the end, we can only draw a blank.

POSTSCRIPT

•◆•

In the late summer of 2012, an archaeological team co-ordinated by the University of Leicester was granted permission to dig several trenches in the car park in Leicester where Richard III's body was believed to have been buried. In the far corner they discovered a skeleton in what was identified as the site of the choir of the nave of Greyfriars Church.

The skeleton, lying around 26¾ inches (68cm) below modern ground level, had been placed in a hurriedly made grave that was irregular in shape, with sloping sides and a concave base, and too short for the skeleton to be fully laid out inside it. Its lower limbs were fully extended, suggesting that perhaps the legs had been laid in the grave first, yet the torso of the remains had been twisted slightly, and the skull had been buried noticeably higher than the rest of the skeleton, propped up against the north-west corner of the grave, as if the body had to be squeezed into the grave pit by bending the neck. The mouth of the body must have fallen open as the remains were being interred, for the skull was uncovered with its jaw hanging open. Rather than the arms lying by the sides of the body, as is the case with most medieval burials, the lower left arm had been draped over the abdomen, the right arm laid over the torso, and the hands crossed, evidence of them possibly having been tied together, right hand over left, by the hip.

As the bones were unearthed by trowel and brush strokes, it became apparent that the skeleton was missing both of its feet. However, it seems that the disappearance of the feet in their entirety can be explained by later disturbance caused by the construction of a Victorian building merely metres away. As the skeleton was removed for further examination, it also became clear that this person had not died of natural causes. The lead archaeologist, Dr Richard Buckley, quickly recognised that the body had suffered 'critical injuries'. When the team announced the discovery of the body to an eager gathering of the press on 12 September 2012 he explained that the skeleton showed signs of 'near death trauma' that 'appears to be consistent with injury from battle'. According to Dr Jo Appleby, Professor of Human Bioarchaeology at Leicester University, 'the skull had a minimum of two injuries. The first was a small penetrating wound to the top of the head that had dislodged two small flaps of bone on the skull's interior. The second was a much larger wound to the occipital bone (or base of the skull): a slice had been cut off the skull at the side and back. This is consistent with a bladed instrument of some sort . . . it should be noted that this did not cut through the neck and that the skull was in its correct anatomical position when excavated.'

No images of the skeleton were released while the university carried out further tests on the bones. On 4 February 2013, at a press conference at Leicester University, it was announced that not only did radio-carbon dating suggest that the remains were those of a male who had lived between 1455 and 1540, testing also showed that the individual had enjoyed a protein-rich diet, with high levels of marine protein detected in the bones. Crucially, DNA tests also matched the bones to the nearest surviving relative of Richard III.

Analysis of the skeleton had confirmed that the individual was male, in his late 20s to late 30s, with a 'gracile or feminine build'. Yet, perhaps most strikingly, from the moment the remains were uncovered, it was clear that the skeleton demonstrated a noticeable curvature of the spine or scoliosis that had most likely occurred at the time of puberty. 'The analysis of the skeleton proved that it was an adult male, but with an unusually slender, almost feminine, build for a man,' Dr Jo Appleby announced at the conference. 'This is in keeping with historical sources which describe Richard as being of very slender build. There is, however, no indication that he had a withered arm – both arms were of a similar size and both were used normally during life.' Without the spinal abnormality, it is estimated that the individual was roughly 5 feet 8 inches (1.72m) high. This would have been above average height for a medieval male; however, the curve in the spine would have taken a significant amount off his apparent height when standing. The spinal disability would have meant that the individual stood up to one foot

(0.3m) shorter, with his right shoulder higher than his left. 'Taken as a whole,' Dr Appleby reported, 'the skeletal evidence provides a highly convincing case for identification as Richard III'.

Ten wounds had been identified on the remains. Eight had been inflicted to the skull area, with two elsewhere on the body. Of course, these wounds are ones that were severe enough to have cut through bone, thereby leaving a permanent mark or damage to the skeleton itself. There could have been other wounds to the body – through soft tissue and organs – of which there is no longer any trace.

The most noticeable wound is at the back of the head, where an entire slice of bone has been sheathed, leaving a flap of bone hanging off still attached to the skull. The slice wound seems consistent with other similar remains found in gravepits at other medieval battle sites, which suggests massive cranial trauma caused by one particular weapon – the halberd. The weapon, mounted on a pole around 6 feet (1.8m) tall, consisted of an axe blade with a spike at its top together with a hook for grappling with and pulling down combatants. It was able to cut clean through bone without leaving any splinters, as can be witnessed on the Greyfriars skull. We can only speculate, but the Burgundian chronicler Molinet describes how, when Richard found himself stuck fast in the marsh into which his horse had leapt, 'one of the Welshmen then came after him and struck him dead with a halberd.' There is also an intriguing line in a poem by the Welsh poet, Guto'r Glyn, written shortly after Bosworth, praising the efforts of Sir Rhys ap Thomas during the battle. One stanza relates how 'He slew the boar, shaved his head' (Lladd y baedd, eilliodd ei ben). This may demonstrate that an understanding of exactly how Richard had been killed, with the back of his head being literally shaved off by the blow from a halberd, was already common knowledge among the Welshmen in Henry Tudor's army who had witnessed the king's final moments.

The halberd wound opening up the skull would have certainly caused almost instant loss of consciousness, with death following shortly afterwards, especially given that the axe blade would have cut into the brain tissue. If the blade had penetrated 2¾ inches (7cm) into the brain, death would have been instantaneous. If this injury had not quite killed Richard, another visible wound would certainly have done so. To the left of the slice wound, in the base of the skull is a smaller injury caused by a bladed weapon, most likely a sword. We know exactly how far the sword had been thrust through the skull, as a mark is present on the inner surface of the skull, directly opposite the entry point, a distance of 4⅛ inches (10.5cm). In effect, the blade had been thrust straight through Richard's brain and did not stop until it impacted with the bone on the other side of the skull.

Three further shallow wounds have been identified on the outer surface of the vault of the skull. Although only slight wounds that shaved away a small area of bone, highly consistent with where the blade of a weapon such as a sword or halberd, the wounds would not have been immediately fatal, but would have bled heavily. More noticeable is a small rectangular or diamond-shaped wound that has pierced through the top of the skull, leaving a visible hole, though not deep enough to have been fatal. It would have been inflicted by a small spiked weapon; the aperture of the hole in the skull is too small to have been caused by a halberd or a poleaxe, but instead seems more likely to have been the result of a rondel dagger, which often bore a diamond-shaped, four-sided blade, being thrust down or pressed into Richard's skull.

Matching this skull wound, there is also small rectangular 'punch mark' on the cheekbone, just below the left eye. Given the delicate nature of the bone around this area, the fact that the wound did not cause more damage suggests that it must have been performed from behind, possibly as someone grappled with Richard, perhaps attempting to stab him in the eye. Strikingly, however, the 'punch mark' is so similar in size and shape to the head wound that it is likely to have been caused by the same weapon that inflicted the square wound that cuts through the top of the skull.

There is also a small cut mark on the lower jaw, caused by a bladed weapon, consistent with a knife or dagger. Of course, none of the wounds to the skull could have been inflicted while Richard was wearing his helmet. Either he had lost his helmet in battle, or else it had been forcibly removed. It may be possible that the cut mark on the jaw was caused by the chin strap to Richard's helmet being deliberately cut away to expose the king's bare head. In this case, Richard's death would have been more of an execution on the battlefield than the result of an injury sustained while fighting. Perhaps Richard, having been brought down off his horse in the marsh, found himself surrounded by Henry

Tudor's Welsh troops. As he continued to fight, he was attacked from behind and held; perhaps his visor was lifted, allowing for the dagger to be gouged into his cheek. Incapacitated, the leather straps of his helmet were forcibly cut away, which also inflicted cuts to his jaw, nicking the jawbone. With his helmet removed, Richard was now at the mercy of his captives: we cannot know the exact sequence of events, but as the halberd axe came crashing down onto the back of Richard's head, before the sword thrust through his brain, death would have been at least swift. Then, perhaps in some kind of ritualistic fashion, the rondel dagger that had been used to inflict the wound to Richard's face was pressed down into the top of his exposed and bloodied skull.

Richard's body would later have been stripped of its armour and, as the Crowland chronicler reported, 'many other insults were heaped upon it,' though the chronicler added, somewhat curiously, these were 'not exactly in accordance with the laws of humanity'. The wounds to the body of the skeleton may reveal what the chronicler had in mind. The two wounds on the postcranial skeleton are likely to have been inflicted after armour had been removed from the body. One, a cut mark on a rib, did not penetrate the ribcage; the other, located on the right pelvis, would have been caused by the blade of a knife or dagger, that must have had been thrust from behind in an upward movement. According to the university's research: 'detailed three-dimensional reconstruction of the pelvis has indicated that this injury was caused by a thrust through the right buttock, not far from the midline of the body'. The sources recording the events after the battle concur, describing how Richard's naked body was flung over the back of a horse as it was carried back to Leicester. Could this have been the perfect opportunity for someone along the route to take a dagger and thrust it into Richard's corpse, performing the ultimate 'humiliation injury'?

What is clear from the Greyfriars skeleton is that, unlike other grave finds of those who died in other battles during the civil wars, such as the mass graves discovered near Towton, the face of the victim had not been touched after death. Unlike many of the Towton deaths, whose faces were deliberately destroyed or hacked apart as part of the 'humiliation injuries' performed to ensure that the bodies might go unrecognised and therefore never returned to their families, it is clear that Richard's face was to be preserved intact. His body, going on public display in Leicester, needed to be recognised as the body of the king. Richard III was dead: there would be no return for the Yorkist king.

The remarkable discovery of Richard's remains beneath a car park in 2012 reminds us that while history can only be the study of the past that survives, we can always hope to make more discoveries, unearthing further relics of the past, whether from the ground or in the archives. The story of Bosworth remains very much alive.

paucis pugnā intermiscent. Tunc Oxoniensis una in parte, confertis turmis, hostes impetū facit: et alij in parte altera, facto
cuneo, simul urgent.

Dum ita inter primas acies utrinq̃ certatur: Ricardus ubi ab speculatoribus, procul, Henricum esse: deinde propius
ac certius cognoscit: inflammatus ira conci-
tat calcaribus equū atq̃ in ipsum, ex altero latere
ultra aciem, ingreditur. Sensit contra se Henricus Ricardum ire:
et quia omnis spes salutis in armis erat: se aciem avide offert.
Ricardus primo impetu aliquot interfectis: et vexillo Henrici humi deiecto: una cum Guillermo Brandon vexillario
cum Ioanne Cheyne homine fortissimo: ima-
gra sui in terra tradidit: etiam sibi ferro ubiq̃ faciens
sustinuit tn Henricus impetum diutius: quam etiam sui putabant:
qui victoria iam penitus diffidebant: donec Guillermus
Stanley cum tribus armatorū milibus: suppetias tulit:
tunc reliquis in fugam coiectis Ricar-
dus inter confertissimos hostes: pugnans confoditur. Interea Oxoniensis post breve certamen: ceteros et qui in prima
acie pugnabant: in fugam vertit: quorum magnus numerus
in ipsa fuga interficitur. Sed multo plures qui iuvari Ricardum secuti erant: facile abstinerent: quippe qui
no salutem sed exitium suo quo obeunt: precabantur.
ex parte Ricardi occubuere in eo praelio circiter mille homines.
inter quos ex nobilitate fuerant: Ioannes Dux Northfolchiæ:
Gualterus Deuereux Dns Ferys: Robertus Brakynbury: Ricardus
capturæ ex alij. Captivorū uero numerus maximus fuit:
quoniam occiso Ricardo: in Henrici potestatem
ultro se tradiderunt: quorū maior pars uino et Ricardo
sponte fecisset: sine periculo: illud ipsum sibi
potuisset et nobilitate ipsorū capti sunt: Henricus Comes Northū-
briæ: et Thomas Comes Surrū. Hic diu post in turri Londinensi
captivus servatus est: illi statim venia est data. ex parte Henrici
Brandon: qui Henrici militare signū ferebat. Dies pugnæ fuit
undecimo kl Septembris, anno dni M. cccc. octogesimo quinto.

+ ihesus Maria × + × ihesus Maria ᵈ ꝯ L·xx·x̄j̄·

(ut ꝓhibent)

Dimicatum est circiter duas horas. Ricardus postᵃ̄ sibi salutem fuga parere ... am qui circa eum erant: ubi uideret militem langui-
de se sequitur ... arma mouere: ac alios clam ꝓelio excedere: fran-
don suspicari portati sunt eum ad fugam: et cum ia manifesto res moli-
nata esset: equū uelocem obtulerunt ... Ille uero qui sciebat populum sibi
infensum esse abiecta spe ... fertur respondisse ipso eo die
aut bellorū aut uite finem facturum ... Adeo magna audacia: magnaꝗ
uis animi in eo fuit: qui ꝓpea certo sciens illum diem aut regnum
sibi deinceps ... daturū ... aut adempturū:
... corona regia sup galeam: usus in certamen descendit ...

Henricus ꝓ adepta uictoria: incredibili letitia affectus: in ꝓximum
collem se recepit: ubi postꝗ collaudauit milites: iussitꝗ curari uulne-
ratos: magnas omnibus proceribus gratias egit: ꝓmisitꝗ se me-
morem beneficioꝗ fore. Sed cum milites eum regem magno cla-
more consalutarent: ac inter spolia, interim corona Ricardi reperta
esset: tunc ita ... acclamantibᵘ̄ omnibus. Thomas
Stanley eius capiti illam coronam imposuit · Post hec collectis
omnibus sarcinis: cum uictore exercitu: ad Leycestriam oppidum ...
sub uesperū illius diei: peruenit: ubi ... reficiendi ... a labore
militem: seꝗ ad iter Londinū uersus parandi ... duos dies moratus
est ... Interim corpus Ricardi omnibus indumentis nudatū, ac dorso equi
re supinē impositum: uia ex parte equi: capite cum brachiis: et ex altera
tibiis ... pendentibus. Leycestriā deportatur: spectaculum sane mise-
rabile ... sed hominis uita dignissimum, postꝗ biduo omnibus aspice-
re uolentibus in publico stetit: in cenouia fratrū ordinis diui francisci
sepultura demandatum est · Regnauit annos duos: et totidem menses:
supra ꝗ diem unū. Statura fuit pusilla: corpore deformi: altero humero
uo eminentiori: facie breui ac truculenta: dum cogitabundus stabat: in
ferius labium ex consuetudine assidue mordebat: quasi ita fera in eo corpu-
sculo nouita in se ipsam seuiret: simul pugionem quem semp gestabat:
deꝓtera manu ... ꝗ uagina recondebat: condebat ꝗ identidem. Ingeniū
uero habuit acutū: sagax: uersutum: ad simulandū atꝗ dissimulandū
aptum: animū aut ... ac ferocem: qui ... se etiā in morte nō defecit:
quam desertutus assui: potius subire uoluit: quā ꝗ turpe fuga: incerti ... for-
situs post paulo morbus uel suplitio interiturus uite parceret. Hunc ...
... animū, magnitudo pralii animi Ricardo dedit: ne regnū flagitio quesitū
diutius possideret. Que res aliis documento sit: qui sibi potentiam et honores
ꝗ malas artes ... nituntur. ✝ A͞men Amen Amen
＋ Benedictus Deus, et d͞n͞s n͞r Iesus Christus. Amen ✝

Polydore Vergil's Manuscript account of the Battle of Bosworth,
Urbini Latini 498 fos. 434v–435 © 2013 Biblioteca Apostolica Vaticana

BIBLIOGRAPHIC ESSAY

Chapter 1: Fortune's Wheel

The family background of the Tudors is covered in R.A. Griffiths and R.S. Thomas, *The Making of the Tudor Dynasty* (Stroud, 1985), chapters 1 and 2. Henry VI's reign and its decline is covered in extensive detail by R. Griffiths, *The Reign of Henry VI* (London, 1981), B. Wolffe, *Henry VI* (London, 1981) and J.L. Watts, *Henry VI and the Politics of Kingship* (Cambridge, 1996). Owen Tudor's relationship with Katherine of Valois is discussed in Griffiths and Thomas, chapter 3; S.B. Chrimes, *Henry VII* (London, 1972) chapter 1 and Appendix A and R.A. Griffiths, 'Queen Katherine of Valois and a missing statute of the realm', *Law Quarterly Review*, XCIII (1977), pp. 248–58. Owen Tudor's arrest is described in Tyrell and Nicholas (eds.), *A Chronicle of London* (1827), p. 123 with further details in *Foedera*, ed. T. Rymer (20 vols, 1704–35), vol. X, pp. 685–6, 709–10 and *Calendar of Patent Rolls (CPR) Henry VI*, vol. III, pp. 182, 225, 283, 285, 344. For Edmund and Jasper Tudor's upbringing see J. Blacman, *Henry the Sixth*, ed. M.R. James (Cambridge, 1919). The Tudor's rise to power is covered in R.S. Thomas, 'The political career, estates and connection of Jasper Tudor, Earl of Pembroke and duke of Bedford (d. 1495)' (University of Wales, Swansea, Ph.D. thesis, 1971); H.T. Evans, *Wales and the Wars of the Roses* (Cambridge, 1915); Griffiths, *Reign of Henry VI* and Griffiths and Thomas, *Making of the Tudor Dynasty*, chapters 3–5.

The course of the civil wars of the fifteenth century is best covered by J. Gillingham, *The Wars of the Roses* (London, 1981) and C. Ross, *The Wars of the Roses* (London, 1981). The most modern popular treatment is T. Royle, *The Wars of the Roses* (London, 2009). For the campaigns, their impact on society, and the nature of war in the fifteenth century, A. Goodman, *The Wars of the Roses: Military Activity and English Society, 1452–97* (London, 1981) and the same author's *The Wars of the Roses: The Soldiers' Experience* (Stroud, 2005) are invaluable, while the individual battles are chronicled in P.A. Haigh,

Military Campaigns of the Wars of the Roses (Stroud, 1995). For Richard, Duke of York, see P.A. Johnson, *Duke Richard of York 1411–1460* (Oxford, 1988).

Margaret Beaufort's background and life is covered in M.K. Jones and M.G. Underwood, *The King's Mother. Lady Margaret Beaufort, Countess of Richmond and Derby* (Cambridge, 1992) and M.K. Jones, 'Richard III and Lady Margaret Beaufort – a re-assessment' in P. Hammond (ed.), *Richard III: Loyalty, Lordship and Law* (London, 1986). Details of Henry Tudor's early life can be found in B. André, 'Vita Henrici Septimi' in *Memorials of King Henry VII*, ed. J. Gairdiner (London, 1858) and H. Owen and J.B. Blakeway, *A History of Shrewsbury* (2 vols, London, 1825). John Fisher's recollections of Henry's birth are printed in *The English Works of John Fisher*, part I (Early English Text Society, extra series, XXVII, 1876) and also J. Gairdiner (ed.), *Letters and Papers illustrative of the Reigns of Richard III and Henry VII*, vol. I (London, 1861), pp. 422–3.

Chapter 2: To Conquer or Die

Jasper Tudor's fortunes and rise to prominence at court can be tracked in the grants awarded to him registered in the patent rolls: *CPR 1452–61*, pp.130, 180–1, 267, 486–7, 494, 532–3, 534, 550, 565, 574, supplemented by R.S. Thomas's thesis. The looming conflict between the houses of Lancaster and York is covered in the works by Gillingham and Royle. The battle of Wakefield has recently been reassessed by H. Cox, *The Battle of Wakefield Revisited* (2010). The account of Owen Tudor's death is in the *Chronicle of William Gregory, skinner*, ed. J. Gairdiner, *The historical collections of a citizen of London in the fifteenth century* (Camden Society, new series XVII, 1876), p. 211. Jasper Tudor's letter is printed in W.W.E. Wynne, 'Historical Papers (Puleston)' in *Archaeologia Cambrensis* I (1846) pp. 145–6. The Yorkists' act of attainder against Jasper Tudor is printed in *Rotuli Parliamentorum* (6 vols., Record Commission, 1767–7), vol. V, pp. 478–81. The grant of Henry Tudor's wardship to Sir William Herbert is recorded in *CPR 1461–67*, p. 114 while details of his upbringing can be found in Vergil, p. 134 (full details in the notes to chapter 3 below), *CPR 1485–94*, p. 332 and André, pp. 12–13.

Edward IV's reign is best covered in C. Ross, *Edward IV* (London, 1974), H. Kleineke, *Edward IV* (2009) and C. Scofield, *The Life and Reign of Edward the Fourth* (2 vols., London, 1923). Many of the principal sources from Edward IV's reign can be found in *Edward IV: A Sourcebook*, ed. K. Dockray (Stroud, 1999). For the most recent account of the battle of Towton and its context, see G. Goodwin, *Fatal Colours: The Battle of Towton 1461*

(London, 2011). The Lancastrian alliance with Louis XI is covered in Scofield I, pp. 261–5, 315–18, while payments by the French king to Jasper Tudor are to be found in Bibliothèque nationale de France (BnF) Fonds Français 6970 fo. 501v, Fonds Français 20,496 fo. 91, with a later pension from October 1469 to September 1470 recorded in Archives nationales (AN) KK 62 fo. 51v and BnF Fonds Français 20,685 pp. 383, 461, 475, 493 and 499 for later years. Thomas's thesis, pp. 209–14, describes Jasper Tudor's raiding in Wales, with his escape documented in National Library of Wales Mostyn MS fo.323v.

Edward IV's marriage to Elizabeth Woodville and the later breakdown between Edward IV and Warwick is covered in Ross, *Edward IV*, chapters 5–7. For Clarence and the re-adeption, M. Hicks, *False, Fleeting, Perjur'd Clarence: George, Duke of Clarence, 1449–1478* (Gloucester, 1980). The evidence for Henry Tudor's movements at Edgecote as described by Richard Corbet can be found in Owen and Blakeway, *History of Shrewsbury*, vol. I, p. 248 and in Westminster Abbey Muniments (WAM) MS 5472 fos. 41v, 43r, 44r, 44v. Margaret's attempts to reconcile her son to the new regime are in WAM 5472 fos. 45v–47r. The details of Henry's visit to Westminster are taken from WAM 12183 fos. 19r–19v, 20v–21r, 21v, 22r, while the account of Henry VI's meeting with Henry Tudor is from Vergil, p. 135.

Chapter 3: Exile

For a detailed account of Edward IV's return to claim the throne in 1471 see *The Historie of the Arrivall of King Edward IV A.D. 1471*, ed. J. Bruce (London, Camden Society Series 1, 1838). For Somerset's visit to Margaret Beaufort and Stafford's actions see Jones and Underwood, *The King's Mother*, pp. 54–5, and WAM 12183 fo. 50, WAM 12189 fo. 58. Details of the battle at Barnet have been taken from *Great Chronicle of London*, ed. A.H. Thomas and I.D. Thornley (London, 1938), p. 216 and printed in *Three Chronicles of the Reign of Edward IV*, (ed.) K. Dockray (Stroud, 1988), p. 16. Barnet and Tewkesbury are given full treatment in P.W. Hammond, *The Battles of Barnet and Tewkesbury* (Gloucester, 1990) and Goodman, *The Wars of the Roses*, pp. 79–83. Sir William Cary's comments on Prince Edward's death are in W. Campbell (ed.), *Materials for a History of the Reign of Henry VII* (2 vols., Rolls Series, 1873–7), abbreviated as *Materials*, vol. I, p. 138. For Henry VI's death see *Warkworth's Chronicle*, p. 18, *Great Chronicle*, p. 220 and W.J. White, 'The Death and Burial of Henry VI', *The Ricardian* VI (1982).

Jasper Tudor's flight through Wales is recorded in *Leland's Itinerary in Wales*, (ed.) L.T. Smith (London, 1906), p. 66 and R. Griffiths, *Sir Rhys ap*

Thomas and his family: a study in the Wars of the Roses and early Tudor politics, (University of Wales Press, 1993), p. 179. His and Henry's arrival in France is covered by Alain Bouchard, *Grandes Chroniques de Bretaigne*, vol. II, p. 420; Vergil, p. 155; Commynes, vol. II, p. 234 (full details below). Sir John Paston's remarks are in J. Gardiner (ed.), *The Paston Letters 1422–1509*, (6 vols., 1904) vol. III, p. 17. Duke Francis's reaction to Jasper and Henry's arrival is in Vergil, pp. 158–9.

Key accounts of Henry's exile appear only in Polydore Vergil's *Anglia Historica*, of which the most accessible translation remains *Three Books of Polydore Vergil's English History*, ed. H. Ellis (Camden Society, 1844). B.A. Pocquet du Haut-Jusse, *Francois II, duc de Bretagne et l'Angleterre* (Paris, 1929), J.L.A. Calmette and G. Perinelle, *Louis XI et l'Angleterre* (Paris, 1930), J. Allanic, *Le Prisonnier de la Tour d'Elven, ou la Jeunesse du Roy Henri VII d'Angleterre* (Vannes, 1909) and H. Marsille, *Vannes au Moyen Age* (Vannes, 1982) are the key French studies. The influence of Henry's early life is discussed in R.A. Griffiths, *King and Country: England and Wales in the Fifteenth Century* (London, 1991) chapter 7 and in A.E. Goodman, 'Henry VII and Christian renewal', *Studies in Church History* XVII (1981), pp. 115–25.

The Earl of Oxford's life has recently been explored in J. Ross, *John de Vere, Thirteenth Earl of Oxford (1442–1513): 'The Foremost Man of the Kingdom'* (Boydell, 2011) but see also C.S. Scofield, 'The early life of John de Vere, thirteenth Earl of Oxford', *English Historical Review* XXIX (1914), pp. 228–45. Richard's treatment of the earl's mother is explored in M. Hicks, 'The Last Days of the Countess of Oxford', *English Historical Review* CII (1988). Oxford's movements after Barnet are tracked in the *Paston Letters*, vol. V, pp. 84–5, 101–2, 186, 188, 189. Oxford's capture of St Michael's Mount is detailed in *Warkworth's Chronicle*, pp. 26–7 and *Paston Letters*, vol. V, p. 201. The earl's attempted suicide is remarked upon in *Paston Letters*, vol. VI, pp. 2–3.

Louis XI's letter to Francis II is printed in Dom H. Morice, *Mémoire pour server de prévues a l'histoire ecclésiastique et civile de Bretagne* (Paris 1742–6), vol. III, cols. 266–70. The description of the robe of black damask is found in Les Archives départementales (AD) Loire-Atlantique, serie B, parchemins non classés, dossier Francois II: '*A monsr. de Richemont pour robbe longue du don de mondit seigneur [le duc] sept aulnes de veloux noir trespoil, val' a IIII reaulx l'aune XXXV l., pour doublez le hault des manches demi tierz de noir val' XXIII d. Et pour le doublez quatre aulnes de taffetas changeant a II realux l'aune, val' X l. fac[on] de chescun, somme XLV l. XIIIs. IIIId A luy pour ung pourpoint une aulne et demie de Damas noir a IIII l. L'aulne et estoffes I escu, VII l. IIs. Xd.*' For the financial records concerning Henry's stay in Brittany, see

M.C.E. Jones, 'For my Lord of Richmond, a pourpoint . . . and a palfrey: Brief Remarks on the Financial Evidence for Henry Tudor's Exile in Brittany, 1471–1484', *Tant d'Emprises, So Many Undertakings: Essays in Honour*, ed. Livia Visser-Fuchs (*The Ricardian*, XIII, 2003), 283–93.

Edward IV's treaty at Picquigny and its accompanying festivities recorded in detail in the memoirs of Philippe de Commynes is conveniently translated in *Memoirs of Philippe de Commynes: The Reign of Louis XI, 1461–83*, ed. Michael Jones (Harmondsworth, 1972). Another increasingly important source is the Crowland Chronicle, reprinted in *The Crowland Chronicle Continuations* ed. N. Pronay and J. Cox (full details in the notes to chapter 4 below).

Henry Tudor's escape from capture by Edward IV's agents is principally recorded in Vergil, pp. 163–6. The story of Henry's fortunate escape has come down solely through the hands of Vergil, writing decades after the event, though a cryptic payment, partially mutilated, survives, shedding further light upon the episode. It is a receipt from Francis ordering for 'the expenses and costs of the Earl of Richmond' to be paid to him when 'he left Brest to go to St-Malo, with two others . . . for the guard and conduct of the same . . . for six days when they were at the said place of St-Malo': Archives départementales (AD) de la Loire-Atlantique B parchemins non classés, dossier Francois II, printed in Jones, 'Financial Evidence for Henry Tudor's Exile', p. 289.

Chapter 4: Usurpation

The key works on Richard III's reign include C. Ross, *Richard III* (London, 1981) and R. Horrox, *Richard III: A Study of Service* (Cambridge, 1989). *Richard III: A Medieval Kingship*, ed. J.Gillingham (London, 1993) contains important articles. P.W. Hammond and A.E. Sutton, *Richard III: The Road to Bosworth* (London, 1985) provides a narrative of Richard's life through contemporary documents. Other works include A.J. Pollard, *Richard III and the Princes in the Tower* (Gloucester, 1991), and essays published in P.W. Hammond (ed.), *Richard III: Loyalty, Lordship and Law* (1986) and R. Horrox (ed.), *Richard III and the North* (Hull, 1986), J. Petre (ed.), *Richard III: Crown and People* (1985) and J. Gillingham (ed.) *The Kingship of Richard III* (1993). Richard's movements during his reign can be found in R. Edwards, *The Itinerary of Richard III* (1983). Richard's coronation is covered in A.F. Sutton and P.W. Hammond (eds.) *The Coronation of Richard III: the Extant Documents* (Gloucester, 1983).

The principal sources for Richard's reign include R. Horrox and P. Hammond (eds), *British Library, Harleian Manuscript 433* (4 vols., London, 1979–83). The Great Chronicle is printed in facsimile in *Great Chronicle of London*, ed. A.H. Thomas and I.D. Thornley (London, 1938). Other key sources for the reign can be found in K. Dockray, *Richard III: a Reader in History* (Gloucester, 1988). The most recent edition of the Crowland Chronicle with parallel Latin-English translation is N. Pronay and J. Cox (eds), *The Crowland Chronicle Continuations 1459–1486* (London, 1986). John Rous's account of the reign is in *Historia Johannis Rossi Warwicensis de Regibus Anglie*, ed. T. Hearne (1716) with a translation in A. Hanham, *Richard III and His Early Historians, 1483–1535* (Oxford, 1975). For Richard's usurpation, Dominic Mancini's account, published as *The Usurpation of Richard III*, ed. C.A.J. Armstrong (2nd edn Oxford, 1969) is a crucial contemporary account, to be supplemented by the Great Chronicle, Vergil and R.F. Green, 'Historical notes of a London Citizen 1483–88', *English Historical Review* XCVI (1981). Thomas More's version of events is published in *The History of King Richard III*, ed. R.S. Sylvester (Newhaven, 1976). Richard's June letter to the city of York is printed in A. Raine (ed.), *York Civic Records*, Yorkshire Archaelogical Society XCVIII, 1939, vol. I, pp. 73–4.

For Henry and Jasper Tudor's removal to Vannes under the guard of Vincent de la Landelle and Bertrand du Parc see AD Loire-Atlantique E 212 no. 16 fo. 13, no.18 fo.9; BnF Fr. 6982 fo. 326v: 'Le Comte de Richemont prisonnier a Elven en janvier 1474', 'Le Comte de Richemont a Vannes en la garde de Vincent de la Landelle octobre 1476', 'Le Comte de Pembrok prisonnier a Josselin avril 1475', 'Le Comte de Pembrok prisonnier a Vannes sous Betrand du Parc, novembre 1476'; Dom Morice, *Mémoires*, vol. II, col. 1777; vol. III, cols. 66, 122–3, 144, 238, 271–2, 391, 427–8; AD Loire-Atlantique B5 fo. 144, B6 fos. 46, 53v, 117, 154v, B7 fo. 68, B8 fo.22v, 82, 83, E 141 p. 21, E 214 no. 37; AD Loire-Atlantique 1 J 142, E 212 no. 16 fos. 4v, 13. Jones, 'Financial Evidence for Henry Tudor's Exile', p. 287. For Henry's movements after 1481 see AD Loire-Atlantique E 133 no. 10, B8 fo. 9v, B 3 fo.7; Dom Morice, *Mémoires*, vol. III, col. 388. Duke Francis's payments for both Henry and Jasper can be found in AD Loire-Atlantique E 212 no. 15, no.16 fo. 4v; L. Maitre, 'Le budget', *Annales de Bretagne*, vol. 5 (1889), pp. 293–319, p. 295; AD Loire-Atlantique 1 J 142; Jones, 'Financial Evidence for Henry Tudor's Exile', 'Financial Memoranda', p. 290. Henry's offerings are recorded in Allanic, p. 38 n.3. Further payments suggestive of Henry and Jasper's freedom are in AD Loire-Atlantique B, parchemins non classés, dossier François II, printed in Jones, 'Financial Evidence for Henry Tudor's Exile', p.290.

Richard III's letter to Duke Francis II is printed in Gairdiner, *Letters and Papers*, vol. I, pp. 22–3; Francis's reply is pp. 37–42.

Chapter 5: Rebellion

The various sightings of the Princes in the Tower are reported in the *Great Chronicle*, p. 234 and Mancini, p. 93. Rumours that both were dead emerge in the *Great Chronicle*, pp.236–7 and C.L. Kingsford (ed.), *Chronicles of London* (Oxford, 1905), p.191. On the possible 'enterprise', Richard's own letter can be found in The National Archives (TNA) C81/1392/1 with the conspiracy referred to in J. Stow, *Annales of England* (London, 1592), p. 459 and Basin, *Histoire de Louis XIII*, vol. III, pp. 234–5. Horrox, *Richard III*, and M.A. Hicks, 'Unweaving the Web: The plot of July 1483 against Richard III and its wider significance', *The Ricardian* 114 (1991) investigate the charges. Richard's nervousness in orders of weapons and commissions to investigate treasons are given in *Harleian 433*, vol. II, pp. 7–9 and *CPR 1476–85*, pp. 465–6.

Margaret Beaufort's dealings with Elizabeth Woodville and the movements of Lewis Caerleon, Christopher Urswick and Reginald Bray are recorded in Vergil, pp. 195–6. For Buckingham's communication with Henry Tudor see *Crowland Chronicle* (CC), p. 163 and *Rotuli Parliamentorum* (RP), vol. VI, pp. 244–9. Duke Francis II's offer of aid for Henry's possible invasion is given in Vergil, p. 197 and proved by AD Loire-Atlantique E 212 no. 18 fos. 17v–19 and British Library (BL) Additional MS 19,398 fo. 33. On Henry Tudor's journey to England see Vergil and I. Arthurson and N. Kingwell, 'The proclamation of Henry Tudor as King of England, 3 November 1483', *Historical Research* 63 (1990).

Richard's stunned reaction to Buckingham's rebellion is found in his letter, TNA C81/1392/6. Horrox, *Richard III*, contains the best account of the rebellion, but see also Griffiths and Thomas. For Cheyney and Daubeney's flight, TNA C82/55/6; for Edgecombe, I. Arthuson, 'A Question of Loyalty' *The Ricardian* VII (1987) p. 404.

Henry's return to Normandy and journey back to Britanny is in Bouchard, *Grande Chroniques*, pp. 459–60 and payments in BnF Clairambault 473. Bouchard gives the Christmas Day ceremony as taking place at Vannes, *Grande Chroniques*, p.459, though Vergil pp. 203–4, the main narrative account, suggests Rennes. Brittany's preparations against Richard are in Dom Morice, *Mémoires*, vol. III, pp. 431–2.

Chapter 6: The Rat, the Cat and the Dog

For Richard's proclamation, see *Harleian 433*, vol. II, pp.48–9. The full text of the *Titulus Regius* is in *Rotuli Parliamentorum* (RP), vol. VI, pp.240–2. Margaret Beaufort's treatment is recorded on RP VI, p. 250, *CPR 1476–85*, pp. 389, 423–8, 501 and *Harleian 433*, vol. I, pp. 173, 186. For the comment on Margaret's patience, BL Additional MS 12060 fo. 22v.

Richard's relationship with his northern gentry is covered by A.J. Pollard, *North-Eastern England during the Wars of the Roses: Lay Society, War and Politics 1450–1500* (Oxford, 1990), K. Dockray, 'Richard III and the Yorkshire Gentry' in Hammond, *Loyalty, Lordship and Law*, W.E. Hampton, 'John Hoton of Hunwick and Tudhoe, County Durham', *The Ricardian* VII (1985), pp. 2–17, Horrox, *Richard III*, pp.178–205, and A.J. Pollard, 'The Tyranny of Richard III', *Journal of Medieval History* III (1977). Marmaduke Constable's rise can be followed through *Harleian 433*, vol. II, pp. 81, 124, *CPR 1476–85*, p. 557 and K. Dockray, 'Sir Marmaduke Constable', in Petre (ed.), *Crown and People*.

Evidence of Richard's reconciliation with the Woodvilles is taken from *Harleian 433*, vol. III, p. 190. For Richard's attempt to strengthen his royal title and confirm the inheritance of his son, see A. Sutton, 'Richard III's "Tytylle and Right": A New Discovery', *The Ricardian* IV (1977), pp. 2–7 and the *Crowland Chronicle*, p. 171. For Edward of Middleham, see *Harleian 433*, vol. II, pp. 24–5 and Hammond and Sutton, pp. 162–3.

Richard's military interests and restocking of the Tower's arsenal are covered in A. Sutton and L. Visser-Fuchs, 'Richard of Gloucester and la grosse bombard', *The Ricardian* X no. 134 (1996), M. Jones, 'Richard III as a soldier' in J. Gillingham (ed.), *Richard III: A Medieval Kingship*, J. Raine, 'The statutes ordained by Richard, Duke of Gloucester, for the college of Middleham. Dated 4 July, 18. Edw. IV, (1478)', *Archaeological Journal*, vol. 14 (1857) and *Harleian 433*, vol. I, pp. 160–1, 175, 268, 288, vol. II, pp. 103, 112, vol. III, p.192 and TNA E404/78/2/33.

William Collingborne's arrest and trial is covered in *Great Chronicle*, p. 236 and Gairdiner, *Richard III*, pp. 189–90. Richard's letter to his mother is BL Harleian MSS 433 fo. 2v and to the Mayor of Windsor, BL Harleian MS 787 fo. 2r. For William Finch's treatment, TNA C255/8/11 m.5. Arrests in Cornwall and the West Country are featured in Horrox, *Richard III*, pp. 275–6 and *Harleian 433*, vol. II, p. 164. The order to prevent ships departing for Brittany is in *Historical Manuscripts Commission* 2nd Report, p. 91.

Henry Tudor's relationship with the French government and the nature of French military assistance for his campaign can be followed in P. Pel-icier, *Essai sur le gouvernement de la Dame de Beaujeu*, 1483–91 (Chartres, 1882) and A. Spont, 'La marine française sous le régne de Charles VIII', *Revue des Questions Historiques* XI, (1894), pp. 387–484 and is also covered in A.V. Antonovics, 'Henry VII, King of England, "By the Grace of Charles VIII of France"' in R.A. Griffiths and J. Sherborne (eds.), *Kings and Nobles in the Later Middle Ages* (Gloucester, 1986); A. Grant, 'Foreign affairs under Rich-ard III' in *Richard III: A Medieval Kingship*, and re-examined in M.K. Jones, 'The myth of 1485 – Did France really put Henry Tudor on the Throne?' in *The English Experience in France 1450–1558: War, Diplomacy and Cultural Exchange*, ed. D. Grummitt (Ashgate, 2002). See also articles by Cliff Davies including 'Bishop John Morton, The Holy See and the accession of Henry VII', *English Historical Review*, CII (1987), pp. 2–30 and 'Richard III, Henry VII and the Island of Jersey', *The Ricardian* IX (1992), pp. 334–42.

Payments by Duke Francis II to the English exiles at Vannes are preser-ved in AD Loire-Atlantique E 212 no. 17 fo. 17v; E 209 no. 23 fo. 7v: '2500l. ... deu des Angloys qui y ont este logez quelx estoient o le sire de Richemont et don't le duc a voulu prenre la charge', and AD Loire-Atlantique E 212 no. 18 fo. 16: 'Aux Angloys que leur a este paye ou moys de mars derrain, savoir au Marquis, IIIIc l, a Messire Edouart de Wudeville, C l., Maistre Halouel, IIc l, a Messire Robert Wlby, C l. A Messire Edouard de Wdville . . . pour employer en la mise de la despense de luy et de ses gens 900 l.' The Breton truce of June 1484 is printed in Rymer, *Foedera*, vol. XII, pp. 221–2. The agree-ment for 1,000 archers to be sent to Brittany is discussed in C.S.L. Davies, 'Richard III, Brittany and Henry Tudor, 1483–1485', *Nottingham Medieval Studies* 37 (1993), pp. 110–26.

Chapter 7: A Confederacy of Rebels

The offering of alms in Vannes cathedral is printed in Allanic, pp. 38 and 49. The main source of Henry's escape is Vergil, though payments by Duke Francis to the remaining exiles to journey to France are in AD de la Loire-Atlantique E212/93 fos. 15r, 17v. Henry's reception in France is documented in *Procés-verbaux de séances du Conseil de Régence du roi Charles VIII*, ed. A. Bernier (Paris, 1836), pp. 128, 148 while Charles VIII's letter is printed in Spont, 'La marine française', p. 393: 'accompagnes de 5 à 600 Engles, en disposition de faire venire d'Autres tant qu'il voldra, pour tenir bon port au roy et recouvrer le royaume de Englettere sur les ennemis de la coronne de France. Et les a le roy benignement recues en son service et doint pour leur entretenement bonne et grande provision'.

Oxford's escape and plots surrounding it are described in J.A. Buchon (ed.) *Chroniques de Jean Molinet* (Paris, 1828), vol. II, p. 406, TNA KB27/908 rex rot 8, Vergil, pp. 208–9. Its effect on French confidence in Henry is reflected in the further payments to his men, in Bernier, pp. 164, 168. The earl's influence over Henry's claim to the throne is in *Molinet*, vol. II, p. 406: 'deux grands seigneurs d'Angleterre entre les autres . . . exciterent le comte de Richmemont de aspirer a la couronne'. M. Jones, 'The myth of 1485', pp. 92–3 and Commynes, p. 354 highlight the problems with the strength of Henry's claim. Henry's letter is BL Harleian MS 787 fo. 2r, with Richard's proclamation and commissions of array printed in *Harleian 433*, vol. III, pp. 124–5. The Christmas celebrations at court are described in CC, p. 173.

Henry's relations with the Beaujeu government are described in Vergil, pp. 209–14 and Pelicier, *Essai*, p. 254. For Richard's loans, CC, p.175 and *Harleian 433*, vol. III, p. 128 with context in Horrox, *Richard III*, pp. 306–7. Reconciliation with former rebels is covered in Horrox, *Richard III*, pp. 293–4, *CPR 1476–85*, p. 528 and *Great Chronicle*, p. 237. For Morton, see Chrimes, *Henry VII*, p. 106.

Chapter 8: The Spiral of Decline

Queen Anne's death is covered in J. Ashdown-Hill, *The Last Days of Richard III* (2011) and in CC, p. 173. Richard's hawking activities are in *Harleian 433*, vol. II, p. 216. Richard's letter to York is in York House Books 2/4 fo. 163v. Henry's reaction to Richard's possible marriage to Elizabeth of York and his attempt to seek support for a Herbert alliance is from Vergil's manuscript of the *Anglia Historia*, Vatican Library, Urb.Lat. 498, fos. 229v–230r. For Welsh prophecies, see G.A. Williams, 'The Bardic Road to Bosworth: a Welsh view of Henry Tudor', *Cymmrodorion* (1986), p. 23 and University College of North Wales, Bangor MS 1267 fo. 10r. Richard's military preparations are documented in *Harleian 433*, vol. II pp. 222–3 and TNA E404/78/3/46.

For Charles VIII's entry into Rouen and Henry Tudor's formal recognition, see Beaurepaire, *Entrée de Charles VIII à Rouen en 1485* (Rouen, 1902), p. 9: 'le conte de Richemont, soy disant roi d'Angleterre', pp. 22–4 and A.E. Goodman, 'Henry VII and Christian Renewal' in *Studies in Church History* XVII (1981), p. 116.

For rumours of Henry's landing at 'Milford' and the subsequent preparations at Southampton, see the Crowland Chronicle and Hammond and Sutton, p. 206. Richard's June proclamation and commissions of array are printed in *Harleian 433*, vol. II, pp. 228–9 and *Paston Letters*, vol. VI, pp.81–4. The commission to Gloucester is in *Harleian 433*, vol. III, pp. 127–8. For the possible list of commissioners, dated May 1484, see *CPR 1476–85*, pp. 397–401. Caxton's dedication is printed in A.T.B Byles (ed.), *The Book of the Ordre of Chyvalry printed by William Caxton*, EETS 168 (1926), pp.121–5. Richard's orders for Chancellor John Russell to hand over the Great Seal are in *Calendar of Close Rolls 1476–85*, nos. 1457–8. For the impact of the seal, see *Paston Letters*, vol. III, no. 894.

Henry's offering at Rouen is in Rouen, AD Seine-Maritime G2 143; 'Ecu d'or d'Aquitaine offert par le roi d'Anglettere, prince de Richemont, quant il vint dans la chapelle de la Sainte Vierge'. For Beton, see Campbell, *Materials*, vol. I, p. 413. Jean Lallement's account roll is BN Nouvelles Acquisitions Françaises 7642, fos. 159v–60: 'A Henry, comte de Richemont, 10,000 l.t. pour partie de 40,000 l.t. a lui ordonées par le Roi pour l'aider a supporter les frais, missies et dépenses qu'il lui convient faire pour l'armée qu'il fait mettre sus pour le passer en royaume d'Angleterre et pour executer certain enterprise qu'il a faite pour le recouvrement d'icellui royaume qui lui appartient et où quell il a bon et apparent droit'. See also BN MS Français 23266 fo.45: '10,000 l.t. pour son passaige en Angleterre'. John Morgan's message is in Vatican Urbs.Lat. 498, fo. 230r. For the role of French mercenaries and the war camp at Pont-de-l'Arche see A. Spont, 'La malice des Francs-Archers' (1448–1500), *Revue des Questions Historiques* LXI (1897), pp. 474–7 and A.V. Antovics, 'Henry VII, King of England "By the Grace of Charles VIII of France"', *Kings and Nobles in the Later Middle Ages*, ed. R.A. Griffiths and J. Sherborne (Gloucester and New York, 1986), 169–84 pp. 183–4. *Molinet*, vol. II, p. 406 and Commynes, pp. 355, 397 add further detail. On Esquerdes, see Mancini, p. 81 and Gairdiner, *Letters and Papers*, vol. I, pp. 18, 20–1 and for Colinet Lebouef, AN JJ 218 no. XIX, fo. 11r. The nature of Scottish support is examined in N. MacDougall, *James III* (Edinburgh, 1982).

Chapter 9: March to War

The location of Henry's landing place is discussed in S.B. Chrimes, 'The Landing Place of Henry of Richmond, 1485', *Welsh History Review* II (1964–5), pp. 173–80. For the knighting ceremony, BL Harleian 78 fo. 31v and standards BL Landsdowne 255 fo. 433r. For Vergil's comment on the composition of Henry's forces, see Vatican Urbs.Lat. 498, fo. 230r. Lewis Glyn Cothi, see G. Mechain and I. Tegid (eds), *The Poetical Works of Lewis Glyn Cothi* (Oxford, 1837), pp. 480–1. Rhys ap Thomas's seventeenth-century

'Life' has been printed with valuable commentary in R.A. Griffiths, *Sir Rhys ap Thomas and his family: A Study in the Wars of the Roses* (Cardiff, 1993). My reassessment of Henry's march is taken from the manuscript of Vergil's *Anglia Historia*, Vatican Urbs.Lat. 498, fos. 230r–231r, in comparison with the first printed edition of 1534. The ballad accounts that cover Henry's march are printed in several forms. 'Bosworth Feilde' can be found in *Bishop Percy's Folio Manuscript. Ballads and Romances*, ed. J.W. Hales and F.J. Furnivall (3 vols, London, 1868), vol. III, pp. 233–59, though its prose version, taken from BL Harleian MS 542 fos.31–3 is printed by W. Hutton, *The Battle of Bosworth Field* (Tempus, 1999). The 'Ballad of Lady Bessie' is printed in *Percy Society Publications* XX (1847).

The Crowland Chronicle is the best source for Richard's final months and reaction to Henry's landing. The reception of the news by Richard is analysed by O.D. Harris, 'The Transmission of the news of the Tudor landing', *The Ricardian* IV, no. 55 (December, 1976), pp. 5–12. Henry's letters to supporters appealing for aid can be found in G. Grazebrook, 'An unpublished letter by Henry, Earl of Richmond', *Miscellanea Genealogica et Heraldica*, 4th Series, V (1914), pp. 30–9 and J. Ballinger (ed.), *The History of the Gwydir Family written by Sir J. Wynn of Gwydir* (Cardiff, 1927). Both are analysed by R. Horrox, 'Henry Tudor's letters to England during Richard III's reign', *The Ricardian* VI, no. 80 (March, 1983), pp. 155–8. Henry's Welsh support and bardic prophesies are analysed in G.A. Williams, 'The bardic road to Bosworth: a Welsh view of Henry Tudor', *Cymmrodorion* (1986), pp. 7–31.

Richard's military attitudes as reflected in his books is discussed in A. Sutton and L.Visser-Fuchs, 'Richard III's books: Chivalric ideals and reality' *The Ricardian* IX, no. 199 (1992). Von Poppelau's observations have been translated in L. Visser-Fuchs, 'What Nicolas von Poppelau really wrote about Richard III', *The Ricardian* XI, no. 145 (1999). Other comments on Richard's reaction are in *The Ballad of Bosworth Field*, p. 243 and *Molinet*, vol. I, p. 407: 'Le roy Richard se vouloit joindre avecq les seigneurs d'Angleterre, pour ester a la descente, mais ils lui manderent: "Ne vous bougez, nous ferons bien"'. Richard's letter to Vernon is printed in *Historical Manuscripts Commission 12th Report, Rutland MSS*, vol. I (1888), pp.7–8. Norfolk's letter to John Paston is in *Paston Letters*, vol. VI, p. 85 with details of Norfolk's muster list from J. Payne Collier (ed.), *Household Books of John, Duke of Norfolk* (1844), pp. 481–92. Thomas Longe's will is in Norfolk Record Office, NCC, Will Register, Caston, fo. 256v.

Richard III's relationship with Thomas, Lord Stanley and Sir William Stanley is examined in M.K. Jones, 'Richard III and the Stanleys' in *Richard*

III and the North, ed. Horrox and 'Sir William Stanley of Holt: politics and family allegiance in the late fifteenth century', *Welsh History Review* XIV (1988). J.M. Williams, 'The Stanley family of Lathom and Knowsley, c.1450–1504: a political study' (University of Manchester M.A. thesis, 1979) is the most comprehensive study of the Stanleys' career. Lord Strange's arrest is covered in CC, p. 179, 'Bosworth Field' p. 239 and its prose version, printed in Hutton, *Battle of Bosworth Field*, p. 126. For William Gruffudd, see E.W. Jones, *Bosworth: A Welsh Retrospect* (Liverpool, 1984), pp. 57–8. Stanley's letter to Scarisbrick is at Lancashire Record Office DDSc/9/1.

Henry's reception at Shrewsbury is recorded in W.A. Leighton (ed.), *The Early Chronicles of Shrewsbury* (1888), pp.249–50 and Owen and Blakeway, *A History of Shrewsbury*, vol. I, pp.246–8. See also Campbell, *Materials*, vol. I, pp. 125–6, 156 and *Bishop Percy's Folio Manscript. Ballads and Romances*, ed. J.W. Hales and F.J. Furnivall, (3 vols., London, 1868) III pp. 319–63, 'The Ballad of Ladie Bessie', p. 353.

Chapter 10: Secret Friends

For the city of York's actions, see York House Books, Books 2/4 fo. 169. For Nottingham, *The Records of the Borough of Nottingham*, p. 238, and Chester, Campbell, *Materials*, vol. I, pp. 9, 110–11, 154, 202. Vergil, pp. 218–21 and *Bosworth Field*, pp. 249–51 cover the events from Lichfield to the battle, with *Great Chronicle*, p. 237 adding further detail regarding the defections from Sir Robert Brackenbury's camp. D. Baldwin, 'Bosworth: two battles or one?', unpublished paper, investigates the supposed altercation before the battle began. Payments to the abbot of Merevale, Witherley, Fenny Drayton, Mancetter, Atherstone and Atterton are given in Campbell, *Materials*, vol. I, pp. 188, 201, 233 with payments for Henry's armour p. 274.

C. Richmond, '1485 and all that: or what was going on at the battle of Bosworth' in *Richard III: Loyalty, Lordship and Law* is an important evaluation of who exactly was present at the battle. For Salazar, see BL Harleian MS 433 fos. 210v, 213, 214, 219 and for comment in Molinet: 'hardy comme ung Hector, soutil comme Ulixes, heures comme Cesar, plus asseurez aveuc ses petis Scipions que n'estoit Achilles avenc ses Mirmidons'; *Molinet*, vol. I, p. 302. Mancini's description of the forces assembled at London is at pp. 99–101. Richard's final night at Ambion is related by both Vergil and the Crowland Chronicle, with added detail provided by *The Historie and Cronicles of Scotland . . . written and collected by Robert Lindesay of Pittscottie*, ed. A.J.G Mackay (Scottish Text Society, 1899–1911), vol. I pp. 196–9. For

Biconell, see W.E. Hampton, *Memorials of the Wars of the Roses* no.265 and *Inquisitions Post Mortem Henry VII*, vol. I, no. 536.

Chapter 11: The Battle

William Hutton's classic but flawed study of the battle, first published in 1788, has been reprinted as *The Battle of Bosworth Field* (Tempus, 1999). Key works include M. Bennett, *The Battle of Bosworth* (Gloucester, 1985) and the indispensable revisionist history by Peter Foss, *The Field of Redemore: The Battle of Bosworth 1485* (2nd edn, Newtown Linford, 1998). Recent studies include M.K. Jones, *Bosworth 1485, Psychology of a Battle* (Stroud, 2002), though its interpretation should be read in conjunction with L. Visser-Fuchs, 'Phantom Bastardy and Ghostly Pikemen', *The Ricardian* XIV (2004), pp. 117–18.

Vergil is the most important source for the battle: Vatican Urbs.Lat. 498, fos. 234r–235r and also the 1534 edition have been used in the interpretation. The 'Spanish Account' of the battle is printed in E.M. Nokes and G. Wheeler, 'A Spanish account of the battle of Bosworth', *The Ricardian* 2, no. 36 (1972), pp. 1–5; see also A. Goodman and A. MacKay, 'A Castilian report on English affairs, 1486', *English Historical Review* 88 (1973), pp. 92–9. Molinet's French account is in *J.A. Buchon (ed.) Chroniques de Jean Molinet (Paris, 1828)* , vol. I, pp. 434–6, with a part translation in Bennett, *The Battle of Bosworth*, p. 161. My own translation is taken from J.A. Buchon (ed.), *Chroniques de Jean Molinet*, vol. I, pp. 407–9.

Richard's book of hours is Lambeth Palace Library MS 474, the devotional prayer is at fos.181–3, printed in Sutton and Hammond, pp. 191–3. The account of Richard's early awakening and the unprepared nature of his camp is in BL Additional MS 12060 fos. 19–20v and CC, p. 181. The incident is discussed in J.W. Verkaik, 'King Richard's last sacrament', *The Ricardian* IX (1992), pp. 359–60. On the Bosworth Crucifix, see J. Ashdown-Hill, 'The Bosworth Crucifix' *Leicestershire Archaeological and Historical Society Transactions* 78 (2004), pp. 83–93.

For the French forces' position, see J.A. Buchon (ed.), *Chroniques de Jean Molinet* (2 vols., Paris, 1828), p. 408: 'Les François pareillement firent leurs preparations en marchant contre les Angles, estans au camp a un quart de lieue'. For Oxford, see J. Ross, pp. 218–19 and William Caxton, *The Book of Fayttes of Armes and of Chyvalrye*, ed. A.T.P. Byles (EETS 1937), p. 291. The modern text of Christine de Pizan is from S. Willard and C.C. Willard (eds), *The Book of Deeds of Arms and of Chivalry* (Pennsylvania, 1999).

For Richard's artillery, see Sutton and Visser-Fuchs, 'Richard of

Gloucester and la gross bombarde', p. 461, J. Raine, 'The statutes ordained by Richard', p. 161. Preparations are in Harleian MS 433, vol. I, pp. 160, 161, 175, vol. II, pp. 112, 268, vol. III, p. 192. See J.A. Buchon (ed.) *Molinet*, vol. II p. 407: 'il avoit environ quarante mille combatants et grande quantite d'engiens volants'. Edward Hall's reflections are in *The Union of the Two Noble Families of Lancaster and York* (London, 1550, Facsimile, 1970), fos. 29d–35, printed in part in Bennett, pp. 167–9.

Richard's orders for Lord Strange's execution are described in CC, p. 181, Hutton p. 129 and 'Ladie Bessie', pp. 360–1. For Oxford's manoeuvre see Vergil, MS: 'Oxoniensis Comes (interim) veritus ne sui pugnando a multitudine omnino circumvenirentur, edicit per ordines ne quis miles a signis quatuor pedes procederet' and 1534 edn: 'Oxoniensis comes interim veritus ne sui pugnando a multitudine circumvenirentur, edixit per ordines, ne quis miles a signis plus decem pedes procederet': *'the Earl of Oxford, fearing that in the fighting his men would be completely encircled by the [enemy's] great numbers, sent an order through the ranks that no soldier was to advance ten feet from the standards'*. From the 1534 edn: 'Quo cognito mandato, cum sese cuncti condensassent et parum a certamine cessassent, adversarii ut territi ob eam rem aliquid fraudis suspicati ipsi quoque parumper pugnam intermiserunt et id quidem multi non gravate, qui malebant regem perditum, quam salvum, ac ideo minus fortiter pugnabant. Tunc Oxoniensis una in parte confertis manipulis, in hostes impetum renovat, et alii in parte altera, facto cuneo, una urgentes integrant pugnam': *'When they heard this command, all his men crowded together and withdrew a short way from the battle. Their opponents as if terrified and suspecting a trick because of this, also stopped fighting for a short time – and many indeed not unwillingly, as they preferred the king lost rather than safe and so were fighting the less energetically. Then Oxford collected his companies together and renewed the attack on the enemy on one side, and others on the other side made a wedge and simultaneously pressed on and renewed the battle.'* See also 'The Rose of England' printed in F.J. Child (ed.), *The English and Scottish Popular Ballads*, vol. III, pp. 331–3, the relevant section for the battle is printed in Bennett, p. 170. Compare Pizan in Willard and Willard, pp. 72–3. For Norfolk's capture at the windmill by Savage, 'Ladie Bessie', p. 361. and also *Molinet*, vol. II, p. 408: 'En ce conflit fut prins le duc de Norford avecq sons fils, et envoye au comte de Richemont, lequel le renvoya au seigneur d'Oxenfort, qui bientost le fit despescher'.

For Molinet's comments regarding the Earl of Northumberland and other noblemen, J.A. Buchon (ed.), *Molinet*, vol II p. 408: 'Le comte de Northombelland estoit, a l'aide du roi Richard, accompagne de dix mille hommes qui debvoient charger sur les Francois; et ne fit rien; ains s'enfuit lui et sa compagnie, et abandonna son roi Richard'; p. 407: 'Alors les grands seigneurs d'Angleterre eurent cause de metre main aux armes, non point pour secourir un roy, mais pour ester quittes de lui, et eux venger des torfaicts qu'il leur avoit faict.'; on Northumberland's possible pact with Henry, p. 408: 'car il avoit entendement avec le comte de Richemont, comme avoient plusieurs aultres qui le laisserent au besoing'. The Earl of Northumberland's relations with Richard are examined in M. Hicks, 'Dynastic change and northern society: the career of the Fourth Earl of Northumberland, 1470–89', *Northern History* XIV (1978) and M. Weiss, 'A Power in the North? The Percies in the fifteenth Century', *Historical Journal* XIX, no.2 (1976). For Thomas Woodshawe, see R. Skinner, 'Thomas Woodshawe, "Grasiour" and Regicide', *The Ricardian* IX, no. 121 pp. 417–25.

Chapter 12: Our Victorious Field

On Richard's burial, see J. Ashdown-Hill, *The Last Days of Richard III* (2011). On Newark: 'Frowyk Chronicle', *The Ricardian* X, no. 126, pp. 86–103. On deaths at Bosworth, L. Boatwright, 'The Buckinghamshire Six at Bosworth', *The Ricardian* XIII (2003) is a seminal work on how reconstruction of the fates of participants in the battle can be done, but see also Hampton, 'John Hoton of Hunwick and Tudhoe, County Durham', pp. 2–17 and Richmond, '1485 and all that'. Individual fates, injuries, rewards and petitions throughout this and subsequent chapters have been taken from Campbell, *Materials*. On Sir Gilbert Talbot, see *The Topographer and Genealogist*, vol. I (1846), p. 510. On rewards to Leicester for treating the wounded, *Materials*, vol. II, pp. 244–5, and William Altoftes, the king's surgeon, *Materials*, vol. II, p. 159. For the injuries sustained at 'Bosard felde', see Bodleian Library Ashmole MS 1500, p. 206. On the Earl of Surrey, P. Hammond, 'The Earl of Surrey after Bosworth', *The Ricardian* X, no. 128 (1995). Henry's order to seize the young Earl of Warwick is in Vergil, see D. Hay (ed.), *Anglia Historia 1485–1547*, p. 2. For William Bracher, see *CPR 1476–85*, pp. 366, 373, 390, 489. Sir James Harrington's treatment is mentioned in Bodleian Library MS Add d.113 fo. 28.

Henry's proclamation is printed in J. O. Halliwell-Phillips, *Letters*, vol. I (1846), pp. 169–70 and *Tudor Royal Proclamations*, ed. P.L. Hughes and J.F. Larkin (New Haven, 1964), vol. 1, p. 3. For Richard's relationship with Westmorland, see *Paston Letters*, vol. VI, pp. 71–2, Harleian MS 433, vol. II, p. 205 and his fate after the battle, H.E. Salter, *Registrum Annalium Collegii Mertonensis*, Oxford Historical Society, 76 (1921), p. 71 and *Materials*, vol.

I, pp. 191, 196. William Berkeley is mentioned in *Calendar of Papal Registers* XIV 1484–92 (1960), pp. 17–21 and on his ambiguity, John Smith of Nibley, *The Berkeley Manuscripts*, pp. 127–8. William Catesby's will is TNA PROB 11/7 Logge fo. 15, printed in D. Williams, 'The hastily drawn up will of William Catesby, Esquire, 25 August 1485', *Transactions of the Leicestershire Archaeological and Historical Society* 51 (1975–6), pp. 43–51. Henry Tudor's visit to Coventry is detailed in Griffiths and Sherborne (eds.), *Kings and Nobles in the Later Middle Ages*, pp. 194–5.

The reaction of the city of York to Richard's death is in York City Archives, House Book, B 2/4 fo. 169v. Coton's mission is described in D. Palliser's article in Horrox (ed.), *Richard III and the North* (1986). Henry's journey to London and reception by the city is covered by D. Hay (ed.), *Anglia Historia 1485–1547*, pp. 3–5 and in Corporation of London Journals IX fo. 84v, 87r. Rewards for supporters and followers fill the pages of *Materials*, vol. I. Oxford University's letter to the Earl of Oxford is printed in H. Anstey (ed.), *Epistolae Academiae Oxon* (1844), pp. 498–501 and see *Great Chronicle*, p. 239. Henry's proclamation of 24 September is printed in A. Raine, *York Civic Records*, vol. I, p. 125, and his letter to Henry Vernon on 17 October is in H. Kirke, 'Sir Henry Vernon of Haddon', *Journal of the Derbyshire Archaeological and Natural History Society* 42 (1920), p. 12.

Chapter 13: Reward, Retribution and Reconciliation

Jasper Tudor's creation ceremony is documented in BL Egerton MS 985 fos. 41v–42r. For the coronation banquet see also BL Egerton MS 985 fo. 45v and for the jousts fo. 48r. On international news of Richard's death, *Calendar of State Papers, Milan*, ed. A.B. Hinds (London, 1912), vol. I, p. 247; *Calendar of State Papers, Venice*, ed. R. Brown (London, 1864), vol. I, p. 156 and *Calendar of State Papers, Spain*, ed. G.A. Bergenroth (London, 1862), vol. I, p. 1. The style of Henry's title is recorded in *Rotuli Parliamentorum*, vol. VI, pp. 268–70. For the Act of Attainder see RP VI, p. 276. P. Cavill, *The English Parliaments of Henry VII 1485–1504* (Oxford, 2009) is a crucial guide to the 1484 Parliament. Roger Wake's petition is taken from TNA C82/5.

On families torn apart by Bosworth, see J. Nichols, *The History and Antiquities of the County of Leicester* (London 1795–1815), vol. IV, p. 567. On the Kendal, Bourgchier, Charlton triangle, *Inquisitions Post Mortem Henry VII*, vol. III, no. 654, *CPR 1485–94*, p. 439, *Materials*, vol. I, p. 216. For the Beverstones, see I. Arthurson, 'A Question of Loyalty', pp. 404–5. The collection of revenues is discussed in Cavill, pp. 36–7.

The papal dispensation for Henry's marriage is printed in *Materials*, vol. I, pp. 392–8. For the battle of Stoke, see M. Bennett, *The Battle of Stoke* (1987) while the fate of Francis, Viscount Lovell is investigated in D. Baldwin, 'What happened to Lord Lovell?', *The Ricardian* VII, no. 89 (1985), pp. 56–65. For Northumberland's death, *Paston Letters*, vol. VI, pp. 127–8, *Materials*, vol. II, p. 447, *Great Chronicle*, p. 242, and comment by John Skelton, *The Complete English Poems*, pp.31–2. For tavern gossip at York, York House Books VII fo. 39r. For Sir Marmaduke Constable's final years, see Dockray, 'Sir Marmaduke Constable', pp. 221–2. The importance of St Armel has been highlighted by M. Jones in *Bosworth: Psychology of a Battle* (2004) and by J.D. Austin in *Merevale Church and Abbey: The Stained Glass, Monuments and History of the Church of Our Lady and Merevale Abbey* (1998) and *Merevale and Atherstone: 1485: Recent Bosworth Discoveries* (2004). The Dadlington warrant is from TNA C82/367/15 with the letter of confraternity also printed in O.D. Harris, 'The Bosworth commemoration at Dadlington', *The Ricardian* VII (1985), pp. 115–31. Henry VII's will is printed in *The Will of Henry VII*, ed. T. Astle (London, 1775). Commynes' comment is from *Memoirs*, p. 397.

Chapter 14: Bosworth Rediscovered

The fierce debate over the location of the battle site was first stoked by C. Richmond, 'The Battle of Bosworth', *History Today* XXXV, no. 8 (August 1985), only to be challenged by D. Williams in *The Ricardian* VII, no. 90 (September 1985). There have been a legion of articles on the subject of the exact location of the battle; however, Peter Foss's work remains the most important and detailed reassessment of the battle site, proved mostly correct by the new archaeological discoveries, which are described in G. Foard, 'Discovering Bosworth', *British Archaeology* (May–June 2010) and G. Foard, 'Have we discovered where Richard died?', *BBC History Magazine*, vol. 11, no. 3 (March 2010). On landmarks such as the windmill, see Westminster Abbey Muniments 14463 and TNA Chancery Proceedings Series II Bundle 56/101. The Dadlington Court Records are in Leicestershire Record Office, 2D71. On the name of 'Sandeford' see T. Thornton, 'The Battle of Sandeford: Henry Tudor's understanding of the meaning of Bosworth Field', *Historical Research* 78 (2005), pp. 436–42.

ACKNOWLEDGEMENTS

This book would not have been possible without the generous and kind assistance of many people, to whom I am extremely grateful. At Weidenfeld & Nicolson, Alan Samson commissioned the book, and Bea Hemming has seen the work through all stages of the editing process. For all their help, both by way of encouragement and in providing assistance in the research and writing of the book, I am also indebted to Jonathan Pegg, Peter Foss, Sean Cunningham, James Ross, Hannes Kleineke, Jessica Lutkin, Tracey Sowerby, Paul Cavill, Louis Daillencourt, Richard Knox, Peter Hammond, Steve Gunn, Carolyn Hammond, Geoffrey Wheeler, Wendy Moorhen, David Baldwin, Lara Eakins, Livia Visser Fuchs, Rosemary Horrox, Michael Jones, Cliff Davies, Erkin Gozutok and Robert Woosnam and the Royal Armouries for sharing their expertise on Richard's wounds. Lydia Wilson has also provided constant support, ever since giving me my first tour of the battlefield sites. I apologise if I have omitted anyone who deserves mention in my thanks, and naturally all errors and mistakes are my own.

In writing *Bosworth* I have been struck by how many people felt able to share with me their expertise and dedication. In particular, Lesley Boatwright devoted hours to transcribing and translating the Latin manuscript of Polydore Vergil's *Anglia Historia*, which I have made use of in my descriptions of Henry Tudor's march through Wales and the battle itself. An excellent scholar of the battle, sadly Lesley died suddenly in late 2012. Though she never had the chance to read this book, it is to her memory that I have chosen to dedicate this work.

INDEX